Prehistoric Quarries and Terranes

Prehistoric Quarries and Terranes

The Modena and Tempiute Obsidian Sources
of the American Great Basin

Michael J. Shott

THE UNIVERSITY OF UTAH PRESS
Salt Lake City

The Defiance House Man colophon is a registered trademark
of The University of Utah Press. It is based on a four-foot-tall
Ancient Puebloan pictograph (late PIII) near Glen Canyon, Utah.

LIBRARY OF CONGRESS CATALOGING-IN-PUBLICATION DATA
Names: Shott, Michael J. (Michael Joseph), author.
Title: Prehistoric quarries and terranes : the Modena and Tempiute obsidian sources of the American Great Basin / Michael J. Shott. Description: Salt Lake City : University of Utah Press, 2021. | Includes bibliographical references and index.
Identifiers: LCCN 2020025422 (print) | LCCN 2020025423 (ebook) | ISBN 9781647690106 (cloth) | ISBN 9781647690113 (ebook)
Subjects: LCSH: Quarries and quarrying, Prehistoric—Nevada. | Antiquities, Prehistoric—Nevada. | Excavations (Archaeology)—Nevada. | Obsidian—Nevada. | Nevada—Antiquities.
Classification: LCC GN799.Q83 S56 2021 (print) | LCC GN799.Q83 (ebook) | DDC 979.3/01—dc23
LC record available at https://lccn.loc.gov/2020025422
LC ebook record available at https://lccn.loc.gov/2020025423

Errata and further information on this and other titles available online at UofUpress.com

Printed and bound in the United States of America.

Publisher's Note

This book makes reference to online appendices,
which can be accessed at the book's home page
at the publisher's website, UofUpress.com.

Contents

Figures

Tables

Online Appendices

Appendix A. Modena and Tempiute
Flake Count and Proportion by Size Class.

Appendix B. Modena and Tempiute
Lithic Terrane Sourcing Data.

Acknowledgments

University of Akron (UA) fieldwork at Modena was funded by the Bureau of Land Management as part of the Lincoln County Archaeological Initiative (Grant No. 2008 NV040 5844FD B005 411C). Lisa Gilbert, Nicholas Pay, Kurt Braun, and Carol Bass of the Bureau's Ely District assisted our efforts, as did Coleen Beck of the Desert Research Institute. Special thanks go to Mark Henderson, formerly of Ely District, for his support and guidance at the project's start. It would not have been possible without his help. Thanks also to Rebecca Campbell of the University of Akron Office of Research Administration for assistance in proposal preparation. I am grateful for assistance provided by Thomas Burke and Bryan Hockett at the Nevada BLM office and Eugene Hattori of the Nevada State Museum.

Farrel and Manetta Lytle, who grew up in and years later retired to Eagle Valley, Nevada, discovered the Modena quarry and reported its location to Ely BLM. Besides that contribution, highly significant in itself, the Lytles served as instrumental collaborators and gracious hosts in subsequent archaeological and geological field investigations. Along with Peter Rowley, the Lytles mapped and drafted the initial report on the Modena quarry, which greatly expedited our work there. Robert Hafey discovered the Tempiute source and reported its location to Ely BLM. He undertook his own investigations at the source and its environs, a foundation that greatly expedited UA work there. Mr. Hafey also graciously hosted our crew during 2010 fieldwork at Tempiute.

Jerrad Lancaster served two seasons on the field crew. He proved the most able fieldworker with whom it has ever been my pleasure to work with. Anne Donkin assisted in the field in 2009 and in preparing the Modena and Tempiute sample designs. My wife, Elisabeth Bacus, participated in 2010 fieldwork and provided key advice, not least on the matter of shipping field samples via Caliente.

Michael Moore conducted obsidian reduction experiments. Elizabeth Mancz assisted in laboratory processing, Meagan Deitering in analysis. Jeffrey Hoyt drew most of the artifact illustrations. Michelle Davis and Eric Olson prepared some original maps. Craig Skinner and Jennifer Thatcher of the Northwest Research Obsidian Laboratory conducted sourcing and hydration analyses.

A number of Great Basin scholars provided useful information, advice, and reports. Grateful thanks go to Jeffrey Altschul, Daniel Amick, Michael Berry, Clint Cole, Karyn de Dufour, Daron Duke, Robert Elston, Mark Estes, Jennifer Farquhar, Richard Hughes, Kathleen Hull, Eric Ingbar, Robert Jackson, Joel Janetski, Eva Jensen, Marc Kodack, E. S. Lohse, Brian McKee, Joseph Moore, Amelia Natoli, Khori Newlander, Bonnie Pitblado, Matthew Root, Alan Schroedl, Matthew Seddon, Geoffrey Smith, Alex Stevenson, Bridget Wall, Robert Wegener, and Matthew Zweifel. Particular thanks are due to Elston and Seddon for excellent earlier studies that improved and enhanced analysis reported here. Cole's substantial research near the Modena obsidian quarry complemented UA investigations and contextualized analysis of that important source. Charlotte Beck and George Jones conducted earlier research that in material ways guided this investigation. Extensive consultation with Daron Duke and Alexander Rogers on obsidian hydration results greatly aided this research. Eric Henderson and Clarence Bush introduced me to Modena in 2004.

Peter Rowley was instrumental in original re-porting of Modena and provided advice during our fieldwork. Andrew P. Bradbury provided critical data that proved instrumental in esti-mating scale of production at Lincoln County obsidian quarries. William Andrefsky provided thoughtful, constructive comments on analyt-ical chapters. The method developed and re-ported here for assigning debris assemblages to reduction segments was developed by my for-mer colleague Desale Habtzghi, now of DePaul University. Andrew Bradbury and an anony-mous reviewer provided constructive criticism that improved the manuscript. The University of Akron Interlibrary Loan service provided a number of important sources.

Parts of Chapter 5 previously appeared as Shott and Habitzghi (2019) and Shott and Olson (2015). Parts of Chapter 7 previously appeared as Shott (2015).

1

Introduction

Approaches to Quarry Studies

Whence came the millions of flaked implements…that cover the hills and valleys of America,
that occur upon every fishing-ground, shell bank, refuse heap, and village site occupied
by the American aborigines, historic and prehistoric? They did not grow to be picked like
ripe fruit from trees, nor could they have been dug up like potatoes from the ground.
Where are the quarries and the shops from which the Indian secured his enormous supplies?
(Holmes 1892:296).

North America's archaeological record is written in stone more than anything else. For 13,000 years or more, people made and used chipped stone tools, many of them bifaces of various kinds. The remnants of their efforts number in the billions and litter the landscape of North America. Tools were worked into particular forms that reflected function as well as time, cultural affinity, and transmission rules. Their abundance and distribution register scale and pattern of prehistoric land use. The debris from production and maintenance of stone tools is found in numbers practically beyond measure, and its quantity and technological character reflect in turn the amount and kind of production. Naturally, stone tools and debris are popular subjects of archaeological analysis and interpretation. In comparatively impoverished records like the Great Basin's, lithic evidence is especially important merely by the circumstance of its relative abundance.

Toolstones considered useful by prehistoric peoples range from quartzite, to fine-grained volcanics, to microcrystalline silicates like chert, and obsidian. Of course, obsidian is a natural glass, not stone. But its hardness and fracture properties, the sharp edges that it forms and holds in tools, in addition to other qualities make obsidian comparable to stone in most respects, and superior in some. Strictly an oxymoron, for practical purposes obsidian truly is a tool*stone*. And obsidian's abundance in volcanic regions made it a popular and common choice of toolstone among ancient knappers and tool users around the world.

Whether chert, obsidian, or another material, toolstone was fashioned into finished tools that reflected patterns of prehistoric activity. Trivially, tools had to be made from naturally occurring toolstone distributed across the landscape. Nodules or cobbles of usable stone might be encountered in isolation or in small numbers in many places, and no doubt many prehistoric tools were made from such chance finds. But prehistoric makers and users of tools usually found it convenient, if not essential, to visit places where toolstone occurred in abundance, either on the surface or in near-surface deposits. At such source locations, toolstone could occur in nodules or cobbles as elsewhere but also in tabular deposits, in the case of chert, or float deposits or flows, in the case of obsidian. People were drawn to where toolstone occurred in abundance, either to procure unmodified raw material or to partly or completely make finished tools. In the process, they transformed toolstone sources into quarries, places where the patterned acquisition, processing, and reduction of raw material to finished or semi-finished tools occurred.

Quarries thus preserve the evidence of repeated instances of toolstone reduction. They register both the kind and amount of stone-tool production processes and the technological organizations and modes of production that ancient people employed in making those tools. When quarry debris or associated organics can be dated, or in the rarer instances when they occur in stratigraphic context, chronological patterns and trends in kind and amount of lithic production can be inferred. Production debris is widely distributed and sufficiently abundant that many studies involve its detailed analysis at occupation sites. Yet no matter how abundant debris may be where people lived, that abundance is multiplied by orders of magnitude at quarries. In addition, later production stages are well represented in assemblages at residential sites and may be as well at quarries, but quarry assemblages almost always contain evidence of early production stages.

History of Quarry Studies

For more than 40 years now, North American archaeologists have analyzed the complete range of the process of tool production and use. That includes everything from cobbles to cores to production debris to tools to resharpening debris. Excepting tools themselves, nowhere is the material evidence of stone tool production nearly so abundant as it is at quarries. Therefore, quarries should figure prominently in such studies; sometimes they do. Yet a notable characteristic of the literature is the comparative paucity of detailed studies of tools and debris at quarries. The history of quarry studies, at least in American archaeology, is adequately documented elsewhere (e.g., Bucy 1974:8–11; Johnson 1993; Root 1992:14–22; Syncrude Canada, Ltd. 1974:69–73; see Hiscock and Mitchell 1993: 3,57 for an Australian account).

In so many ways a pioneer of lithic analysis, William Henry Holmes conducted the first systematic quarry study when his detailed examination of the Trenton Gravels, a complex of quarries and workshops in New Jersey, discredited claims for an American Paleolithic. In the process, Holmes developed the concept of the reduction sequence (e.g., 1894a), which undergirds the modern analytical reduction model (Collins 1975; Shott 2003), and showed how cobbles progress from raw to partly transformed stages in the course of their reduction to finished tools. The crude tools of the Trenton Gravels and elsewhere were revealed as unfinished preforms—tools only partly reduced from raw form. Crude thus meant unfinished, not old or a reflection of the quality of the cultures that produced the tools. (The Trenton Gravels controversy was echoed in the Desert West, nearly a century later, in claims for great antiquity from Manix Lake [Bamforth and Dorn 1988].)

After helping to resolve the Paleolithic debate, Holmes visited and described chert quarries in Washington (1894a) and Oklahoma (1894b), and obsidian quarries in central Mexico (1900). Little of note transpired in the next 50 years (but see Mills 1921). Bryan (1950) fashioned a curious reversal in lithic analysis when he concluded that major eastern North American sites like Flint Ridge were not quarries but factories where toolstones were imported and tools and the debris from their making and maintenance accumulated in great numbers owing to the concentration of people and production that occurred there. Few archaeologists found Bryan persuasive (Bucy 1974:10–11; Johnson [1993:152] called Bryan's argument "a minor side track" made prominent only because it was published by a major university), and today few if any doubt that quarries were places of toolstone acquisition and centers of tool production, factories all right but not in Bryan's sense.

Despite this consensus and the production-stage perspective that dominates American lithic analysis, quarries remain relatively uncommon subjects. Partly this may owe to the daunting complexity of deposits that they sometimes contain, partly to the often confusing mixture of deposits of different nature made at different times, and partly to the sheer, overwhelming abundance of evidence, mostly debris, that they always contain. Quarries are "understudied, probably because of the variety of problems they seem to present" (Singer 1984:35; see also Beardsall 2013; Burke 2007:63; Doelman 2008; Ericson 1982:133; Syncrude Canada 1974:69; Torrence 1986:165), and their analyses require careful planning and patience. As Davis and colleagues put it, "archaeologists had been loathe to tackle the study of quarries.... The enormous volume of waste flakes, the great scale of some quarries, and the expected lack of datable materials have discouraged quarry excavations" (1995:39). Confessing a "love-hate" view of quarries, Cobb called their analysis archaeology's "worst nightmare" (2000:121) for the sampling and analytical challenges they pose and the scarcity of contextual data for their interpretation.

However daunting the challenges, the comparative neglect of quarry analysis is lamentable. For decades if not longer, American archaeologists have approached the analysis of lithic production and assemblages of both tools and flakes from the perspective of Holmes's reduction sequence (1894a; see also Collins 1975; Shott 2003). Since about 1980, the concept of technological organization (e.g., Binford 1979) has complemented the reduction-sequence perspective by drawing attention to the cultural factors (e.g., mobility, task-group structure, land-use patterns) affecting the nature, length, and segmentation across the landscape of the tool-making and -using practices that comprise reduction sequences. Save in presumably rare cases of export of raw cobbles from quarries and in the considerable use of secondary cobbles, all reduction sequences begin at quarries. This simple fact alone makes quarries "the logical place to begin the study of a stone-tool-using culture" (Ericson 1984:2; see also Burke 2007:63). Some may end there as well, although most likely begin at quarries and continue elsewhere across the landscape. This much accepted, analysis of quarries is "key to understanding manufacturing technology, and the organisation of production and stone distribution [and] the first step in a lithic analysis should be

to identify the factors that influenced the formation and composition of a quarry assemblage" (Doelman 2008:2). If lithic reduction begins at quarries, then we must study quarries more thoroughly than has been customary in the past, whatever the difficulties that the effort entails.

If Americanist quarry studies trace back to Holmes, they have been hampered not only by the sheer scale of quarry assemblages but also by three specific shortcomings (Syncrude Canada 1974:70–71). First is the general failure to use probabilistic sampling to ensure representative samples. Failure to acquire samples using probabilistic controls can lead to "sample bias...that presents a misleading view of the quarry and prejudices the interpretation of the quarry assemblage" (Doelman 2008:156). Second is the relative neglect of flake debris, despite or perhaps because of the copious quantities of them encountered at quarries. Third is an underdeveloped theoretical approach to the study of quarry production. These limitations are echoed in Australia, where Hiscock and Mitchell (1993:75–78) called for several specific steps—detailed mapping, data collection and analysis, methods to estimate volume of quarrying and production, and characterization of quarry reduction processes and intended products—that resemble those followed here. This study concerns two obsidian quarries in Lincoln County, Nevada.

Modena and Tempiute

UA's project, funded by the Lincoln County Archaeological Initiative (LCAI) administered by the Nevada office of the Department of the Interior's Bureau of Land Management, was conceived in substantial part to address these deficiencies. The subjects of the study were the archaeological deposits at the Modena, Tempiute, and Kane Springs obsidian quarries (Figure 1.1; Shott 2016). Kane Springs results being limited, Modena and Tempiute are the focus here. Data collection was guided by formal probability sampling. At the outset, flake debris was accorded importance in analysis comparable to that of quarry products like biface preforms, redressing a situation in quarry studies,

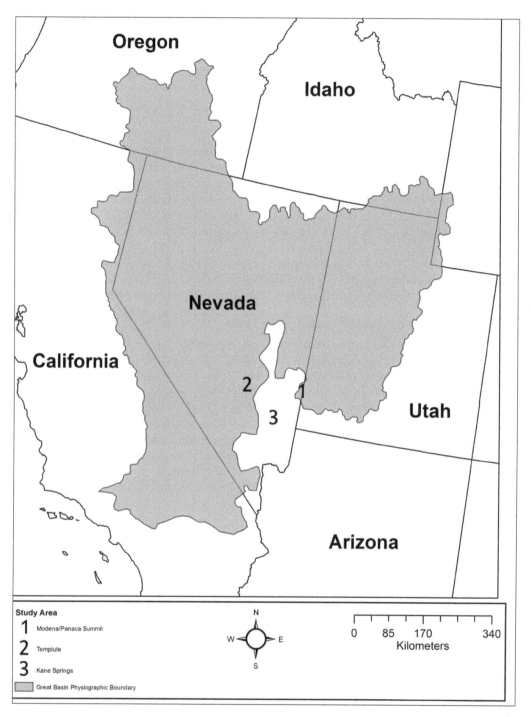

FIGURE 1.1. Location of the Modena and Tempiute Quarries. The Kane Springs quarry complex, a subject of UA investigations, is also shown.

admittedly more common when expressed than in recent years, "that debitage is seldom analyzed and reported" (Ericson 1984:2).

There is no doubting the challenges that quarry analysis poses to archaeology's scarce allotments of labor, time, and funds, but one purpose of this study is to suggest a few surprisingly economical methods that might lighten the analytical load. They derive in part from the second renaissance in quarry analysis led by Ahler (1986) in his study of the massive Knife River quarries of the Middle Missouri Valley. Ahler devised and illustrated the value of a set of related techniques that he called "mass analysis" (1989a, 1989b), the sorting of the copious flake debris found at quarries into a series of size classes and subsequent analysis of proportions by class or the ratio between classes. Ahler's mass analysis was later included as a variant of Andrefsky's (1998:126) "aggregate analysis." Recognizing that empirical debris assemblages often are time-averaged mixtures of material produced and deposited using different reduction modes at different times for different purposes, Root (1992, 1997) developed statistical methods to parse such mixed assemblages into their original constituent reduction modes. A somewhat related variant of mass analysis—also employed here—involved fitting proportions of debris sorted by size class to mathematical models (e.g., Brown 2001; Shott 1994; Stahle and Dunn 1982), which were interpreted to represent ranges of reduction stages or continua. As a result, the current study, possibly for the first time, allocates proportions of flake assemblages to successive stages in biface-preform reduction. Combined with experimental controls, methods reported here enable not only the aggregate description of large flake assemblages (e.g., "mostly core reduction" or "mostly biface production with some core reduction") but apportion those assemblages more finely by proportion and mode (e.g., "23% early-stage biface reduction, 64% late-stage reduction, 13% other" or "12% early-stage and 31% late-stage biface reduction, and 56% core reduction"). Mass analysis itself can be time-consuming; it may require less time and effort in processing than do other ways of characterizing debris as-

semblages, but to exploit its potential requires both experimental controls and extended analysis. No matter how efficient it may be, no one should undertake mass analysis in the mistaken belief that it is easy.

Biface preforms are abundant, especially at Modena. Analysis tested stage versus continuum models of biface production (Shott 2017), favoring the latter. The process is characterized by continuous variation in the rate at which preform weight declines with volume, with analysis providing continuous measures of reduction degree, not merely subjective judgments about reduction "stage." Reduction is complex but can be understood as an allometric process, in part by using surprisingly simple measures.

In addition to Ahler's methodological innovations, the second renaissance of American quarry studies demonstrated the relevance of quarry data to sophisticated theoretical models of human behavior. In this respect, Great Basin scholars led the way. For instance, the distance-to-source data, so popular and so easily acquired with the advent and widespread use of instrumental methods, is not unambiguous data amenable to simple interpretation. Instead, analysis of such distributions must specify modes and organizational contexts of acquisition (Ingbar 1994:50). Realizing the need to link empirical data like distance-to-source values to explanatory theory, Elston (ed. 1992) and colleagues linked quarry data to a number of behavioral-ecology models (see particularly Elston 1992a), applying and testing the models in a series of studies conducted for the Tosawihi chert quarry of northern Nevada. Later, from an end-user perspective, Beck and colleagues (2002; see also Kessler et al. 2009) tested one of those models, the Field Processing Model, in Paleoarchaic assemblages in the Grass and Little Smoky Valleys of east-central Nevada. Accordingly, preform analysis was organized partly as a formal test of the Field Processing Model (FPM), following from pioneering work (Beck et al. 2002; Elston 1992a, 1992b) on other Great Basin quarry and "habitation" assemblages (see also Miller [2018] for the American southeast).

No one who has visited Modena or Tempiute can help but be impressed by the sheer quantity of debris found there. But how much reduction of how many raw cobbles to produce how many end products, whether finished tools or reduction-stage preforms, does such immense quantities of debris reflect? A casual response is "a lot." But using experimental data it is possible to at least roughly convert enormous quantities of debris to impressively large numbers of cobbles and products. One goal of this study was to develop a systematic approach to converting raw amounts of debris to estimated numbers of starting and end products, including cores, flakes, and exported preforms. Using these methods along with probabilistic samples of quarry assemblages, archaeologists can resolve casual judgments of quantity ("a lot" or "a little") into numerical estimates of separate quantities of cores and finished products.

Often, toolstones can be distinguished from one another by color, texture, diagnostic inclusions, or other visible qualities, but the range of variation within sources and the sometimes considerable overlap between them can complicate visual identification. More rigorous instrumental physical-science methods can reliably distinguish toolstones and identify archaeological specimens with specific geological sources. When this is possible, scale and pattern of prehistoric land use or distribution systems can be revealed in the detailed mapping of distance between archaeological occurrences and originating quarries. From the perspective of sites in the landscape where tools were used and eventually discarded, such as "habitation" sites, the number of distinct toolstone sources and their distance from the sites implicate land use, although even in supposedly simple sociopolitical groups like hunter-gatherers of the prehistoric Great Basin unsuspected complexities of organization and mode of acquisition may prevail. The Great Basin has a respectable tradition of such studies (e.g., Jones et al. 2012). But what goes for "habitation" sites goes as well for quarries: the pattern and scale over which quarry toolstone is distributed reveal something of prehistoric land use, while changes over time in that pattern and scale reveal chronological trends in land use. Unfortunately, there is little

tradition of quarry-centered distribution studies in the Great Basin and neighboring areas (but see Elston, ed. 1992; Ericson 1982), although this situation is changing (Haarklau et al. 2005).

In pursuing these research lines, this study employs the concept of the archaeological *terrane*, "the area or surface over which a particular rock or rock group is prevalent" (American Geological Institute 1976:429, cited in Elston 1990a:155, 1992a:35); see also Ericson's similar concept of "regional lithic production system" [1984:4].) Such a terrane is characterized by the knapping and other relevant physical properties of the toolstone but also by its abundance, distribution, and the form in which its cobbles, flows, or formations occur. A terrane is also characterized by the scale and pattern of a toolstone's spatial distribution beyond its source area as the result of its use, and by the inferred modes and rates of its acquisition. To the extent possible, often assisted by contextual data, a terrane also may be characterized by chronological trends in its spatial distribution and technological character.

Recent Great Basin research addressed the problem of calibrating obsidian-hydration dating (OHD) results to radiocarbon time (e.g., Rogers and Duke 2014; Seddon 2005a). An integral part of this research project is obsidian-hydration dating of preforms from Modena and Tempiute, whose calibration to the radiocarbon time scale may eventually improve its precision. UA's study is one example of the use of OHD results in conjunction with distributional studies to map, at least in a preliminary way, the scale and pattern of quarries' distribution zones and to begin to interpret them with respect to acquisition modes and chronological trends. Accordingly, this study and other recent ones (e.g., Connolly, ed. 1999) follow in some of these lines of research. It has several purposes. One is basic mapping of debris deposits. A larger purpose, however, is to advance the theoretically and methodologically informed anthropological study of prehistoric quarry behavior using the considerable data provided by Modena and Tempiute.

2

Previous Research in Lincoln County

Lincoln County, including the vicinities of the Modena and Tempiute sources, has a fairly long but uneven history of archaeological research. Fowler and colleagues (1973:4–6) summarized the 1869 "Morgan Exploring Expedition" and other little-known early work in the region. In the 1920s and 1930s, Harrington (1933) worked extensively in the Moapa valley south of the project area, but also in Lincoln County at Etna Cave (Figure 2.1; see also Wheeler 1973). Wheeler himself accumulated a large collection from 26LN6 in the Panaca Summit Archeological District, and reported substantial obsidian workshop debris there (Schweitzer 2001). Unfortunately, that site's accessibility along Nevada SR 319 made it a popular attraction, such that only a sparse scatter of material was observed there in 2000 (Schweitzer 2001). Best known for its perishable industries, Etna also contained a lithic assemblage including mid- to late-Holocene types (Wheeler 1973:Figure 36). Although claims for great human antiquity there and at nearby Tule Springs did not bear close examination, they at least documented a considerable prehistoric record. Since then southwestern Utah has drawn more archaeological interest (Fowler et al. 1973; Janetski 1981) than has adjacent Nevada, yet even in the former, there is a need for more research. As Cole put it, "The Escalante Desert in western Utah remains very poorly understood" (2012:143).

The first modern systematic archaeological studies in Lincoln County occurred in the late 1960s at the O'Malley and Conaway shelters (Fowler et al. 1973; see also Hull 2010: Appendix A). O'Malley, in the Clover Mountains about 25 km southeast of Caliente, contained a mid-Holocene to late prehistoric record that included substantial Fremont pottery (Fowler et al. 1973:16–18) and Humboldt, Pinto, Gympsum, and Elko Series types, and late prehistoric notched arrowpoints (e.g., Desert Side-Notched; Fowler et al. 1973:21–27). The lithic assemblage also included some production-stage biface preforms (Fowler et al. 1973:29–30) resembling those found in abundance at Modena and to a lesser degree at Tempiute (Fowler et al. 1973:Figures 8–14).

Conaway, near Etna Cave along Meadow Valley Wash in Rainbow Canyon, about 15 km southwest of Caliente, was occupied from about 2,000 BP to European invasion (Fowler et al. 1973:Table 19). It yielded a modest ceramic assemblage along with Elko Series notched/stemmed bifaces, and late prehistoric Rose Springs, Cottonwood, and Desert Side-Notched arrow points (Fowler et al. 1973:Figure 27). Although its assemblage is smaller than O'Malley's, Conaway has a higher proportion of obsidian in both finished tools and flake debris (Fowler et al. 1973:63). A similar sequence was found at Stuart Rockshelter, where several Pinto points were dated to approximately 3900–4000 rcyBP (Shutler et al. 1960:13, Plate 7).

Busby (1979) excavated Civa Shelter II in the northwest corner of Lincoln County, north of Hiko and Slivovitz Shelter in adjacent Nye County, all in Coal Valley. The relatively shallow

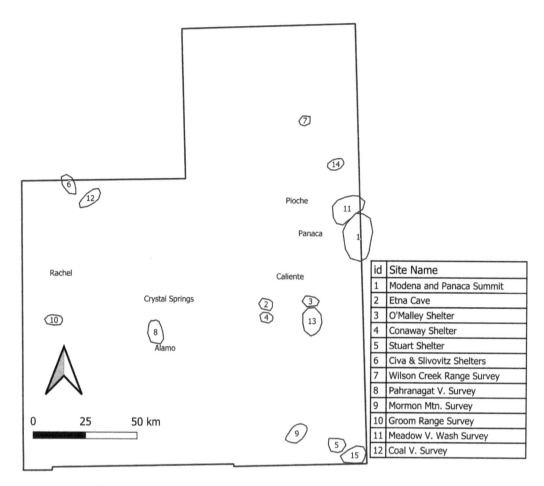

FIGURE 2.1. Location of previous field projects in and near Lincoln County.

and primarily later prehistoric deposits at these shelters, as well as nearby open sites, were dominated by varieties of chert but also included substantial numbers of obsidian points (Busby 1979: 57–59, 110–111, 148–151). Civa II and Slivovitz are perhaps the two largest excavated assemblages nearest to the Tempiute source. More recently, Jones and colleagues (2012:357–358) surveyed sections of the floor of Coal Valley.

Much of the lithic assemblage at O'Malley and Conaway, and perhaps at Etna, is obsidian (Fowler et al. 1973:Figures 7–13, 27; so too at nearby Stuart [Shutler et al. 1960:Figure 4, Plates 7–8]), but work at those sites predated sourcing and OHD studies. Later studies showed that Conaway is dominated by Modena and Kane Springs obsidian in roughly equal

proportions (Skinner and Thatcher 2005:Table D2), O'Malley mostly by Modena, although Hull (2010:43) noted a range of types; no Tempiute obsidian is reported at O'Malley, but some of the modest number of unknown specimens may be from a recently documented obsidian source in the Clover Mountains. Etna was not included in Skinner and Thatcher's (2005) sample, and Hull's (2010:60) account of that collection's tortured history suggests that much of it is lost. To date, obsidian specimens from Civa II and Slivovitz Shelters evidently have not been sourced or otherwise analyzed. Visual inspection of their obsidians suggested to Hull (2010: 81–82) that Tempiute was indeed very common.

Brooks and colleagues (1974; cited in Cole [2012:110]) surveyed approximately 1,000 ha in the Wilson Creek Range north of Modena. One significant finding was the abundance of chert tools and debris in this obsidian-rich landscape. In the late 1970s, Crabtree and Ferraro (1980) surveyed several parcels in the Pahranagat Valley situated between Alamo and Ash Springs, reporting a modest range and number of prehistoric occupations. Lithic assemblages there were dominated by local cherts, particularly varieties described as "brown to buff red...[or] very dark brown" (Crabtree and Ferraro 1980:48), with only small amounts of obsidian. The research occurred before sourcing was common, so Crabtree and Ferraro (1980:49) could point out the area's proximity to the Kane Springs sources but could not document which sources were represented in Pahranagat Valley assemblages.

Several investigations in the 1980s and later followed another hiatus. These projects included a probabilistic survey of Mormon Mountains on the eastern flank of Lower Meadow Valley Wash that reported obsidian of unspecified origin, including flakes and bifaces from at least three sites (Rusco and Muñoz 1983: 54–55). They also included fairly extensive survey and excavation near Panaca Summit and eastward along the margins of Nevada SR 319 (Elston and Juell 1987), as well as a survey of a fiber-optics line (Seddon et al. 2001) that largely encompassed Elston and Juell's survey area, and limited research in the Clover Mountains. Survey in the Groom Range near Rachel identified about 200 sites, mostly middle Holocene in age or later (Reno and Pippin 1986:Figure 5-1, Table 5-1), including several small chert or fine-grained volcanic quarries (Reno and Pippin 1986:125–126).

The lithic assemblage at 26LN21, on Nevada SR 319 near the Utah border, was dominated by a "gray banded obsidian" but also included a "mahogany obsidian" (Elston and Juell 1987: 161). So too did the assemblages from nearby 26LN3356 and 26LN3357 although the latter includes no mahogany obsidian (Elston and Juell 1987:166, 173). Both of these descriptions fit material from nearby Modena, as discussed in Chapter 4. Whatever other functions these sites served (which can be difficult to infer from

the limited material record [Seddon 2001b]), the size and character of their lithic assemblages, particularly flake debris, suggest that they were workshops for the processing of early-stage to middle-stage bifaces and other tools (Elston and Juell 1987:161, 166). Notably, "debitage representing the earliest stage of reduction...is scarce...suggesting that initial processing most likely took place elsewhere" (Elston and Juell 1987:161). So far as this conclusion concerns Modena obsidian, it implicates a staged process of obsidian reduction that confines initial work to the source and its immediate environs and middle- to later-stage reduction to more distant locations like these sites. 26LN3357 also contained a check dam for water control (Elston and Juell 1987:171–172).

Nearer to Panaca Summit itself, 26LN3359's lithic assemblage was dominated by what probably is Modena obsidian, including its mahogany variant, and its character suggests late-stage processing (Elston and Juell 1987:181–183). 26LN1775 is a set of deposits generated by complex, mostly late prehistoric, occupations, that is, an accumulation or palimpsest (Seddon 2001b:347). There, chert is more abundant than obsidian (which again is gray and banded, so perhaps Modena) and the debris assemblage reflects late-stage processing or resharpening of finished points (Elston and Juell 1987:206). Although Panaca Summit sites along Nevada SR 319 were occupied over a considerable time range and for a variety of purposes, many of them include intermediate- to late-stage processing of obsidian.

Seddon and colleagues (2001) revisited several of Elston and Juell's sites. The difference in number and type of artifacts recovered in the two investigations (e.g., Shurack 2001:110) is less important than the fact that both documented substantial mid-Holocene or later occupation of the Panaca Summit Archeological District. SWCA documented intact buried deposits at 26LN1775 (Shurack 2001) and 26LN3357, including abundant obsidian debris at depths of 60 cm or more below surface (Stokes et al. 2001:132–139), and the extensive sourcing and OHD conducted in SWCA's investigation (e.g., Seddon 2001a) gave some indication of patterns of occupational intensity through time. Hull (2010:32–37) also revisited and sampled Panaca Summit Archeological District sites.

Across the Panaca Summit Archeological District, Modena comprised 95% or more of obsidian assemblages (Seddon 2001a:Table 4.3), although two then-unknown materials, one of which could be Tempiute, occurred in small numbers. In Seddon's (2001b) extensive effort to identify dimensions of assemblage variation interpretable as different site types, 26LN3357—particularly Block 2—stood apart from the general pattern amid the Panaca Summit Archeological District assemblages for the abundance of obsidian debris there (2001b:351). Otherwise, assemblage size influenced assemblage composition (Shott 2010), suggesting that most sites in the area are complex accumulations of many occupations for many purposes.

Cole (2006, 2012) conducted a large-scale sample survey centered in Meadow Valley Wash north and west of the Modena source but including some 500 × 500 m units near the site. Cole also reported results of excavation at Sand Dune, a Fremont pit house north of Ursine in Meadow Valley Wash approximately 25 km northwest of Modena (2012:544–592), and at Waterfall, an open site and set of small rockshelters approximately 15 km west of Modena (2012:594–680). Cole's survey provided a wealth of data on the distribution of obsidian by amount, technological class, and diagnostic point type for comparison to material recovered at the Modena source itself, as discussed in subsequent chapters.

Jones and colleagues (2012:357–358) reported results of survey work on the floor of Coal Valley, approximately 25 km northeast of Tempiute. That work was designed to test and refine their model of obsidian and other toolstone "conveyance zones," and documented heavy local use of both Tempiute and Modena obsidian. Kremkau and colleagues (2011; see also Natoli et al. 2011) conducted baseline investigations at sites in Pine and Mathews Canyon Reservoirs east of Caliente and south of the Modena source. Limited diagnostic artifacts spanned a wide range of regional prehistory (Kremkau et al. 2011:Figure 55; Natoli et al. 2011), although most dated from the middle Holocene to late prehistory. Fair quantities of obsidian, mostly debris identified as biface-reduction or core-reduction flakes, were found (Kremkau et al. 2011:Tables 8–35). At the time of their fieldwork Modena was the nearest obsidian source known, but the recent discovery of another source in the Clover Mountains cautions against attributing most or all obsidian found in Pine and Mathews Canyons to that source (Kremkau et al. 2011:163). Birnie and others' (2003) survey near State Line Canyon, about 25 km north of Modena, documented Archaic, Fremont, and one Numic occupation. Zeier and Reno (2012) investigated several prehistoric sites between Deer Creek and Fay, also north of Modena. They (2012:113–117) reported modest quantities of obsidian flake debris and nondiagnostic bifaces, but sourced no samples. Giambastini and Tinsley (2002) documented mostly mid-Holocene occupation in a survey area near Mesquite, about 90 km south of Modena. Site types included small chert and quartzite quarries. Modena obsidian was found in the small set of sourced artifacts there (Giambastini and Tinsley 2002:97). Vicari (2013) reported on geoarchaeological aspects of SWCA's survey from Clark through Lincoln and Nye into White Pine County.

On balance, previous research in and near Lincoln County suggests a remarkable continuity in hunter-gatherer adaptive practices and land-use systems from the mid-Holocene to European invasion (e.g., Schweitzer and Seddon 2001:358). Late prehistoric Fremont occupation appears culturally distinct and represents mixed horticultural and foraging practices, but continuity in some respects as well, such as toolstone procurement.

Beyond the immediate environs, survey work in the Escalante Desert documented a range of Archaic through late prehistoric occupations and considerable obsidian assemblages (Janetski 1981). Later in the same area, the massive Kern River project included extensive fieldwork in southwestern Utah, east of Modena (Reed et al. 2005a, 2005b). A transect survey that followed a similar route across southern Nevada into western Utah also produced significant evidence of the use of Modena and Tempiute obsidians (Bernatchez et al. 2013; McKee et al. 2013). Hull (2010:Table 2) listed other investigations as well. Several, particularly in Washington County, produced large quantities of Modena obsidian.

Previous Research at Project Sites

Before UA's project began, the recently discovered Modena quarry had witnessed only brief archaeological activity. Since UA fieldwork was completed, Modena in particular but also Tempiute have been the subjects of several LCAI projects of differing nature and scope; the Modena quarry rapidly became a very popular subject.

Jackson and colleagues (2009:118–124) obtained raw cobbles for source characterization, and also briefly described 42IN737 and other workshops in Utah east of the Modena quarry, including 42IN110, from which a fluted point of obsidian was reported (Copeland and Fike 1988:Figure 1-2); unmodified natural cobbles also occurred at several sites (Jackson et al. 2009:122–123). Clarence Bush and Shott reconnoitered Modena in 2004. Shott and Elisabeth Bacus made a brief visit in 2005 to undertake preliminary sampling at the two densest clusters, A and B. Mr. Lytle assisted in these visits, and in later fieldwork. In 2012 Brigham Young University began a three-year investigation at the Modena quarry and its environs. These efforts were focused partly on mapping but also on detailed in-field sourcing to gauge the range of geochemical variation in local obsidian (Talbot and Richens 2012). Like UA investigations, they mapped the distribution of quarry debris at Modena.

Geological and possibly archaeological samples collected from the vicinity of the Modena source were reported by Jackson and colleagues (2009:123, Appendix A-32-33, Appendix B) and

Hull (1994:Table 7-2). Also, Hughes (2012) collected cobbles at and near Modena for sourcing analysis. His sample locations 12-6 to 12-8 were not mapped. To judge from descriptions, 12-6 is chiefly a source of raw cobbles of modest size probably somewhere between the quarry itself and the state line, 12-7 (as well as a possible rock ring) probably either Clusters A or B at Modena proper, and 12-8 (located west of 12-7 as the field party "were walking back to the truck" [Hughes 2012:2]) probably Cluster F. Rowley and others (2002) made the first detailed report on the Modena quarry itself. Relevant details of this work are discussed in Chapters 3 and 4, where Rowley and colleagues' report is treated as the first stage of systematic fieldwork at the site.

Hafey (2003) discovered and reported the Tempiute source as part of his larger study of archaeological remains in a 200+ ha zone of Sand Spring Valley. His excavation in what we identify as Cluster N-2 revealed a modest depth of deposit (Hafey 2003:7) and dense distributions of obsidian flake debris (Hafey 2003:11). Hafey's discovery of the quarry and its subsequent source characterization were instrumental in clarifying the distribution of toolstone sources in the southern and central Great Basin (e.g., Jones et al. 2003) and constitute a significant contribution to regional research.

Hughes (2005:B15) collected geological specimens from Tempiute. To judge from his Figure B18, Hughes sampled one of the clusters mapped by Hafey and sampled by UA. Hull (2010:51–53) collected samples from the Tempiute source and also visited 26LN4891, on the pluvial lake in Sand Spring Valley, from which a Western Stemmed Tradition/Great Basin Stemmed Series (WST/GBSS) point previously was reported.

Clerico (1978; cited in Reno and Pippin 1986:68) documented "large sites" 26LN706 and 26LN707 in a linear survey area from Penoyer Springs, east of Tempiute, to the bed of pluvial Sand Spring Lake. This area runs near if not across the Tempiute source; Reno and Pippin reported "fist size" obsidian nodules "extensively worked by aboriginal knappers" (1986:68). It is possible that this survey discovered the Tempiute quarry before Hafey's work which, nevertheless, was the first to document the source area in detail and to call it to the attention of researchers.

In his investigations in Sand Spring Valley, Hafey (2003:15) collected modest artifact samples from the Tempiute source and from other sites. Several specimens, mostly used and/or retouched flakes and biface preforms, were submitted for sourcing and OHD, as reported in later chapters. Not surprisingly, most artifacts are sourced as Tempiute obsidian, while several finished but damaged, broken, or depleted bifaces were from other sources. Neither Groom Range obsidian artifacts nor obsidian Clovis points from private collections in that area (Reno and Pippin 1986:105) have been sourced.

The undeniable value of previous research does not obscure some aggregate shortcomings—of circumstance, not commission.

Selective private collection has impoverished some sites of diagnostic points, and the concentration of modern activity and therefore archaeological investigation along Nevada SR 319 must be complemented by work elsewhere in the region (Schweitzer and Seddon 2001:359; see also Dames and Moore 1994:21–26 for accounts of extensive and selective collection of diagnostic points from the Wild Horse Canyon obsidian source in Utah, and, farther afield, Johnson et al. [1995:12] on Obsidian Cliff being "pilfered unrelentingly" over many years). In the aggregate, previous research in the region provided a good view of intermediate-stage and later processing and maintenance of stone tools but little information on quarry and near-quarry workshop patterns of reduction and processing. In part, investigations at Modena and Tempiute, as briefly summarized in Chapter 1 and elaborated in following chapters, were designed to redress these gaps in research and data.

3

Obsidian and the Modena and Tempiute Quarries

This study concerns two of the several obsidian sources in Lincoln County, Nevada—Modena or Panaca Summit, and Tempiute (see Figure 1.1). Both were exploited, to varying degrees, by prehistoric residents of the Great Basin as toolstone quarries for the production of preforms and tools. This chapter discusses the geological origin and relevant current characteristics of each source area. Before describing each study site, the concept of toolstone "source" requires consideration.

Obsidian

Varieties of chert are the most common toolstones used in prehistory. Chert's popularity owes partly to its material properties relevant to knapping—its workability—but partly also to its abundance and wide distribution. Chert is a microcrystalline silicate (Luedtke 1992:5) that forms in many sedimentary deposits and, as a result, occurs naturally in many parts of the world.

Although chert is common in Great Basin lithic assemblages so too are other toolstones, including obsidian and fine-grained volcanics. Obsidian is volcanic, a silicate that forms in the rapid cooling of rhyolite ejected from calderas during magma events. Obsidian may be locally abundant, but its continental and global distributions are more limited than are chert's. For long periods, the Great Basin was tectonically active; consequently, obsidian is widely distributed in the region (Grayson 2011:296–298; Jones et al. 2003:Figure 1; Skinner 1983:14–16,

Figure 4). Sources are fairly abundant in the northwestern Great Basin and in the south-central hydrographic Great Basin (Grayson 2011:Figure 9.5; Haarklau 2005), as is perlite, a mineral of similar origin and chemical composition (Nevada Bureau of Mines 1964:Figure 47). Few obsidian sources lie in the Great Basin's north-central and northeastern chert "core" (Thomas 2014).

Chert is highly variable in color, luster, grain, and inclusions. Although obsidian is somewhat variable in these respects as well (and highly variable in trace-element composition, which is crucial to its suitability for sourcing by xero-radiography [XRF] or other methods), most obsidians are gray to black in color, highly lustrous and reflective once the weathered cortex is removed, and, because obsidian is noncrystalline, both homogeneous—possessing the same properties throughout its matrix—and isotropic—possessing the same mechanical properties in all directions (Luedtke 1992:86; Shackley 2005:185; Skinner 1983:36–41). In McCutcheon and Dunnell's (1998:263) terms, obsidian's *groundmass* is uniform and its inclusions are both rare and uniformly distributed compared to many cherts. In Elston's (1990b:Table 34) terms, obsidian has higher plasticity than chert.

In mechanical properties, therefore, compared to chert, obsidian generally is more plastic or elastic (i.e., has lower Young's modulus values and higher Poisson-ratio values) and has less compressive strength. Obsidian's values for tensile strength, fracture toughness, transverse bending, density (Skinner [1983:39] reported density between 2.13–2.46 gm/cm³), and hardness (Skinner [1983:37] reported Vickers hardness of 500–900 kg/mm², with a mode ca. 700 kg/mm²) generally fall within the range of cherts (Duke and Haynes 2009:155; Luedtke 1992:Table 6.2; Nelson et al. 2012). Many knappers consider most obsidians more workable than most cherts, and obsidian's noncrystalline structure means that knapped obsidian forms a sharper edge than knapped chert (Shackley 2005:185). Yet toolstone quality depends upon intended use, and users might trade abstract knapping or performance quality for access and other circumstances (e.g., Duke 2013). Variation among obsidians also was recognized by, for instance, the Pomo who distinguished between local sources suitable for production of arrow points or for flake tools for general cutting purposes (Heizer and Treganza 1944:294). Where available, obsidian points often were preferred to chert or other materials (Ellis 1997:50; Elston 1990b:Table 42), presumably for their superior target penetration ("the great superiority of the obsidian point in cutting animal material" [Pope 1923:56]). However, obsidian also is brittler than most cherts, so it tends to greater susceptibility both to edge damage and to fracture (Elston 1990a:156–157).

Unlike chert, obsidian contains little or no water when it forms. However, exposed obsidian hydrates as a function of time, a property that enables estimation of the age of exposure (on knapped surfaces, the age of the flake or tool's production, not the age of geological formation) by obsidian hydration dating (OHD). Intrinsic variation among obsidian sources, local variation by elevation and climate, and depositional and postdepositional history of obsidian cobbles and the flakes and tools struck from them greatly complicate OHD as a dating method, a subject revisited in detail in Chapter 9.

What is a Source?

Owing to its geological history, the Great Basin contains many obsidian sources (Grayson 2011: 296–298; Haarklau et al. 2005). This comparative abundance did not escape the notice of

the region's prehistoric inhabitants, who used obsidian on a regular basis. Nor has it escaped the notice of archaeologists who have encountered obsidian assemblages of varying size and composition at a wide range of prehistoric occupation sites and assemblages of very large size indeed at obsidian quarries.

Nominally, Modena and Tempiute each is a distinct source. But obsidian and other toolstone sources can vary widely in spatial extent and stratigraphic depth and "source" has both spatial and geochemical referents. At one extreme, a source may consist of a single, discrete flow or occurrence, whether exposed or embedded in volcanic or sedimentary formations. Many obsidian sources probably arose in this manner; some chert and other toolstone sources occurring in sedimentary deposits may be similar. At the opposite extreme, the complexities of volcanic processes can produce small obsidian clasts broadcast across large areas, even varying in grain size with distance from vent source (Elston and Zeier 1984:18–21; Shackley 2005:25; Skinner 1983:22).

Whether an obsidian or other toolstone source originally was discrete, its later geological history may alter its distribution. Exposed flows can weather, fracture, and erode, the fragments then scattering over considerable distances in valley gravel trains. Modena cobbles, for instance, occur in quantity 30 km or more downstream of the source. Elsewhere, secondary deposition on scales of 100 km or more are documented (Church 2000:670; Shackley 2002:56–57, 2005:26), although Skinner (1983: 54) considered cobbles of usable size to be rare more than 40 km downstream of most obsidian sources. Shackley's description of "nodules as large as two to three centimeters" (2002:56) suggests that water transport over considerable distance does indeed reduce many cobbles to very small, possibly not usable, size (see also Church 2000:670). Also, broadcast and originally buried cobbles may gradually be exposed by erosion, making a chemical source of obsidian progressively more widely distributed. Finally, depending upon an area's volcanic history (or a chert or other toolstone area's geological history), two or more chemically and geologically distinct sources may co-occur (e.g., Jones et al. 2003:15; Shackley 1994).

Thus, obsidian and other toolstone sources may be single point sources, single diffuse sources, or multiple point or diffuse sources. Not all sources are alike. Frahm (2012) contrasted the several distinct obsidians found in stratified sequence and dramatic context at Newberry with the diffuse and complex intermingling over broad areas of distinct sources at Glass Buttes (on the latter condition, see also Moore 2009:59). Newberry is a multiple source whose constituents overlap at effectively a single point. Glass Buttes, on the other hand, is a complex, multiple diffuse source. Similarly, Coso is comprised of several sources, not a single one (Eerkens and Rosenthal 2004; Elston and Zeier 1984; Hughes 1990:2), as is Mono-area obsidian (Hughes 1990), so any identification to the level of "Coso volcanic field" or "Mono Lake" may obscure significant behavioral patterning. How finely we resolve sources both spatially and geochemically influences the patterns of prehistoric distribution and use that we infer (e.g., Ericson and Glascock 2004).

"Source" emerges as a complex, even problematic term, and its use here engages these complexities. Modena, for instance, is a complex toolstone source; the main area of occurrence is fairly discrete but, as above, broadcast clasts or secondary deposits can be found 30 km or more downstream (Jackson et al. 2009:118, Figure 14.1). Modena obsidian occurs in cobbles of sufficient size and quantity to produce debris fields that qualify as workshops at locations from 5–10 km (Jackson et al. 2009:122–124, Figure A-31) to approximately 15 km southeast of the site proper (Umshler 1975:4, 31). Still, Modena cobbles in secondary contexts are apt to be mechanically reworked and therefore smaller than those occurring at the main source, much like the progressive reduction in stream-bed cobble size that Skinner (1983) suggested and Cherry and colleagues (2010:150–152) documented with distance from their Armenian obsidian source.

Visits to Modena by Shott with Martin Bush and Eric Henderson in 2003–2004 revealed debris easily exceeding 1 flake or artifact per square meter in a continuous distribution for at least 2 km west and northwest of the main site. Like Bodie Hills and other major sources (e.g., Ericson 1982), the main obsidian concentration at Modena is of impressive size and volume (although not nearly of the scale of Yellowstone's Obsidian Cliff [Johnson et al. 1995], St. Helena [Heizer and Treganza 1944:304], or Glass Mountain in California [Shackley 2005:8]), yet detailed regional mapping carried out in the Bodie Hills vicinity (e.g., Halford 2008:48) (and useful near Modena) should considerably increase the number of quarry/workshop locales and expand the source's documented spatial scale. In particular, it would be extremely valuable to map the abundance and distribution of Modena tools and debris continuously over a considerable distance from the source—circa 50–75 km—in areas where redeposited secondary cobbles do not complicate the supply situation.

Tempiute, in contrast, seems a notably discrete source, essentially confined to Hafey's and our small study area. Tempiute lies on an alluvial fan that declines to the west and north, and the braided channels and gravel trains found there indicate significant surface erosion that probably divided an original contiguous distribution of obsidian into the quasi-discrete clusters now evident on the site's surface. Whatever the case, surely obsidian clasts have washed out of Tempiute. Perhaps, though, the small original size of Tempiute cobbles rendered unusable the broken clasts that eroded and washed out, at least over short distances, from the site. As a result, Tempiute amounts to a point source of obsidian toolstone.

Besides its spatial extent and chemical and geological origin, any source also can be characterized by the amount and quality of its toolstone and the size of the cobbles or packages in which it is found. This study addresses the question of the scale of production at Modena and Tempiute. As brief summary descriptions, Modena cobbles were fairly large and, in the aggregate, comprised an abundant source of considerably high knapping quality. Cobbles

FIGURE 3.1. View of Modena Area A looking upslope.

from Tempiute are much smaller, and yielded volumes of worked material much smaller in total than Modena.

Modena

Modena was identified as a major source well before the discovery of the quarry's location. Until then, "persistent rumors and local legends" (Weide 1970:192) and the unmistakable local abundance of material placed the source only somewhere between Panaca Summit and the town of Modena. The quantity of Modena float cobbles found downstream in Gold Springs Wash, well into southwestern Utah, long encouraged the assumption that the main source was located there (Hull 2010:85; Janetski 1981:31); indeed, several map references placed the source in Utah (e.g., McKee 2009; Nelson 1984:Figure 1; Nelson and Holmes 1978:Figure 5; Seddon 2001a:Figure 4.5, 2005a:Figure 24-1; cf. Hull 1994:Figure 7-5, who located the main source in the vicinity of Panaca Summit yet also reasoned "that the primary geologic occurrence of this material may extend across the Utah-Nevada border to the west of the town of Modena" [1994:7–3]; Westfall et al. 1987:87). Nelson and Holmes (1978:74) even referred to an Iron County, UT site, 42IN223, as a Modena quarry. Hughes (2005:255) also expressed uncertainty about both Modena's specific source and its float distribution. Even recently, Duff and colleagues (2012:Table 1), Hughes (2010:Figure 10.1; see also Hughes and Bennyhoff 1986:Figure 2), Kodack (1997:258), Martin (2009:154), Origer (2012), McGuire and Ahlstrom (2012:221), McGuire and colleagues (2014:Figure 5.7), Pitblado (2003:146, 257), Stevenson (2008), Westfall and colleagues (1987:87), and Zeier and Reno (2012:133) located the source in Utah or described it as a secondary alluvial deposit. Harper (2006:73) placed the source at or near Panaca Summit, or between there and the town of Panaca.

In September 1998, local residents Farrel and Manetta Lytle chanced upon Modena while hiking. Approaching one of the main concentrations of debris, Area A in this report, the Lytles were momentarily blinded by shafts of early morning sunlight striking and reflecting off the obsidian fragments. Mr. Lytle, a retired geochemist with extensive research experience and an interest in physical-science methods applied to archaeology (e.g., Lytle 2003, 2010; Lytle and Pingitore 2004), at once recognized the significance of the discovery. A BLM Ely District site steward, he reported the location.

At Mount Edziza in British Columbia, "dense lobes of obsidian fragments festoon the steep scree slope" (Fladmark 1984:145). So too at Modena. As elsewhere (e.g., Bowers and Savage 1962:11; Fladmark 1984:145; Heizer and Treganza 1944:303; Parkman 1983:257; Singer and Ericson 1977:172; Torrence 1986:167–168), major clusters of obsidian occur at Modena in sufficient quantity to form loose, unconsolidated scree deposits (Hughes [2012:1–2], cited in Rogers and Duke 2014:Appendix C, described "huge quantities of manufacturing debris litter[ing] the ground"), the largest and densest of which are visible from the air. On the ground, Modena is fairly heavily forested, and no such cluster is visible in a single view. Figure 3.1 shows part of the spatial extent of Area A. (Similarly, Mt. Edziza is "visible from the air as a marked black smear over the grey-green alpine tundra" [Fladmark 1984:145].) Also like other obsidian quarries, at Modena the tread of footsteps across the thick talus slope is "immediately filled by the sliding, tinkling slivers of glass" (Holmes 1900:410) and "flake and preform debris is so dense that in patches it is like walking on cornflakes" (Bickler and Turner 2002:15), except that these cornflakes are black, have sharp edges, glisten in the sun, and radiate the midday heat so intensely as to be felt through the thick soles of field boots.

Modena consists of three dense scree deposits of this nature and a variable distribution and abundance of obsidian debris surrounding them. The scree deposits, labeled A, B, and F to follow Rowley and others (2002:Figure 1), mark the locations of dense, original concentrations of obsidian cobbles that probably were partially knapped in place. To judge from the remarkable density of debris that comprises them, the scree deposits are authentic activity clusters, that is, products of organized, cumulative human activity. Surrounding debris fields are places where sparser cobble deposits were worked, partly reduced cobbles or tool blanks were taken for further reduction, or some combination of the two. Modena is a structured quarry landscape, not a random debris field.

Talbot and Richens (2012) mapped Area A's boundaries to encompass roughly twice the area of obsidian concentration mapped by UA, although their southern boundary corresponds to a smaller concentration at the foot of the slope that Area A occupies. There is indeed a concentration of debris at that area, and discontinuous debris distribution between it and the southern boundary of Area A as mapped in Chapter 4.

The Modena source is situated in the Cedar Range (Talbot and Richens 2012:2) or White Rock Mountains (Best et al. 1989:Figure 4), a series of low mountains east of the Wilson Creek Range and north of the Clover Mountains, about 25 km east of Panaca, Nevada. It lies near the western margin of the Escalante Desert watershed (Environmental Protection Agency 2012), in a national land-cover forest-woodland zone (U.S. Geological Survey 2011). The main source area lies within the hydrographic Great Basin (Grayson 2011:Figure 2.1) near the Escalante Desert (itself occupied mostly by semi-desert [U.S. Geological Survey 2011]). Pinyon-juniper (*Pinus spp., Juniperus osteosperma*) forest with a significant understory dominated by sagebrush (*Artemisia spp.*) and greasewood (*Sarcobatus spp.*) covers the quarry area. Local fauna are mostly endemic to the Great Basin (including Great Basin rattlesnakes in some abundance in the quarry environs), but wild horses were commonly observed during fieldwork. Lytle reported pumas in the area.

Modena cobbles are found well downstream of the main source in the gravel train of Gold Springs Wash (Cole 2012:49; Hull 2010:32; Jackson et al. 2009; Janetski 1981:31; Rowley et al. 2002:1; Seddon 2001a; Umshler 1975). They "cover more than 20 miles, between Panaca, NV and Modena, UT" (Moore 2009:63), and occur as a "remarkable scatter of lithic debitage that runs from the eastern border of the Panaca

Summit Archaeological District…to Site 26Ln6 at Nine Mile Rocks" (Seddon 2001b:337), south of the source and partly outside of the Gold Springs Wash drainage. In the Panaca Summit vicinity, Modena obsidian probably was carried in by prehistoric inhabitants, but some may occur naturally as float. Stream transport of obsidians over considerable distance is documented elsewhere in southern Nevada (Johnson and Wagner 2005:36) and the American West (Church 2000:670–671; Halford 2001:32). In nearby Utah even much of what is defined as the Wild Horse Canyon obsidian source itself is a secondary alluvial deposit as much as 5 km downstream of the primary deposit (Dames and Moore 1994:21-26, 21-31).

Yet secondary deposits of Modena obsidian may not be as extensive as widely believed. Walling and colleagues suspected, but did not document, local supplies of obsidian at their Quail Creek study area 80 km southeast of Modena, because some archaeological obsidian there occurred as "stream tumbled pebbles" (1988:408). This suggests the possibility that Modena or other obsidians can be quite widely distributed in stream deposits. Modena is among the nearest sources to Quail Creek, but obsidian from the site was not sourced, and the worked secondary cobbles found could have been imported; indeed, Walling and others cited a local lapidary on the *absence* of "any concentrated obsidian source in the vicinity" (1988:409). Toolstone in secondary contexts like gravel trains is not necessarily identical in relevant physical properties to material in original context (Church 2000; McCutcheon and Dunnell 1998), and it is uncertain if the generally smaller and possibly reworked cobbles found at distance from the source are comparable to those from Modena itself.

The source is known mostly or interchangeably as "Modena" or "Panaca Summit," although McKee and colleagues (2010) called it "Modena/Panaca Pass." Early sourcing studies (e.g., Nelson 1984:Figure 1; Nelson and Holmes 1978; Umshler 1975:4, Figure 1) identified it as Modena, usage that persists to the present (e.g., Duke 2011; Hughes 2005; Jackson et al. 2009;

Johnson and McQueen 2012; Moore 2009 [originally 2002]:63). "Panaca Summit" came into use chiefly via Elston and Juell's (1987; see also Seddon 2001b) research at and near that topographic feature and is used preferentially by Rogers and Duke (2014). Seddon and others (2001:Figure 4.5) plotted distinct sources at Panaca Summit and Modena. Hull (2010:32) distinguished Panaca Summit as an area of intensive occupation near, but not at, the Modena source, although she also noted (Hull 2010:32–37) that unworked obsidian cobbles, presumably of Modena provenance, occur in small quantities at Panaca Summit, perhaps as tephra. Moore (2009:65) considered occurrences in the vicinity of Panaca Summit to be float. Talbot and Richens (2012:Figure 11) collected raw nodules in the vicinity of the quarry, as well as 5 km or more to the south and, in smaller numbers, somewhat to the north, distances consistent with the range over which tephra may be deposited during volcanic eruption (Skinner 1983:55). Zeier and Reno (2012:115–116) reported "thumb-sized" nodules (also reported as 50 mm [<2 in] in maximum dimension) near Deer Creek about 10 km north of the Modena quarry, and identified that area as an obsidian source.

For its historical primacy and to avoid confusion with the extensively investigated sites near Panaca Summit to which Modena data are compared in several passages here (Elston and Juell 1987; Seddon et al. 2001), in this study "Modena" signifies both the source and its secondary distributions, chiefly to the southeast. It confines "Panaca Summit" to sites at and near that topographic feature. Other names include Piñon Point and Dry Valley (Northwest Research Obsidian Studies Laboratory Source Catalog 2012).

Source Geology

Modena obsidian occurs in Tschanz and Pampeyan's (1970:Plate 2) Tvt ("tuffs and tuffaceous sediments") or TKvu ("volcanic rock, undifferentiated") units. Tschanz and Pampeyan's minerals survey did not include obsidian, but they (1970:122) noted that circa 1950 Lincoln County accounted for roughly half of American perlite production; their Plate 1 showed one perlite source situated only kilometers from the Modena obsidian source. Modena lies near the margins of the 32–27 mya Indian Peak Caldera (Best et al. 1989:1078–1085; Rowley et al. 2002:3; Williams et al. 1997:Figure 1), but at the base of rhyolite lava flows of the Steamboat Mountain Formation of considerably younger age. The latter is dated locally to circa 11.7 mya (Rowley et al. 2002:5; Williams et al. 1997; see also Johnson and Haarklau 2005:127).

Rowley and colleague's (2002:Figure 1) detailed mapping distinguished the obsidian member "Tslo" as a basal constituent of the Steamboat Mountain rhyolitic lava. Modena Area B lies in the vicinity of Rowley's largest "Tslo" zone; Areas A and F adjoin smaller mapped sections of that unit. Rowley and colleagues considered Modena obsidian "to have been deposited as a discontinuous lens that represent the base of some parts of the rhyolite lava-flow members" (2002:5). Because they could not identify a discrete flow deposit at Modena or significant numbers of raw cobbles, the authors (Rowley et al. 2002) concluded that the source was substantially exhausted in prehistory owing to intensive exploitation.

Depletion is not a surprising fate for very small toolstone sources like the Highland Chert Quarry in the Groom Range south of the Tempiute source (Reno and Pippin 1986:126), but may have also occurred at larger sources (e.g., see Amick [1991:80–81] for Buckboard Mesa, Eerkens and Rosenthal [2004:27] and Hartwell et al. [1996:57] for the Coso volcanic field, Parkman [1983:256] for the Annadel source in central California, Skinner [1983:93] for Washington State sources, and farther afield, Foley and Mirazón Lahr [2015] for Libyan Paleolithic landscapes). Yet some obsidians occurred originally as lenses or veins in rhyolitic domes. As the rhyolite weathered and eroded over geological time, the more resistant obsidian formed a lag deposit, or float (Skinner 1983:22). Some obsidian sources, for instance in the extensive Coso Volcanic Field (e.g., Elston and Zeier 1984:14, 18; Gilreath and Hildebrandt 1997:7), include both flow or large-cobble material and extensive

FIGURE 3.2. Unmodified Modena obsidian cobble.

distributions of float in primary or secondary context. This variation may have characterized Modena originally, although the highly vesicular obsidian common in the Coso Volcanic Field (Elston and Zeier 1984:20) was not observed frequently at Modena; whatever the case, Talbot and Richens's (2012) recent work in areas surrounding the main quarry deposits suggests that some raw obsidian remains in the vicinity.

Geochemically, Modena obsidian is relatively homogeneous, no surprise in an Indian Peak caldera complex "marked by cyclic eruptions of petrographically similar, compositionally zoned, lithic-rich rhyolites" (Best et al. 1989: 1089). As a result, Nelson and Holmes (1978:69) considered Modena (their "Sources 7a and 7b") to be easily distinguished from other obsidian sources in the region. Yet the complex's five-million-year history and complicated tectonic character suggests at least the possibility of detectable geochemical variation across its occurrence zone (Nelson and Holmes 1978:1089). Recent research is testing the range of geochemical variation and its spatial patterning in the quarry vicinity (Rogers and Duke 2014; Talbot and Richens 2012).

Whatever its original form, Modena occurs today as cobbles that range from perhaps 100–200 mm in maximum dimension down to 50 mm or less, approximately the size range of perlite or marekanite. Near the quarry, Hughes (2012:1) reported cobbles as large as 100 × 100 mm. There are few that exceed those dimensions on the surface of the main concentration, but some may be found there (Figure 3.2) and in the larger source area in arroyos or on eroding hillslopes. At sample location 12-7, Hughes (2012:2) reported cobbles as large as 150 × 100 mm, with others up to 100 × 100 mm at his location 12-8. To judge from Hughes's (2012:1–2) account, his location 12-7 is almost certainly Area A, and his location 12-8 is Area F. F. Lytle (personal communication, 6 January 2004) reported at least one unworked cobble that approached 600 mm in maximum dimension in downstream secondary context. Jackson and colleagues reported cobbles "up to 27 cm in diameter" (2009:121) exposed in recent tree throws at the main quarry concentrations, and collected several cobbles, either from the main quarry source or a sample unit located about 4 km to the east, the larger of which measured approximately 100 mm in maximum dm (Jackson et al. 2009:Figure C-18). Yet little in the Modena vicinity approaches the "clasts up to 70 cm in diameter" (Dames and Moore 1994:21–26) reported at Wild Horse Canyon. Elston and Juell reported "fist-sized" cobbles (1987:5) at Devil's Gap on the Nevada-Utah line, and Hull (1994:Table 7-1) reported unmodified Modena cobbles ranging from 138–1,649 g at several locations near the quarry. Talbot and Richens (2012:Figure 5) reported cobbles in quantity in the quarry vicinity and surrounding areas. Mapping and measurement of raw cobbles was not a priority of UA investigations, but our own investigation encountered surprisingly few cobbles at the quarry proper, and none that exceeded approximately 150 mm in maximum dimension.

Weathered Modena cobbles generally bear an irregular brown cortex. Modena obsidian's matrix is gray to black, often banded, translucent and vitreous. Hull described archaeological specimens at the nearby Panaca Summit Archeological District, presumably from Modena, as "semi-translucent black (distinct to indistinct) banded glass, semi-translucent black to gray cloudy or speckled...lacking bands, and black opaque obsidian" (2010:33; see also Hull 1994:7–14). Obsidian in some areas of the source contains noticeable mahogany veins (Shott 2016: Figure 3.8), a quality also noted by Hull (2010: 37), Jackson and colleagues (2009:121), and Moore (2009:20). Whether these varieties at Modena occurred as tool-quality cobbles is unknown, although no preform found there bore mahogany veins. (The presence of red to mahogany obsidian at Modena may complicate the frequent identification of such obsidian as Brown's Bench [e.g., Jones et al. 2012:362], and mahogany variants also are reported in the vicinity of Wild Horse Canyon in Utah [Dames and Moore 1994:21–72] and at Obsidian Cliff [Johnson et al. 1995:5].) According to Shackley (2005:186; see also Skinner 1983:36–37, 52), obsidian is iron-enriched and therefore many sources produce sometimes considerable amounts of mahogany-veined obsidian, particularly as the product of oxidized magnetite (Skinner 1983:52). Bush

(2004; see also Hull 1994:7–14; Jackson et al. 2009:123) considered Modena to be of relatively high knapping quality, specifically comparing it favorably to Mineral Mountain.

Modena's Terrane

Knapped obsidian occurs in "astronomical quantities" (Cole 2012:268; see also Talbot and Richens [2012:8] on the "general ubiquity of bifacial and other...lithic artifacts") at Modena and in at least a 10 km radius surrounding the source, and Cole (2012:424) reports copious surface deposits of worked obsidian as far as 15 km to the north and northwest. Zeier and Reno (2012:115–116) also reported small cobbles of natural obsidian within that radius. Yet other toolstones exist in the region. White quartzite and silicified rhyolite cobbles are common in gravel trains, and varieties of chert are reported in the northern part of Cole's (2012:48) survey area, within approximately 30 km of the Modena source, and at Panaca Summit less than 20 km from the source (Elston and Juell 1987:5). In addition, these and other siliceous toolstones are not uncommon in archaeological sites in the region (e.g., Elston and Juell 1987; Fowler et al. 1973; Seddon et al. 2001).

Like many Great Basin obsidians, Modena occurs in high frequency at sites within 50–100 km of the source (McKee 2009; McKee et al. 2010, 2013; Seddon 2005b), a region which might be considered its core *terrane*, the area over which a toolstone is dominant (Elston 1990a:155; 1992b:35). But it also is fairly common over 150 km to the northwest (e.g., Jones et al. 2003) and occurs in small amounts at distances approaching 200 km to the north at Danger Cave (Umshler 1975), 400 km to the west at Death and Owens Valleys, California (Basgall and Delacorte 2003, cited in Johnson and Haarklau 2005:127), on the Kaibab Paiute Reservation and Grand Canyon National Park in Arizona (Nelson 1986, cited in Hughes and Bennyhoff 1986:253) and exceeding 500 km at Chaco Canyon, New Mexico (Duff et al. 2012: Table 1) to the southeast. A more detailed study of Modena's terrane appears in Chapter 10.

Tempiute

This obsidian source lies in Sand Spring Valley. Identified as CrNv 04-8912 in IMACS and 26LN4775 in the Nevada site files, Tempiute was discovered by Robert Hafey in the course of his extensive field studies in the valley. Like the Lytles at Modena, Hafey was a gracious host to UA work at Tempiute.

Hafey (2003) reported the site area as consisting of at least 10 quasi-discrete obsidian concentrations. His own survey in what he called cluster N2 (a nomenclature followed in UA investigation) encountered a nearly 7,000 m^2 "dense concentration" (2003:4) of obsidian flakes, tools, and unaltered cobbles. Tempiute was reported as "Unknown B" in G. T. Jones and colleagues' (2003:15) distributional study. Among others, Rogers and Duke (2014) called it Timpahute or the Timpahute Range.

The Tempiute obsidian bed lies on Tschanz and Pampeyan's (1970: Plate 2) Qol ("older alluvium"; "QTg") unit near a section of their QTI ("intermediate lake beds") in Sand Spring Valley, northeast of pluvial Penoyer Lake. Hughes (2010:170) called the source "Timpahute." The source apparently was his Location HO3-28 (Hughes 2005:B15), described both as deflated and not an "actual primary outcrop," although HO3-28 as marked lies slightly west of the quarry. The site is deflated and does indeed lack evidence of flows. However, the many small (<50 mm maximum diameter) unmodified cobbles found there suggest that the "abundant evidence" (Hughes 2005:B15) of prehistoric use from the dense debris field at Tempiute was of at least somewhat larger cobbles that also occurred there; Hughes (2005:B15) and Johnson and Wagner (2005:34) reported cobbles as large as 80 × 100 mm. The latter also concluded that Tempiute obsidian is in situ, weathering out of a perlite deposit that underlies the Plio-Pleistocene alluvial fan on which the source rests.

Tempiute lies in semidesert land cover (U.S. Geological Survey 2011) and is dominated by a scrub community, notably sagebrush and rabbit brush (*Asteraceae spp.*). Fauna are mostly endemic to the Great Basin. We observed no pumas during fieldwork, but they are reported by Hafey and other local residents. Badgers and antelope are found in the area, and coyote scat is common. At the source in 2011, we earned the dubious distinction of first confirmed sighting of a Mojave Green rattlesnake (*Crotalus scutulatus*) in Sand Spring Valley.

Skinner and Thatcher (2005:Table A-3-1) described Tempiute obsidian as black, uniform, faintly banded, translucent and vitreous, with microphenocryst inclusions. Cobbles they examined possessed smooth cortex. To Hull "visual characteristics are highly variable, including semi-translucent black with distinct parallel bands, semi-translucent black with indistinct bands, translucent brownish-black obsidian with a slightly cloudy appearance, translucent brownish-black obsidian…[with] rare black speckles, and opaque black glass with minor phenocrysts" (2010:52).

Tempiute clusters are fairly dense deposits of both cobbles of toolstone quality and much smaller perlite or marekanite. Tempiute cobbles weather to a hydrated, flat or matte black. Few cobbles observed exceeded 50 mm in maximum dimension; the largest observed measured approximately 60–70 mm. In his investigation, Hafey reported cobbles "measuring up to 20 cm in length" (2003:7). Reno and Pippin (1986:83) summarized earlier reports of "fist-sized" raw obsidian cobbles between Penoyer Spring and the pluvial lake bed of Sand Spring Valley, presumably Tempiute obsidian considering its proximity. It is possible that supplies of larger cobbles were depleted prehistorically, leaving only smaller cobbles. Like Modena, Tempiute may have been substantially exhausted, as were smaller chert quarries nearby (Reno and Pippin 1986:126). Certainly its export to places 200 km or more distant (e.g., Jones et al. 2003) suggests scarcity elsewhere (Reno and Pippin [1986:125] noted the paucity of toolstone in the region) and heavy use of the source as a result. In general, however, the modest size of individual flakes at Tempiute suggests that even worked specimens were fairly small, most perhaps in the range of the 60–90 mm although, as above, some cobbles may have reached 100 mm in maximum dimension. Presumably less desirable than large cob-

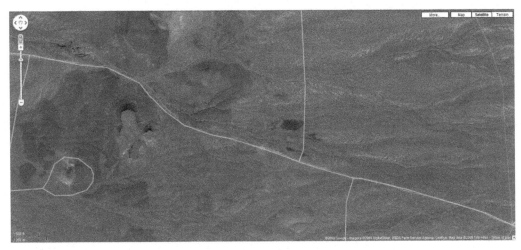

FIGURE 3.3. Satellite image of Tempiute source and environs.

bles, even obsidian nodules approaching the size range of perlite can be knapped (Ballenger and Hall 2010).

Tempiute consists of spatially discrete clusters of varying size, sharply distinguishable from intervening areas of markedly lower obsidian density. These dense obsidian surface deposits are plainly visible on aerial imagery, as are somewhat less dense concentrations of almost entirely naturally fractured obsidian about 500 m south (Figure 3.3). The source's spatial structure, however, probably does not reflect prehistoric patterns of activity. Instead, what are visible today as clusters probably are erosional remnants; most intervening areas are active or abandoned seasonal channels. Tempiute was already scoured by erosion before people began to quarry its obsidian, in which case they simply exploited the obsidian available on those remnants, or erosion began during or after use (perhaps especially after grazing began), in which case some original deposits are washed away, or some combination of the two. Whatever the case, the spatial structure visible at Tempiute—dense clusters of worked and naturally fractured obsidian sharply defined against a background of much lower obsidian density—probably is an artifact of erosion, not organized human activity at the source.

By count and volume, much of the obsidian at Tempiute is small, crudely fractured cobbles with heavily rounded edges and noticeable surface sheen that suggests thick hydration bands. These pieces lacked definable platforms and distinguishable interior and exterior surfaces. If they were of human origin they would fall in the broad category of "shatter." But their heavy rounding and great weathering, in contrast to the much fresher edges of the considerable quantities of unquestionably cultural obsidian at Tempiute, clearly identify them as natural products. What is more, some shatter occurs among the cultural debris at Tempiute, but no heavily rounded specimens bore platforms, bulbs of percussion, or extensively faceted faces as did most flake debris. If weathering and rounding were the product of great age in cultural debris at Tempiute, then some—presumably a large fraction—of that debris should bear platforms or other recognizable traits that betray its cultural origin. The fact that none of the heavily weathered material possessed such traits argues strongly against their cultural origin. Instead, these fragments almost certainly are the product of natural weathering, to which Tempiute obsidian appears to be prone. For instance, Hafey encountered Tempiute cobbles that "crumpled when touched" (2003:9) and illustrated naturally occurring pseudo-artifacts of Tempiute found at the source.

Naturally fractured stone is not uncommon at quarries in the Great Basin and elsewhere.

Elston and Zeier (1984:75) called the resemblance of naturally fractured obsidian to debris of cultural origin "geological mimicry". In their tests at Sugarloaf in the Coso Volcanic Field, admittedly on near-surface versus more deeply buried strata, they too distinguished cultural material from considerable quantities of naturally fractured obsidian. Even in basalt, a tougher toolstone than obsidian "irregular random retouch...can occur by natural processes such as frost heave or other mass movements of deposits which contain large quantities of flaking detritus" (Bucy 1974:10). Elsewhere, at the Hatch Quarry in Pennsylvania, half or more of all fractured material was identified as natural in origin (Andrews et al. 2004:68–71).

Modena and Tempiute in Comparative Perspective

Europeanist archaeology distinguishes quarries—toolstone sources exploited only on the surface—from mines, where toolstone was excavated by pits (Bosch 1979; Torrence 1986: 164–165). Americanist thought makes no such distinction. If it did, Modena and Tempiute would be quarries, not mines. Excavation pits are reported at Tosawihi (see Ingbar [1992:Figure 90] on the dense distribution of large quarry pits at its Locality 36), at some California obsidian quarries (Jackson 1990:82, 85; Parkman 1983:256; see also Heizer and Treganza [1944:303], although that source reported relatively few obsidian sources containing visible pits), and in abundance at Obsidian Cliff in Yellowstone National Park (Johnson et al. 1995:Table 1). Excavation pits also are common at obsidian quarries exploited intensively by complex societies (e.g., Suyuc Ley 2011:132–133).

We observed no unambiguous quarry pits at Modena or Tempiute. Neither were pits or spoil piles reported at Wild Horse Canyon (Dames and Moore 1994) or Buckboard Mesa (Amick 1991). Apparently, these obsidian sources were substantially surface occurrences, and any excavation presumably was shallow and in pursuit of single or few cobbles near the surface (e.g., F. Lytle [personal communication, 6 January 2004] observed shallow depressions in Modena Areas A and B "where it appears that

mining was attempted"). Wilke and Schroth (1989:146–148) considered pits a hallmark of quarries, among a larger set of attributes that include patterned reduction practices, staging of desired end products like biface preforms, and long-distance transport. To this might be added the sheer volume of toolstone to work and the volume of resulting debris from that working.

Whatever their differences in quantity of toolstone and volume and kind of reduction they witnessed, Modena and Tempiute are substantial quarries by any reasonable standard. Both include extensive debris fields from the reduction of cobbles and staged production of tools, evidence of failure or breakage in some of those stage preforms, few finished products, and little evidence of occupation for purposes apart from toolstone reduction. These are recognized features of toolstone quarries (Clark 1989:216; Hiscock and Mitchell 1993:19–28). Chapter 8 reports in detail on estimates of volume of reduction and biface production and the methods used to reach them.

Like many quarries, Modena is surrounded by dense, extensive palimpsest deposits from associated workshops, "places where an activity, or group of similar activities, are carried out" (Clark 1989:213 [my translation]) that involve repeated performance of activities well in excess of immediate need. In particular, Areas A, B, and F lie on fairly steep slopes. The slope crests near Areas A and B in particular are thick with quarry debris, suggesting that many prehistoric knappers took raw cobbles or partly reduced cores from the primary deposits on the slope face to the flatter crests for further reduction. A similar scenario may have played out at an Australian lithic quarry, where "the area of greatest slope gradient occurred on the outcrop and below on the scarp face.... After large flakes or prepared blocks were produced they were removed from the outcrop and most were transported to the flat, upper area north of the outcrop" (Doelman 2008:143) for further work.

Adams and MacDonald (2015:212) used Wilson's (2007) "attractiveness equation" to characterize the Obsidian Cliff source in Wyoming. Many of Wilson's terms are subjective, so strict application of that equation seems unwise.

Broadly, in Wilson's (2007:398) terms, Modena A and B are "very extensive" (more than 100 m in diameter), and Modena F is nearly so. Modena clusters are vastly larger than most aboriginal quarries documented in interior Australia (Hiscock and Mitchell 1993:Figure 4.1). They also are "very abundant (more than 50% of the surface area of the sources consists of potential raw material)" (Wilson 2007:399). In fact, Modena A, B, and F might be termed "superabundant" along with other Great Basin and western obsidian sources because they are extensive areas that consist of nearly 100% coverage by raw toolstone or, as at Modena A, B, and F, mostly knapped material.

Despite their considerable extent and truly impressive density of debris, Modena clusters are modest in broadest comparative context; central Mexico surface deposits of obsidian cover much larger areas (Holmes 1900:409), probably reflecting some combination of the natural abundance of obsidian there and its intensive exploitation by labor specialists within state-level societies possessing large populations. Even within North America's Mountain West—a region occupied prehistorically by relatively sparse hunter-gatherer populations—other sources are much more spatially extensive (e.g., Davis et al. 1995:Appendix C; Gilreath and Hildebrandt 1997; Singer and Ericson 1977:172–173). On balance, Modena is a fairly large, extensive obsidian toolstone source, and Tempiute a significant but considerably smaller source.

4

Fieldwork and Data Collection

Fieldwork at Modena and Tempiute was designed to acquire the data needed to meet several research goals. First, we wished to map the distribution of main obsidian deposits. Second, we wished to acquire data for two research purposes. One was the testing and further development of the Field-processing Model (FPM; Beck et al. 2002; Elston 1992a), which applies behavioral-ecology theory to explain patterns and modes of exploitation of major toolstone sources. The second involved the information residing in the debris that is so abundant at quarries, both to further test the FPM and to demonstrate more broadly the interpretive potential of debris assemblages. After briefly discussing previous work at each quarry, this chapter describes UA's field design and its implementation, and evaluates the results of sampling of the dense and complex deposits at the quarries.

UA Sample Design

Obsidian deposits at Modena and Tempiute were dense and relatively spatially extensive. Complete data recovery, either in the field or by recovery and laboratory analysis, was wildly impractical even if desired. Obviously, sites and their debris assemblages required sampling. One purpose of the UA investigation was to sample such dense deposits with reasonable efficiency. For this purpose, we designed a probabilistic sample for each sample domain, the latter defined by combinations of natural and cultural patterning described for the particulars of each site in its relevant section. Based on the view that the number of observations or sample units is a more valid measure of sample adequacy than the aggregate size of those units (Nance 1981:165)—the same rationale that justifies valid samples of a few thousands from voting electorates measuring in the hundreds of millions—we devised samples that measured approximately 0.5–1% by area of those sample domains but that simultaneously included considerable numbers of sample units.

Sample domains—areas or clusters at each site—were defined in the first stage of fieldwork in 2009. After each domain, *qua* area, was circumscribed and recorded as a shapefile, its area in m² was calculated, and a 1 m² grid imposed over it. Sample units then were selected by simple random sampling, the most advisable probabilistic sampling method when little or no prior information on relevant sampling properties like varying density or technological character is available, as was the case at Modena and Tempiute that had seen only limited previous investigation.

Partly as an economy measure and partly to gauge the efficacy of small sample fractions, we designed a two-stage sample strategy. Stage-1 sampling involved collection units that covered 1% of each sample domain (assuming sample units of 1 m², from which we departed in many cases as described below), all worked obsidian including debris and tools being recovered, bagged, and removed for laboratory analysis. Stage-2 sampling covered approximately 1.5% of each domain and involved no collection of debris, instead simple counts and aggregate weight of worked obsidian found in each unit. Any preforms or points found in Stage-2 sampling, whether of obsidian or not, were collected. In this way, the research design produced two independent probabilistic collection samples of formed artifacts like preforms but only one collected sample of flake debris.

Stage-1 and Stage-2 samples were drawn independently, such that sample units from the two could be and often were near one another but did not coincide. Besides efficiency, the two-stage sample design made it possible to compare independent samples in order to gauge their fidelity to a single underlying surface distribution of archaeological remains.

Samples were drawn before data collection on the assumption that all sample units, for both Stage-1 and Stage-2 work, would measure 1 m on a side. Earlier reconnaissance showed that artifact densities in each sample domain were high but variable. Therefore, the research incorporated flexibility by permitting sample units to be reduced in size in the field, as density on the ground advised. Most such reduced units measured 0.25 m², while some in especially dense deposits were as small as 0.125 m². Obviously, for interpolation and the production of density-contour maps all count and weight values from sample units smaller than 1 m² were scaled to that size. Thus, values from units of 0.25 m² in size were multiplied by four, those from units of 0.125 m² by eight.

Built-in flexibility by unit size was justified by the judgment, noted above, that number of sample units is more salient than the size of those units (Nance 1981). Strictly, this practice complicates the design of both sample stages, because virtually all domains at both Modena and Tempiute were sampled by combinations of units of varying size. Scaled or normalized count and weight from units that measured less than 1 m² technically are subsamples or cluster samples, that is, samples of samples. The estimation of population parameters like overall count, weight, or density from cluster samples is somewhat more complicated than is estimation from simple random samples (Nance 1983). Because many UA sample units did in fact measure 1 m² and because in-field observation and judgment of local debris density at such small spatial scales (like 1 m²) justifies the assumption of essentially uniform distribution at that scale, Stage-1 and Stage-2 samples are treated as simple random ones for purposes of estimation.

As described above, Stage-1 and Stage-2 sample units were selected randomly after initial reconnaissance. In the field, each sample unit was located by GPS unit and initially marked by a pin flag labeled with its N and E coordinates. At Modena, forest cover and fairly rugged topography (Figure 4.1) complicated satellite triangulation, often necessitating waits of a minute or more before sample areas could be fixed. Tempiute being more open (Figure 4.2), this problem rarely occurred. In some cases, sample units could not be placed at the specified location because it was occupied by a tree (at Modena) or a large sagebrush bush (at Tempiute). In those cases, new units were selected by offsetting, typically by one or two meters and, in a few cases, three or more, depending upon local ground conditions. This new location then was used for sampling. Accordingly, original and actual sample units do not always correspond exactly.

Upon locating each sample unit, its size was determined from the density of debris visible. Particularly within Modena Areas A, B, and F and Tempiute Areas N2, N5, and N6, some sample units were reduced to 0.25 m² or even 0.125 m² owing to their artifact density. At both quarries, once units were selected and located, the same procedure was followed. First, a 1 m² wooden or aluminum frame was placed at the pin flag that marked the sample unit's location. After its southwest corner was placed at the sample unit's grid coordinates, the frame was oriented to magnetic north by a Silva or Brunton compass. If the unit size was 0.25 m², a distance of 50 cm was marked by pocket tape along each margin of the frame at the pin flag location and straight lines drawn by string or straight edge were extended to their intersection. This defined the southwestern one-quarter

FIGURE 4.1. Topography and ground cover at Modena.

FIGURE 4.2. Topography and ground cover at Tempiute, and sample collection in progress.

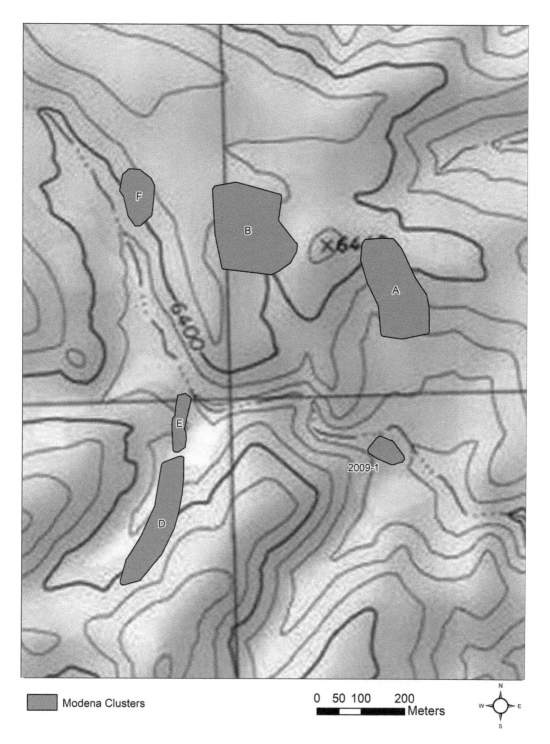

FIGURE 4.3. Major areas at Modena.

of the unit as the sample location. If unit size was 0.125 m², the same procedure was followed by marking at distances of 25 rather than 50 cm along frame margins.

For Stage-1 units, sampling then consisted of simple collection of all artifacts approximately 6 mm or greater (>¼ in) in medial dimension within the limits of the entire 1 m² or the specified fraction. This size threshold was imposed to correspond to the mesh size most commonly used in North American excavations, so that UA data would be broadly comparable to data-recovery norms. It also served as a practical measure, because inordinate time could be devoted to collection of vanishingly small flake debris. For size control, we used manufactured plastic basins whose bases were fitted with ¼-inch mesh hardware cloth.

Artifacts were bagged by unit and bags labeled with the unit's UTM coordinates and size. Bagged samples were removed from the field each day, for eventual shipment to UA for analysis. For Stage-2 units, obsidian debris and any worked preforms or tools present were collected and bagged. After completing the sample, contents were counted and their aggregate weight measured on a hanging balance graduated in 20 g intervals; flakes then were returned to the unit. Again, preforms or finished tools of any toolstone that were found in Stage-2 units were retained for analysis after other unit contents were returned to the ground.

Modena

As noted above, Modena was reconnoitered in 2003. In 2005, limited random samples were drawn from what Rowley and others (2002) called Areas A and B. Given Modena's spatial extent and impressive artifact density, Rowley and colleagues' area designations were retained for purposes of UA sampling. Figure 4.3 shows Modena sample domains. For spatial control, the WGS84 datum was used in those visits and in 2009–2011 UA investigations. Visits in 2003 and 2005 made clear several salient points. First, Modena's debris field is immense, extending for several kilometers in every direction (see also Cole 2012:268; Jackson et al. 2009:268; Tal-

bot and Richens 2012:8). Attempting to define the boundaries of a "site" of this magnitude would be an enormous undertaking. Second, continuous scree deposits of primary quarry debris occur at the locations that Rowley and colleagues (2002:Figure 2) labeled Areas A, B, and F. Accordingly, these areas became the chief but not sole focus of UA investigation. Third, although Modena's debris field is far too large to be systematically sampled as a unit, several areas of relatively high obsidian-debris density lie near Areas A, B, and F.

There is scarcely a square meter within 3 km or more of Areas A, B, and F that does not contain at least one obsidian flake (Cole 2012: 268; Jackson et al. 2009:123–124). Ideally, the best sample strategy for Modena would be to randomly or systematically sample the complete site, treating only A, B, and F as particular sample domains by virtue of their tremendous debris density. But Modena's great spatial extent and generally high artifact density made this approach impractical. Fortunately, Rowley and others (2002:Figure 2) mapped several areas near the central zones of A, B, and F, which therefore served as quasi-"natural" sample domains. These include Areas D and E (Rowley et al. 2002:Figure 2). However, our examination on the ground of other zones mapped by Rowley and others did not persuade us either of their spatial discreteness or unusually high debris density. UA's 2009 reconnaissance, on the other hand, identified and mapped an area of dense debris south of Area A that was labeled 2009-1. For comparison to Areas A, B, and F and in view of the site's tremendous extent and density, we defined and mapped Areas D, E, and 2009-1 and sampled them in the same way that the UA research design specified for the central zones of Areas A, B, and F.

Talbot and Richens (2012) included Area A within a larger area of twice or more its size extending downslope to the southeast. Although in places the debris density within this larger field approaches the level of Area A as we defined it, that distribution is patchy or discontinuous. To some extent this patchiness may owe to forest cover, which in places can make it difficult to trace the extent of obsidian debris fields. Again, there is scarcely a square meter in this section without at least several flakes, but we preferred a more conservative definition, confining Area A to the upslope portion of that described by Talbot and Richens (2012). Obviously, this treatment is conservative as well for the estimation of flake quantity and other measures of production at Modena (Chapter 8).

Transect Samples

Although the assemblage of preforms accumulated from probabilistic sample units and chance discoveries was substantial, to increase it further a series of judgmentally placed transects were surveyed across the northern, upslope sections of Areas A and B, extending to the ridgetop above those two areas. This effort yielded 13 additional preforms in Area B and its vicinity, 17 in the vicinity of Area A, and 16 in transects that traversed that area (Shott 2016:Figures 4.5–4.6). Similar transects also were surveyed across Area F, yielding 14 preforms (Shott 2016:Figure 4.7), and part of Area D where they yielded 12 preforms. For some analysis in Chapter 6 and 9, preforms found in transects in or near Areas A, B, and F are identified as "vicinity-A," "vicinity-B," and "vicinity-F," respectively. These samples being judgmental or selective, obviously they cannot be used to estimate the number of preforms at Modena.

Overall, preforms were found at Modena in several ways. Some were found by chance, some in the transects described above, and some in Stage-1 or Stage-2 sample units.

Other Cultural Remains

In the course of fieldwork, UA crews sometimes encountered by chance artifacts or features not directly relevant to our research design. Pottery was noted occasionally but neither recorded or collected at the Modena site and in its environs at several places during 2004–2005 reconnaissance. UA's 2009–2011 fieldwork encountered one sherd. In 2005, we also encountered several metates and one mano, most in or near Area A but one well to the south, as well as several points and point fragments. None of these artifacts was collected.

Stone Circles. The Modena quarry is a naturally rocky area, and prehistoric residents of the Great Basin sometimes erected circular stone rings or circles. In several places, particularly in and near Areas A and B, we encountered configurations of angular to subangular volcanic cobbles and boulders that, because they formed ambiguous circles or ovals, suggested human agency. At least one at Modena, in the vicinity of Area A, was fairly persuasive about its cultural origin (Figure 4.4), others less so. Great Basin archaeologists frequently interpret such features as rock circles, but elsewhere at quarries possible structural remains are treated as evidence of labor specialization and corresponding investment in capital facilities (e.g., Torrence 1986:49). Eerkens and colleagues defined rock circles as "circular to ovoid in plan, between 2 and 4 m in diameter, and hav[ing] a shallow deposit of charcoal-rich earth visible against a background of lighter-colored soil" (2004:17). Their own illustration (Eerkens et al. 2004:Figure 2) suggests some ambiguity in the recognition and definition of circles. Elston and Zeier (1984:59–60, 72) reported rock circles or circular depressions identified as structures, several measuring from 3.5–4 m in diameter, at the Sugarloaf Quarry complex; Dillian (2002:208) documented similar features at Glass Mountain.

In the project area's vicinity, Reno and Pippin (1986:151–157) reported 25 rock circles in the Groom Range. Some are unmistakable (e.g., Reno and Pippin 1986:Figures 5-12, 5-15), others ambiguous (e.g., Reno and Pippin 1986:Figure 5-16). Nearer to Modena, Cole reported 11 complex and 14 simple rock circles (2012:Table 8.1). Cole's (2012:Figure 9.1) example of a complex rock circle, which he tentatively interpreted as remains of a structure, is unmistakable, but his simple rock circle (2012:Figure 9.2) seems ambiguous, at least for such a boulder-strewn area as the Modena source. But at the nearby Waterfall Site, Cole (2012:613, Figure 14.16) reported several stone circles lying at least in part on exposed bedrock in a context that implicates human agency.

Their abundance in the Groom Range and Meadow Valley attest to the common prehistoric practice of constructing rock circles,

FIGURE 4.4. Probable stone circle in Area A at Modena. Handheld GPS unit shown for scale.

almost certainly unrelated to quarrying activities. Rock circles are interpreted either as piñon-nut caches or as temporary structures (Cole 2012:257–258; Reno and Pippin 1986:159; Simms 1989:17). In either case they are interpreted as chiefly late prehistoric Numic features (Cole 2012:241–242; Eerkens et al. 2004; Simms 1989), although Reno and Pippin (1986) found little evidence by which to date rock circles in the Groom Range. Supporting the cache interpretation, most circles in Cole's (2012:277) Meadow Valley survey area and in the Groom Range (Reno and Pippin 1986:159) lay in piñon-juniper woodlands, and they often were constructed in rocky landscapes because "locating them near bedrock would inhibit rodent invasion" (Simms 1989:17). Certainly most of the possible stone circles at Modena were placed either near bedrock outcrops or partly on obsidian debris fields, so are unlikely to be even temporary shelters for any but the most ascetic. Elsewhere in the Great Basin features of similar

form and scale have been interpreted as hunting blinds (Delacorte 1985:Figures 3–5).

Rings were not abundant at Modena, nor were similar features common at other major obsidian quarries like Glass Mountain (Dillian 2002:208). All possible rock circles were found in the course of investigation for other purposes, and most were encountered against a dense background of naturally occurring boulders and cobbles. We recorded the locations of rock circles, but neither mapped them in detail nor excavated them (in any event, excavation was impossible where circles stood on exposed bedrock); nor did we identify orientation of possible entryways (Eerkens et al. 2004:22), if in fact such were visible, or determine ratios of inner to outer ring diameters (Vierra 1986, cited in Simms 1989:18) that might distinguish residential structures from caches. It is possible that rock circles at Modena were of Cole's complex variety and thus served as structures, but their ambiguity on the ground made them an elusive subject. Most lacked the "crisply defined line of rocks on both the inner and outer margins" that Simms (1989:18) considered typical of house rings, as opposed to the diffuse scatters of cache structures necessitated to retrieve stored contents. The metates encountered in 2005 fieldwork are consistent with caching but, arguably, also with extended residence.

Recognizing rock circles in a landscape where natural boulders are scarce and the substrate is sandy is straightforward, as are those cases where two or more courses of stones remain in place (e.g., La Pierre 2007:Figures 2, 4; Simms 1989:17). Modena's natural boulders occur in profusion, however, rendering identification of rock circles inherently ambiguous; constructed courses of stone at Modena were not observed. Tempiute is sandy, and cairns (Hafey 2003), but no rock rings, are documented from its environs, the latter's absence perhaps expected as the site does not lie in the pinyon-juniper ecozone where nut-cache rock rings might be expected. On balance, the dense, confusing scatters of irregular volcanic cobbles at Modena probably are evidence of piñon-nut caching, an overlay upon the site unrelated to its use as an obsidian quarry and indicating nothing about labor specialization in quarrying. Moreover, considering Modena's occupational history, as reported in Chapter 9, combined with the late-prehistoric popularity of rock circles, whatever human activity that these jumbled scatters may indicate likely occurred after the site substantially was abandoned as a quarry.

Sampling Results

Count and weight of flake debris by sample unit for both Stage-1 and Stage-2 samples were processed in ARC GIS. (Flake inventories by Modena area are reported in Shott [2016: Appendices B and C].) Results of mapping are discussed by major area, with Stage-1 count and weight distributions shown in Figure 4.5 for Areas A, B, and F only. In this figure and in Figure 4.7 for Tempiute, square sample units are shown as circles, and are not to scale. Density interpolation maps do not always show maximum extent of areas as defined in the field,

instead encompassing the smallest polygon defined by the distribution of sample units.

Area A. Like Areas B and F, at the site scale Area A is a relatively discrete area whose boundaries roughly correspond to the limits of areas of sustained, intensive reduction. Count and weight distributions both show diffuse higher density areas along Area A's western and northwestern boundaries, measuring approximately 130 × 45 m (Figure 4.5a). This area lies near the top of the slope from which Area A descends, and near a field of ridgetop debris in which a number of preforms was found. Other, smaller and more discrete, peaks are visible along Area A's eastern and southern boundaries, each measuring roughly 45 m in diameter as shown in Figure 4.5a. However, these peaks may be map distortions of highly variable count/weight density by sample unit. The eastern peak is comprised mostly of two closely spaced units. The southern peak is formed by a single sample unit; another unit 4 m east had a very small debris sample. In general, count and weight distributions are similar, suggesting no significant patterning either of low-count, high-weight flakes or vice versa. Interpolation maps from Stage-2 sampling at Area A are similar to Stage-1 results (Shott 2016:4.13b). Analysis in Chapter 5 assigns 64% of Area A flake debris to reduction Stage 1, indicating mostly early-stage reduction there.

Area B. Highest density modes in Area B occupy its northeastern sector. As in Area A, the high density area adjoins the ridgetop from which Area B descends. The highest densities identified in Stage-1 sampling lay near the area's northern and eastern borders (Figure 4.5b). The results of Stage-2 sampling differed somewhat, count and weight modes found at individual sample units form a north-trending arc from the north-center of the area to its northern boundary (Shott 2016:Figure 4.14b). Debris densities fall off substantially downslope, to the south, a pattern not reflected in Stage-1 sampling. Analysis in Chapter 5 assigns 63% of Area B flake debris to reduction Stage 1, indicating mostly early-stage reduction there.

Modena Cluster A

Modena Cluster B

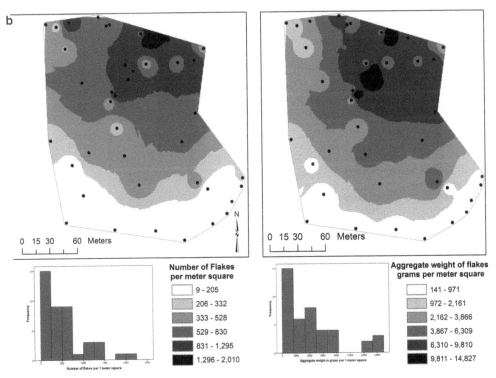

FIGURE 4.5. Count and weight distributions in Modena Areas A, B, and F: a. Stage-1; b. Stage-2.

Modena F - Stage 1

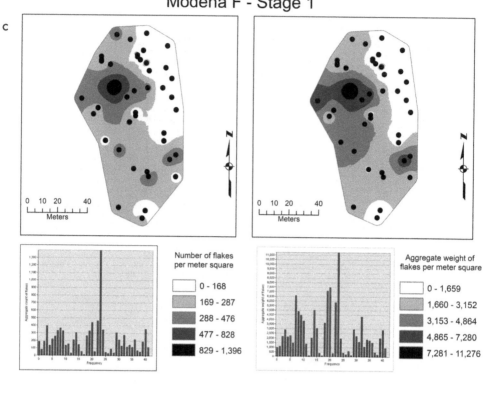

Modena E - Stage 1

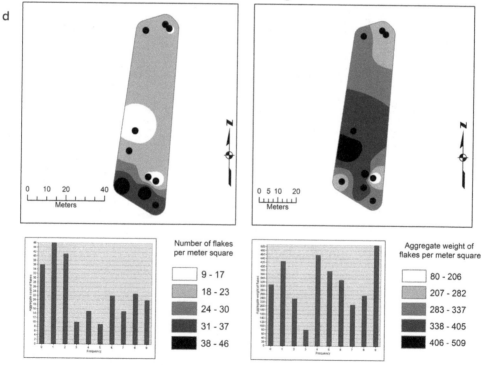

FIGURE 4.5. (cont'd.) Count and weight distributions in Modena Areas A, B, and F: a. Stage-1; b. Stage-2.

Modena F - Stage 1

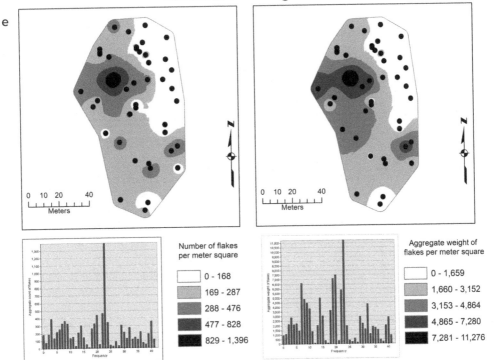

Number of flakes per meter square

☐	0 - 168
☐	169 - 287
☐	288 - 476
■	477 - 828
■	829 - 1,396

Aggregate weight of flakes per meter square

☐	0 - 1,659
☐	1,660 - 3,152
☐	3,153 - 4,864
■	4,865 - 7,280
■	7,281 - 11,276

Modena Cluster F

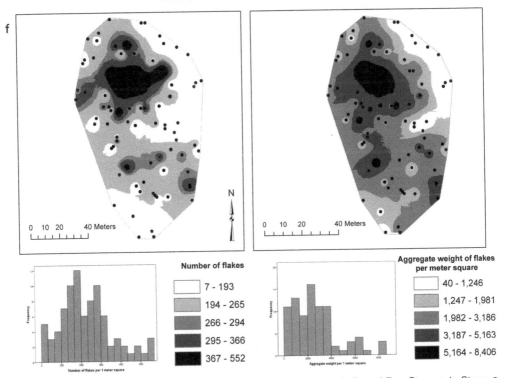

Number of flakes

☐	7 - 193
☐	194 - 265
☐	266 - 294
■	295 - 366
■	367 - 552

Aggregate weight of flakes per meter square

☐	40 - 1,246
☐	1,247 - 1,981
☐	1,982 - 3,186
■	3,187 - 5,163
■	5,164 - 8,406

FIGURE 4.5. (cont'd.) Count and weight distributions in Modena Areas A, B, and F: a. Stage-1; b. Stage-2.

Area D. Area D lies obliquely across a northeast-southwest trending ridge, and generally declines in elevation to its north. It is elongated north-south, extending for about 270 m, but spans roughly 60 m east-west. It shows a small density mode in Area D's east-central area, and generally higher densities to the north.

Unlike Areas A, B, and F, Area D and other demarcated Modena zones are subjectively identified areas of relatively high local debris density. Not located at the main cobble sources that gradually were reduced to the dense talus slopes of Areas A, B, and F, Area D and others may represent workshops. Although Area D's count/weight densities are significantly lower than Areas A, B, and F, the debris patterning does not resolve clearly into discrete workshop areas (Shott 2016:Figure 4.15). Analysis in Chapter 5 assigns 55% of Area D flake debris to reduction Stage 1, indicating roughly equal incidence of early- and later-stage reduction there.

Area E. This area extends northward from Area D. The Stage-1 distribution has a north-south range of roughly 100 m, the Stage-2 distribution roughly 140 m. In the Stage-1 sample, the count peaks in the southernmost units. The weight mode, however, lies in a unit somewhat to the north. As discussed in Shott (2016:82), this unit's weight mode owes to one flake each in the 50.8 mm (2 in) and 38.1 mm (1½ in) fractions. Stage-2 count density, but not weight density, is higher than in Stage-1 (Shott 2016:Figure 4.16). A southern mode in both count and weight corresponds fairly closely to the southern density mode revealed by Stage 1 sampling. A central mode, in weight but not particularly in count, has no equivalent in Stage-1 sampling. Analysis in Chapter 5 assigns 73% of Area E flake debris to reduction Stage 1, indicating mostly early-stage reduction.

Area F. Like Areas A and B, Area F consists of an extensive talus deposit of obsidian debris—a pavement of loose glass—lying on a slope. Stage-1 (Figure 4.5c) and Stage-2 samples (Shott 2016:Figure 4.17b) reveal similar patterns. A prominent mode in both count and weight

measuring approximately 50 m east-west by 50–60 m north–south lies north of Area F's center. The northeastern segment shows consistently low densities. Secondary density modes are visible to the southeast of the chief Area F mode; in Stage-1 units these are determined especially by weight. In the Stage-2 units, density modes quantified broadly by count and especially weight were visible across the southern one-third.

Like Areas A and B, highest count-weight modes lie near the north end of Area F. However, F differs slightly in that highest densities do not occur along its northern margin, which does not extend to the top of the ridge from which Areas A and B extend downslope. In none of these three dense talus deposits do the highest densities lie downslope; instead, fine debris of <12.7 mm (<½ in) fractions apparently traveled downslope beyond the main concentrations. Analysis in Chapter 5 assigns about two-thirds of Area F flake debris to reduction Stage 1, again indicating mostly early-stage reduction.

Area 2009-1. This area lies across an intermittent stream from the foot of the slope on which Area A lies. Stage-1 sampling shows density modes in its south-central part, and smaller modes near the center and in the northwest (Shott 2016:Figure 4.18a). Stage-2 sampling revealed a broader, multimodal density peak across Area 2009-1's south-center (Shott 2016:Figure 4.18b). An isolated mode, determined largely by count, was identified within a Stage-2 unit in the west-center of Area 2009-1, and equally isolated modes lie at its northern boundary. Analysis in Chapter 5 assigns 77% of Area 2009-1 flake debris to reduction Stage 1, again indicating mostly early-stage reduction.

Tempiute

As noted in Chapter 3, Tempiute is a set of dense obsidian debris fields and naturally occurring obsidian separated by areas of relatively sparse obsidian scatters, which probably are lag or secondary deposits lying in erosion channels. Unlike Modena, defined Tempiute artifact areas are discrete zones with sharp boundaries, although it is likely that there was a single original debris field subsequently subdivided by erosion into a set of apparently discrete deposits. Although Tempiute's sparser debris field extends for hundreds of meters, it is much smaller and much more sharply delimited than is Modena's.

UA crews mapped 10 areas of fairly dense obsidian debris at Tempiute, using the WGS84 datum. (Flake inventories by Tempiute area are reported in Shott [2016:Appendices D and E].) UA also sampled one of the smaller, sparser concentrations that lie several hundred meters to the south. But close inspection of the southern concentrations revealed that they are dominated by naturally fractured obsidian, with only minor amounts of cultural debris. This is also the case in surrounding areas and on the surface between the southern concentrations and Areas N1–N10. On the other hand, the main toolstone areas at Tempiute, labeled N1–N10 (Figure 4.6), include densities of naturally fractured material roughly comparable to those found to the south, but they are interspersed with substantial amounts of cultural debris. Accordingly, UA investigations focused upon Areas N1–N10 at Tempiute.

Count and Weight
Distributions by Area

Area N-1. Samples from eight Stage-1 units were collected here. Extensive Stage-2 sampling revealed a count/weight density mode in the area's eastern one-third (Shott 2016:Figure 4.21). More isolated modes, especially determined by count, lie southwest to northeast across the western half of Area N-1. Analysis assigns nearly equal proportions of reduction Stage-1 and Stage-2/3 debris to this area (see Chapter 5).

Area N-2. This large debris field was sampled by 35 Stage-1 and 77 Stage-2 units. The Stage-2 interpolation map reveals a high-density band around its east-center that, particularly in the count distribution, extends to the south (Figure 4.7a). Fairly high densities also extend to its eastern boundary. Area N-2's western one-third has lower count and weight densities, although large flakes create isolated weight modes in several units. Analysis in Chapter 5 assigns 60% of Area N-2 debris to reduction Stage 1.

Area N-3. This small area was sampled by nine Stage-1 and 17 Stage-2 units. Count and weight densities are highest along its southern border, particularly in Stage-2 units (Shott 2016:Figure 4.23). A nearly contiguous count mode occurs to the north. Chapter 5 shows that Area N-3 is dominated by reduction Stage-1 debris.

Area N-4. Another small remnant debris field, Area N-4 included five Stage-1 and six Stage-2 units. The distribution is markedly bifurcated. One Stage-2 unit revealed an isolated count/weight mode at the area's eastern extreme, with other modes at the southwest and the northwest corners (Shott 2016:Figure 4.24). According to analysis detailed in Chapter 5, Area N-4 is dominated by reduction Stage-1 debris.

Area N-5. UA crews collected materials from 27 Stage-1 units and 58 Stage-2 units in this area. A roughly triangular count/weight density mode occupies the eastern part of its Stage-2 interpolation map (Figure 4.7b). When considering count alone, zone extends westward; by weight, it resolves into secondary modes to the south and north. Like most other Tempiute areas, analysis in Chapter 5 assigns most analyzed debris from Area N-5 as reduction Stage 1.

Area N-6. Area N-6 is the single largest Tempiute debris field (Figure 4.7c). Because of extensive Stage-1 sampling of 44 units, Stage-2 sampling was not conducted here. The western half of Area N-6 is sparsely populated by obsidian debris, with one small density mode. In contrast, N-6's eastern half is a broad, fairly high-density zone extending from the area's northern to southern boundaries. There, count and weight distributions are fairly consistent. As for most Tempiute areas, Chapter 5 analysis shows that Area N-6 is dominated by reduction Stage-1 debris.

Area N-7. This small area immediately north of Area N-6 was sampled by five Stage-1 and 14

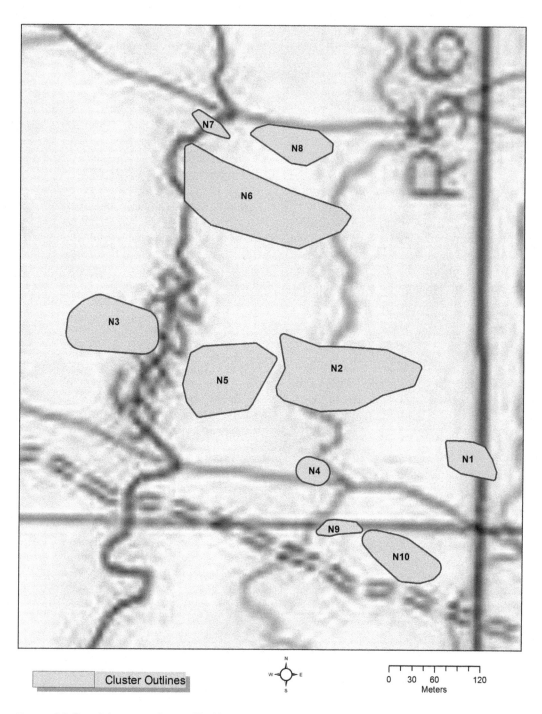

FIGURE 4.6. Tempiute mapped areas N1–N10.

Tempiute Stage 2 - Cluster N2 Interpolation by Weight and Number of Flakes

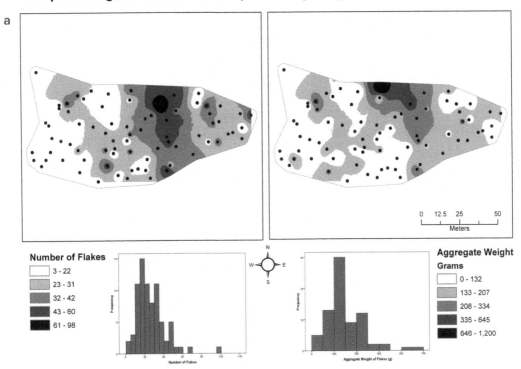

Number of Flakes
- 3 - 22
- 23 - 31
- 32 - 42
- 43 - 60
- 61 - 98

Aggregate Weight
Grams
- 0 - 132
- 133 - 207
- 208 - 334
- 335 - 645
- 646 - 1,200

Tempiute Stage 2 - Cluster N5 Interpolation by Weight and Number of Flakes

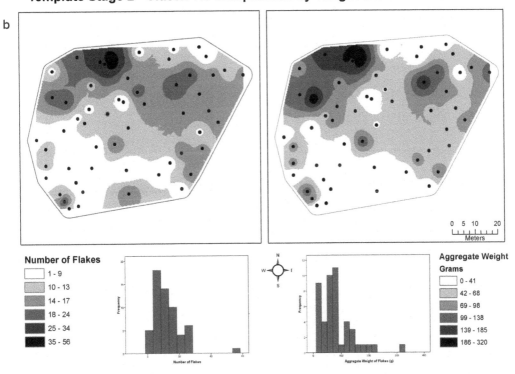

Number of Flakes
- 1 - 9
- 10 - 13
- 14 - 17
- 18 - 24
- 25 - 34
- 35 - 56

Aggregate Weight
Grams
- 0 - 41
- 42 - 68
- 69 - 98
- 99 - 138
- 139 - 185
- 186 - 320

FIGURE 4.7. Count and weight distributions for selected Tempiute areas: a. N2; b. N5; c. N6.

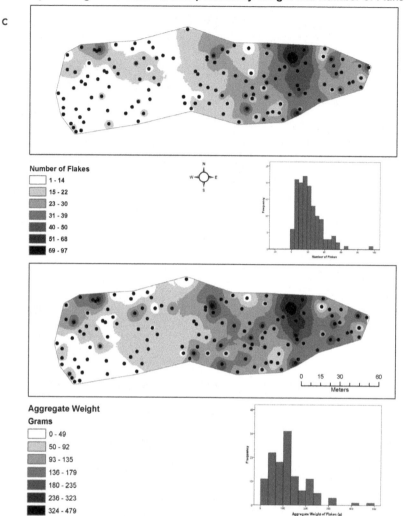

FIGURE 4.7. (cont'd.) Count and weight distributions for selected Tempiute areas: a. N2; b. N5; c. N6.

Stage-2 units. Its highest Stage-2 sample count/ weight densities occupy N-7's eastern half, trending toward the higher density zone of N-6 (Shott 2016:Figure 4.27). Chapter 5's flake analysis assigns nearly all of this area's small analyzed debris sample to reduction Stage 1.

Area N-8. This area also is a small zone just north of Area N-6 and, like Area N-7, probably originally formed part of a single larger debris field centered on N-6. It was sampled by 11

Stage-1 units only. Chapter-5 analysis assigns about two-thirds of this area's debris to reduction Stage 1, a somewhat lower proportion than in most Tempiute areas.

Area N-9. This area nearly adjoins Area N-10 in the southeast corner of the Tempiute quarry. Five Stage-1 and 10 Stage-2 units were collected there. Congruent high-density count and weight modes from Stage-2 sampling occupy the western half of Area N-9 (Shott 2016:Figure 4.28).

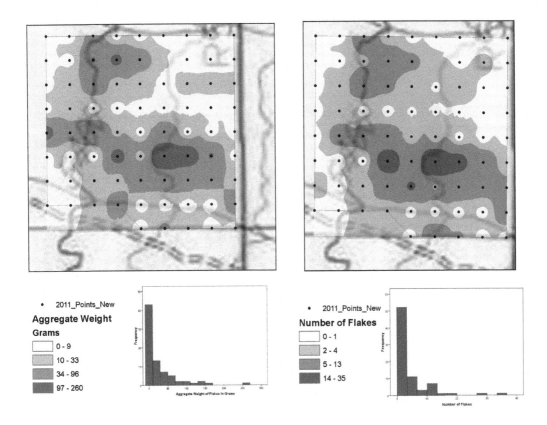

FIGURE 4.8. Results of 50-m Grid Sampling across the Tempiute Quarry.

Its eastern half is sparsely covered in obsidian debris. As Chapter 5 indicates, Area N-9 flake debris is dominated by reduction Stage-1 specimens.

Area N-10. Marking the southeastern extent of the main Tempiute debris field, Area N-10 was sampled by 10 Stage-1 and 19 Stage-2 units. The Stage-2 distribution features a western density mode in weight only, and joint count/weight modes in its south-center (Shott 2016:Figure 4.29). As discussed in Chapter 5, most Area N-10 flakes are assigned to reduction Stage 1, similar to that found in N-9 and other Tempiute areas.

Further Investigations at Tempiute

After sampling of N1–N10 at Tempiute, UA crews conducted two additional surveys in this vicinity. The first gauged the background dis-

tribution and density of flake debris between defined sample areas. The second surveyed a series of linear transects in a search for preforms, diagnostic points, and any other artifacts besides obsidian debris.

To sample the background density and distribution of flake debris across the larger area in which Tempiute lies, we imposed a grid that encompassed Areas N1–N10, then sampled it at 50 m intervals. At each interval all flakes found within a 1 m² area were counted, and their aggregate weight recorded. Flakes were not collected. Recalling that much of the ground surface lying outside of defined debris fields at Tempiute is heavily eroded, the background density and distribution sampled by this effort almost certainly underestimates original density and distribution. The resulting density-contour map is similar by count and weight (Figure 4.8), both of which show two modes from south to north that correspond to Areas N2 and N5, and N6–N8, respectively.

UA crews then resurveyed the entirety of the same sample domain in linear transects at 10 m intervals. This effort produced nearly half of Tempiute's small preform assemblage.

Discussion

Count or weight density modes identified in interpolation maps should not be interpreted as the results of discrete knapping episodes at either Modena or Tempiute. Particularly in Areas A, B, and F but to a lesser extent in other Modena sampled areas as well, obsidian debris deposits are far too dense and abundant to be the product of isolated episodes. Instead, Modena and Tempiute areas are best interpreted as long-term accumulations of debris from many discrete knapping events that varied in volume, span(s) of the reduction continuum represented, and technological reduction modes. That is, Modena and Tempiute areas are accumulations, not discrete depositional events.

Whatever models may help explain the extent and spatial pattern of individual knapping debris scatters, it is clear that variation in knapper position (e.g., Newcomer and Sieveking 1980:349), certainly in microtopography, probably in technology or reduction mode, and possibly in toolstone cobble size and fracture mechanics all contribute in complex ways to the structure of debris fields. We have no models, behavioral or otherwise, to accommodate so large a set of independent variables and their complex interactions to account for the spatial structure of Modena's and Tempiute's primary and secondary debris fields.

Nor can patterns in the distribution and abundance of obsidian debris easily be interpreted as a function of slope, such that, for instance, tops of slopes were impoverished while foots of slopes became enriched in obsidian debris. Both the discussion above of the relationship of highest density modes to slope in several Modena areas and some analysis to follow fail to reveal any simple, deterministic correlations between debris distributions and slope.

Stage-1 to Stage-2 Interpolations

As above, one purpose of UA's two-stage sample design was to provide two independent datasets for comparative analysis. If the two samples provide similar information then future studies can maximize sample efficiency by concentrating on non-collection samples supplemented by more selective collection strategies. Thus, one secondary purpose of UA investigation was to test the two-stage design for the samples' fidelity to one another. This section describes some results of analysis of the comparability of two-stage sampling.

Also as above, Stage-2 sampling collected only count and aggregate weight per sample unit. Therefore, the two samples can be compared only for these measures. One way to do so is by examining their point estimates of obsidian count and weight, averaged across units within each sample domain. (For discussion of number of flakes and for the "analytical core unit" concept [Carr and Bradbury 2001], see Chapter 8.) Interpolation is another way to evaluate samples that differ in the exact location of their units. That is, interpolated values for obsidian count or aggregate weight from one sample stage at each point location of units in the other stage can be compared. Selected results of this assessment are reported here.

Very high correlation within narrow ranges should not be expected in data subject to variation by prehistoric human behavior, the winnowing effects of slope discussed above, and the vagaries of sampling. Yet the somewhat noisy patterns nevertheless are grounded in significant patterns (e.g., in Area B, for count $r = 0.50$; $p < 0.01$; for weight $r = 0.43$; $p = 0.02$). This result justifies regression of Stage-1 observed values upon Stage-2 interpolated ones, separately for count and weight.

Details of regression results are unimportant since correlation is already established, and there is no need to use regression results to predict already-known Stage-1 counts. Standardized residuals measure degree and direction of the departure of Stage-1 counts from values predicted from regression upon interpolated values. Again using Area B as an example, count and weight residuals clearly pattern, with rising dispersion at high positive values on both variables. Thus, correlation between count and weight residuals grows more diffuse as both variables increase, surely a reflection of technological character or flake-size distribution such that high sample-unit counts can include small flakes and high weights large ones. Considering count alone, as observed values rise so do standardized residuals. To judge from analysis of Modena Area B, correlation between observed and interpolated counts is strongest at relatively low values. To the extent that the samples identified local peaks or troughs in their count or weight distributions, the same results did not necessarily occur in the other stage sample. That is, Stage-1 and Stage-2 samples are most comparable in measuring the overall pattern of variation in obsidian count and weight density, less so in local details. Stage-1 standardized residuals for Area B shows some spatial patterning (Figure 4.9). Negative residuals lie mostly at the northern, upslope extreme of Area B, positive ones mostly at the margins of the area. On balance, Stage-1 and Stage-2 samples differ mostly at Area B's upper zone, perhaps in part from winnowing effect and in part from simple stochastic variation.

There is some variation in interpolation results by area. Modena Area F represents one extreme, where both count and weight correlate significantly (for count $r = 0.61$; $p < 0.01$; for weight $r = 0.78$; $p < 0.01$) and pattern relatively tightly. As in Area B, standardized residuals pattern fairly closely ($r = 0.54$; $p < 0.01$), especially with removal of one extreme positive outlier ($r = 0.60$; $p = 0.01$). They show a similar, admittedly more diffuse, tendency to dispersion at high positive values. Therefore, again, observed and interpolated values are not just absolutely closer, itself a function of scale, but also relatively closer, at lower values. Unlike in Area B, however, in Area F there is no significant correlation between observed count and its standardized residual. A spatial plot of Area F Stage-1 unit standardized residuals (Figure 4.9) shows patterning similar to Area B. Again, most negative standardized residuals lie in the north-

ern half of the area, admittedly somewhat nearer the center compared to Area B, and positive standardized residuals lie on Area F's margins.

Area D is a considerably larger, relatively long, and narrow area that lacks the dense scree deposits of Areas A, B, and F and presumably the original concentrations of workable obsidian cobbles that underlaid those areas. There, the relationship between observed and interpolated values is, as in the case of Area B, somewhat diffuse and therefore noisy, owing to several sources of variation. Again, however, correlations are significant (for count, $r = 0.48$; $p < 0.01$; for weight, $r = 0.52$; $p < 0.01$) between Stage-1 sample values and those interpolated from Stage-2 sampling. Standardized residuals of count and weight pattern very closely in Area D ($r = 0.87$; $p < 0.01$), more so than in Area F. As in Area B, observed Stage-1 counts from Area D correlate significantly with standardized residuals ($r = 0.88$; $p < 0.01$), showing more dispersion of count values in lower ranges for the standardized residual. A spatial plot for Area D does not clearly pattern in the distribution of high negative or high positive standardized residuals.

In two areas at Tempiute selected for analysis, N2 and N5, there is no significant correlation between Stage-1 observed and Stage-2 interpolated values (for N2 count, $r = 0.10$; $p = 0.56$ and for N2 weight, $r = 0.08$; $p = 0.64$; for N5 count, $r = 0.15$; $p = 0.45$ and for N5 weight, $r = -0.05$; $p = 0.80$). Removal of a high-count outlier in Area N2 does not improve correlation, in fact, it slightly reduces it. Because observed and interpolated count/weight values in these Tempiute areas do not correlate, regression is not justified.

In sum, observed Stage-1 and interpolated Stage-2 count and weight values correlate at Modena, although not to the same degree or in the same way in all areas studied. The absence of correlation in the only two Tempiute areas studied suggests some degree of uncontrolled variation between stage samples there. Nevertheless, the fairly strong pattern of correlation at Modena indicates that the two independent samples largely capture and model the same pattern of spatial variation in obsidian count

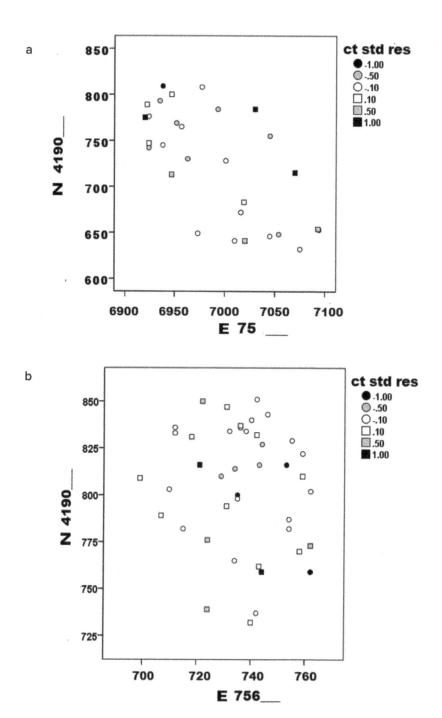

FIGURE 4.9. Distribution of Stage-1 count standardized residuals at Modena Areas B and F.

and weight, itself suggesting fidelity between Stage-1 and Stage-2 sampling. In similar future projects, collection samples might be safely limited to relatively few units and generally low volumes. Non-collection sampling instead might serve as the basis for modeling the distribution and abundance of surface artifact distributions.

Surface Processes and Downslope Artifact Movement

Modena occupies a dissected upland, and its densest obsidian deposits lie on fairly steep, forested slopes. Tempiute rests on an alluvial fan of modest slope populated by scrub vegetation. Accordingly, the sites differ considerably in slope, aspect, soil, and plant community. Yet both consist of concentrations of irregular particles—flakes—that are subject to a range of natural geological processes. Playing out over very long periods, these processes can systematically alter the surface assemblages of quarries. Characteristics of the Modena and Tempiute assemblages suggest that they have been so altered.

On slopes, particularly the fairly steep ones at Modena, gravity and sheetwash are the likeliest taphonomic agents. Except on the steepest of slopes and for the most spherical of cobbles, gravity alone is unlikely to move artifacts (e.g., Rick 1976), nor should sheetwash much alter assemblages that lie on perfectly flat upland surfaces. Instead, it is the combination of sheetwash's flow and the steepness of slopes on which artifacts of different sizes lie that selectively move smaller pieces over greater distances, in the process altering the size distribution of surface assemblages like those at Modena and Tempiute. As Fanning and Holdaway put it, "small artifacts will move farther and predominantly down slope as a result of hillslope hydrologic processes" (2001:676; see also Byers et al. 2015:384; Sheppard and Kleindienst 1996: 176–179).

These processes and their effects on arid landforms are well documented. On hillslopes in southeastern Spain, median diameter of rock fragments varied directly with slope, meaning steeper slopes held fragment assemblages of larger median size (Poesen et al. 1998:334, Fig-

ure 8), although rock type also affected the relationship. Synthesizing a substantial literature, Parsons and colleagues concluded that "as the weathering particles become finer, they are preferentially transported downslope by hydraulic processes, so that usually the proportion of fines increases and the proportion of coarse debris decreases" (2009:233–234). The profiles of hillslopes often comprise shallow curves rather than straight lines, and therefore slope itself varies continuously in ways that complicate its effects. Nevertheless, similar slopes (of regression lines of median diameter upon hillslope, not hillslope itself) over similar ranges of values of both fragment size and hillslope characterized a number of studies that involved different areas and rock types, suggesting a robust pattern (Abrahams et al. 1985:351, Table 5; Byers et al. 2015:Figure 2; Fanning and Holdaway 2001; Sheppard and Kleindienst 1996:176).

Sheetwash (Petraglia and Potts's [1994: 229] "overland flow") and erosion channels or rills ("concentrated runoff" to Parsons et al. 2009:245) act upon archaeological sites as they do natural deposits, such that sites lose "the smaller fractions of artifacts at a higher rate than the larger fraction" (Smith 2001:59). Yet Smith's size-distribution data suggest that source sites and eroded artifacts captured in sediment traps differed only in subtle ways; Chapter 5 discusses this matter in detail. Although sheetwash and the particle transport that results can occur regularly and over the entirety of slopes, a three-year study in New Mexico found that most transport by far occurred in only three summer monsoon storms, that the volume of artifacts and finer sediment transported was substantial, and that gentler natural processes like snow melt transported relatively little material (Smith 2001:48, Figure 9, Table 5). Thus, the most powerful erosive events are relatively few and spasmodic (see also Cameron et al. 1990:62). A recent study of alluvial fans at the Nevada Test Site identified sheetwash as the most common surface process that has the effect of "winnowing sand and silt out of surface deposits and leaving a coarser lag" (Dickerson et al. 2015:552).

Experimental studies corroborate geological findings. Winnowing of flakes by size, and secondarily by shape, was clearly demonstrated in controlled flume experiments that measured both distance and settlement time (Byers et al. 2015). There, movement during individual events fell in the range of 1–4 m, but aggregate effects of many events would multiply the effect many times over. After four years of monitoring 43 experimental scatters' natural alteration, Schick found that "smaller debitage was particularly vulnerable to fluvial winnowing and removal…so that even relatively low velocity currents which did not move larger cores or flakes…would most often remove some portion of the very small debitage" (1987:96). Her analysis (1986:Table 2) suggested that, in all geomorphological contexts but the most stable, the smallest size fractions (up to 20 mm, slightly smaller than the largest, 25.4 mm [1 in], fraction used in this study) are reduced by 50% or more just over her four-year monitoring period. The slopes on which Tempiute and especially Modena lie are unlikely to resemble Schick's most stable contexts, so the winnowing rates that she reported may apply as well there.

Similarly, Petraglia and Nash's (1987) experiments in New Mexico's Jemez Canyon were designed to monitor the taphonomic effects of gravity, sheetwash, and other fluvial processes. Greatest taphonomic bias occurred at their Site B, which was located on a hillslope to examine the joint effects of slope and erosion (1987:120). In general, artifact movement occurred as a negative exponential function of size and suggested a size threshold of 15 g (Petraglia and Nash 1987:120, Figure 5) above which movement was unlikely. Reid and Frostick (1985; see also Bertran et al. 2012:Figure 23; Petraglia and Potts 1994:241–242) also documented considerable downslope movement in their Koobi Fora study area. They stressed the independent effect of artifact shape (1985:147–148), suggesting that cylindrical and spherical objects of any given size are likelier to move than are relatively flat objects like flakes. In experiments on a cultivated surface, many flakes were transported by fluvial processes, some over a distance of 50 m

or more, and thin, flat flakes "were preferentially transported downslope" (Allen 1991:47). Hartley's (1991:59–60) and Robins's (1999:Table 2) similar experiments also showed considerable movement, again differentially by smaller experimental flakes. Isaac's (1967:36) experiments showed that smaller flakes were more susceptible to transport than larger ones. Sheppard and Kleindienst's (1996:176–177) experiments identified winnowing effects chiefly upon flakes of maximum dimension <25 to 30 mm.

Finally, archaeological studies further corroborate geological conclusions. Impoverished fine fractions of debitage at Kalambo Falls implicated "fluvial disturbance and winnowing" (Schick 1992:1). Compared to unwinnowed experimental controls, Sheppard and Kleindienst (1996:Figure 3) documented considerable bias in flake-size distributions of empirical assemblages subject to fluvial winnowing, shifting modes of distributions from the smallest size interval to those >30 mm. Sheetwash and wind differentially transported smaller lithic artifacts in the Australian desert (Cameron et al. 1990: 66), and for the Simpson Desert, Barton concluded that "the low percentage of material in the smallest size class (0.5–1 cm) is expected, indicating that these samples have been winnowed by wind and water" (2001:261; see also Barton 2008:61). Flake assemblages at a Cameroonian rock shelter were winnowed by runoff as a function of slope (Lavachery and Cornelissen 2000:158). Bertran and colleagues (2006; Bertran et al. 2012) compiled extensive sets of flake debris from experimental reductions of various technological modes. These varied to some degree in flake-size distributions—the only basis for distinguishing reduction modes by mass analysis. Yet the range of variation (e.g., Bertran et al. 2012:Table 4) in intact, undisturbed experimental flake-size distributions was exceeded by various archaeological assemblages. Bertran and colleagues used ternary diagrams to illustrate the departure of empirical assemblages from experimental standards, both toward their enrichment in some cases but usually impoverishment of fines (2012:Figures 15, 20). They also documented progressive downslope concentration of fines (e.g., 2012:Figure 9). In particular for hillslopes like Modena, these analysts concluded that "the best hypothesis that can explain sorting is the impact of overland flow" (Bertran et al. 2012:3165). At Annadel, Parkman (1983:256) reported downslope movement and resulting taphonomic damage to obsidian flakes, presumably from combinations of gravity and sheetwash. For a project area that traversed Lincoln County, Vicari's comparison of surface and excavated assemblages concluded that "most sites…have been affected by erosional processes that selectively expose larger artifacts at the surface" (2013; see also Dickerson et al. 2015).

Besides sheetwash on slopes, burial by natural agents can also bias archaeological assemblages. In actualistic experiments on Utah landforms broadly similar to Modena and Tempiute, Hartley concluded that "smaller artifacts will be underrepresented in surface assemblages, due to their greater potential for burial" (1991:63 and Figure 1; see also Root 2004:90). Elsewhere, vertical movement of artifacts by natural processes can be extensive. This too acts most strongly upon smaller artifacts, such that "size is a critical variable in settling velocities" (Michie 1990:37; see also Figure 10).

In summary, natural processes systematically transform surface assemblages like those at Modena and Tempiute. The most influential processes probably are sheetwash and other forms of fluvial transport, particularly on Modena's relatively steep slopes. But natural burial processes also remove artifacts from the surface. In combination, these processes implicate the systematic removal and redeposition of fines which, in this context, mostly are flakes in smaller size fractions. Modena and Tempiute assemblages probably are affected by taphonomic size bias that differentially removed smaller flakes. As abundant as they are, these surface assemblages have been exposed for millennia to natural taphonomic processes that have steadily impoverished them of smaller artifacts.

Chapter 5 explores this matter in detail, and attempts to estimate the magnitude of resulting size bias. Part of that analysis involves the compilation of flake-size distributions from the sites and their comparison to equivalent data from experimental reductions of several modes and degrees. Of course there is considerable variation in flake-size distribution among the experimental modes. But in a set of sources that reported a range of experimental reduction modes, the proportion of flakes always varied inversely with size interval; the smaller the size interval, the higher the proportion. As Chapter 5 documents, however, in empirical flake-size distributions from Modena and Tempiute, the count proportion of 6.4 and 12.7 mm (¼ and ½ in) flakes was considerably lower than comparable figures from any experimental sources, even the earliest-stage experiments. Other experimental sources consulted but not discussed in Chapter 5 (e.g., Behm 1983) also reported significantly higher proportions of flakes by count in their 6.4 and 12.7 mm (¼ and ½ in) fractions. On balance, experimental studies document a strong winnowing bias in surface flake assemblages on hillslopes, which acts to impoverish the finer fractions that are abundant in excavation and experimental samples at the expense of coarser ones.

Clearly, Modena and Tempiute are anomalous in their low proportion of flakes in the finest or smallest size classes. It is conceivable that smaller flakes were overlooked in collection units, but UA crews were repeatedly reminded to collect all flakes lying on the surface of units regardless of their size. (My own past experience with large assemblages of small flakes [e.g., Shott 1994, 1997a] counselled both the critical value and the preponderance of smaller size fractions. In UA fieldwork, despite taking particular pains to collect the smallest flakes to the ≥6.4 mm (¼ in) threshold, I was surprised by their comparative paucity.) The considerable difference between archaeological and experimental size distributions could be explained by collection bias only if UA crews had neglected to recover many thousands of 6.4 and 12.7 mm (¼ and ½ in) fraction flakes since, because smaller-fraction debris almost always is most numerous such that its selective winnowing only moderately increases the proportion of coarser-fraction debris even in lag deposits (Petraglia and Potts 1994:231).

One way to investigate possible taphonomic size effects is to plot measures of particle size against slope and elevation. Two measures of possible taphonomic size-sorting were used, mean weight and the proportion of all flakes by count in the 25.4 mm (1 in) size class. Of course the size distribution of flakes within debris fields owes to complex cultural patterning as well as natural processes; taphonomic winnowing contributes to, but does not alone determine, spatial structure of archaeological deposits. All else equal, however, if slope-dependent winnowing occurred then both mean weight and 25.4 mm (1 in) proportion should positively correlate with slope, as such winnowing preferentially removes smaller flakes. This would have the joint effect of increasing the mean weight of untransported flakes and leaving larger size fractions progressively more abundant.

Modena Area F is a dense debris field that lies on a fairly steep slope. Mean weight of obsidian flakes there correlates with slope ($r = 0.22$; $p = 0.05$; $r_s = 0.40$; $p = 0.01$; expressed in degrees, following Fanning and Holdaway 2001:676), as does the proportion of flakes in the 25.4 mm (1 in) class more ambiguously ($r = 0.23$; $p = 0.13$; $r_s = 0.35$; $p = 0.02$). Tempiute N6, like the rest of that site, occupies a more modest slope than does Modena F. Mean weight there correlates more weakly with slope ($r = 0.23$; $p = 0.14$), better after removal of one positive outlier ($r = 0.30$; $p = 0.05$; $r_s = 0.32$; $p = 0.04$), as does the proportion of flakes in the 25.4 mm (1 in) class ($r = 0.30$; $p = 0.24$; $r_s = 0.38$; $p = 0.13$).

To judge from these examples, there are observable size-sorting effects upon flake assemblages as a function of slope, more at Modena than Tempiute. Modena and Tempiute assemblages most closely resemble Petraglia and Potts's Case 3, "lag situation (winnowed)" (1994: 237) scenario. Nevertheless, percent-variance explained is low and results do not reach conventional significance levels in some cases. Taphonomic winnowing is one among a number of factors (e.g., variation in prehistoric reduction modes carried out between the quarries at

different times, differences in cobble size, spatial structure of sites, etc.) that conditioned the size and flake-size distribution of quarry flake assemblages.

Fanning and Holdaway (2001) modeled flake movement in Australian desert assemblages as a function of artifact maximum dimension, surface slope, and relative elevation. The more advanced, but possibly less robust, multiple regression that achieved significant results in their case were more equivocal for Modena and Tempiute. For instance, using backward stepwise regression and mean weight as dependent variable (as per Fanning and Holdaway [2001: 676–677], relative elevation, but not slope, for Modena F was entered, while results were opposite for Tempiute N6. Using the same procedure with the proportion of 25.4 mm (1 in) fraction flakes as dependent, both Modena F and Tempiute N6 entered slope, but results reached conventional significance level only for Fanning and Holdaway's dependent variable "flake maximum dimension," not the mean weight and proportion of flakes in the 25.4 mm (1 in) fraction as here. Nor was any attempt made to regress clast measures against nominal states like macromorphology and ground cover, because each of these essentially was constant within Modena and Tempiute. Thus, following Fanning and Holdaway (2001:676–678) macromorphology would be "hillslope" for all Modena clusters and "low-slope alluvial fan" for all at Tempiute, while vegetation cover was constant among clusters at each site. Whatever explains the difference from Fanning and Holdaway's results, taphonomic winnowing of small flakes is evident at Modena and Tempiute among the myriad of factors that in complex combination generated the assemblages.

Not surprisingly, flake-weight distributions are skewed in both assemblages (Figure 4.10). At Modena, 67% of flakes are lighter than the 15 g threshold identified by Petraglia and Nash (1987); 85% of Tempiute flakes are lighter than 15 g. Clearly, most flakes in both assemblages are below this threshold yet remain on the slope surface. But the difference between quarry and experimental flake-size distributions suggests

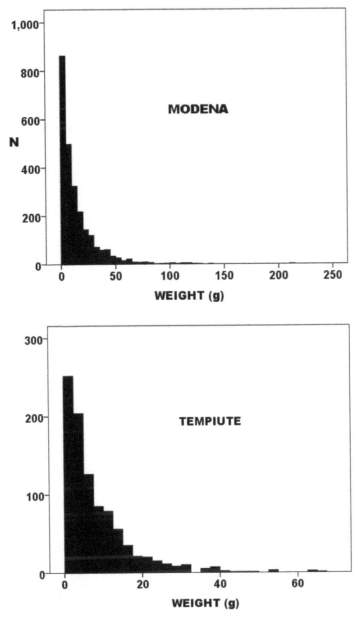

FIGURE 4.10. Modena and Tempiute flake-weight distributions.

that many more small flakes once were present on the surface at Modena and Tempiute. At both sites, mean flake weight by size class is less than 15 g for all fractions except 25.4 mm (1 in), although the means of the 19 mm (¾ in) fractions approximate that figure. Combined with sources cited in Chapter 5, these values suggest that 6.4 mm (¼ in) and possibly 12.7 mm (½ in) fractions are systematically underrepresented in quarry surface assemblages.

Bertran and colleagues (2012) documented considerable taphonomic bias in archaeological flake-size distributions compared to experimental controls. As above, they used ternary

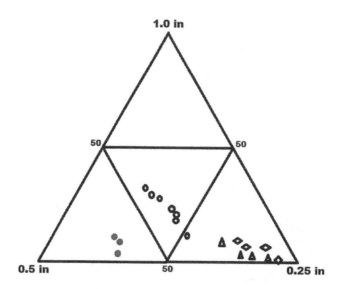

FIGURE 4.11. Ternary diagram by size fraction of Stahle and Dunn (1982) (diamonds), Root (1992) (triangles), and original Modena (open circles) and Tempiute (solid circles) flake assemblages.

diagrams to depict the direction and degree of departure of empirical from experimental assemblages, most of which showed coarsening (i.e., overrepresentation of large size fractions) in empirical assemblages as a product of winnowing (e.g., Bertran et al. 2012:Figure 20; Bertran et al. 2006:Figure 18). Figure 4.11 shows a coarsening of flake-size distributions for major areas at Modena and Tempiute, compared to Stahle and Dunn's (1982) and Root's (1992) experimental knowns. Both sites' assemblages are displaced from the high concentration in the smallest fraction that is characteristic of experimental distributions, Tempiute's somewhat more than Modena's. Modena assemblages are also drawn closer to the largest, 25.4 mm (1 in), fraction compared both to Tempiute and experimental assemblages.

Spatial Distribution
of Modena Preform Assemblages

As above, preforms were discovered in UA investigations either by chance, by selective transect samples in several areas, or by Stage-1 and Stage-2 probabilistic sampling. The latter samples can be used to estimate the total population of preforms. At Modena, Areas A and F had suf-

ficiently large samples for estimation. Area B's Stage-1 sample was fairly high; no other Modena area yielded more than one preform in sample units. Too few preforms were found anywhere at Tempiute for valid estimation, so analysis here is confined to Modena areas.

Besides estimating the size of the preform population at Modena areas, results of which are reported in Chapter 8, probabilistic sampling was used to identify the underlying models that govern preform spatial distributions. Samples on a grid, like UA sample units at Modena and Tempiute, are a form of quadrat sampling. In quadrat sampling, to gauge fit to model spatial distributions Poisson is a suitable baseline model that describes a random distribution of the objects of interest (Harvey 1966:84). Individual quadrats—sample units—are characterized by the number of elements they contain. Since many contain no elements of interest, they have counts of 0. Presumably fewer units contain 1 element, fewer still 2 elements, and so on. Model-fitting proceeds by calculating the mean number of elements—preforms in this case—per sample unit. Then the Poisson model is used to calculate expected number of units having 0, 1, 2…preforms, in other words a frequency distribution of preforms per unit. Finally, the expected Poisson is compared to the observed frequency distribution, with fit gauged by χ^2 (Harvey 1966:89–92).

For most purposes, incidence of preforms per unit must be scaled to 1 m² units, because many sample units were fractions of that figure. Scaling amounts to multiplying the observed incidence per unit by a factor that corresponds to unit size. If, for instance, the unit measured 0.25 m², the factor is four, because four such units sum to 1 m². Most sample units at Modena Area A and all at Area F were 0.25 m², and were thusly scaled by a value of four. As a result, the frequency distribution of preforms per scaled sample unit would have few values of 1–3 in Area A and none in that range in Area F. Such frequency distributions are questionable to fit to any model distribution, and almost certainly would produce results that did not fit a Poisson model, indicating either a uniform or, more likely, clustered distribution.

Therefore, for purposes of model-fitting, counts per sample unit were not scaled to 1 m² unit size. Instead each sample unit was treated as equivalent to the complete 1 m² in which it lay. As a practical matter, this treatment assumed that all preforms located within the 1 m² from which the unit was drawn were recovered, a reasonable assumption since preforms adjacent to the actual sample unit probably would be observed. (Several were noted and collected just beyond the borders of units in the course of Stage-1 or Stage-2 sampling at Modena.)

Ten preforms were recovered in Stage-1 sampling in Area A (the two found in Stage-2 sampling are omitted as insufficient for estimation), with seven in Stage-1 sampling and six in Stage-2 sampling in Area F. Frequency distributions of preforms per unit were fitted to the Poisson model, which is given as (Harvey 1966:84):

$$P_x = e^{-\lambda} \lambda^x / x!$$

where x is the number of preforms per unit, λ is the mean number of preforms per unit, and e is the base of Naperian logs. P_x is solved for each value of x to produce the model's expected values. In turn, expected values form the frequency

distribution for λ governed by a random spatial distribution.

In Area A, the frequency distribution of preforms found in Stage-1 probabilistic sampling is highly nonrandom, instead corresponding to a clustered distribution. The highest divergence between observed and expected frequencies occurs at $x = 3$, where observed frequency is disproportionately high. In Area A, preforms are not distributed randomly but instead patterned by prehistoric activity ($\chi^2 = 39.1$, p<0.01). The pattern clearly is peripheral to the area itself (Figure 4.12a), identifying clusters along its southeast margin and at its northwest corner, adjacent to the upland area that was the subject of judgmentally placed transects. Although this evidence is limited, it does suggest that most preforms in the vicinity of Area A either were produced from suitable flake blanks that were removed from the main quarry deposit to adjoining workshops, or were transported there after initial working at the locus of the cobbles from which they derived.

In Area F, the frequency distribution of preforms found in Stage-1 probabilistic sampling is random ($\chi^2 = 3.4$, p>0.05), and the distribution of Stage-2 specimens nearly so ($\chi^2 = 5.0$, p<0.05). In the Stage-2 sample, the greatest disparity between observed and expected frequencies is at $x = 1$, where half as many as expected occur. If anything, this result suggests a uniform or dispersed distribution, not a clustered one. Certainly no large, distinct clusters are evident in the map of Area F preform distribution (Figure 4.12b). Compared to Area A, there is no pronounced clustering in the spatial distribution of preforms but instead a random one to judge from Stage-1 sample results, tending toward perhaps a uniform one to judge from Stage-2 results.

Conclusion

Modena and Tempiute were sampled probabilistically in two stages within areas defined as major debris scatters. In general, but not in all salient details, the two probabilistic samples produced similar results. Resulting data permitted estimation of raw quantities of debris

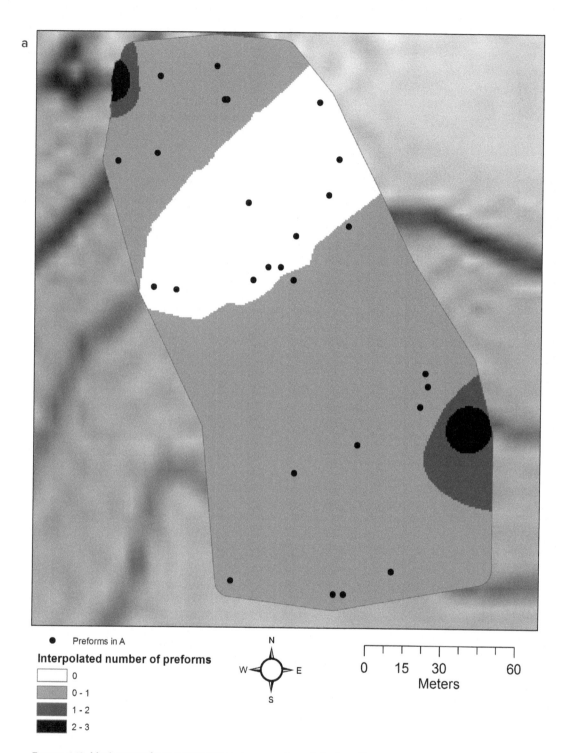

a

●   Preforms in A

Interpolated number of preforms

☐   0

☐   0 - 1

■   1 - 2

■   2 - 3

N
W   E
S

0   15   30   60
Meters

FIGURE 4.12. Modena preform interpolation maps: a. Area A; b. Area F.

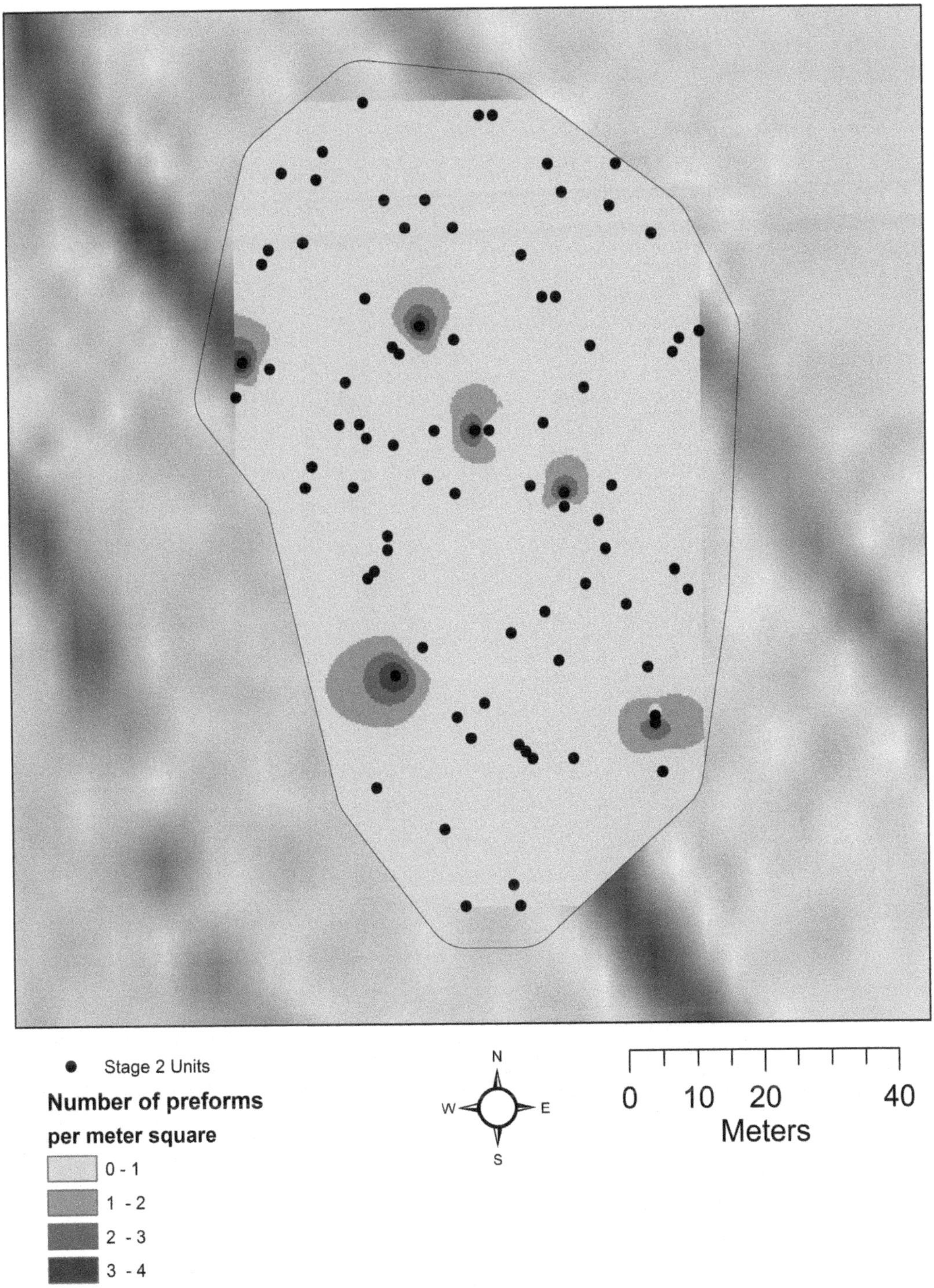

FIGURE 4.12. (cont'd.) Modena preform interpolation maps: a. Area A; b. Area F.

and other artifact types. In addition, systematic transect sampling for preforms was undertaken in and near major Modena areas and across the entirety of the Tempiute quarry.

Stage-1 debris samples and all recovered preforms were laboratory-processed for analysis reported in subsequent chapters. In large measure, these data form the basis for the analytical chapters to follow. Nevertheless, natural taphonomic processes that biased the surface record must be taken into account before analysis. Surface relief and the winnowing effect of sheetwash probably have biased the extant record against smaller artifacts, particularly small-fraction flakes. They have not, however, biased the distribution of preforms at Modena which, as distribution analysis here demonstrates, varies across the site.

5

The Reduction Process
and Analysis of Flake Debris

The debitage produced in making stone tools
is perhaps the world's first hazardous waste.
(Whittaker and Kaldahl 2001:32)

This chapter describes and analyzes the by-products of toolstone reduction. The category encompasses abandoned or exhausted cores, and the flake debris found, as at quarries elsewhere, in great abundance at Modena and Tempiute. Whether or not lithic debris is hazardous waste, core and especially flake assemblages reveal important dimensions of prehistoric quarrying behavior when analyzed in detail.

Cores

Lithic reduction starts from natural or unmodified cobbles. During the reduction process, these cobbles become cores. In biface industries, cores may be difficult to distinguish from bifaces, as exhibited by Ataman and Bloomer's (1992) work at the Tosawihi quarry, where they stated only "cores *not* exhibiting biface morphology are considered here" (1992:217). However, given the small size and indeterminate technological character of Modena and Tempiute core assemblages, no attempt was made to apply Ataman and Bloomer's (1992:218) typology of assayed pieces, split nodules, block and spheroidal cores, or "possible" cores. Instead, three basic core types—split/tested, block or polyhedral, and biface, in approximate order by degree of reduction—were defined.

Split/tested cobbles are specimens bearing facets on one face only, with cortex on the remaining one (if the original cobble was spheri-cal) or more faces. They are the product of splitting raw cobbles either to test them or to work one or both split halves. Block/polyhedral cores bear facets over all, or nearly all, of their surfaces, and two or more platforms often perpendicular to one another. Biface cores approach the form and technology of biface preforms, as Ataman and Bloomer (1992) noted. They bear two opposing faces separated by a nearly continuous, if sinuous, edge. Opposing faces are not symmetrical; although both faces are faceted, they may differ in scar density and pattern. A miscellaneous category "other" includes irregular cores or core fragments that could not be assigned to any defined type.

Cores also were coded for presence/absence of cortex, for weight and major dimensions, and for number of platforms. Few core platforms at Modena were unfaceted, so platforms also were coded for number of facets, platform facet patterning, and minimum and maximum length of platform facets.

Modena

Only 18 cores were found at Modena, most in Stage-1 units (Shott 2016:Table 5.1). Most by far were found in Areas A and B; despite its similarity in context and artifact density, no cores were found in Area F. Only one of two found in Area D occurred in a Stage-1 sample unit. Modena is not unique in its comparative scarcity of cores.

TABLE 5.1. Dimensions and platforms by core type at Modena. ANOVA *F* and attained significance *p* reported.

		n	mean	F	p
Dimension 1	split	7	52.1		
	polyhedral	7	58.4		
	biface	4	52.5		
				0.58	0.57
Dimension 2	split	7	39.9		
	polyhedral	7	47.7		
	biface	4	45.5		
				3.00	0.08
Dimension 3	split	7	29.3		
	polyhedral	7	42.6		
	biface	4	21.3		
				14.8	>0.01
Weight (g)	split	7	68.7		
	polyhedral	7	139.0		
	biface	4	55.7		
				5.93	0.01
Plat. 1 scars	split	7	2.9		
	polyhedral	7	1.7		
	biface	4	4.0		
				2.32	0.13
Plat. 2 scars	split	2	2.5		
	polyhedral	4	1.0		
	biface	4	4.8		
				2.82	0.13

Across the vastness of the Tosawihi quarry landscape, only 130 cores were found (Ataman and Bloomer 1992:Table 76), and only 35 across five quarry-workshop sites at Newberry Crater (Connolly ed., 1999:Tables 6.6, 7.5, 8.5, 9.17).

Such a small core assemblage has limited potential for technological analysis. As a general observation, most Modena cores probably were extensively reduced and therefore probably exhausted, as at Tosawihi (Ataman and Bloomer 1992:223), or were too small to bear much reduction. Certainly the presence of two or more platforms on many cores suggests extensive use, while the presence of cortex on most suggests that many began as small cobbles.

Core type did not pattern with number of platforms ($\chi^2 = 6.2$; $p = 0.19$; Shott 2016:Table 5.2), although the result is equivocal because all nine cells had expected values <5. Despite the absence of statistical significance, standardized residuals >|1|, suggesting association, were found for split-cobble cores and single platforms and biface cores and two platforms, which are essentially a matter of type definition. Number of platforms was independent of block/polyhedral cores, that is, cores of that type could bear any number of platforms.

Some coded attributes patterned by core type (Table 5.1). The longest dimension of cores did not differ by type, but block/polyhedral cores had significantly longer second and third dimensions than did split or biface cores, probably due to their reduction from unsplit original cobbles. Biface cores, however, were substantially reduced in the process of transforming them to that condition. Split-cobble and biface cores did not differ in dimensions. Block/polyhedral cores also weighed more than other core types. Biface cores bore significantly more facets on their first and second platforms than did block/polyhedral, although they did not possess more than split-cobble ones. (Too few cores had third platforms for ANOVA to be conducted.) There were no significant differences in dimensions, weight, or scar count by number of core platforms.

Only Areas A and B yielded sufficient cores to characterize their spatial distribution and to estimate the size of their overall core assemblages. Areas A and B together produced 15 cores from eight sample units, an average of nearly two per unit. Six units produced Area A's 11 cores, and two yielded Area B's four specimens. The same scaling of sample-unit size and frequencies used in Chapter 4's quadrat analysis of preforms was used here. Clearly, the spatial distribution of cores within these areas is clustered, that is, nonrandom. Rescaling, as in Chapter 4, further increases clustering. Fitting adjusted frequency distributions of cores per unit to the Poisson model that approximates a random distribution, gauged by χ^2 fit, failed for both areas (for A, χ^2 = 94.5; df = 3; for B, χ^2 = 40.5; df = 3; for both, p < 0.010). Accordingly, the distribution of cores per unit is nonrandom and, to judge from mean number of cores per unit, highly clustered in Areas A and B.

The adjusted mean number of cores/m² in Stage-1 samples is 1.64 for Area A, 0.97 for Area B. Multiplying these means by the number of 1 m² units in each area yields point estimates of 49,298 cores (95% confidence limits 0–110,020) in Area A, 30,522 (95% confidence limits 0–84,014) in Area B. Although our fieldwork recovered relatively few cores, the estimated number present just in Areas A and B is substantial. These estimates must be qualified, however, because UA's research design was directed toward sampling for preforms and par-

ticularly flakes, which are vastly more abundant and more widely distributed than are cores and so are sampled more efficiently. The relatively small number of cores encountered in Stage-1 units projects to a substantial core assemblage at Modena, but the sample does not allow precise estimates. The upper confidence limit for both areas is more than twice the point estimate. Because UA's sample design was efficient for flakes, but not necessarily for cores, these estimates of core numbers are not comparable to those determined by a more thorough sampling of considerably larger populations of flakes.

Tempiute

Six cores were found at Tempiute (Shott 2016: Table 5.1). Only one fell in a sample unit. This assemblage is far too small for analysis or interpretation.

Flake Analysis

Ingbar and colleagues note that "the technical challenges presented by the sheer volume of material in quarries can be met only by active development of efficient analytical techniques" (1992:76). This is certainly true of quarry industrial debris like cores and flakes, which demand attention precisely because of their great abundance. All analysis strives for validity, but any that confronts the sheer abundance of flake debris at quarries is forced to contemplate approaches that also are pragmatic and efficient.

By any measure—number, volume, mass—flakes are by far the most abundant artifact category at Modena and Tempiute. This is no less true of most quarries, and often equally true of lithic assemblages at a full range of site types across terranes. In the past, however, archaeologists rarely invested much thought or effort in the analysis of flake debris; only in recent decades have they begun to rectify their neglect (Shott 1994). A major focus of UA's research design is the field-processing model (e.g., Beck et al. 2002; Elston 1992a). For this purpose, the stage preforms analyzed in Chapters 6 and 7 are the most directly relevant artifact category. Yet the size and character of flake assemblages also are relevant to testing the field-processing model, and to other legitimate goals of quarry analysis, including scale and organization of production. This chapter examines flake assemblages in some detail, in equal part to further test the field-processing model and to gauge the inferential potential of lithic debris.

Philosophy of Flake Analysis

Flakes are by-products typically left where detached, whereas the tools that were the objects of reduction or maintenance often were removed for use elsewhere. By combinations of their abundance and characteristics, flakes can reveal both the amount and kind of tool production and use that occurred in places where the tools did not remain so cannot be found. Even if it was made elsewhere and carried to several places during its use history, a stone tool can only be discarded and found in one place, leaving a trail of production and resharpening flakes across the landscape throughout its life. Among other values, flakes help estimate donor curation (*sensu* Schiffer 1975; see also Shott 1995)—the carrying of tools from sites for use elsewhere. In this sense, flakes become the footprints that mark the pattern and scale of movement of tools across landscapes.

Tool making and using, and the flakes that result, involve two principal dimensions of variation: kind and amount. Various *kinds* of reduction produce various finished tools. This variation can be further subdivided into kinds of tool(s) produced and portions of the reduction continuum from original core to completion registered in debris. For example, bipolar reduction for the production of flake tools and the thinning of bifaces are kinds of behavior. Edge production and thinning represent reduction stages or spans of reduction continua. Whether a sample registers one tool made or 50, or early versus late reduction "stages" matters a great deal to our understanding of past behavior. Inferring *amounts* is not necessarily independent of inferring kinds of tool-making behavior because what is made affects how much debris is produced in the making. Thus, inferring amounts of tool-making and -using

behavior requires simultaneous inference to kind of behavior.

Approaches to Flake Analysis

The tension produced in the simultaneous contemplation of the abundance and information content of flake assemblages naturally encouraged archaeologists to consider several approaches. Breadth in analytical approaches is a good thing, but it acts against standardization. Quarry and other studies of flake debris use a variety of methods, and "no standards of classification have been accepted which allows any uniformity in the typology" (Syncrude Canada 1974:74). As a result, the considerable literature on quarry analysis accumulated in recent decades has produced only limited comparison of results.

After a long period of essentially ignoring flakes, Americanist archaeologists devised sometimes extensive sets of attributes to code and dimensions to measure in individual flakes starting with the work of Wilmsen (1970), if not earlier. Magne (1985:128; see also Magne and Pokotylo 1981) assigned flakes to reduction stages in experimental data chiefly by scar count on platform and exterior surface. Yet so far as attributes and dimensions are thought to reflect reduction stage, Mauldin and Amick (1989; see also Morrison 1994:91–99, 130) found that some—degree of cortex cover, exterior-surface scar patterning, and platform size—correlated weakly with stage. (Platform scar count also may pattern ambiguously, because the small size of many platforms severely limits the number of facets they may bear.) Mauldin and Amick (1989:73) suggested instead that such attributes and dimensions might pattern with flake size in ways that indirectly reflected stage. Similarly, the presumed association between platform and exterior-surface facets did not bear out in detailed analysis of flake debris from sites near Casa Diablo. Single-platform flakes often exhibited many exterior-surface scars while multiple-platform ones often had few exterior-surface scars, and advanced-stage biface thinning flakes sometimes possessed cortex (Skinner and Ainsworth 1991:161, 164, 165). Such complexity counsels the use of joint approaches. Since the analysis of flakes and flake assemblages became a serious pursuit about 40 years ago, three approaches, complementary in some respects, emerged at ascending scales: attributes and dimensions of flakes, typological assignment of flakes as discrete wholes, and properties of the size distribution of flake assemblages (Shott 1994; Steffen et al. 1998:135–139).

Attribute Analysis. Attribute analysis has made important contributions to resolving the nature of reduction as either a continuous process or sequence of discrete stages, and segments of reduction continua or sequences represented by flake assemblages. Besides Wilmsen (1970), examples are almost too numerous to mention and the range of questions addressed broad (see Andrefsky, ed. 2001; Shott 1994). Attribute analysis has demonstrated sometimes complex patterned variation according to reduction segment or stage in classic studies like Magne's (1985; see also Fish 1981; Goldstein 2018; Riley et al. 1994:Table 44). In general, flake attributes change or vary as reduction proceeds because dimensions become smaller and mass decreases on average (although considerable variation in crude flake size occurs along the reduction continuum). Flakes steadily bear less cortex cover, they become more extensively faceted both on platform and exterior surface, and they often show increased incidence of platform preparation like abrasion (e.g., Wright 1980).

But attribute analysis can reveal more. As one example, attribute approaches have been used to determine the nature of reduction (i.e., continuous or staged) and to gauge the degree or stage of reduction. Bradbury and Carr (1999), Braun and colleagues (2008), Ingbar and colleagues (1989), and Shott (1996b; see also Shott et al. 2000) used different sets of attributes to model continuous reduction and to estimate segments of the continuum represented. Bradbury and Carr's model (1999:112) identified platform facets, flake width, and exterior-surface scar density (scars/g) as attributes that reliably predicted removal order in reduction continua. Shott (1996b:17) obtained similar results using

exterior-surface scar count, flake weight and platform width. Braun and colleagues (2008: 2158) identified flake-scar direction and degree of cortex cover relative to flake size as further important variables. In the process, these studies suggest that exterior faceting combined with attributes that measure size effectively model continuous variation in reduction, a conclusion that can help inform analysis of the Modena and Tempiute assemblages.

Flake Typology. Another common method of flake analysis is typological, the assignment of flakes to specific technological types. Some typological approaches define types by reduction stage (e.g., primary, secondary, tertiary; see Elston and Juell 1987:29–30) thought to correspond to distinct segments of reduction continua. Others define types by reduction modes (e.g., core reduction, biface production, blade production, bipolar reduction; see Dames and Moore 1994:Tables 21-11, 21-17). Another common variant combines elements of stage and mode typologies, particularly when applied to successive stages of biface production from edging to thinning to finishing.

In Great Basin archaeology, Flenniken (2003, 2006; Roberts and Flenniken 2008) is among the most prominent advocates of technological typology. In bifacial reduction, for instance, this approach often defines four successive stages: core reduction, edge preparation, percussion bifacial thinning, and pressure bifacial thinning. It also includes nondiagnostic fragments, a default category that consists of "potlids, shatter, and flake fragments, with cortex or without cortex" (Roberts and Flenniken 2008:48)—individual pieces by whose nature or fragmented condition lack attributes of presumed technological affinity. The four stages are distinguished variously. The first is characterized by the presence and amount of cortex cover but also by "interior debitage" (i.e., flakes that lack cortex cover; Roberts and Flenniken 2008:48) that possesses particular (but unspecified) platform attributes (presumably large size and two or fewer platform facets), exterior scar counts (presumably few) pattern (presumably irregular or multidirectional), and longitudinal and transverse section forms (presumably triangular to irregular).

Notably, flakes in the first, core-reduction, stage either must possess cortex or, if they are interior flakes, must lack it. Accordingly, an essential character of some first-stage flakes is the presence of cortex and for others its absence. Flakes of the second stage possess platforms characterized by their multifaceting and location, location of the bulb of percussion, exterior scar count (presumably high) and direction (presumably less multidirectional than first-stage flakes), flake termination (presumably feathered or hinged but perhaps either in high proportion), longitudinal and transverse section forms (presumably flatter and more regular than first-stage flakes), and presence or absence of detachment scar. Third-stage percussion bifacial thinning flakes have, like second-stage ones, multifaceted platforms, but also platform lipping and (again unspecified) location, exterior-surface scar count (presumably higher than earlier stages) and pattern (presumably more nearly alternating or subparallel compared to earlier stages), terminations (presumably mostly feathered), longitudinal and transverse section forms (presumably flatter and more regular than earlier-stage flakes), and again presence or absence of detachment scars. Flakes of the final, pressure-thinning, stage again are distinguished by multifaceted platforms and something diagnostic of their location, exterior scar counts (presumably higher than in earlier stages) and pattern (presumably more nearly alternating or subparallel compared to earlier stages), terminations (presumably feathered), "platform-to-long axis geometry" (presumably longer for their width; Roberts and Flenniken 2008:48), longitudinal and transverse section forms (presumably flatter and more regular than earlier-stage flakes), and again presence or absence of detachment scars.

Some advocates of technological typology consider a third approach described below—analysis of flake-size distributions—invalid when applied to more than one toolstone because "size, shape, and quality of the original raw materials may have influenced reduction strategies", because its statistical analysis is "not capable of 'interpreting' data" and, finally, because metric analyses common to attribute and size-distribution approaches "do not take into account crucial variables like raw material type, quality, shape, and flakeability" (Roberts and Flenniken 2008:47; see also Scott 1991). The third criticism amounts to a restatement of the first one. There is no doubting the importance of raw material characteristics. Yet it is unclear how the technological-typology approach is better suited to analysis of two or more toolstones, because the technological attributes essential to their approach themselves can vary by toolstone independently of reduction stage or mode (e.g., Morrison 1994:100, 105, 113). Neither have proponents of this approach explained why statistical inference is less capable of interpreting data than is typology, or of how or why the apparently invalid measurement of flake attributes is more susceptible to variation with the cited causes than is typology. What's more, a considerable body of evidence shows patterning of size-distribution (i.e., mass-analysis) data with reduction stage (e.g., Ahler 1989a, 1989b; Ammerman and Andrefsky 1982; Morrow 1997:51, 59; Shott 1994 and sources cited therein). Altogether, Roberts and Flenniken are neither persuasive about the merits of their approach nor necessarily valid in their criticism of alternatives.

Reduction stages may be successive and so occupy segments of a continuum, but stages often are conceived as categorically distinct entities. Thus, Roberts and Flenniken's first-stage flakes are largely distinguished by the presence of exterior-surface cortex, a categorical trait, although some lack cortex but qualify for first-stage status by virtue of their platform attributes and exterior faceting. As Hatch noted, "The assumption that [cortical] categories represent an invariant sequence of flake removal is imprecise because there is no technological dependency between them and core reduction" (1998:43; see also Morrison 1994:26). Further evidence comes from the Oldowan industry, as a study of common technological classification of Oldowan flakes did not pattern significantly with removal order, a measure of degree of reduction, in experimental data (Braun et al. 2008:2157).

In schemes like Roberts and Flenniken's, successive stages are treated as discrete and qualitatively different yet are mostly distinguished by interval- or ratio-scale variables like number of exterior-surface scars, the size and faceting of platforms, or the proportions of discrete traits like termination types. So far as discrete attributes like section form are considered, they are not clearly treated in nominal fashion or as an essential trait for membership in the stage, but instead as varying by type proportion (i.e., continuously) between stages.

Typological analysis of flakes appeals for its apparent combination of efficiency and validity. The simple inspection of flakes followed by their assignment to one or another type certainly requires less time and effort than does recording of individual flake attributes or the size-distribution analysis described below. Assuming that the types defined and specimens assigned to them are replicable, such that different analysts almost always would agree on type assignments (i.e., interobserver consistency); are valid, such that flakes of a given type are produced either exclusively or primarily in one reduction stage and/or mode; and are comprehensive, such that all flakes produced in any combination of stage and mode are substantially identical and equally diagnostic, then the typological approach is justified.

Unfortunately, none of these assumptions is warranted. Blind tests of replication between analysts in typological assignments do not inspire confidence in the approach (e.g., Howell 1996; Shott 1994:77–78; Sullivan and Rozen 1985). As Ingbar and others put it, "your biface thinning flake may be our core platform preparation flake" (1989:117; see also Ahler 1986:43, 1989b:211; Bradley and Sampson 1986; Morrison 1994:21; Railey and Gonzales 2015; Steffen et al. 1998:142–143 on lack of consistency in flake and technology terminology). Regarding the popular primary-secondary-tertiary (PST) flake model, lack of standardization between analyses means that "primary or secondary flakes of one

study would be classified as secondary or tertiary flakes in another" (Hatch 1998:44). Blind tests of the PST model yielded a 63% agreement rate, while those of qualitative flake typologies produced a 56% rate that is barely superior to a coin toss (Howell 1996). Another study found that incidence of cortex is affected by core size (Bradbury and Carr 1995).

There is also the matter of comparability between typological schemes. Flake typologies differ considerably in technological emphasis (e.g., core reduction biface production, bipolar reduction) and detail (number and nature of types defined). Two flake assemblages typed in different ways cannot be compared to one another, defeating a main purpose of flake analysis. (See Railey and Gonzales 2015 for a critique of the wide range of approaches and types used in Southwestern archaeology.) At Hunchback Shelter, for instance, Greubel and Andrews (2008:Table 4) defined three types (besides "indeterminate")—debris, biface-thinning, and core reduction—while for Coral Canyon Flenniken (2003:117–119; 2006:101) defined four types (besides "undiagnostic") spanning a single reduction continuum from initial core reduction to pressure flaking. Comparison of data resulting from those analyses is thusly hampered. Elsewhere, Dames and Moore (1994: Tables 21-11, 21-17) used different typologies for different sites in the same project, complicating comparison even within that project.

Although they themselves assigned flakes to technological types, Buck and colleagues (1994) analyzed the Midway Valley quarry at the Nevada Test Site to show, for example, that most flakes from a block-core reduction episode either were classified as shatter or indeterminate, and that "there is not a direct correspondence between individual flakes and reduction types" (1994:46; see also Amick 1991:40). Ahler (1986:71) reported shatter in all reduction modes replicated, and biface-thinning flakes present only in soft-hammer, not in hard-hammer, replications. In a dataset that overlapped with Ahler's, Root (1992:Tables 6.1–6.2) reported shatter in several reduction modes. Furthermore, Ahler found (1989b:211) that a flake-blade production sequence could not yield blades while bipolar reduction could, in addition to the production of bipolar flakes via biface-thinning replications. Magne (1985:104; see also Morrison 1994:108–114) generated what he identified as biface-retouch flakes in bipolar reduction experiments, perhaps not surprising considering how poorly controlled the application of force is in that reduction mode.

Presence and amount of cortex figures prominently in technological-typology approaches (e.g., Roberts and Flenniken 2008:48), yet one experimental replication alone showed that both early-stage "core reduction" flakes may lack cortex while much later-stage flakes may possess it (Shott 1996b; see also Hatch 1998:43; Mauldin and Amick 1989:71–73; Morrison 1994:25–26,130; Skinner and Ainsworth 1991:164). To Bradbury and Franklin, cobble size seriously complicates the equation of cortex with early reduction stages "because the percentage of cortical flakes is directly related to the size of the original nodule" (2000:49; see also Braun et al. 2008:2155; Hatch 1998:43; Tomka 1989) independently of stage or degree of reduction. Coding for degree of cortex cover also is subject to measurement error (Hatch 1998:44; Shott 1994:74–75). As stated above, the size and form of flakes vary by reduction stage and mode, as well as other factors (e.g., toolstone quality, cobble size and form, hammer type, knapper skill, or context) that greatly compromise the validity of flake typologies (Hatch 1998:43). Assuming that particular flakes were the product of specific stages or modes of reduction fails to control for the many complicating factors.

Sullivan and Rozen (1985), in the course of criticizing typological approaches, proposed an "interpretation-free" alternative to formal typology that identified types like complete flakes and shatter. Intended to improve flake typology, Sullivan and Rozen's approach was itself compromised by lack of inferential validity (Morrison 1994:28; Shott 1994:78–79). Mauldin and Amick (1989:83–84; see also Morrison 1994:118–127), for instance, found great variation in the proportion of Sullivan and Rozen flake types by reduction episode in their ex-

perimental data. A typological approach would attribute the variation to reduction mode, but mode was held constant experimentally; instead, variation was a function mostly of cobble size and form, which is not typically the goal of typological inference. In Pelcin's (1996:50) controlled experiments, core reduction had *lower* proportions of shatter while tool production had *higher* proportions of complete flakes, the opposite of Sullivan and Rozen's expectation. Austin's (1999), Kotcho's (2009:216–219), and Morrison's (1994:114–117) use of Sullivan and Rozen's approach to distinguish core versus tool reduction yielded ambiguous results. Separately, Austin (1999) and Kotcho (2009) found only slight differences in flake-type proportions between reduction modes, not the sharp differences postulated by Sullivan and Rozen (1985). Morrison's (1994) quartzite experiments yielded virtually identical results for all reduction modes tested. Altogether, studies inspired by their work compromise the value of Sullivan and Rozen's approach.

Typology often uses a fraction of all flakes to identify reduction stages and modes, ignoring the majority of flakes as "nondiagnostic" (Bradbury and Carr 2009:2791; Bradley and Sampson 1986:39; Flenniken 2003, 2006; Morrison 1994:109; Roberts and Flenniken 2008:46; Wills 2013:Tables 26–30). Nearly 70% of technologically classified flakes at Hunchback Shelter were labeled "indeterminate" (Greubel and Andrews 2008:Table 4), leaving technological inference for the assemblage to typological assignment of fewer than one-third of specimens. Similarly, Flenniken's (2003, 2006) analysis at Coral Canyon near St. George, Utah—which included considerable obsidian, much of which probably was Modena (Roberts and Eskenazi 2006:97)—classified approximately a third of the recovered flakes (e.g., at 42WS1219, 710 flakes were assigned to types and 1,543 were deemed "undiagnostic" [Flenniken 2003:Tables 6.17–6.18; see also Flenniken 2006:Appendix F]). Wills's (2013) analysis of Laurel Lake, an assemblage dominated by Bodie Hills obsidian, yielded similar results. Of the 4,349 flakes found, 1,845 (42.4%) were classified as shatter or fragments and were not analyzed; of the remaining 2,504 flakes 1,670 (66.7%) were classified either as "small nondiagnostic" or "general interior" flakes (Wills 2013:Table 29). "Small nondiagnostic" flakes were produced "in all reduction technologies" (Wills 2013:109). Additionally, "general interior" flakes lacked cortex, had "no other diagnostic attributes…[and] can also be produced by a wide range of reduction activities" (Wills 2013:110). Altogether, the materials seemed to convey only the broadest information about reduction practices, and indeed, Wills (2013:201) advocated combining these "types." More specific, and presumably diagnostic, technological flake types comprised about 20% of the Laurel Lake assemblage.

Mass Analysis

Attribute analysis parses individual flakes into constituent segments and characters. Typological analysis places individual flakes into discrete types thought to correlate with reduction stage and mode. Yet the abundance of flake debris is a two-edged sword; despite the information it can deliver it also can tax our ability to process, code, and measure sufficient numbers of flakes to properly characterize large assemblages. One response to this dilemma involved the sorting of entire assemblages of flakes by size classes and the characterization of those assemblages by the proportional distribution of flakes among the classes. This is size-distribution or "mass" analysis, developed and popularized by Ahler's (1986, 1989a, 1989b) pioneering work. Mass analysis is efficient even on the largest assemblages. It uses all specimens and produces assemblage-level data and statistics that characterize size distribution and facilitate comparisons (Beardsell 2013:78–79). Yet mass analysis elides variation among individual flake, mitigated by judicious coding of "minimal attribute sets" (Ammerman and Andrefsky 1982:163; Shott 1994:79–81) on at least samples of large assemblages.

Mass analysis is common enough that there is some variation in practice. For example, there may be variation in the number and threshold values of size classes, in number and type of experimental reductions used as controls, or

in analytical methods used. Possibly the best-known approach is Ahler's (1986, 1989a, 1989b), based on his extensive experiments with Knife River Flint from North Dakota. Ahler used simple ratios but also discriminant analysis to distinguish between reduction modes. Other forms of mass analysis plotted count proportion against size class and modeled variation by linear regression (Stahle and Dunn 1982, 1984; see also Patterson 1990; Shott 1994), or fitted flake-size distributions to the exponential and Weibull models (Stahle and Dunn 1982:88–89). Bertran and colleagues (2006; see also Bertran et al. 2012:Figures 4, 20) used ternary diagrams to depict variation in size distributions.

Andrefsky (2007) strongly criticized mass analysis, partly because its popularity owed to what he considered the modest investment of time and effort in it. Like any method, mass analysis can be misused; anyone who uses it because it seems easy misunderstands its value and the nature of archaeological analysis in general. Mass analysis, properly understood and implemented, actually is both tedious and time consuming, and at least as labor intensive as other methods. Certainly this is true at the level of analysis, as opposed to size sorting and other aspects of data processing, which in mass analysis requires fairly extensive efforts.

Andrefsky (2007) identified three problems that, either separately or in combination, he considered fatal to mass analysis: variation by individual, by material (which can be important in several ways but which Andrefsky legitimately reduced to variation by size and form of original cobbles), and by postdepositional mixing. (Beardsell [2013:81] argued that Andrefsky did not consider toolstone variation, reduction mode, and variants of mass analysis besides Ahler's approach.) I address each of these variations below.

Individual Knappers

Andrefsky's criticism derived in part from Redman's (1997) experimental study, which did not involve size distributions or mass analysis in any form. Redman (1997:76–81) found considerable variation between knappers in some, but not all, metric attributes of flakes. Until there is comparable study of individual variation in producing flakes of different "type," it remains unknown how much individual variation is a problem for mass analysis in particular or for flake analysis in general. When Andrefsky (2007:394) conducted his own size-distribution analysis of Redman's and other experimental data, he confined treatment to "relatively simple" bipolar reduction, documenting individual variation in weight distribution; Andrefsky did not examine variation by count, nor did he explore count or weight variation by other reduction modes. (See Morrison [1994] on the greater reliability of count than weight data.) However simple bipolar reduction is, it is a questionable model for testing mass analysis, particularly for obsidian (Andrefsky 2007:395) whose brittle nature and isotropic character make it unlikely to require bipolar reduction. (Admittedly, Price and others [2009:76] reported obsidian bipolar cores from a Mojave Desert site, and small amounts of obsidian bipolar debris occur near an andesite source in British Columbia [Hall 1998:306].) Also, bipolar technology's poorly controlled nature and massive force application make it among the most variable in resulting debris, so not necessarily a valid judgment concerning other reduction modes. At Modena and Tempiute, bipolar reduction is rare, to judge from the character of the flake assemblages. Amick (1991:39) reached the same conclusion for the Buckboard Mesa quarry, while Wills noted that near the Bodie Hills obsidian source "bipolar flakes were present in a very small quantity" (2013:199). Nor is flake typology valid for bipolar debris, as the technique appears to produce some flakes of other types (e.g., Magne 1985; Morrison 1994). It would be interesting to examine Redman's and others' data for variation among individuals in attribute analysis. This is not to deny the possible role of individuals as sources of variation, but to question its pertinence to mass analysis alone among flake-analysis methods. Clearly, we need more experimental data on the effects of individual knappers on flake assemblages analyzed typologically, by size distribution, or in any other way.

Cobble Size and Form

The size and form of raw toolstone cobbles may be considerable (e.g., Bradbury and Franklin 2000; Sturgess 1999:85) and, as with individual variation, deserves study to gauge its effects on a full range of mass-analysis and flake-typology data. Andrefsky's (2007:395) critique involved two obsidian cobbles that differed in weight by a factor of nearly three and which, in bipolar reduction, yielded significantly different weights per size class. Bipolar reduction is of doubtful relevance to obsidian reduction as noted above. Yet Andrefsky's data (2007:Table 3) showed only slight differences in *count* by size class, particularly in the more numerous, smaller size classes ≤12.7 mm (≤0.5 in); variation in larger classes is difficult to gauge considering their small sample sizes. Bradbury and Franklin (2000:45) noted the effect of cobble size particularly on the incidence of cortex on flakes, and their classification of experimental assemblages by reduction mode improved with removal of cortex variables. They also found that larger packages, whether tabular or nodular, yielded more reliable results (Bradbury and Franklin 2000:47). Modena cobbles vary somewhat but are large in general; although the few raw cobbles found at Tempiute may not be a representative sample, this source probably occurs mostly in small cobbles. Accordingly, package size should have greater effects at Tempiute than Modena. Cobble size may be significant, but again a balanced approach is to compile and analyze large datasets in which various analytical approaches are compared, not just one criticized on the strength of limited experiments. Otherwise, differences between toolstones themselves might be a significant source of variation, especially between cryptocrystalline to fine-grained materials like chert versus coarse-grained volcanics or quartzite. Fortunately, our data are naturally controlled for toolstone, because each quarry's debris assemblage may safely be assumed to consist almost entirely of the local obsidian.

In their study, which controlled for toolstone variation, Anderson and Hodgetts (2007:237) reported good mass-analysis results.

Mixing

However internally homogeneous and externally distinctive flake assemblages may be—whether produced by, for instance, core reduction or biface production, itself an empirical question—archaeological deposits of any size are almost certainly the mixed result of various fractions of various reduction episodes of various modes. We cannot change how the archaeological record formed. Without discussing it in great detail here, it suffices to note there have been serious efforts to gauge and control for the effects of mixing (e.g., Root 1992:232–258; Shott 1997a), efforts in some ways extended here. Readers may judge for themselves how persuasive those efforts are, but this part of Andrefsky's critique raises a legitimate concern that is confronted directly in this study.

Discussion

Andrefsky (2007; see also Root 2004) expressed reasonable reservations about mass analysis, certainly to the extent that some may use it as an analytical shortcut. On balance, however, his criticism is not entirely persuasive and certainly pertains as well to other approaches, at least in part. A better strategy is to compile existing experimental data or to conduct new experiments that control variation by knapper, material, cobble size, and form, and that analyze both distributional and typological data at once. Certainly Bertran and colleagues (2006) found relatively few effects of toolstone and other factors except for reduction mode, Beardsell (2013) identified only modest impacts of various factors in mass analysis of quartz industries. After detailed analysis of experimental data, Bradbury and Franklin concluded that "mass analysis effectively separates core reduction from tool production across a wide variety of chert types and was most powerful in identifying general trends in reduction trajectories" (2000:47; see also Bradbury and

Carr 2009), findings that lends confidence to its use.

Other Criticisms of Mass Analysis

While Andrefsky's critique of mass analysis is the most notable, he is not the only one to question the method. Scott (1991) criticized mass analysis because, apparently, empirical assemblages that seemed to vary considerably in reduction stage and mode all produced size distributions in which the smallest fraction—6.35 mm (0.25 in)—had the highest count. Scott (1991:173) did not describe her statistical methods in detail, but reported use of the F-ratio, so perhaps compared difference in mean count by size fraction using ANOVA. Apparently, Scott considered reduction stages or modes to sort out only by frequency mode, that is, in which of the size fractions contained the most flakes. However, most experimental and empirical debris samples are dominated numerically by the smallest size fraction. The key distinction is in often slight proportions between size fractions within individual samples and their distributions, not coarser differences in mean counts per fraction. Also, ANOVA may be a less effective statistical approach to size-distribution data than regression (e.g., Root 1992; Shott 1994; Stahle and Dunn 1982, 1984) and discriminant analysis (e.g., Ahler 1986, 1989a; cf., Ingbar et al. 1992:78).

Morrison (1994:130) found significant differences between reduction modes in mean and size distribution of flake weight but not count. In particular, ratios of flake counts in size classes (e.g., the ratio of G4 to combined G1–G3) did not pattern clearly with reduction mode. Also, quartzite and obsidian cobbles reduced in the same way generated very different size distributions, apparently by count. Morrison's results may owe to a difference in toolstone (cf., Bradbury and Carr [2009] and Bradbury and Franklin [2000], who considered cobble size more influential, and Schick [1986:28, Figure 3.5] who found little variation at all by toolstone), but a number of factors may influence the form of flake-size distributions. Besides the undeniable effects of toolstone, there is also the size and form of cobbles, the type of reduction mode, and the number and size of intended products. As above, compiled experimental data (e.g., Bertran et al. 2006; Bertran et al. 2012) from a range of studies that varied considerably in salient respects found little difference in toolstone and other factors.

Ingbar and colleagues (1992:61–62; see also Bloomer and Ingbar 1992) applied Ahler's mass analysis, along with technological flake classification and perhaps the first empirical application of Weibull analysis (Stahle and Dunn 1982), to the Tosawihi quarry debris, but then partly disavowed results. The authors' dissatisfaction owed to several factors. First, there were some differences in the number and nature of reduction segments or stages between their experimental designs and their technological classification. Second, Ingbar and colleagues (1992:78) suggested that mixing between reduction modes in empirical assemblages complicated mass analysis results, which is undeniable but equally applicable to technological classification (i.e., flake "types" can occur in different reduction modes, and a single mode can contain a range of "types"). Finally, however, the authors disliked mass analysis because it produced results substantially at odds with technological classification, which they always accepted as valid by "presuming…that the technological characterizations are correct" (1992:80). Starting from that premise, any disagreement between technological classification and any other analytical method is proof not merely of difference but of the latter's flaws. It is possible that mass analysis performed poorly in Ingbar and colleagues' analysis, but their detailed, innovative study actually documented differences between analytical approaches, not their preferred one's superiority.

Addressing the Mixing Problem

The mixing problem that Andrefsky (2007:396), Ingbar and colleagues (1992), and others (e.g., Ahler 1989a; Austin 1999; Bertran et al. 2012; Root 1992; Shott 1997a; Sturgess 1999:87) raised is confronted at some length here. This is not to doubt its relevance or possible gravity, but to suggest that this criticism of mass analysis is best confronted by serious attempts to account for it. Until the detailed, comparative study proposed above is conducted, and recalling that mass analysis involves all flakes not merely the fewer than half that typological studies typically involve, its use here is justified.

Single flakes cannot be mixed, but assemblages of them can be mixed from reduction of different cobbles in different ways at different times. Although some debris assemblages may be in their primary context, as a starting point archaeologists should assume that debris samples are the aggregate of more than one knapping episode of more than one reduction mode. As Steffen and colleagues put it, "mixing is not a problem to be overcome…[but] an intrinsic part of the archaeological record" (1998:141). In this perspective, our challenge is to devise methods to parse mixed assemblages into their constituents, not invoke mixing as a counsel of despair that prevents analysis.

Even when different episodes of the same reduction mode contribute to aggregates, they may represent partial, often different, segments of that mode. A sample that consists of all the debris generated in one complete episode of, say, reducing a large flake blank to a biface of any given size and form may differ from one that consists of all debris of one such episode plus the first half of another episode of the same mode, plus the middle third of another episode of the same mode. A potential fatal flaw to mass analysis would be a mixed assemblage of Types A and B reduction that its analytical methods identified as Type C. Fortunately, limited experimental studies to date suggest that reduction modes are fairly robust, in the sense that simulated mixing of, for instance, bifacial reduction with other reduction modes preserved the signal for bifacial mode (Bradbury and Carr 2004:79; cf. Bradbury and Carr 2009:2791, where some modes swamped other modes' signals), and simulated mixing of different replications of the same reduction mode consistently produced results identified with that mode (Bradbury and Carr 2009:2791). For mass analysis to work, it must be able to control for the effects of mixing in the accumulations that are most flake assemblages.

Such mixed assemblages accumulate when various knappers occupy the same place at the same or different times. They also can accumulate in secondary discard, when varying fractions of several reduction episodes of various modes are deposited together. Ratios between flake counts in different size classes may distinguish primary and secondary deposits (e.g., Behm 1983), but the complexities of discard suggest that such simple measures are at best partial solutions (Clark 1986; Steffen et al. 1998:144). Characteristic proportions (e.g., of count in the 6.35 mm [¼ in] fraction) identify modes, and values from empirical assemblages that fall between distinct modes' norms might identify mixing (Bradbury and Carr 2009:2792). Carr and Bradbury (2001:137) estimated the percentage of bifacial reduction in mixed experimental assemblages (measured by count) by multiple regression, expressing the value as a function of the percentages of 6.35 mm (¼ in) flakes, and flakes with zero and two exterior-surface scars (all measured by count), and percentage by weight of 6.35 mm (¼ in) flakes.

Using Ahler's experimental assemblages as controls or "calibration sets," Root (1992) simulated mixing of varying degree between different flake assemblages, employing multiple linear regression (MLR) to parse mixtures into their constituent reduction modes. This approach, applied by Root (1992) and Shott (1997a) to archaeological assemblages and discussed at some length below, controls at least to some extent for the complicating effect of mixing. Even if methods like these identify mixed assemblages, however, they cannot allocate their constituents to the reduction modes that produced them. In another attempt to address mixing, Stahle and Dunn (1982:90–93, 1984) used experimental controls and constrained least-squares analysis to allocate empirical archaeological assemblages to their constituent original or pure modes. Although their results were good generally, their method allocated some mixed assemblages somewhat inaccurately (1982:Table 1).

Whatever the difficulties of Root's MLR method in disentangling mixed assemblages, the mixing problem is not unique to mass analysis. Austin (1999:57–59) used discriminant functions to evaluate experimentally mixed assemblages of flakes characterized typologically, not by size distribution. Yet, by its nature, the complexity of fracture mechanics can yield flakes considered diagnostic of modes other than the one in which they were produced (Bradbury and Carr 2009:2791–2792). Flake typology assumes a strict correspondence between specific flake attributes and reduction modes that experimental controls and archaeological data do not support. (For instance, in one bipolar reduction experiment, only 20 of the 146 flakes produced were classified as bipolar [Bradbury 2010:77; see also Morrison 1994:109].) In flake-typological approaches, therefore, a single technological reduction mode can appear to be technologically mixed, and a mixed assemblage could appear to be pure. In sum, debris assemblages accumulated from mixtures of kinds and segments of reduction modes pose analytical challenges to all flake-analysis methods, not to mass analysis or any other one alone. The challenge is to confront and grapple with the limitations, seeking solutions without denying the problem.

Mass or size-distribution analysis is validated experimentally, not least by Ahler (1986, 1989a, 1989b; see also Hall 1998:71; Morrow 1997:56; Root 1992:251–254; Shott 1994) and empirically (e.g., Anderson and Hodgetts 2007; Barton 2008; Bickler and Turner 2002; Hiscock and Mitchell 1993:30; Ingbar et al. 1992; Kahn et al. 2009; Shott 1997a). Discriminant analysis of experimental data distinguished between most reduction modes in Ahler's (1989a) and Root's (1992) analyses. Root's (1992; see also Kohler and Blinman 1987) MLR method and Stahle and Dunn's (1982, 1984) constrained least-square method can parse size-distribution data in mixed assemblages into their constituent modes. Yet Morrison's (1994) experiments suggested significant differences between obsidian and quartzite, no surprise considering the materials' very different mechanical properties. Owing to assemblage size or its analytical virtues, mass analysis was a method of choice in quarry studies elsewhere (e.g., Ahler 1986; Bickler and Turner 2002; Ingbar et al. 1992; Toohey 1999). For the Yucca Mountain source area in Nye County, obsidian "flake percentages by size grade [were] more meaningful in terms of interpreting the reduction process" (Haynes 1996:118) than was flake typology.

Mass analysis can quantify flakes by count or weight. Weight produced better results than counts in some experimental studies (e.g., Morrow 1997:56), count better than weight in others (e.g., Morrison 1994; Stahle and Dunn 1984:31); count can produce better results in pure stage samples, weight better in experimentally mixed ones (e.g., Root 1992:248, 254). Certainly both may be used (Shott 1994:101), but Bertran and colleagues (2012:3149) favored count as less sensitive to erratic variation in large fractions and to taphonomic winnowing effects. Stahle and Dunn (1984:31) favored count on theoretical grounds, which their analytical results corroborated. Similar logic guided analysis here. Finally, mass analysis is valuable in designing valid sampling strategies for the analysis of large flake assemblages, because it "provides an easily replicable way to assess the degree of variability present in an assemblage" (Milne 2009:59).

Summary

No single approach to the analysis of flake debris is ideal for all purposes. Instead, different approaches should be used as analytical goals and the methods' strengths justify. Flake typology is questionable for the several reasons listed above, not least the ambiguity and lack of consistency with which types are defined and flakes assigned to them, and because typological approaches often fail to accommodate many empirical specimens. The comprehensiveness of any approach that omits up to half of all specimens is questionable at face value. The virtues of attribute analysis are fairly clear, even if that approach is also time consuming. Mass analysis is no more susceptible to mixing problems than is typology. Mass analysis "is not a panacea for the flake-ridden" (Bloomer and Ingbar 1992:231), a failing it shares with all approaches.

Of course there are no panaceas, only methods useful to greater or lesser degree. Mass analysis and attribute analysis are two valid approaches whose value in combination is explored in this study.

Toolstone Effects

Trivially, not all toolstones are alike. Obviously, Modena and Tempiute are different obsidian sources. Morrison's (1994) study of quartzite and obsidian may compare extremes in which differences are as clear as they are expected. For the Great Basin, quartzite is a less common and therefore less relevant material than are chert and varieties of fine-grained volcanics like basalt. Just as all toolstones are not alike, neither are all cherts, although in general chert lies between refractory materials like quartzite and brittle ones like obsidian (Luedtke 1992:Table 6.2). So far as it concerns their flaking qualities, not even all obsidians are alike. Yet obsidian's nature justifies the assumption that differences between Modena and Tempiute obsidians are relatively minor.

Bradbury and Franklin's (2000) study of several chert sources found little difference in flake-assemblage characteristics attributable to toolstone. Instead, no matter the grain or quality of the toolstone, internal flaws and especially cobble size and form (tabular vs. nodular) conditioned results independently of material. In particular, reduction of large tabular cobbles yielded higher correct-classification rates than small nodular ones (2000:47; see also Bradbury and Carr 1995, Tomka 1989). Indeed, Bradbury and Franklin (2000:50) found significant differences in flake assemblages of the same material but different cobble sizes, and little difference between cobbles of similar size composed of different toolstones. Therefore, it was not the mechanical properties of the toolstone (although Bradbury and Franklin [2000:49] did suggest that chert and obsidian differ significantly so may not be comparable) but the size and form in which it occurred naturally that influenced results.

Modena and Tempiute obsidians occur as nodules. Because the quarries may be depleted, form and particularly size of remaining natural cobbles are not necessarily representative of cobble size distributions before prehistoric use. Assuming any reasonable degree of knappers' selection, in fact, remaining unmodified cobbles should be atypical. Nevertheless, evidence and selective recent collection in the Modena vicinity, cited in Chapter 3, suggest that Modena nodules could have been fairly large. By comparison, Tempiute natural cobbles probably were smaller. Bradbury and Franklin's (2000) results suggest that cobble form is important, with tabular pieces being preferable to nodules, but also that larger cobbles yield flake assemblages more consistently identifiable to mode and stage. If so, then Modena may be more suitable for mass analysis than is Tempiute.

Bradbury and Franklin (2000:50) emphasized the value of large sample sizes and the use of mass-analysis or size-distribution data in combination with judicious attribute coding and analysis. Fortunately, UA's research design supplied suitably large debris samples, and our analytical protocol included attribute coding alongside mass analysis. On balance, past research suggests the wisdom of using chiefly experimental data from obsidian and fine-grained chert to interpret structure in flake assemblages like Modena and Tempiute. Roughly controlling for toolstone quality in this way, some combination of carefully conducted size-distribution analysis and selective attribute coding seemed both the most efficient and valid of approaches to the large flake assemblages encountered. Results should reflect differences in cobble size more than each source's flaking qualities.

Flake-Assemblage Analysis

"The humble flake has proved that it can hold its own with a story to tell when the signs can be read" (Turner and Bonica 1994:27). Accordingly, this study combines the virtues of efficient mass analysis—surprisingly time-consuming, especially in analysis—with consideration of selected attributes coded on a selection of flakes—undeniably time-consuming. There is good evidence that patterns of both attribute variation (Fish 1981:379; Goldstein 2018; Magne 1985;

Riley et al. 1994:Table 44; Turner and Bonica 1994:6) and flake-size distributions (Ahler 1986, 1989a, 1989b; Shott 1994; Stahle and Dunn 1982; Sturgess 1999; Turner and Bonica 1994:Table 3) correlate with reduction mode and reduction segment/stage. Moreover, this combination was used in somewhat different ways but to good effect in earlier studies of Great Basin obsidian quarries (e.g., Byram et al. 1999) and elsewhere (e.g., Trubitt 2007), and in experimental studies (e.g., Bradbury and Carr 2004). In summary, "the size grading technique, particularly when coupled with other attribute analysis including the recording of cortex coverage and dorsal scar complexity, offers a viable alternative to" (Kahn et al. 2009:142) flake typology. UA's approach to debris assemblages thus involved analysis of individual flake attributes and flake-size distributions. Analytical protocols are described here.

Attribute Analysis

For analysis, intact flakes only (Shott 2016:Appendices J–K; Modena n = 2,549, Tempiute n = 942) were coded for a set of standard attributes that largely duplicated earlier analyses (e.g., Magne 1985; Shott 1994:79–81; Wilmsen 1970: 14–19). Dimensions and other metric variables included weight (g), axial length, maximum perpendicular width, platform width and platform thickness (Shott 2016:Figure 5.1). Following Bradbury and Carr (1999:112), exterior-face facets ≥2 mm in length divided by weight was defined as "scargm" (for scars/g). This variable recognizes that exterior-face faceting tends to increase during reduction while flake size simultaneously tends to decline. That is, it corrects for the limiting effect of declining size on the number of facets, thus roughly controlling for the countervailing effect of declining flake size upon increasing faceting.

Count variables included platform facets and exterior-face facets ("scar count"; among facets on the platform, again only those ≥2 mm in length were counted). Discrete attributes included platform type (intact or hinged, i.e. much or all of the platform removed by hinge fracture, probably at the moment of flake detachment; facets, obviously, could not be counted on hinged platforms), presence/absence of exterior-face cortex, and termination type (feather, hinge, step). All linear dimensions were recorded in millimeters. Flakes also were coded for condition (intact, proximal, medial, distal, lateral). Intact flakes retained both the platform and the distal edge, the latter usually taking the form of a feather or hinge termination. Snap-fracture terminations of intact flakes can be difficult to distinguish from flakes broken during or after detachment. We followed a conservative practice by treating any flake with a snap-fracture termination as intact, so long as it could be assumed, owing to its length or other characteristics, to have been intact but acknowledge the possibility that some intact snap-fracture flakes may have been misclassified as broken.

Lateral fractures extend from proximal to distal poles and are roughly normal to flakes' longitudinal axes. Flakes bearing lateral fractures but that retained recognizable proximal and distal ends were coded as whole/lateral; lateral fractures on flake fragments were coded as that fragment type and further specified as lateral.

Mass Analysis

All Modena and Tempiute Stage-1 flake samples were size-sorted, intact flakes separately from broken ones. Although archaeology mostly uses the metric scale, the American scholars who largely developed the mass-analysis approach (Ahler 1986, 1989a; Root 1992) size-sorted through nested sieves, as was done in the UA laboratory. Because nested sieves available in the United States almost exclusively are manufactured to the British Imperial scale, these archaeologists—and UA—adapted to this reality and used intervals of 1 in, ½ in, ¼ in and ⅛ in (25.4 mm, 12.7 mm, 6.35 mm, and 3.175 mm, respectively; hereafter listed by the metric equivalent first). These values obviously form a geometric series defined by halving. The UA research design omitted the 3.175 mm (⅛ in) class, which is uncommon in the excavated archaeological flake assemblages for which most mass analysis is intended. Rather than a geometric series, processing in UA's laboratory

sorted flakes by count and weight in size classes of 50.8 mm, 38.1 mm, 25.4 mm, 19.05 mm, 12.7 mm, and 6.35 mm (2 in, 1½ in, 1 in, ¾ in, ½ in, and ¼ in). Flake counts were extremely low in the two largest classes, which were pooled into the 25.4 mm (1 in) fraction for analysis. Thus, UA analysis sorted by arithmetic series, at 6.35 mm (¼ in) intervals from 25.4 mm to 6.35 mm (1 in to ¼ in), designed to capture somewhat more finely the variation between 25.4 mm and 12.7 mm (1 in and ½ in) classes.

As in all size-sorting schemes, the size classes listed above are nominal. Using nested sieves with square meshes and sorting specimens individually by hand, flakes were sorted by medial dimension whose effective thresholds are found as $d\sqrt{2}$ (Bertran et al. 2012:3149; Ozbun 2011:236). For UA size classes 25.4 mm, 19.05 mm, 12.7 mm, and 6.35 mm (1 in, ¾ in, ½ in, and ¼ in), actual sorting thresholds were 35.9 mm, 26.9 mm, 18.0 mm, and 9.0 mm, respectively (1.414 in, 1.061 in, 0.707 in, and 0.354 in, respectively).

It is common to observe that size classes like those listed above fail to capture the smallest flakes that can occur in great abundance. Ozbun (2011:239), for instance, cited one experimental replication in which 98% of flakes passed through the 6.35 mm (¼ in) screen. This much is undeniable (e.g., Behm 1983; Fladmark 1982) but there are good reasons to confine analysis to flakes trapped in ≥6.35 mm (¼ in) mesh screens. First, the vast majority of archaeological field projects process sediment through 6.35 mm (¼ in) mesh, not finer meshes. Conformity to archaeological practice makes experimental and empirical data comparable; use of finer sizes defeats comparability. Second, very small flakes often are fragments of larger flakes or are detached from snap or step fractures of larger flakes. At least in percussion flaking, they are not usually the single results of individual blows, as are many larger flakes. Third, there is no theoretical lower limit to flake-fragment size, and fragment numbers almost certainly rise as whatever preferred size threshold declines. If for perhaps dozens of flake fragments at the 6.35 mm (¼ in) fraction there are hundreds at, say, the 3.175 mm (⅛ in) fraction and probably thousands at the 0.79 mm (1/32-in) fraction. How much new information can be extracted from such exponentially rising numbers at exponentially declining flake size is unclear, or at least has not been studied in detail. The considerable effort required to systematically collect "microdebitage" begs the question of where the point of diminishing return lies in flake-debris studies (Shott 1994:102). Nor is there any theoretically grounded warrant for any minimum flake size, whether 6.35 mm (¼ in) or finer. Yet there is robust patterning and great information content in experimental and empirical flake-size distributions truncated at 6.35 mm or 3.175 mm (¼ in or ⅛ in) intervals (e.g., Ahler 1986, 1989b; Bertran et al. 2012; Root 1992; Shott 1994; Stahle and Dunn 1982) that amply justifies use of these thresholds.

Experimental Control Datasets

Analysis of flake assemblages was informed partly by several experimental datasets, whose salient properties require description before presenting results. Experimental data were taken from Root's (1992) replications of various reduction modes using mostly Knife River Flint, Stahle and Dunn's (1982, 1984) replications of points in Boone chert, and UA's experimental reduction of several Glass Butte cores to preforms.

Stahle and Dunn

Stahle and Dunn (1984:3; 1984:Tables 4a–d) analyzed flake debris from reduction of Boone chert nodules to produce replica Afton points (1984:Figure 1), which they described as either or both dart points and knives. For analysis, they divided the resulting debris into four successive stages (Stahle and Dunn 1982:85; 1984:4–5). The first "involved removing cortex, bedding planes and other imperfections" (Stahle and Dunn 1984:4) by hard hammer. Stage-2 hard- and soft-hammer percussion removed remaining cortex and began the edging and thinning process. Both hammers continued to be used in Stage 3, which completed the thinning process, while soft-hammer percussion

and pressure flaking occurred in Stage 4 to finish edges and haft element. Stahle and Dunn's Stage-1 assemblages "failed to recover some of the Stage-1 flakes produced when the cores were tested for imperfections at the quarry site" (1984:9). Thus, some flakes from the earliest reduction step, cobble testing, were omitted. This omission reduces the comparability of Stahle and Dunn's experimental data to Root's cobble-testing reduction mode. Because such cobble testing should be common at quarries, it also somewhat reduces the comparability of their data to Modena and Tempiute samples.

Root

Root (1992) explored methods for assigning assemblages to reduction modes and, significantly, for allocating mixed archaeological assemblages to constituent modes. His (1992:91–98) experimental data involved about 230 separate reductions of Knife River Flint cobbles, grouped by technological modes. Most experiments were carried out by Root or other experienced knappers but some by what Root (1992:95) called "novices." It is unclear from Root's account how different the results of skilled and unskilled knapping were for any given reduction mode; apparently, all knapping by mode was combined for analysis regardless of skill level. Technological modes included:

1. cobble testing to gauge suitability for extensive knapping, involving relatively few flake removals (37 experiments);
2. hard-hammer unprepared core reduction to produce flake blanks "suitable for use as unretouched or marginally retouched tools or for use as blanks that could be chipped into" bifaces or other tools (41 experiments; Root 1992:95);
3. hard-hammer tabular-core reduction to produce thick flake blanks suitable for finishing into bifaces and other tools (8 experiments);
4. hard- and soft-hammer prepared core reduction, also to produce flake blanks, particularly "large, straight, expanding" (Root 1992:95) ones for conversion to bifaces (17 experiments);

5. hard-hammer bifacial tool edging from tabular cobbles, whose goal was to produce Callahan (1979) Stage-2 bifaces, i.e., creating edges but not yet thinning the preform (35 experiments);

6. soft-hammer primary and secondary bifacial thinning, whose goal was to produce Callahan Stage-4 bifaces (25 experiments);

7. hard- and soft-hammer and pressure-flaking small-tool production from flake blanks, involving "two quite different experiments" (Root 1992:98), one of soft-hammer knapping of flake blanks produced in the hard-hammer unprepared core reduction experiments listed above (n = 7) and also of pressure flaking of similar blanks (7 experiments), and one of hard-hammer and pressure flaking of a blank to produce a Besant point (n = 1);

8. bipolar core reduction, designed to yield "flakes usable directly as tools or as blanks for reduction into tools" (48 experiments; Root 1992:96).

Except for the bipolar experiments, modes are listed above in approximate reduction-sequence order. Modes 2 and 3 essentially are variants of early-stage reduction to produce flake blanks for subsequent finishing into tools, differing apparently in the wider range of (mostly) larger blocky to tabular cores reduced in Mode 2. Mode 4 appears to involve reduction of raw cobbles, mostly by soft-hammer with hard hammers confined to platform preparation (Root 1992:96). Mode 5 also involved reduction of cobbles, in this case directly to Callahan Stage-2 bifaces. That is, the cobbles were reduced to preforms rather than being used as the source of large flake blanks, which were themselves treated as preforms. Thus, Modes 1–4 represent variations by degree and hammer of reduction of cobbles. Modes 5–7 represent successive later steps in the reduction process, although Mode 7 is somewhat heterogeneous. In fact, the Callahan Stage-2 preforms completed in Mode 5 were subsequently thinned in Mode-6 experiments. As discussed in Chapter 6, archaeological data suggest that Callahan Stage 3 was the most common objective

of reduction at Modena and, to some extent, at Tempiute. Similarly, preforms in our own experimental data were reduced approximately to that stage. Thus, Modes 1–4 in Root's experiments can be treated as variants of early-stage reduction and Modes 5–6 as variants of intermediate-stage reduction of biface preforms, and for this reason may possess special relevance to analysis of Modena and Tempiute assemblages. Mode 7 is likely to represent only a minor aspect of lithic processing at these quarries.

Bipolar reduction represented by Mode 8 involves massive, poorly controlled force that is effective—it produces usable flakes and flake blanks—but inefficient (e.g., Flenniken 1981; Shott 1989) because it wastes a great deal of toolstone in the process. For several reasons, bipolar reduction is particularly unlikely to be represented at Modena or Tempiute. First, bipolar reduction is perhaps most common, certainly most effective, on small cobbles that otherwise could not be knapped, and/or in circumstances of raw-material scarcity. Second, Modena cobbles probably were fairly large, although Tempiute cobbles may have been small. Third, material scarcity does not arise at toolstone quarries. An additional consideration is the complicating effect of including Root's bipolar experimental data in analysis, as described below. For these reasons, bipolar data were excluded from consideration. (UA's single bipolar experiment quickly ended with the massive failure of the cobble and no suitable flake blanks.) This is consistent with Bradbury and Carr's (2004:32–33) approach in interpreting their experimental data, in which bipolar data did not pattern clearly and in which predictive results from bipolar experiments was poor. Likewise, Root's separate categories of "skilled" and "expert" biface thinning were combined as a single mode, as were unprepared and prepared core reduction. Root separated cortical and non-cortical flakes in analysis; here those subsets were combined. The result was four major modes—cobble testing, core reduction, biface edging, and biface thinning—that encompass the range of reduction characteristic of most quarry assemblages.

UA

UA experiments were conducted using cobbles acquired from the BLM source at Glass Butte, Oregon, a common source for experimental knapping of obsidian. Seven cobbles were reduced by Michael Miller, an experienced knapper, to produce Callahan Stage-3 preforms (Stage-2 preforms using Beck et al.'s [2002] terminology). It proved impossible to maintain the flow or continuity of reduction while attempting to collect and number each removal in sequence. As an expedient, Miller's reduction was stopped at 30-second intervals (admittedly, a lesser break in continuity), and all flakes struck in that interval were collected as a group. Assisted by detailed notes that Miller dictated to a transcriber, the resulting debris assemblages were divided into three successive groups, *qua* stages. Stage 1 spanned initial core reduction to the production of usable flake blanks. Stage 2 began with the first removals from those blanks. Stages 2 and 3 together, somewhat arbitrarily as is always the case with stage schemes, simply spanned the first and second halves, respective of reduction of the flake blank to a successful Callahan Stage-3 preform. Stone hammers were used throughout the experiment, so there was no natural stage "break" by hammer type. Typically, Stage 2 spanned five to six 30-second intervals, Stage 3 another five to six intervals. Some blanks were not successfully completed, failure always occurring within the time range of Stage 2; flakes from those failures accordingly were assigned to that stage. In all, 1,878 flakes were collected from seven cobbles, 284 assigned to Stage 1, 1,147 to Stage 2, and 447 to Stage 3 (Shott 2016:Appendix L).

Correspondences among Experimental Sources

Stahle and Dunn's and UA's experiments began with cobbles that were reduced to flake blanks for subsequent finishing. Stahle and Dunn's flake blanks were heat-treated before further reduction (1982:85). They (1982:85) defined four successive reduction "stages" somewhat arbitrarily—always the case, acknowledged here—in UA experimental data. "Stage" 1 involved initial reduction to the production of suitable flake blanks. "Stages" 2 and 3 subdivided subsequent reduction equally by timed interval, not by number of flakes struck. As a result, "Stage" 2 counts many more flakes than does "Stage" 3. Aggregate flake data usually are distributed somewhat differently by count and weight (Shott 1994:92), and these and other experimental sources emphasize counts over weights. Accordingly, I used only count data in analysis.

Experimental data were grouped into a small set of modes that encompass most or all of the relevant reduction continuum thought to characterize Modena and Tempiute assemblages. This treatment resembles Carr and Bradbury's (2004:31–35) research, with experimental data similar to the datasets used here. In several permutations, they pooled reduction modes and flake-size classes and used discriminant and classification analysis to make mode assignments. As was done here, they omitted bipolar reduction because of its technological heterogeneity and also its poor classification results (2004:32–33). Carr and Bradbury found generally best results—over 96% correct classification—by combining various reduction modes into three successive ones: 1) cobble test and core; 2) biface edging; and 3) biface thinning and small-tool production and by pooling size classes into 6.35, 12.7, and 25.4 mm (¼, ½, and 1 in) classes (2004:33–35, Table 2.12). Carr and Bradbury's approach suggests the wisdom of consolidating both reduction modes and flake-size classes into fewer, broader groups, a suggestion that Stahle and Dunn (1982:93) also made and that was followed here. Shott (2016:Table 5.5) presented counts of Stahle and Dunn's and UA datasets by Ahler/Root's size classes. Stage divisions, *qua* reduction modes, in other experimental sources do not correspond strictly to Root's experiments.

Thus, Stahle and Dunn's experimental data covers all but the earliest reduction processes of Root's data and extends somewhat beyond Root's reduction modes. Stages 1–3 of UA experimental data approximate Root's cobble-testing, core-reduction, and edging modes, respectively. Admittedly, these correspondences do not themselves pattern perfectly with plots of 6.35 mm (¼ in) count against 6.35 mm (¼ in) weight proportions reported in later analysis. There, Stahle and Dunn's Stage 2 as well as Stage 1 is slightly closer to Root's core-reduction than edging mode, and Stahle and Dunn's Stage 3 aligns with Root's thinning mode while their Stage 4 lies in an advanced position compared even to Root's thinning mode.

Attribute Analysis
UA Experimental Flakes

UA experimental data have value only for comparative purposes, representing successive reduction intervals or "stages" whose patterning may help interpreting variation in Modena and Tempiute assemblages. Three stages were defined in UA experimental data (Shott 2016: Tables 5.7–5.8). Stage 1 extended from the start of each cobble's reduction until removal of the first flake blank designated for use as preform. Mean time span in reduction of failed preforms was 1 minute and 30 seconds; debris from all failed preforms was assigned to Stage 2. Otherwise, Stage 2 encompassed one-half of the cumulative time from flake-blank definition to finished Stage-3 preform. Stage 3 therefore encompassed the second half of the cumulative time that followed the end of Stage 1.

All ratio-scale variables pattern significantly as expected by defined stage (Shott 2016:Table 5.9, Appendix L). Size measures (weight, length, width, platform dimensions) all decline by stage. Scar count, platform facets, and scargm all increase by stage. Using Tukey's least-significant different (LSD, henceforth) test, all pair-wise tests for significant difference between defined stages are significant except between Stages 1 and 2 for platform facets. Therefore, flake attributes pattern predictably with reduction stage.

Categorical attributes also pattern by stage. Normal platforms are rare in Stage 1, where hinged and especially ridged platforms are common, and hinged platforms are rare in Stage 2 ($\chi^2 = 36.4$; $p < .001$). Flake termination type also patterns by stage ($\chi^2 = 44.9$; $p < 0.01$), feather terminations being rare in Stage 1 and dominant in Stage 3, while hinge terminations pattern in-

versely. Incidence of exterior-face cortex is high in Stage 1 and low in Stage 3, while incidence of noncortical flakes patterns inversely ($\chi^2 = 250.9$; $p < 0.01$). This pattern resembles Riley and colleagues' (1994) results, in which cortex was confined almost entirely to their Early Biface stage, but noncortical flakes were distributed equally across stages. Like Riley and others (1994) and Shott (1996b), UA experimental data show that noncortical flakes occur early in the reduction process and that cortical flakes can occur much later. Incidence of broken flakes is high in Stage 1 and low in Stage 3; again, intact flakes pattern inversely ($\chi^2 = 17.0$; $p < 0.01$).

Associations between categorical attributes are variable. Termination and platform type are unassociated ($\chi^2 = 3.6$; $p = 0.46$). Cortex cover and platform type are associated ($\chi^2 = 6.2$; $p = 0.04$); incidence of cortex is high in ridged platforms, while incidence of cortex is low in normal ones. Association disappears in Stage 3. Flake condition and platform type are weakly associated ($\chi^2 = 3.9$; $p = 0.14$); ridged platforms tend to occur on broken flakes. Cortex and termination are associated ($\chi^2 = 24.4$; $p < 0.01$); feather termination is associated with noncortical flakes, hinge terminations with cortical ones. However, this association occurs only among Stage-2 flakes. Exterior-face cortex and flake condition are not associated ($\chi^2 = 6.0$; $p = 0.20$) across all stages; in Stage 1, intact flakes tend to lack cortex and broken ones tend to bear it.

Stage Identification by Discriminant Analysis
Preexisting stage assignments of flakes in UA experimental data were used in an attempt to define classification functions of unknown "stage" for flakes at Modena and Tempiute by means of discriminant analysis (DA). Although other experimental datasets were used in other analyses of Modena and Tempiute assemblages, only the UA dataset among them was coded for the individual flake attributes that this approach requires.

Presnyakova and colleagues (2015) used DA to distinguish Paleolithic "Mode 1" core reduction/flake production from "Mode 2" biface-reduction flakes. Classification functions then

TABLE 5.2. Discriminant Analysis of UA Experimental Data.

Variable	Stage 1		Stage 2/3		Function Coefficient	Box's M (sig.)	Wilks' λ (sig.)
	Mean	sd	Mean	sd			
exterior scar density	0.0062	0.0069	0.011	0.009	0.732	293.6 (0.000)	0.942 (0.000)
weight	16.14	37.47	4.71	19.07	−0.649		
length	30.11	19.82	24.33	15.40	0.506		
width	28.54	19.55	20.96	12.28	−0.310		

could be used to classify flake debris by stage. Assumptions of the method are described in detail elsewhere (e.g., Shott 1997b:90–92). Briefly, DA makes three assumptions: the validity of a priori groups like the stages defined in our experimental data, multivariate normal data distributions, and equal covariance matrices between groups. In this analysis, stage definitions and assignments are asserted, and somewhat imposed, upon the continuum of variation that characterizes reduction. Because the boundary between Stage 1 and Stage 2 was comparatively unambiguous, DA sought only to distinguish Stage 1 from combined Stage-2/3 flakes, which had the added virtue of promoting stability of results by confining analysis to only two groups. (In any circumstance, exploratory DA using three stages failed to distinguish satisfactorily between stages, yielding very similar group centroids and scatters of cases on the two discriminant functions that extensively overlapped among stages. Correct classification was roughly 42%.) With two levels of the dependent variable "stage," a single discriminant function was produced. The second assumption is unimportant for descriptive purposes but relevant if, as here, results are extended to other datasets. Results are robust under mild skewness but are sensitive to higher skewness (Shott 1997b:91). Box's M tests for validity of the third assumption. Stepwise variable entry may bias results, so most DA was conducted using simultaneous entry, equal prior probabilities, and cross-validation. (Proportional or weighted prior probabilities assigned 95+% of flakes to Stage 2/3.)

The first DA entered flake weight, axial length, and width as size measures, cortex presence/absence as a technological variable, and scargm as a faceting variable. Generally, flake size and incidence of cortex should fall by stage while faceting should increase. Details of analysis are irrelevant because this first attempt was discarded. Among UA experimental flakes, 140 fall into Stage 1 and 971 into Stages 2/3. In this DA, 327 flakes were assigned to Stage 1, more than double the actual number, and 784 to Stages 2/3. Cross-tabulation showed that this iteration of DA essentially sorted flakes by cortex presence/absence. Therefore, a second DA omitted cortex.

A third permutation included platform width and platform scars because Magne (1985) suggested they were useful in distinguishing stages. It produced almost identical results. Accordingly, the simpler analysis of four variables is reported. (Magne also considered cortex useful for the purpose of distinguishing stages, contrary to results of this analysis.) All mean values of discriminating variables by assigned stage differ significantly. Results show that, not surprisingly, neither group means nor group covariances are equal (i.e., Wilks' λ and Box's M both are highly significant; Table 5.2). From their absolute values, exterior scar density and weight are the most influential discriminating variables, and their values differ in sign as expected given the inverse relationship between faceting and weight across the reduction sequence. However, ln-transformation of discriminating variables did not significantly alter results. Results are not entirely satisfactory, because only 69.3% of flakes (83 of 140 [59.2%] in Stage 1 and 687 of 971 [70.8%] in Stages 2/3) were correctly classified.

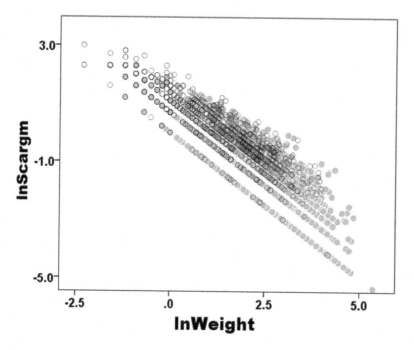

FIGURE 5.1. Ln-exterior-facets versus ln-weight by DA stage assignment. Shaded circles = DA Stage 1, open circles DA Stage 2/3.

A cross-plot of log-transformed exterior scar density and weight, the two most influential variables, shows some separation but also considerable overlap between inferred stages (Figure 5.1). To some degree, reduction stages arbitrarily parse a complex pattern of continuous variation in flake characteristics, so it is no surprise that DA results are significant but not definitive. They are a useful heuristic exercise for application to Modena and Tempiute, but not conclusive evidence of stages or clear boundaries between them.

Intact UA Experimental Flakes

Analysis of archaeological flakes from Modena and Tempiute was confined to intact specimens only. For comparability, this section reports results of analysis of only intact experimental flakes. Some results differ from analysis of all UA experimental flakes, although the correlations among variables are exactly the same. Metric variables by stage pattern substantially as they did among all flakes. Again, all LSD pair-wise results are significant except between Stages

1 and 2 and Stages 2 and 3 for platform facets, Stages 1 and 2 in platform width, and Stages 1 and 2 in scargm.

Categorical variables pattern by stage as does the all-flake dataset, except that both hinged and ridged platforms are common in Stage 3. Associations among categorical variables differ somewhat from the complete dataset. Again, termination and platform type are not associated ($\chi^2 = 2.5$; $p = 0.64$), except that hinged platforms co-occur with hinge terminations. Cortex and platform type are weakly associated ($\chi^2 = 3.6$; $p = 0.17$). Again, cortex and termination are associated ($\chi^2 = 22.0$; $p < 0.01$).

Attribute Analysis: Modena

As in experimental flakes, all metric and faceting attributes are highly correlated. Metric attributes all covary positively; scargm covaries inversely with all of them. Most metric attributes are right-skewed; already-high correlations are somewhat improved among log-transformed variables. Log transformations also tend to linearize bivariate plots (e.g., Figure 5.2), which

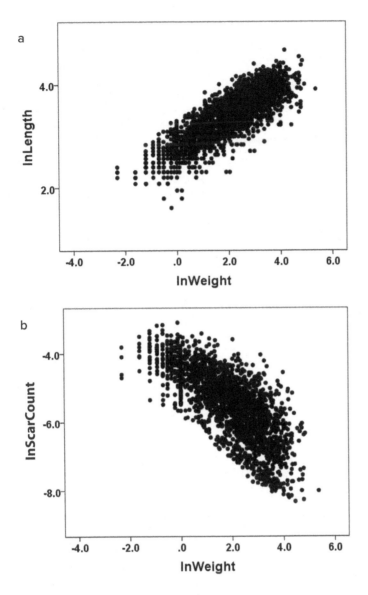

FIGURE 5.2. Modena flakes: a. Ln-lengh versus ln-weight (g); b. ln-scar count versus ln-weight (g).

helps explain the higher correlation coefficients in log-transformed data. Mean values for dimensions, weight, and faceting variables appear in Table 5.3. As in the experimental assemblage, exterior scar count at Modena varies inversely with flake size, such that flakes tend to become more extensively faceted as they decline in size during the reduction process. The relationship between scar count and weight also is linearized in ln-transformed variables.

Metric attributes differ between cortical and noncortical flakes (Table 5.4). In all cases, cortical flakes have higher mean values, that is, they are larger. Faceting variables, in contrast, provide higher mean values among noncortical flakes. Not surprisingly, size declines from what often are called "primary" flakes (100% exterior cortex) to "secondary" (<100% cortex) ones. Metric attributes also differ by termination type (among more than 2,500 flakes, only 47

TABLE 5.3. Modena and Tempiute Flake Metric and Faceting Variables Mean and Standard Deviation (s.d.).

Modena	n	mean	s.d.	Tempiute	n	mean	s.d.
weight (g)	2515	14.8	18.2	weight (g)	945	8.3	8.9
length	2514	33.4	14.6	length	945	29.2	11.0
width	2514	30.5	12.6	width	945	25.5	10.3
plat. width	2249	12.3	8.3	plat. width	799	9.4	5.7
plat. thick.	1934	5.1	3.7	plat. thick.	690	3.8	2.3
plat. scars	1999	1.1	0.9	plat. scars	735	0.7	0.7
scars	2512	3.7	2.8	scars	945	2.9	2.2
scargm	2512	0.006	0.006	scargm	945	0.005	0.006

TABLE 5.4. Modena and Tempiute Flake Metric and Faceting Variables by Cortex Category. Student's t and attained significance p reported.

		Modena				Tempiute			
		N	mean	t	p	N	mean	t	p
weight (g)	noncortical	929	6.7	22.1	<0.01	264	4.0	13.1	<0.01
	cortical	1,585	19.6			681	9.9		
length (mm)	noncortical	929	27.3	17.6	<0.01	264	25.3	7.3	<0.01
	cortical	1,585	36.9			681	30.7		
width (mm)	noncortical	929	25.2	17.9	<0.01	264	21.7	8.1	<0.01
	cortical	1,585	33.7			681	26.7		
plat. width (mm)	noncortical	227	11.5	3.8	<0.01	227	9.4	0.1	0.89
	cortical	572	12.8			572	9.4		
plat. thick. (mm)	noncortical	928	4.6	5.0	<0.01	195	3.6	1.6	0.12
	cortical	1,583	5.5			495	3.9		
plat. scars	noncortical	928	1.4	12.0	<0.01	195	0.9	6.7	<0.01
	cortical	1,583	0.9			540	0.6		
scars	noncortical	923	4.7	15.2	<0.01	264	4.1	11.6	<0.01
	cortical	1,581	3.1			681	2.4		
scargm	noncortical	923	0.009	3.8	<0.01	264	0.01	10.9	<0.01
	cortical	1,581	0.004			681	0.004		

bore step terminations, so analysis is confined to feather and hinge terminations). In all cases, hinge-terminated flakes have higher mean values; larger flakes tend to terminate more often by hinging than do smaller ones. Neither platform nor exterior facets differ significantly in mean between termination types, but scargm does; in this case, flakes with feather terminations have higher values, meaning they are more densely faceted.

Attributes differ by number of exterior-surface facets, all decline in mean from 0 to 1 and some decline steadily with number of facets (Table 5.5); in general, flakes become smaller as faceting rises. However, several size and facet-ing variables have slightly higher mean values among flakes with 3+ exterior-surface facets. This interval covers a wide range of exterior-surface facets, up to 23, and larger values probably are somewhat positively correlated with size. Platform dimensions decline in size in flakes with 0–3+ facets, but the differences are not significant. Pair-wise differences also fail to reach significance in LSD tests.

These results suggest the interaction of several tendencies. Not surprisingly, flake size tends to decline and faceting to rise as reduction advances. But a countervailing tendency is for larger flakes (with larger platforms), all else equal, to bear more facets. This interaction is

TABLE 5.5. Modena and Tempiute Metric and Faceting Variables by Exterior-Surface Facets. ANOVA *F* and attained significance *p* reported.

Variable	Facets	Modena					Facets	Tempiute				
		N	Mean	sd	F	p		N	Mean	sd	F	p
weight	0	201	23.6	24.3	27.9	<0.01	0	143	11.9	10.2	12.0	<0.01
(g)	1	294	18.9	22.9			1	131	9.5	13.3		
	2	400	13.6	17.6			2	177	6.4	6.5		
	3+	1,617	13.1	15.4			3+	494	7.6	7.4		
length	0	200	35.2	14.5	8.7	<0.01	0	143	29.5	10.5	4.2	<0.01
(mm)	1	294	36.5	16.4			1	131	28.2	12.2		
	2	400	31.2	15.5			2	177	26.9	9.5		
	3+	1,617	33.1	13.9			3+	494	30.1	11.3		
width	0	200	35.1	14.5	12.2	<0.01	0	143	27.7	9.3	5.1	<0.01
(mm)	1	294	31.9	13.1			1	131	23.7	8.9		
	2	400	29.1	13.0			2	177	24.4	9.6		
	3+	1,617	30.1	12.2			3+	494	25.4	9.3		
plat.	0	166	13.0	9.4	1.0	0.39	0	113	9.1	5.4	0.7	0.55
width	1	259	12.9	8.3			1	109	8.8	4.7		
(mm)	2	366	11.9	8.3			2	153	9.4	5.9		
	3+	1,458	12.2	8.1			3+	424	9.6	5.9		
plat.	0	137	5.5	4.9	1.1	0.37	0	102	3.9	2.4	0.1	0.99
thick.	1	232	5.4	3.8			1	103	3.9	2.6		
(mm)	2	319	5.0	3.5			2	126	3.9	2.4		
	3+	1,246	5.1	3.5			3+	359	3.8	2.2		
plat.	0	154	0.5	0.7	40.0	<0.01	0	121	0.5	0.6	12.0	<0.01
scars	1	241	0.8	0.8			1	107	0.7	0.7		
	2	326	0.9	0.9			2	133	0.6	0.6		
	3+	1,278	1.2	0.9			3+	374	0.8	0.7		
scargm	0	201	0.0	0.0	206.0	<0.01	0	143	0.0	0.0	103.0	<0.01
	1	294	0.0016	0.0			1	131	0.002	0.0		
	2	400	0.0044	0.0			2	177	0.004	0.0		
	3+	1,617	0.0075	0.01			3+	494	0.008	0.01		

s = standard deviation

partly clarified or resolved by faceting variables. Scargm rises steadily with exterior facets.

Differences in metric and faceting attributes by platform type are limited because, by definition, hinged platforms lack platform dimensions while ridged ones lack all but platform width. Although there are differences in mean values of size variables between all three platform types, none of those differences were found to be significant by LSD pair-wise comparison between normal and hinged platforms. ANOVA also failed to find significant differences between platform types. Flakes with ridged platforms are heavier and wider than others. All metric attributes decline from zero to two platform facets; platform size, however, rises slightly from 1 to 2 platform facets. Metric attributes, however, increase as flakes from two to three or more facets, although LSD pair-wise comparisons show that none of these increases are significant. Both faceting variables increase steadily with platform facets, although the LSD test for scargm from two to three platform facets is not significant. Cortical flakes are significantly associated with ridged platforms, noncortical ones with normal platforms (χ^2 = 21.8; p < 0.01). Cortical flakes and termination are not associated (χ^2 = 0.2; p = 0.92), nor is platform type with termination (χ^2 = 3.6; p = 0.46).

Attribute Patterning Across Modena Areas

Metric and faceting variables differ significantly in mean across Modena clusters, although the fairly large number of clusters and the relatively low sample sizes in some contribute to this result. A more robust comparison and more robust test is to compare the quarry areas A, B, and F to workshops D, E, and 2009-1. In that comparison, the quarry group might be expected to have higher values for size and lower ones for faceting. In fact, metric or size variables do not differ between these groups, although platform size (but not faceting) is significantly larger in the workshop group. Although faceting variables pattern as expected, the difference in their means is not significant.

Discriminant/Classification
Analysis of the Modena Assemblage

Stages can be defined and assigned in experimental data, but can only be inferred in archaeological data. Using SPSS's Outfile command, classification functions defined in DA of UA experimental data were applied to the Modena flake assemblage. Confining comparison to intact specimens, assigned Stage 1 size variables have lower means among experimental flakes than Modena ones. In exterior scar count, the mean for experimental flakes is slightly lower than the Modena mean, but in scar density the experimental value is higher; experimental flakes are smaller and more faceted for their size than are Modena ones. In platform attributes the two datasets are similar in thickness and scar count, although experimental flakes have narrower widths on average than do Modena flakes; their somewhat smaller size is reflected in experimental flakes' narrower, but not thinner, platform and higher scar count. On balance, experimental flakes have smaller, more faceted platforms. Modena flakes show a higher incidence of cortex than do experimental ones;

termination types do not differ between datasets. Flake-size distributions differ somewhat, the experimental assemblage having a higher proportion in the lowest, 6.35 mm (¼ in), fraction, the Modena assemblage a higher proportion in the 19.05 mm (¾ in) one.

In assigned Stage 2/3, experimental flakes have lower means in all size and platform variables as well as exterior scar count. Only in exterior scar density does the mean experimental value exceed Modena's. Again, therefore, smaller experimental flakes are more extensively faceted. There is a higher incidence of cortex in Modena than in experimental flakes, and as before, termination types do not differ between datasets. In flake size, again the distributions are complementary with the experimental assemblage having a higher proportion in the 6.35 mm (¼ in) fraction and the Modena one a corresponding higher proportion in the 12.7 mm (½ in) and 19.05 mm (¾ in) fractions; proportions in the 25.4 mm (1 in) fraction are nearly identical.

Table 5.6 summarizes Modena results for major metric variables, all of which differ in mean between assigned Stages 1 and 2/3. The mean for cortex is determined by the arbitrary coding variable (0 = no cortex, 1 = cortex present). Because more flakes assigned to Stage 1 bear cortex, the mean is higher in that case. Despite the clear association of cortex with Stage 1 (χ^2 = 365.9; p < 0.01), it is noteworthy that significant proportions of Stage-1 flakes lack cortex and significant proportions of Stage-2/3 ones possess it, consistent with UA and other (Shott 1996b) experimental data.

Not surprisingly, flake-size distributions differ by predicted stage assignment (χ^2 = 858.6; p < 0.01; Table 5.7). The 25.4 mm (1 in) fraction is dominated by assigned Stage 1, the 6.35 mm (¼ in) fraction by assigned Stage 2/3. Interestingly, termination type is not associated with assigned stage (χ^2 = 1.79; p = 0.41) even though hinge terminations a might be expected to occur mostly in Stage 1 and feather terminations mostly in Stage 2/3.

Stage assignment of flakes patterns with defined Modena clusters (χ^2 = 21.5; p = 0.002;

TABLE 5.6. Mean Attributes of Modena and Tempiute Flakes by DA-Assigned Stage. Student's *t* and attained significance *p* reported.

| | Modena | | | | | |
| | Stage 1 | | Stage 2/3 | | | |
	N	mean	N	mean	t	p
weight	1,642	20.1	873	4.83	21.8	<0.01
length	1,641	36.2	873	28.0	14.1	<0.01
width	1,641	36.2	873	19.9	46.1	<0.01
exterior scars	1,639	0.0029	873	0.011	33.5	<0.01
plat. width	1,446	14.1	803	9.1	16.5	<0.01
plat. thickness	1,238	5.9	703	3.1	13.4	<0.01
cortex	1,641	0.76	873	0.38	19.9	<0.01
	Tempiute					
weight	371	10.4	222	4.3	10.7	<0.01
length	371	29.5	222	28.7	0.8	0.41
width	371	29.5	222	18.6	18.0	<0.01
exterior scars	371	2.3	222	4.1	9.9	<0.01
plat. width	306	10.6	192	9.0	3.3	<0.01
plat. thickness	272	4.1	160	2.1	1.8	0.08
cortex	371	0.83	222	0.5	8.5	<0.01

TABLE 5.7. Modena and Tempiute Flake-Size Distribution by Assigned Stage.

| | Modena | | | |
	Size		Class	
Assigned (mm)	25.4	19.7	12.7	6.35
Stage (in)	1	3/4	1/2	1/4
1	638	520	384	100
2/3	9	109	367	388
	Tempiute			
Assigned (mm)	25.4	19.7	12.7	6.35
Stage (in)	1	3/4	1/2	1/4
1	53	131	131	56
2/3	1	24	95	102

Shott 2016:Table 5.20), but standardized residuals attain the conventional significance value of |1| mostly in small clusters with low sample sizes. Among larger clusters, only Area D patterns significantly (by having fewer Stage 1 and more Stage 2/3 flakes than expected); Area F has a significant standardized residual only for Stage 2/3, where the negative value indicates underrepresentation. A more effective and statistically more valid test compares combined quarry loci A, B, and F to combined workshop zones D, E, and 2009-1. That result shows little patterning ($\chi^2 = 1.8$; $p = 0.18$; Fisher's Exact $p = 0.19$; Shott 2016:Table 5.20). Only one cell, combined workshop loci with assigned Stage 2/3, attains a standardized residual of |1|, positive in this case as expected. Stage 2/3 flakes pattern weakly with workshop loci, Stage 1 flakes with quarry loci.

Attribute Analysis: Tempiute

Mean attributes for metric and faceting variables of Tempiute's assemblage appear in Table 5.3. As in experimental and Modena flake assemblages, metric and faceting variables all are positively correlated, except for exterior facets with all other variables. Almost all original variables are skewed or otherwise non-normal in distribution, although again, ln-transformation roughly normalizes those distributions, linearizes cross-plots, and improves correlation.

As above and in both experimental and Modena flake assemblages, Tempiute scar count patterns are inversely related to flake size; again, ln-transformation linearizes the pattern. Flake-size attributes differ by presence/absence of cortex, although platform size attributes do not (Table 5.4). Noncortical flakes have lower means in all size attributes. All faceting variables, including platform facets, differ significantly by cortex category, with cortical flakes having lower values. As in the experimental and Modena assemblages, Tempiute noncortical flakes are smaller and more extensively faceted.

Some size and faceting variables differ by platform type. Weight and width differ significantly, although LSD tests indicate that the only significant pair-wise difference in both cases is between ridged and normal platforms; length does not differ by platform type. As in the Modena assemblage, ridged-platform flakes are heavier and wider, but not longer, than flakes with other platform types. Given the nature of platform types, comparisons of their platform dimensions and faceting is meaningless. Platform types differ by exterior-surface facets, although the only significant pair-wise results are between ridged platforms and the other types separately; normal and hinge platforms do not differ. Ridged platforms bear significantly fewer facets than do other platform types. Differences are not significant in scrgm, although again ridged platforms have a lower mean value. Incidence of cortex is higher among ridged platforms than other types.

Hinge-termination flakes are larger in plan dimensions than feather-termination flakes, but not in weight (Shott 2016:Table 5.23). (As at

Modena, low counts in other termination types justify focus upon these two common terminations alone.) No platform or faceting variable is associated with termination type. Overall, the pattern of Tempiute flakes according to termination type resembles Modena's in length and width, but not weight. Hinge-termination flakes possessed larger platforms in the Modena assemblage, yet these differences are not significant among Tempiute flakes. In neither assemblage do most faceting variables pattern with termination; although scargm values are higher among feather-termination flakes in both, the difference attains significance only at Modena.

Flake-size variables pattern inversely with number of exterior-surface facets (Table 5.5), although width increases slightly in flakes with 2 to 3 facets. Platform size and scar-count are not significantly associated with exterior-surface facets. Not surprisingly, scargm patterns positively with exterior facets. Overall, the relationships between flake characteristics and exterior-surface facets are similar between the Modena and Tempiute assemblages, although Modena platform facets are also associated with exterior-surface facets.

At Tempiute, mean size and faceting differ significantly by number of platform facets (Shott 2016:Table 5.25). In all variables, however, means increase in those flakes with one to two platform facets, which indicates that the significant difference lies between flakes bearing no platform scars and those that contain one or more scars. Most pair-wise LSD comparisons do not yield significant differences. Flakes without platform facets are larger in size and in platform size, but are less faceted than are flakes whose platforms bear scars. Compared to Modena, Tempiute flakes do not bear as many scars, and size patterns less complexly with platform facets. Whereas metric variables tended to decrease steadily with platform facets at Modena, in the Tempiute assemblage the significant size distinction is between platforms without facets versus those with facets. The two assemblages demonstrate generally similar patterns by platform facets in exterior-facet variables. Cortex cover is significantly associated with platform type (χ^2 = 24.5; p < 0.01) because ridged plat-forms are strongly associated with cortex. Cortex cover is not significantly associated with termination type, however (χ^2 = 4.4; p = 0.11). There is no relationship between platform type and termination type (χ^2 = 2.2; p = 0.69).

Attribute Patterning
Across Tempiute Areas

Metric and faceting variables differ significantly across all Tempiute areas. This result is somewhat misleading, because the number of areas makes it relatively easy for F to attain significance. The best and most statistically valid comparison is between areas with the highest sample sizes, N1, N5, and N6. Among these three areas, analysis of flake weight differences barely reaches significance; LSD shows that the difference is significant only between N1 and N6. Length and width do not differ among the three areas. In platform width and thickness, material from N1 possesses larger values, whereas N5 and N6 values are similar to one another. N1 again has a larger value when considering platform scars than N5 or N6, whose means are not significantly different. The same pattern is found in exterior-surface scar count and scargm. Altogether, N1 flakes are heavier but not larger in plan size; they possess larger and more extensively faceted platforms and exterior surfaces than N5 and N6 flakes.

Discriminant/Classification
Analysis of Tempiute Flakes

Predicted stages from UA experimental data were applied to the Tempiute flake assemblage, as they were at Modena. As at Modena, all measured and coded Tempiute flakes were intact, while UA experimental data included broken flakes.

Again confining analysis to intact experimental flakes, assigned Stage-1 Tempiute flakes have significantly lower means for weight, length, and width than do experimental ones, as well as for platform size, scar count, and exterior-surface faceting variables. Incidence of cortex is higher among Tempiute flakes. Unlike Modena, Tempiute Stage-1 flakes are smaller,

less extensively faceted, and likelier to bear cortex than are experimental ones. Flake-size distributions differ greatly, the experimental assemblage skewing toward the 6.35 mm (¼ in) fraction, with lower than expected frequencies in 12.7 mm (½ in) and 19.05 mm (¾ in) fractions, while Tempiute flakes are underrepresented at the smallest size class and overrepresented in intermediate ones. This difference is somewhat greater than that revealed in the comparison of the experimental and Modena assemblages. On balance, Tempiute flakes assigned to Stage 1 are smaller but *less* faceted than experimental ones, and have a size distribution skewed to intermediate rather than smallest fractions.

Among Stage-2/3 flakes, Tempiute specimens are considerably larger than experimental ones. Although the two datasets do not differ significantly in platform width, Tempiute flakes have thicker platforms that are less extensively faceted. Tempiute flakes also possess more exterior-surface facets although their facet density (scargm) is slightly lower. Incidence of cortex is much higher in Tempiute Stage-2/3 flakes than in experimental ones. As in the case of flakes assigned to Stage 1, the Tempiute flake-size distribution is skewed toward intermediate size classes, whereas the experimental distribution is skewed toward the smallest, 6.35 mm (¼ in), fraction. In general, Tempiute flakes assigned to Stages 2/3 are larger, less extensively faceted, and likelier to bear cortex than experimental ones.

Table 5.6 summarizes Tempiute results for metric variables, most of which differ in mean between assigned Stages 1 and 2/3. Unlike Modena, flake length does not differ significantly between assigned stages, although platform thickness does. As at Modena, the Tempiute cortex mean is determined by the arbitrary coding variable (0 = noncortical flake, 1 = cortical flake). Because more flakes assigned to Stage 1 bear cortex, the mean is higher in that case. Despite the clear association of cortex with Stage 1 and absence of cortex with Stage 2 (χ^2 = 119.8; p < 0.01), again it is noteworthy that substantial proportions of Stage-1 flakes lack cortex and substantial proportions of Stage-2/3 flakes possess it.

TABLE 5.8. Modena and Tempiute Flakes in Assigned Stages 1 and 2/3. Student's *t* and attained significance *p* reported.

Variable	Site	Stage 1					Stage 2/3				
		N	Mean	sd	t	p	N	Mean	sd	t	p
weight (g)	Modena	1,642	20.1	20.2	14.3	<0.01	873	4.8	5.8	2.71	<0.01
	Temp.	594	10.8	10.1			351	4.0	4.0		
length (mm)	Modena	1,641	36.2	14.0	12.4	<0.01	873	28.0	14.3	0.58	0.59
	Temp.	594	29.6	10.0			351	28.4	12.6		
width (mm)	Modena	1,641	36.2	11.6	14.8	<0.01	873	19.9	6.2	4.13	<0.01
	Temp.	594	29.4	8.8			351	18.4	5.4		
plat. width (mm)	Modena	1,446	14.1	9.0	10.7	<0.01	803	9.1	5.5	3.29	<0.01
	Temp.	493	10.3	6.1			306	8.0	4.5		
plat. thick. (mm)	Modena	1,231	5.9	4.0	11.9	<0.01	703	3.9	2.6	2.70	<0.01
	Temp.	436	4.1	2.4			254	3.4	2.0		
plat. scars	Modena	1,291	1.0	0.9	8.9	<0.01	708	1.3	0.9	7.41	<0.01
	Temp.	474	0.6	0.6			261	0.9	0.6		
scars	Modena	1,639	3.2	2.7	8.5	<0.01	873	4.7	2.6	5.44	<0.01
	Temp.	594	2.3	2.2			351	4.0	1.9		
scargm	Modena	1,639	0.003	0.003	1.1	0.27	873	0.011	0.007	2.81	<0.01
	Temp.	594	0.003	0.003			351	0.0097	0.008		
cortex	Modena	1,641	0.76	0.42	4.3	<0.01	873	0.4	0.49	4.3	<0.01
	Temp.	594	0.84	0.36			351	0.5	0.51		

TABLE 5.9. Summary of Principal Components Analysis of Modena and Tempiute Assemblages Combined.

PC	Eigenvalue	Cumulative % variance	Variable Loading				
			weight	length	width	scars	scargm
1	2.624	53.5	0.852	0.812	0.826	−0.090	−0.740
2	1.262	77.7	0.190	0.186	0.181	0.948	0.510
3	0.535	88.4	0.194	−0.511	0.441	0.113	0.168

As at Modena, it is not surprising that flake-size distributions differ by predicted stage assignment (χ^2 = 112.7; p < 0.01; Table 5.7). The 25.4 mm (1 in) fraction is dominated by assigned Stage-1 flakes, the 6.35 mm (¼ in) fraction by assigned Stage 2/3, as was the case in the Modena assemblage. As at Modena, termination type in the Tempiute assemblage is not associated with assigned stage (χ^2 = 0.2; p = 0.70) even though hinge terminations might be expected to occur mostly in Stage 1 and feather terminations mostly in Stage 2/3.

Stage assignment of flakes is associated with defined Tempiute areas (χ^2 = 114.6; p < 0.00; Shott 2016:Table 5.29), but standardized residuals reach conventional significance of |1| mostly in small areas with low sample sizes. Confining analysis to the larger clusters N1, N5, and N6, patterning persists (χ^2 = 78.2; p < 0.00). N1 has significantly more Stage-2/3 flakes, N5 and N6 significantly more Stage-1 flakes.

Comparing Modena and Tempiute by Assigned Stage

At both Modena and Tempiute, roughly two-thirds of flakes are assigned to Stage 1, one-third to Stages 2/3. At both quarries, therefore, the assemblage is dominated by flakes that probably were produced at earlier intervals or stages of reduction. In assigned Stage-1 flakes, Modena specimens have significantly higher means in all size variables, as well as in both platform and exterior-surface scars (Table 5.8). The assemblages do not differ significantly in scargm, which roughly controls for size when measuring faceting. Incidence of cortex is significantly higher at Tempiute, probably owing to the smaller size of Tempiute cobbles. Over-all, Modena flakes are larger and bear more exterior-surface facets although the two assemblages do not differ in facet density (i.e., scargm). Despite their similar proportions in DA-assigned Stage-1 and Stage-2/3 flakes, the Modena and Tempiute assemblages differ greatly in flake-size distribution (χ^2 = 130.9; p < 0.01). Modena is significantly overrepresented in 25.4 mm (1 in) fraction flakes, Tempiute in flakes in the 6.35 mm (¼ in) and 12.7 mm (½ in) fractions.

Among assigned Stage-2/3 flakes, again Modena mean values exceed Tempiute ones in most size variables (but not length), and in all faceting variables (Table 5.8). In this assigned stage, Modena has a significantly higher mean value even in scargm, unlike results for assigned Stage 1. In general, again Modena flakes are larger and more extensively faceted than Tempiute ones, with a lower incidence of cortex. In assigned Stage 2/3, the Modena and Tempiute assemblages differ only equivocally in flake-size distribution (χ^2 = 7.1; p = 0.07). Standardized residuals exceed |1| only in the 19.05 mm (¾ in) fraction, where Modena is overrepresented and Tempiute underrepresented, and marginally (standardized residual = −1.1) in the 25.4 mm (1 in) fraction for Tempiute only. In sum, differences in flake-size distribution in assigned Stage 2/3 are modest and occur mostly in intermediate size classes.

Principal-component Analysis

Principal-component analysis (PCA) reduces larger numbers of original variables to smaller sets of mutually orthogonal, independent dimensions, which can be interpreted as underlying axes of variation. PCA (using the correlation matrix) of the size variables weight, length, and width, and of the faceting variables exterior-surface scars and scargm, for Modena and Tempiute combined produced results summarized in Table 5.9. PC1 has high positive loadings for all size variables and a high negative one for scargm. PC1 simultaneously describes large size and low faceting; it captures early segments or stages of reduction, which, in these datasets, accounts for more than half of total variance. PC2 has low loadings for size variables but high positive ones for faceting variables. It describes smaller, more extensively faceted flakes, and captures approximately one-quarter of total variance. PC3's eigenvalue is <1, the conventional significance threshold, but describes mostly shape variation (flakes that are wide but not long nor particularly large), with a low degree of faceting. It accounts for little more than 10% of total variance. The separate Modena and Tempiute assemblages pattern similarly on PC plots, although the range of Tempiute's variation is encompassed by Modena's wider variation in all pairs of plots. Separate PCA of Modena and Tempiute produced very similar eigenvalues, cumulative-variance explained, and variable loadings, so the structure revealed in both assemblages together also characterizes each separately.

In the Modena assemblage, a possible salient distinction is between primary quarry clusters A, B, and F and secondary workshop areas D, E, and 2009-1. Separate PCA of these two sub-groups yielded eigenvalues, %-variance explained, and variable loadings almost identical to one another and to the entire Modena assemblage as a unit. In PCA of three size and two faceting variables, there is no appreciable difference in structure of the data between primary quarry areas and other portions of the site.

Summary of
Data Reporting and Statistics

Overall, at both Modena and Tempiute metric dimensions are strongly correlated, faceting varies inversely and cortex presence positively with flake size, and faceting inversely with cortex. Platform type patterns weakly with metric dimensions and discrete attributes. DA classi-

fication, defined in analysis of the UA experimental dataset, assigns most flakes in both assemblages to the earlier stage. There are no robust differences in relevant flake-technological variables between areas at either quarry.

The physical and technological constraints of toolstone reduction partly explain the strong patterning in these datasets. Analysis to this point also suggests that both the Modena and Tempiute assemblages are characteristic of earlier reduction intervals or stages, as would be expected at quarries. But this judgment need not rely on assumption or casual treatment. Instead, relatively simple data display and analysis describe central tendencies in these datasets and gauge the pattern and strength of correlation within them. Similar treatment of other quarry debris assemblages will improve the comparability of results and promote the compilation of larger, analyzed datasets that in turn can be used to address methodological issues and theoretical models in the study and interpretation of hunter-gatherer toolstone quarries. Some lines of such comparable treatment, based on earlier studies of flake assemblages and intended to encourage more thorough, detailed analysis of quarry data, are described in the sections that follow.

Flake-Size Distibutions

Flake-size distributions by count, proportion, and cumulative proportion are reported by area for Modena and Tempiute (Table 5.10). Flake-size distributions for each Stage-1 sample are compiled in Appendix A. For clarity of presentation, only the distributions for N2, N5, and N6 are shown for Tempiute. Other areas there have roughly similar but, owing to small sample sizes, more variable figures. Counts and proportions are presented both for all flakes and for intact flakes only. Modena and Tempiute plots of proportions appear in Figure 5.3.

A notable characteristic of flake-size distributions is the comparatively low proportions at the smaller size fractions, particularly the 6.35 mm (¼ in) class. Experimental datasets described above have much higher proportions in the 6.35 mm (¼ in) fraction, and in many cases somewhat higher proportions in 12.7 mm (½ in)

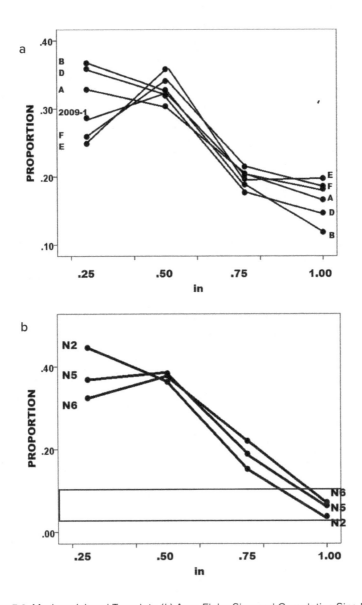

FIGURE 5.3. Modena (*a*) and Tempiute (*b*) Area Flake-Size and Cumulative Size Distributions.

and 19.05 mm (¾ in) fractions as well. Proportions of 6.35 mm (¼ in) fraction flakes in Root's dataset range from 0.6727 to 0.8853; in Stahle and Dunn's that fraction exhibits an even higher and narrower range. Although the UA dataset's 6.35 mm (¼ in) fraction is somewhat lower than other experimental sets, it nevertheless exceeds Modena and Tempiute area figures by a factor of two or more. Other experimental data (e.g., Behm 1983:Table 1) also have much higher 6.35 mm (¼ in) fraction proportions. Before an-

alyzing flake-size distributions, this discrepancy must be addressed.

Taphonomic Winnowing of Flake Assemblages

Clearly, Modena and Tempiute flake assemblages are impoverished in 6.35 mm (¼ in) and 12.7 mm (½ in) flakes compared to experimental controls. Chapter 4 suggested that some combination of slope and sheetwash produced this taphonomic effect. Whatever the cause, the

TABLE 5.10. Modena and Tempiute Flake-Size Distributions by Count, Proportion, and Cumulative Proportion.

Count

Area	25.4 mm[a]	19.05 mm	12.7 mm	6.35 mm	Σ
Modena					
All Flakes					
A	458	558	837	905	2,758
B	215	342	593	667	1,817
D	160	194	350	394	1,098
E	45	45	82	57	229
F	434	501	795	605	2,335
2009-1	40	45	72	63	220
Intact Flakes					
A	145	137	174	108	564
B	91	92	113	89	385
D	79	69	133	230	511
E	23	16	32	21	92
F	207	176	223	288	894
2009-1	20	17	21	17	75
Temp.					
All Flakes					
N1	18	78	240	319	655
N2	52	210	500	614	1,376
N3	26	29	47	35	137
N4	4	24	24	53	105
N5	40	119	238	232	629
N6	35	108	188	159	490
N7	3	5	21	30	59
N8	13	12	33	18	76
N9	11	20	29	34	94
N10	5	22	80	39	146

Proportion

Area	25.4 mm	19.05 mm	12.7 mm	6.35 mm
All Flakes				
A	0.1662	0.2023	0.3035	0.3281
B	0.1183	0.1882	0.3264	0.3671
D	0.1465	0.1767	0.3188	0.3588
E	0.1974	0.1965	0.3581	0.2489
F	0.1860	0.2146	0.3405	0.2591
2009-1	0.1820	0.2045	0.3273	0.2864
Intact Flakes				
A	0.2571	0.2429	0.3085	0.1915
B	0.2363	0.2390	0.2935	0.2312
D	0.1555	0.1352	0.2595	0.4505
E	0.2500	0.1739	0.3478	0.2283
F	0.2324	0.1969	0.2494	0.3221
2009-1	0.2675	0.2267	0.2800	0.2267
All Flakes				
N1	0.0275	0.1191	0.3664	0.4870
N2	0.0378	0.1526	0.3634	0.4462
N3	0.1897	0.2117	0.3431	0.2555
N4	0.0380	0.2286	0.2286	0.5048
N5	0.0636	0.1892	0.3784	0.3688
N6	0.0714	0.2204	0.3837	0.3245
N7	0.0510	0.0847	0.3559	0.5085
N8	0.1711	0.1579	0.4342	0.2368
N9	0.1170	0.2128	0.3085	0.3617
N10	0.0343	0.1507	0.5479	0.2671

Cumulative Proportion

Area	25.4 mm	19.05 mm	12.7 mm	6.35 mm
All Flakes				
A	1	0.8339	0.6316	0.3281
B	1	0.8817	0.6935	0.3671
D	1	0.8543	0.6776	0.3588
E	1	0.8035	0.6070	0.2489
F	1	0.8141	0.5996	0.2591
2009-1	1	0.8182	0.6136	0.2864
Intact Flakes				
A	1	0.7429	0.5000	0.1915
B	1	0.7636	0.5247	0.2312
D	1	0.8452	0.7101	0.4505
E	1	0.7500	0.5761	0.2283
F	1	0.7685	0.5716	0.3221
2009-1	1	0.7333	0.5067	0.2267
All Flakes				
N1	1	0.9725	0.8534	0.4870
N2	1	0.9622	0.8096	0.4462
N3	1	0.8102	0.5985	0.2555
N4	1	0.9619	0.7333	0.5048
N5	1	0.9364	0.7472	0.3688
N6	1	0.9286	0.7082	0.3245
N7	1	0.9492	0.8644	0.5085
N8	1	0.8289	0.6711	0.2368
N9	1	0.8830	0.6702	0.3617
N10	1	0.9658	0.8151	0.2671

	Intact Flakes						Intact Flakes					Intact Flakes			
N1	10	39	71	61	181	N1	0.0552	0.2155	0.3923	0.3370	N1	1	0.9448	0.7293	0.3370
N2	27	99	177	141	444	N2	0.0609	0.2230	0.3986	0.3176	N2	1	0.9392	0.7162	0.3176
N3	14	17	23	19	73	N3	0.1917	0.2329	0.3151	0.2603	N3	1	0.8082	0.5753	0.2603
N4	2	11	4	30	47	N4	0.0426	0.2340	0.0851	0.6383	N4	1	0.9574	0.7234	0.6383
N5	25	59	101	111	296	N5	0.0845	0.1993	0.3412	0.3750	N5	1	0.9155	0.7162	0.3750
N6	16	43	83	84	226	N6	0.0713	0.1903	0.3673	0.3717	N6	1	0.9292	0.7389	0.3717
N7	1	3	9	21	34	N7	0.0295	0.0882	0.2647	0.6176	N7	1	0.9706	0.8824	0.6176
N8	4	4	19	9	36	N8	0.1111	0.1111	0.5278	0.2500	N8	1	0.8889	0.7778	0.2500
N9	5	9	7	26	47	N9	0.1064	0.1915	0.1489	0.5532	N9	1	0.8936	0.7021	0.5532
N10	1	12	35	30	78	N10	0.0129	0.1538	0.4487	0.3846	N10	1	0.9872	0.8333	0.3846

[a] Measurements given in mm correspond to 1 in, ¾ in, ½ in, and ¼ in, respectively.

TABLE 5.11. Surface and Subsurface Flake-Size Distributions, Count and Proportion of Remnant and Transported Flakes, and Estimated Rate of Winnowing by Three and Four Flake-Size Classes.

Source	Context	Count			Proportion		
		6.35 mm	12.7 mm	25.4 mm	6.35 mm	12.7 mm	25.4 mm
Amick 1991	surface	126	82	8	0.583	0.379	0.037
	subsurface	115	19	1	0.852	0.141	0.007
Seddon 2001	surface	1,031	705	31	0.583	0.399	0.018
	subsurface	2,900	524	11	0.844	0.153	0.003
Byram et al. 1999	subsurface	41,792	7,301	499	0.843	0.147	0.01

	Proportions			Counts			
	6.35 mm	12.7 mm	25.4 mm	6.35 mm	12.7 mm	25.4 mm	Total
surface	0.583	0.389	0.026	111.9	74.6	5	192.3
subsurface	0.848	0.147	0.005	848	147	5	1,000
prop. orig.				0.132	0.507	1	
1/prop. orig.				7.578	1.971	1	

	Proportions				Counts				
	6.35 mm	12.7 mm	19.05 mm	25.4 mm	6.35 mm	12.7 mm	19.05 mm	25.4 mm	Σ
surface	0.583	0.269	0.125	0.023	126.7	58.5	27.2	5	217.4
subsurface	0.848	0.076	0.044	0.005	848	76	44	5	1,000
prop. orig.					0.149	0.597	0.555	1	
1/prop. orig.					6.711	1.675	1.801	1	

Imperial equivalents of size classes are as follow: 25.4 mm = 1 in; 19.05 mm = ¾ in; 12.7 mm = ½ in; 6.35 mm = ¼ in.

pattern and degree of bias in surface assemblages remain to be gauged so that their original size distributions can be estimated. One way to accomplish this would involve a program of excavation at both sites and comparison of flake-size distributions of the surface and subsurface assemblages. But excavation was not part of the UA research design.

The approach used here starts from the understanding of surface winnowing processes discussed in Chapter 4, in which the probability of removal is inversely related to artifact size. Thus, smaller flakes are disproportionately subject to winnowing. The approach applies this understanding to the differences observed in flake-size distribution between surface and subsurface obsidian assemblages in the southern Great Basin. Other toolstone quarries, in the Great Basin and elsewhere, have dense surface distributions, so this approach may be useful in other settings.

Two studies of obsidian assemblages in the region involved both surface collection and excavation, and reported flake-size distributions for both contexts. Amick (1991:Tables 6-2–6-4; see also Walsh 1991:Table 8-2) reported combined obsidian and chert flake-size distributions from 26Ny2894 at the Nevada Test Site. Seddon and colleagues (2001:Tables 4.11, 4.15, 4.17, 4.32, 4.35, 4.39, 4.48, 4.50, 4.55, 4.57, 4.59, 4.65, 4.68, 4.73, 4.75, 4.81, and 4.82) reported obsidian flake-size distributions from various sites and contexts in their Panaca Summit study area, which was presumably dominated by Modena obsidian. (Farrel and Burton [2010:Tables 2,5] reported similar data for very small obsidian assemblages at Mammoth Lakes, California.) Amick (1991) and Seddon and colleagues (2001) both observed proportions across the three size classes used here; their differences between surface and sub-surface contexts are similar (Table 5.11). Byram and others (1999:Table 10.2) reported flake-size data for excavated, but not surface, contexts at the large Newberry Crater obsidian assemblages. Their subsurface proportions are remarkably similar to those reported by Amick (1991) and Seddon and colleagues (2001), particularly in the 6.35 mm (¼ in) class.

Surface to subsurface comparisons of chert flake assemblages in Sturgess's (1999:Table 4.2) Arctic study area showed similar proportions by size class. In summary, a robust pattern is evident in the size distribution of flake assemblages from surface and subsurface contexts. Although all buried sites once were surface ones, those remaining on the surface probably have experienced longer and more intensive taphonomic size sorting than have buried sites.

At Buckboard Mesa, Amick (1991:35) attributed differences in size distribution of surface and subsurface assemblages to downward migration of small flakes and fine sediments into the substrate. At Yucca Mountain, obsidian and other toolstone flake-size distributions were dominated by fractions near 25.4 mm (1 in) and progressively impoverished in smaller fractions, to an even greater degree than at Modena and Tempiute (Haynes 1996:Figures 6, 8, 10). Rather than collection bias, the paucity of small fractions in flake-size distributions therefore implicates the role of natural taphonomic processes like sheetwash and gravity in systematic size biasing of surface assemblages.

Smith (2001) studied surface erosion processes in a New Mexico watershed occupied by several archaeological sites. Sediment traps placed downslope of the sites and monitored over a three-year period measured the quantity and rate of transport of artifacts from sites to secondary downslope contexts. Smith (2001: Tables A.1 and A.2) reported data for a range of artifacts including flakes, mostly of obsidian but some of basalt and chert. Flake proportions by size class were very similar between the site and transported assemblages, especially in smaller size fractions (Table 5.1). That is, they did not indicate that sheetwash and other natural factors have altered the character of assemblages on the sites' surfaces. Recalling, however, that these sites themselves have experienced erosion and other taphonomic effects for centuries or more, the similarity in recent flake-size distributions is not surprising. A possibly more informative way to interpret Smith's data is to express flake proportions by context across size class, rather than by size class across context. The lower section

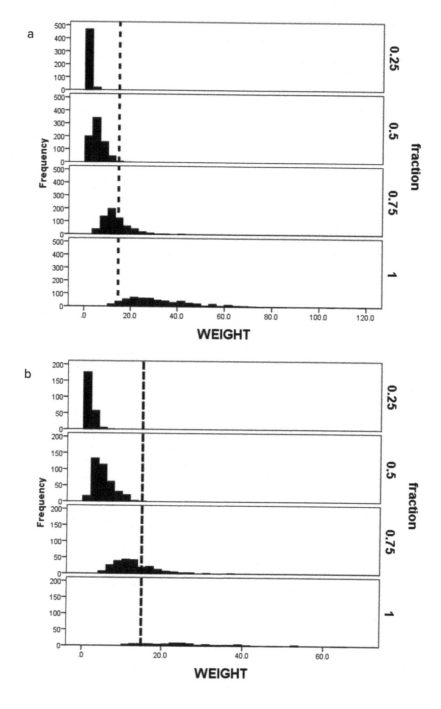

FIGURE 5.4. Flake-weight distribution by size fraction: a. Modena; b. Tempiute.

of Table 5.11 shows the results. Although sample sizes are very small in the 19.05 mm (¾ in) and 25.4 mm (1 in) fractions, these figures suggest that most flakes in the 25.4 mm (1 in) class stay put, more than half are transported in the 19.05 mm (¾ in) class, and more than 70% are transported in smaller size classes. Recalling that Smith's study spanned only three years, it suggests very high rates of winnowing of size classes below 25.4 mm (1 in).

Table 5.11 suggests that surface assemblages are impoverished and that the rate of impoverishment varies inversely with size class. Proportions in 12.7 mm (½ in) and 25.4 mm (1 in) fractions are considerably higher in surface than subsurface context, presumably as lag effects. That is, as smaller flakes are differentially winnowed from the surface by the taphonomic processes discussed in Chapter 4, proportions of other fractions must increase as in any closed mathematical array. This does not mean that flakes in the larger fractions are *not* subject to removal by sheetwash or other taphonomic processes, merely that they are much *less* susceptible than are the smallest, 6.35 mm (¼ in), fraction.

Figure 5.4 corroborates this conclusion for Modena, and Tempiute follows a closely similar pattern. The 6.35 mm (¼ in) and 12.7 mm (½ in) fractions lie almost entirely below the value of 15 g that Petraglia and Nash (1987:120) identified as a threshold above which particle movement was unlikely and below which it was very likely. Accordingly, taphonomic winnowing should be especially strong in these sizes. The 19.05 mm (¾ in) fraction is roughly bisected, although at both sites its mode also lies below the 15 g threshold; Taphonomic winnowing is modest but not insignificant there. Finally, 25.4 mm (1 in) fractions lie mostly above the threshold, so winnowing effects in those fractions should be slight. Again, this does not mean that all 6.35 mm (¼ in) and 12.7 mm (½ in) flakes must be winnowed, obviously not the case at Modena or Tempiute since many were collected. Rather, it suggests that many flakes in those fractions are winnowed at higher rates than those in larger fractions.

Degree of winnowing at Modena and Tempiute can be estimated using Table 5.11's data; lacking surface data for comparison to subsurface data, Byram and colleagues (1999) cannot be used. Amick's (1991) data are from a quarry, and Seddon and colleagues' (2001) are from workshops at some distance from the main quarry, Modena. The datasets can be pooled, which gives greater weight to the larger numbers in Seddon's Panaca Summit assemblages. An alternative takes midpoint value between each source's proportion by size fraction. Taking this approach, Table 5.11 also shows "typical" surface and subsurface proportions, and counts that match those proportions in a hypothetical assemblage of 1,000 flakes. (Even buried assemblages recovered only through excavation once were on the surface, but I assume minimal winnowing before burial, thus treating subsurface proportions as typical of original debris assemblages at their formation.) Of course even large flakes are subject to at least slight winnowing, but for simplicity's sake Table 5.11 assumes no winnowing in the 25.4 mm (1 in) fraction. Because that fraction comprises 0.005 of all flakes in the original subsurface assemblage, the original assemblage must be reduced to 192.3 flakes before the 25.4 mm (1 in) fraction's proportion rises to the figure of 0.026 found in the subsurface assemblage (i.e., 5/192.3 = 0.026). Thus, the original subsurface assemblage is reduced by more than 80% by winnowing. Proportions for other flake-size classes are found by multiplying 192.3 by class proportions in the surface assemblage.

Table 5.11 shows counts across the three size fractions where assemblage n = 192.3. It also shows the proportion of the original assemblage in each fraction that remains in the winnowed surface assemblage ("prop. orig."). Finally, the table shows a multiplication factor by which count by size class in the winnowed assemblage gives count in the original assemblage (found by dividing 1 by the proportion of original assemblage in each fraction). Because this exercise assumed no winnowing in the 25.4 mm (1 in) fraction, of course that fraction's multiplication factor is 1. Using the Amick and Seddon datasets, count of 12.7 mm (½ in) flakes is nearly halved in the winnowed assemblage, while the count of 6.35 mm (¼ in) flakes is reduced by a factor of nearly 7.6.

As suggestive as these figures are, unfortunately they aggregate flakes by size over three classes (6.35 mm, 12.7 mm, and 25.4 mm [¼ in, ½ in, 1 in, respectively])) rather than the four classes of UA's dataset. This has the effect of exaggerating the count and proportion in the 12.7 mm (½ in) class because it incorporates all flakes under 25.4 mm (1 in), including those that would fall in the 19.05 mm (¾ in) fraction. Neither Amick (1991) nor Seddon and colleagues (2001) reported flake count in the 19.05 mm (¾ in) class, so the original four-interval size distributions cannot be recovered. Disaggregating the 12.7 mm (½ in) and 19.05 mm (¾ in) fractions can only be accomplished by estimation. Among nonlinear models available in SPSS, the logarithmic fits flake-size distributions best. (It also provides the best fit for flake-size distribution in UA experimental data.) Subsurface cumulative proportions in the 6.35 mm (¼ in) and 25.4 mm (1 in) fractions were fitted to the logarithmic model (fit statistics are meaningless when n = 2) and cumulative proportions for the 12.7 mm (½ in) and 19.05 mm (¾ in) classes were estimated from the resulting model.

Table 5.11 also shows proportions (calculated from cumulative proportions) in the estimated four-fraction size distribution and corresponding counts in a hypothetical assemblage of n = 1,000. After obtaining these figures, the procedure described above to produce Table 5.11's estimates were repeated. As before, no taphonomic loss was assumed for the 25.4 mm (1 in) class. In this case, however, the difference in the 25.4 mm (1 in) fraction's proportion between surface and estimated subsurface or original assemblage extended from 0.023 to 0.005, not 0.026 to 0.005 as previously used. This difference yields an estimated winnowed assemblage of n = 217.4 (1,000 / (0.023/0.005)). Again, the proportion of the original hypothetical assemblage of 1,000 flakes retained in the winnowed assemblage, this time of 217.4 flakes, was estimated from proportions in the surface

assemblage. Table 5.11 also shows the proportion of the original assemblage retained in the winnowed one by each size class, and the multiplication or conversion factor required to reconstitute the original from the winnowed assemblage taking account of taphonomic bias against smaller flakes.

Table 5.11 shows a similar conversion factor for the 6.35 mm (¼ in) fraction, and a slightly lower one for the 12.7 mm (½ in) fraction using four size classes. Again, of course, the assumption of no winnowing in the 25.4 mm (1 in) fraction yields a conversion factor of 1.0. The 19.05 mm (¾ in) fraction's conversion factor is surprisingly high. These are the factors by which observed count by size fraction in surface assemblages must be multiplied to account for taphonomic winnowing. As discussed in Chapter 4, slope is a key variable by which winnowing acts. Ideally, differences in slope between areas at Modena and between Modena and Tempiute should be taken into account in this procedure, but that is possible only with data acquired for that purpose. Therefore, the same conversion factor was applied to all Modena and Tempiute flake assemblages even though 6.35 mm (¼ in) count proportions at Tempiute are somewhat higher than at Modena, implicating lower winnowing rate. This likely has the effect of slightly overestimating the winnowing rate on steeper slopes and slightly underestimating it on lower ones. Appendix A compiles results.

For comparative size distribution and, when possible, for attribute analysis reported below, taphonomically corrected counts and proportions from Modena and Tempiute are used. Taphonomically corrected cumulative flake-size distributions by size fraction for both sites appear in Table 5.12.

Comparative Attribute Analysis

Comparative analysis of Modena and Tempiute to other flake assemblages and experimental data begins with attributes of individual flakes then continues by studying the properties of flake-size distributions. In both kinds of analysis, the chief objective is to infer the mode(s) of reduction represented in flake assemblages.

TABLE 5.12. Taphonomically corrected Modena and Tempiute Flake-Size Distributions.

	25.4 mm	19.05 mm	12.7 mm	6.35 mm
Modena				
A	1.000	0.9488	0.8364	0.6792
B	1.000	0.9659	0.8682	0.7101
D	1.000	0.9572	0.8639	0.7067
E	1.000	0.9304	0.8050	0.5918
F	1.000	0.9355	0.8015	0.6031
2009-1	1.000	0.9398	0.8180	0.6360
Tempiute				
N1	1.0000	0.9933	0.9413	0.7929
N2	1.0000	0.9903	0.9201	0.7651
N3	1.0000	0.9336	0.8003	0.5998
N4	1.0000	0.9910	0.8934	0.8029
N5	1.0000	0.9819	0.8849	0.7049
N6	1.0000	0.9783	0.8575	0.6626
N7	1.0000	0.9879	0.9517	0.8105
N8	1.0000	0.9382	0.8356	0.5738
N9	1.0000	0.9660	0.8547	0.7051
N10	1.0000	0.9886	0.8986	0.5949

25.4 mm = 1 in; 19.05 mm = ¾ in; 12.7 mm = ½ in; 6.35 mm = ¼ in.

Analysis of flake attributes was conducted only for intact flakes. Analysis that involved flake-size distributions was drawn from actual data, but also in some cases by using estimated original size distributions before the effects of taphonomic winnowing. Methods of estimation were described in Chapter 4 and above in this chapter.

Multivariate Attribute Analysis

As described above, in Magne's (1985; see also Magne and Pokotylo 1981) classic experimental data and attribute analysis weight, overall size, platform and exterior-surface faceting, and cortex cover patterned consistently with degree or stage of reduction. In fact, Magne (1985:128) argued that the two faceting variables sufficed to assign flakes to stages, and his final classification system relied exclusively upon weight and platform facet count: 0–1, 2, and ≥3 facets indicating early, middle, and late reduction stages, respectively (1985:Figure 14). Similarly, Fish (1981:379) identified "primary knapping" with high incidence of platform and exterior cortex.

No matter the breadth and rigor of Magne's analysis, this result seems somewhat rigid; scar count may vary more complexly. Since Magne's experimental work was performed in the 1980s, scar density has been identified as, in some ways, a more valid measure (e.g., Bradbury and Carr 1999; Turner and Bonica 1994).

Elsewhere, Trubitt (2007:75–80) distinguished quarry from workshop debris in archaeological data. Not surprisingly, she found that mean flake weight was higher for quarry flakes and that the distribution of weight skewed more to high size classes at quarries. She also found that 31% of quarry debris by count bore cortex, compared to 5% of workshop debris. Finally, platform-bearing flakes at quarries mostly had 0–1 platform scars, while those at workshops mostly had ≥2 platform scars, which Trubitt (2007:80) assimilated to Magne's (1985:Figure 14) platform-scar reduction sequence.

Magne's model, which parses three reduction stages by number of platform facets, is tempting for its simplicity. However, Bradbury and Carr's (2004:69) analysis of a much more comprehensive experimental dataset showed that platform faceting better predicted stage in core reduction, while exterior faceting better predicted stage in tool production. More generally, Bradbury and Carr (2004:75–76, Table 1) synthesized results to identify ranges of values of several flake attributes by reduction mode that correlate broadly with reduction stage. Table 5.13 is drawn from their results. In these data, the sequence from core reduction to finishing involves steady increase in the percentage of flakes that bear 2+ platform facets and in the percentage of all flakes that fall in the 6.35 mm (¼ in) fraction and steady decline in mean flake weight in the 6.35 mm (¼ in) fraction.

Characterizing Modena and Tempiute assemblages in Bradbury and Carr's terms, most areas show similar values (Table 5.13). The range of those values in the percentage of flakes bearing 2+ platform facets characterizes all Modena assemblages in the edging to thinning modes, Tempiute ones to core reduction or edging. In percentage of flakes in the 6.35 mm (¼ in) fraction, all samples fall mostly in the

TABLE 5.13. Flake Attribute Patterning with Reduction Mode. Source: Bradbury and Carr (2004:Table 1).

Reduction Mode	%2 + facets[a]	Mean wt. (g) 6.35 mm fraction	% Count 6.35 mm fraction
core reduction	1	0.9	60
biface edging	12	0.6	83
biface thinning	26	0.3	95
biface finishing	75	0.3	100
Modena			
A	18	1.3	68
B	22	1.1	71
D	28	1.2	71
E	31	1.7	59
F	25	1.6	61
2009-1	17	1.4	64
Tempiute			
N2	12	1.5	60
N5	6	1.4	58
N6	6	1.7	61

6.35 mm = ¼ in.
[a] Exterior-surface facets.

core-reduction mode, and in mean weight of 6.35 mm (¼ in) flakes they exceed even the highest value among Bradbury and Carr's experimental modes. Thus, if Modena and Tempiute were classified by mean weight and proportion by count of the 6.35 mm (¼ in) fraction, the assemblages would be characteristic of early stage reduction, as seems fitting for quarry assemblages. According to platform faceting, however, Modena and Tempiute would be classified as somewhat later stage assemblages

Completeness Analysis: Modena

Ingbar and colleagues (1989; see also Bradbury and Carr 1999; Goldstein 2018:92, Figure 5; Shott 1996b) used flake-debris data to demonstrate that reduction is better understood as a continuum, not a sequence of discrete stages. In their data, flakes that were ordered by removal from cores varied not so much by stage—all flakes within a given stage being very similar or identical in the variables defining that stage— but by continuous degree. Ingbar and colleagues expressed removal order as a linear or log-linear function of several continuous attributes of

flakes. Bradbury and Carr's model, perhaps best because it alone predicted removal number in absolute, not relative order, expressed reduction number as a function of platform facets, exterior-face facets relative to area, and flake weight. Bradbury and Carr (1999:112) used experimental data to define the following model that expressed a flake's relative position in a reduction continuum:

%complete = (0.0898*platform scars) +
   (0.0713*ln(max. width)) +
   (0.1638*ln(exterior scars/weight))

where %complete is the flake's position in the reduction continuum from 0% (first flake removed) to 100% (last flake removed). Mackay (2004) applied this expression to several nonquarry toolstone debris assemblages; most toolstones were distributed between approximately 50–100% (i.e., the second half) of the reduction continuum. Goldstein (2018:92) also applied the expression to a Kenyan obsidian quarry.

Applied to UA experimental data, Bradbury and Carr's expression gives significant results that pattern as expected, mean values increasing by stage ($F = 71.2$; $p < 0.01$; for all LSD pairs $p < 0.01$; see also Shott 2016:Table 5.45, Figure 5.17). Unlike in Mackay's (2004) data, however, some specimens register negative values for %complete. Fortunately, these are relatively few (41 of 776 = 5.3%), and Bradbury and Carr's (e.g., 1999:Figure 6) own data also yielded some negative values. Rare negative values are nothing more than an artifact of the method or this study's combination of Bradbury and Carr's core-reduction and blank-production stages. The main point is that, in the UA experimental assemblage, %complete patterns consistently by stage but overlaps considerably. Stages 1 and 3 occupy early and advanced positions, respectively, while Stage 2 spans virtually the entire reduction continuum.

Bradbury and Carr (2014) reported a different estimator of percent completeness, designed to increase applicability by accommodating already-existing data. The expression, called "%complete2" here, omits metric data such as flake length, and is expressed as (Bradbury and Carr 2014:27):

%complete2 = (0.08068*((exterior facets +
  platform facets)/size class) +
  (0.058073*(size class/weight))

where size class is standard flake-size classes in cm (2.54, 1.907, 12.7, 6.35 cm) and weight is individual flake weight (g). In UA experimental data, %complete2 by stage patterns as expected, with the mean value rising by stage ($F = 65.1$; $p < 0.01$; for all LSD pairs p < 0.01; Shott 2016:Table 5.45). The overall pattern of results resembles that for %complete although, as in Bradbury and Carr's (2014:Figure 3) own data, %complete2 ranges are somewhat higher, exceeding 1, and lack negative values. Also, there is better separation between Stage 3 and earlier stages in %complete; the range of %complete2 values in Stage 2 completely overlaps and slightly exceeds Stage 3's range.

The two %complete measures are highly correlated ($r = 0.88$; $p < 0.01$), and regression through the origin of %complete2 upon %complete yields a slope coefficient of 1.034, well

within one standard error of 1, signifying unit change. Bradbury and Carr (2014:26) interpreted %complete2's higher range to include resharpening of finished tools, activities not represented in UA experimental data, and unlikely to occur in more than neglible amounts at Modena or Tempiute. Rather than resharpening, the higher upper limit of %complete2 may simply owe to its high lower limit. Because %complete better distinguishes Stage 3 from earlier stages and because UA analysis, like Bradbury and Carr's, troubled itself to measure flakes, %complete is used here in preference to %complete2.

Completeness Analysis by Stage

Modena and Tempiute flakes assigned to Stage 1 have a significantly lower mean value (0.11) than do combined Stages-2/3 flakes (0.39; $t = 31.5$; 1-tailed $p < 0.01$), although ranges overlap extensively. As above, Bradbury and Carr's %complete predictor may exaggerate flakes' actual location in the reduction continuum. Accordingly, Stage-1 flakes may occupy an actual range and hold a somewhat lower mean value, indicating very early reduction processing. Stage-2/3 flakes occupy a higher range that corresponds to early to middle reduction segments of the reduction continuum.

Mean values by area differ somewhat (Figure 5.5; $F = 6.0$, $df = 6$; $p < 0.01$). LSD p values <0.05 distinguish Areas A, B, and D (means of 0.12 and 0.40, 0.14 and 0.39, and 0.09 and 0.45 for Stage 1 and 2/3, respectively) from F and 2009-1 (means of 0.08 and 0.35, and 0.04 and 0.33 for Stage 1 and 2/3, respectively), and Areas E (means of 0.11 and 0.44) and F from 2009-1. Thus, quarry areas A and B differ from quarry area F while workshop Area D resembles A and B and workshop Area E resembles F. Area 2009-1 has a mean value considerably lower, not higher as workshops might be expected to have, than quarry areas A, B, and F, although low sample sizes in Areas E and 2009-1 qualify this observation. Mean %complete values crosscut the quarry-workshop divide at Modena. In general, however, Bradbury and Carr's model suggests that the Modena flake assemblage

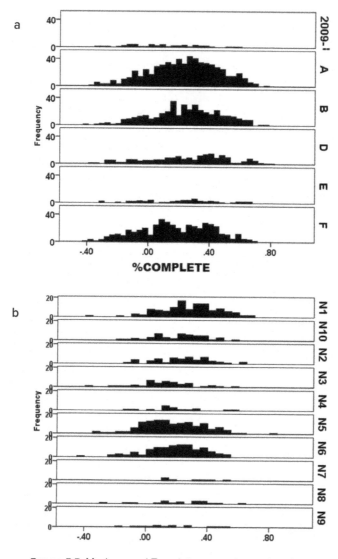

FIGURE 5.5. Modena and Tempiute %complete values by area.

occupies early to intermediate stages of the reduction continuum. In every Modena area, the Stage-1 mean is significantly lower than the mean for Stages 2/3. In this measure as well as others, data pattern consistently with location in the reduction continuum.

Completeness Analysis: Tempiute

As at Modena, %complete range and mean at Tempiute differ by discriminant-function inferred flake stage (Shott 2016:Figure 5.17). Again, flakes assigned to Stage 1 have a signifi-

cantly lower mean value (0.12; Shott 2016:Table 5.45) than do flakes assigned to combined Stages 2/3 (0.33; $t = 15.9$; 1-tailed $p < 0.01$), although ranges overlap extensively.

Mean values by large areas at Tempiute vary slightly ($F = 18.3$; $df = 10$; $p < 0.01$). LSD p values <0.05 distinguish N1 from Areas N2–N6, N12, and S5, which is to say from most other Tempiute areas, Area N2 from N3, N5, N6, and N3 from N6, N7, N8, N10, and S5. Only Areas N1, N5, and N6 have fairly large sample sizes. A more robust analysis confined to these areas still shows significant differences ($F = 10.5$; $df = 2$; $p < 0.01$), but LSD $p < 0.05$ only between N1 (means of 0.17 and 0.40 for Stages 1 and 2/3, respectively), N5 (means of 0.11 and 0.35 for Stages 1 and 2/3, respectively), and N6 (means of 0.12 and 0.29 for Stages 1 and 2/3, respectively); the latter two are not different. Area N1 has a significantly higher mean %complete value, indicating somewhat more advanced reduction there.

As at Modena, for every major Tempiute area mean %complete values differ between stage assignments of 1 and 2/3 resulting from discriminant analysis. Again in every case, the Stage-1 mean is significantly lower than the mean for Stages 2/3. In both assemblages, therefore, %complete values pattern with discriminant-analysis results.

Completeness Analysis:
Comparing Modena and Tempiute

Finally, Modena and Tempiute flake assemblages can be compared for their %complete values. The value of such comparison is questionable when original cobble size almost certainly and flaking quality possibly differed between the sources. Nevertheless, for comparison, the sites show remarkably similar distributions in form and range (but not in frequency; Shott 2016:Figure 5.22). Mean values do not differ significantly ($t = 0.4$; $df = 1,254.3$; $p = 0.35$). As aggregate assemblages, Modena and Tempiute do not differ in %complete estimates.

Predictor Equations

Carr and Bradbury (2001) examined patterning in several measures of flake-size distribution or mean flake attributes of mixed flake assemblages from core reduction, biface production, and uniface production, a good example of use of both mass and attribute analysis. For instance, they demonstrated a strong inverse correlation between the proportional contribution of biface reduction to a mixed assemblage and the proportion of flakes with no platform facets, and an equally strong positive correlation between the proportion of biface reduction and the proportion of flakes bearing 0 or 1 exterior facets (2001:Figures 8.1 and 8.2, respectively).

Such clear patterning encourages the expectation that mixed flake assemblages can be apportioned among the reduction modes that comprise them.

Overall, Carr and Bradbury's best predictor of the proportion of biface reduction in a mixed flake assemblage was found as a function of several measures of flake-assemblage composition. Their expression (2001:137; a significant flaw in the published version—omission of the last component's coefficient of 1.245—was corrected by A. Bradbury [personal communication 15 Jan. 2020]) is:

%biface-production = (1.431*%6.35 mm count)
　+ (1.438*%2-exterior-scar flakes) −
　(0.447*%6.35 mm weight) −
　(1.245*%0-platform-scar flakes) − 0.393.

Carr and Bradbury (2001:138) derived a similar prediction equation for the proportion of core reduction present in a mixed assemblage, as follows:

%corereduction = (2.275*%0-
　1-exterior-scar flakes) +
　(0.329*%6.35 mm weight) −
　(1.558*%6.35 mm count) −
　(1.427*%2-exterior-scar flakes) − 0.214.

UA's coding scheme includes the variables that form these equations. Accordingly, Bradbury and Carr's percentage-estimates of biface production and core reduction can be calculated for study sites. Table 5.14 shows estimates for Modena assemblages. Taphonomically corrected flake-size distributions were used for this analysis, whose results suggest that biface reduction is considerably more common than is core reduction. Also, although the two prediction equations are independent and do not necessarily produce complementary estimates, for most assemblages the percentages are nearly complementary, usually summing to between 93% and 99%. (Sums significantly exceed 100% for Areas B and 2009-1.) Considering the three reduction modes of Bradbury and Carr's study, it is unlikely that uniface production accounts for much flake debris, so this estimation method suggests, not surprisngly, that core reduction

TABLE 5.14. Modena Estimated %Core
and %Biface Production. Source:
Carr and Bradbury (2001:137).

Area	% Core	% Biface
A	17.8	77.9
B	17.1	96.0
D	26.2	73.6
E	46.3	46.3
F	23.4	71.4
2009-1	71.0	70.5

%Biface figures in this table corrected
Feb. 2020 per A. Bradbury's report of
typo in published equation.

and biface production account for most flake debris in Modena assemblages.

Besides their bivariate analyses described above, Byram and others (1999:137) used a variant of multiple linear regression to predict reduction stage from debris-assemblage compositional and dimensional data. Their expression was:

Stage = 6.048 – (0.124*G2%count) – (0.023*G2 mean weight[dg]) – (0.091*G3 mean weight[dg]).

For Modena, the input values for the equation's variables well exceeded values from their experimental data reported by Byram and colleagues (1999:Table 10.4). As a result, solving this prediction equation using Modena archaeological data yielded negative values. These results are meaningless, since no debris assemblage can represent, for instance, Stage 2. For what it is worth, inserting g for dg in Byram and others' equation produced interpretable results, assemblages from all Modena areas returning values in the range of 2.0–2.5, meaning early to intermediate Stage 2. Either the range and pattern of Modena data do not resemble Byram and colleagues' experimental data, or differences in scaling of the predictor equation complicate comparison.

Altogether, Modena archaeological data do not pattern as do Byram and others' experimental data. Either the technological processes that generated Modena debris assemblages differed

significantly from those used in Byram and colleagues' experiments or there are differences in scaling or measurement between the datasets. Even Modena data corrected for taphonomic winnowing do not conform to Byram and colleagues' patterns, being much heavier even in the fairly narrowly constrained 6.35 mm (¼ in) and 12.7 mm (½ in) fractions.

Discriminant Analysis

Ahler (1986) pioneered the use of discriminant analysis to distinguish the flake debris assemblages generated by different technological modes. Discrimination occurred on the basis of variables like count or weight ratios between size fractions and count or weight proportions by size fractions. One product of discriminant analysis is classification functions by which empirical flake-size distributions may be assigned to one or another technological mode by particular coefficients applied to variables like those listed above. Neither Ahler nor Root (e.g., 1992) reported coefficients of the resulting classification functions, so their results cannot be used to classify Modena or Tempiute assemblages.

Fortunately, Ingbar and colleagues (1992: Table 5) reported such classification functions based on Ahler's experimental dataset supplemented by their own replications of several Tosawihi chert reduction modes. Their discriminating variables included mean weight of flakes in the G3 (6.35 mm [¼ in]) fraction, weight proportion of the G3 fraction, count proportion of the G0 (50.8 mm [2 in]) fraction, count proportion in the G2 (12.7 mm [½ in]) fraction, weight in the G1 (25.4 mm [1 in]) fraction divided by weight in the G3 fraction, and count in the G1 fraction divided by count in the G3 fraction. Discriminant analysis produces separate classification functions for each technological mode studied, which range from core reduction to edging and early and late thinning in Ingbar and colleagues' data. Classification proceeds by calculating an empirical assemblage's result for each function, assigning each to the highest result. Analysis was conducted upon taphonomically corrected size distributions from major areas at Modena and Tempiute. Quarry assemblages like Areas A, B, and F at Modena and perhaps Tempiute clusters should classify as Ingbar and others' core-reduction technological mode, or perhaps edging. Workshop assemblages like Modena's D, E, and 2009-1 might classify as edging or thinning technological modes.

Yet most Modena and Tempiute assemblages classify to Ingbar and colleagues' early-thinning mode, Modena 2009-1 to core reduction. By comparison, UA experimental data subdivided into Stages 1 and 2/3 as separate discriminant-analysis reported pattern consistently. UA Stage 1 classifies into Ingbar and others' core reduction, Stages 2/3 into a later stage, early thinning. On balance, Ingbar and colleagues' classification functions suggest variability among debris assemblages, falling into only two of their four reduction modes.

Root's analysis was similar to Ingbar and colleagues' and involved many of the same experimental datasets. Root (1992:23) considered discriminant and classification results to be better for later-stage reduction modes than for earlier ones like core reduction and edging. Certainly his earlier technological modes had similar means on most classification functions (1992:Table 6.12), suggesting that discriminant analysis did not distinguish them as clearly and unambiguously as it did later reduction modes. Also, classification results for the core-reduction and early-thinning modes often are very similar, while results for the edging mode are slightly lower (Shott 2016:Table 5.51). Only late thinning yields classification scores that are substantially lower. For assemblages dominated by earlier reduction modes, classification scores might be expected to be highest for those modes and correspondingly lower for later modes. Conversely, for assemblages dominated by later modes, classification scores for those modes should resemble one another and considerably exceed scores for earlier modes. Instead, core reduction and the early thinning usually return the highest scores. That is, Ingbar and colleagues' classifications produce similar values for three technological modes that range from core reduction

to early thinning, and variation in magnitude of classification scores does not pattern clearly with reduction mode.

Summary

This section compared Modena and Tempiute flake data to prior studies that sought to characterize assemblages by measures, mostly means and proportions, drawn from individual flake attributes. Yet complex, time-averaged assemblages and the complex patterns of attribute variation and covariation that reside in them may not be characterized adequately using only bivariate methods. When three or more attributes were included in analysis, often involving count or weight proportions (especially in the 6.35 mm [¼ in] fraction), results located most Modena and Tempiute assemblages in early and, to a lesser extent, middle segments of the reduction continuum. Thus, results were broadly concordant across methods, experimental datasets, and details of analysis. The conclusion lends confidence to each method separately, which may be further tested in other quarry assemblages, and to inferences about the Modena and Tempiute assemblages drawn from their application collectively.

Comparative Analysis of Flake-Size Distributions

To this point, comparative analysis has involved individual flake attributes. Yet comparative analysis is also useful for examining flake-size distributions and the mass analysis methods developed to characterize them. Mass analysis can be applied to entire flake assemblages or on subsets defined by attributes like cortex presence/absence or platform or exterior-surface facet intervals. Permutations of such data are many; here, analysis is confined to entire flake assemblages for comparison to experimental datasets. Although Root's (1992) experimental data were subdivided by cortex presence/absence, Stahle and Dunn's (1982, 1984) data were analyzed as complete assemblages. Besides narrow comparability, the validity of mass-analysis of subdivided assemblages is unclear. The size distributions of, for instance, cortical and non-cortical flakes should differ by virtue of that technological attribute. That is, the key distinction in the analysis of aggregate assemblages undertaken here is by reduction mode or segment of the reduction continuum, not by subdivision of flake assemblages by technological attributes. Accordingly, no subdivision of the assemblages was attempted in analysis.

Weibull Plots

In their study of experimental data that partly guided the approach to analysis here, Stahle and Dunn (1984:10–12) fitted their cumulative counts and proportions to three mathematical models: Weibull, exponential, and extreme value. (The exponential is a special case of the Weibull distribution where the Weibull shape parameter $\beta = 1$ [Stahle and Dunn 1984:11].) They argued that these distributions may be suitable to model the allocation of fragments of brittle solids like obsidian to size classes, reasoning that they "graduate the fraction of fractured samples as a function of increasing stress" (1984:11). Although all three models fit Stahle and Dunn's data in their test of linearized versions of each model, the Weibull performed best (1984:Table 6). They showed plots of linearized Weibull functions, $\ln(-\ln(1-c_i))$ where $c_i =$ cumulative proportion at each flake-size class, by stage against ln of each size class— 0.3175 mm, was their smallest size class (1982:Figure 2; 1984: Figure 3). Stahle and Dunn's data and analysis thus provide statistical and theoretical warrant for use of the Weibull expression to model flake-size distributions by count and weight. Shott (1997a:Figure 6) previously used linearized Weibull plots to compare Stahle and Dunn experimental data to archaeological flake assemblages from a residential site.

At Tosawihi, Ingbar and colleagues (1992: 63–65) fitted both their experimental controls and selected archaeological flake samples to Stahle and Dunn's Weibull model. They too produced regression plots of linearized Weibull functions across flake-size classes. Ingbar and colleagues did not, however, report the exact figures used in their Weibull plots. This means that approximation of their successive reduction modes from mass reduction to edging, to early and then late thinning, had to be approximated by eye and ruler from their (1992) Figure 30a. The approximation qualifies comparison of Ingbar and colleagues' results to Stahle and Dunn's or other data. Broadly, Stahle and Dunn's Stages 1–4 may approximate a similar reduction sequence of successively more advanced segments to Ingbar and colleagues' mass reduction, edging, and early and late thinning.

Figure 5.6 plots Stahle and Dunn's experimental data. Because UA data are truncated at the 6.35 mm (¼ in) size class, the figure's abscissas are of $\ln(d-1/4)$. Stahle and Dunn's regression-fit statistics are very high (for all stages, $r^2 \geq 0.98$; $p < 0.01$) so are not reported in detail; the Weibull model fits these data very well. Stahle and Dunn's Stages 1–4 span a somewhat wider range on the plot, but correspond to Ingbar and colleagues' data (i.e., Ingbar et al.'s linearized plots all fall within the range of Stahle and Dunn's plots), in sequence (i.e., each successive reduction mode in both experimental datasets to the left of the preceding one), and in slope. Although scaled somewhat differently, they also closely resemble the pattern found in Ingbar and others' Figure 30a. Thus, Stahle and Dunn's and Ingbar and colleagues' separate datasets pattern similarly in Weibull plots, and both datasets serve as models for Modena and Tempiute.

Modena and Tempiute regression-fit statistics are as high as Stahle and Dunn's so again are not reported. Figure 5.6 plots Modena and Tempiute, respectively, against Stahle and Dunn Stages 1–4. Modena areas show similar slopes (Area F's slightly steeper than others') to Stahle and Dunn data, particularly their Stages 1–2, but fall in a relatively narrow band to the right of all Stahle and Dunn stages, including their Stage 1. Accordingly, placement of linearized Weibull lines for all Modena areas suggests even earlier reduction than Stahle and Dunn's Stage 1. By itself, this conclusion is not surprising since, as noted above, Stahle and Dunn's data lacked the earliest cobble-testing model for their experiments. But the linearized Weibull plot for

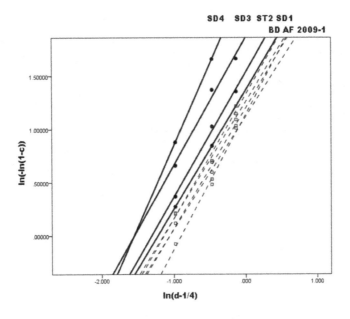

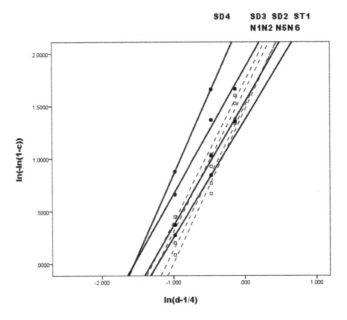

FIGURE 5.6. Comparative linearized Weibull plots of Stahle and Dunn (SD) stages 1–4. Comparison to Modena (top) and selected Tempiute (bottom) areas.

Ingbar and others' mass-reduction mode intersects Stahle and Dunn's Stage-1 plot, so it too is somewhat more advanced compared to Modena plots. Major areas at Tempiute are slightly nearer Stahle and Dunn plots in slope and placement, falling mostly in the range of the latter's Stages 1–2. Interestingly, the Tempiute pattern is fairly similar to the linearized Weibull plots of residential-site flake assemblages that Shott (1997a:Figure 6) reported.

Like Modena samples compared to Stahle
and Dunn's dataset, Ingbar and others' own archaeological samples fell below (i.e., to the right
of) even their earliest mass-reduction mode
(1992:Figure 31a). They believed that this pattern arose because their mass-reduction mode
included the reduction of flake blanks, not just
cobbles (1992:64); if so, then Ingbar and others'
mass-reduction mode actually may be more
similar to Stahle and Dunn's biface-reduction
Stage 1, which also started from flake blanks and
which may not be an entirely accurate model
for quarry assemblages. In that case, at least the
Modena samples' results suggest that they represent earlier or less advanced reduction than
either Stahle and Dunn's or Ingbar and others'
earliest mode, although Tempiute samples
match those datasets' earliest modes fairly well.

Evidence from Modena's Area B supports
this inference. Plotted against Stahle and Dunn's
Stages 1 and 4 limiting distributions and Root's
cobble-testing distributions, the slope and location of Modena B's plot are similar to Stahle
and Dunn's Stage 1 but also overlap with Root's
cobble-testing distribution (Shott 2016:Figure
5.26d). Tempiute plots also seem similar to
both, especially Root's cobble-testing mode. On
linearized Weibull plots, accordingly, study assemblages more nearly resemble Root's cobble-
testing mode than Stahle and Dunn's Stage 1.
Whatever the explanation, linearized Weibull
plots of study assemblages place them in comparative context to experimental datasets of
known reduction modes. Broadly, all represent
early reduction segments or modes.

Mass Analysis
of Mixed Assemblages

Preceding analysis takes no account of the complex mixing of reduction modes that probably
characterized the Modena and Tempiute assemblages. Instead, it treated each assemblage as a
unitary aggregate. As noted previously, archaeological flake assemblages like Modena's and
Tempiute's probably accumulated over considerable time spans. Therefore, they are likely to
be the mixed result of many different episodes
and modes of reduction. Mixing by reduction

mode is a reality that analysis must confront.
As argued above, the mixing problem besets all
approaches, not just mass analysis. Accordingly,
discriminant analysis of Modena and Tempiute
assemblages suggested varying combinations
of flakes identified as Stage 1 versus Stage 2/3,
and some attribute analysis suggested that assemblages were somewhat varying mixtures of
core-reduction and biface-production modes.
That is, various analyses to this point indicates
the probability of mixing of reduction modes or
stages in assemblages. This section addresses the
mixing problem in size-distribution analysis.

Before undertaking mass analysis of archaeological assemblages, which, as stated, are very
likely to be mixed in surface deposits at Modena
and Tempiute, experimental data described
above were used to evaluate two alternative approaches, derived from two of the experimental
sources. Experimental data being controlled,
mixtures of various reduction modes in various
proportions are easily created on paper or computer, although toolstone difference may complicate results. These experimental mixtures can
be used as inputs to test the ability of analytical
methods to parse them among their constituent reduction modes. The first method tested
is Root's multiple linear regression (MLR) approach. The second is a variant of Stahle and
Dunn's constrained least-squares regression
(CLSR). Each is described before analysis of
experimental and archaeological data.

MLR

Root (1992:216–217; 1997) used MLR to parse
mixed debris assemblages into their constituent
reduction modes. (Kohler and Blinman [1987]
used the same method to partition mixed sherd
assemblages in producing a ceramic seriation.
Shott [1997a] applied Root's approach to an
archaeological debris assemblage from Iowa.)
Root's original modes, replicated in Knife River
Flint from North Dakota, included cobble testing, unprepared and prepared core reduction,
biface edging, and skilled and expert biface
thinning. He also included data on bipolar reduction and flake-tool production. These data
were used selectively and sometimes by aggre-

gating modes that Root separated, as described above. Here, analysis is confined to four successive modes from start to end of the reduction process: cobble testing, core reduction to produce flake blanks, biface edging, and biface thinning.

Root (1992:Tables 6.1–6.2, 1997:Table 4) presented and analyzed data by both count and weight. As above, I used only count data. In analysis, I also combined Root's cortical and noncortical counts and proportions. Root sorted flakes through four size classes ("size-grades"): G1 (≥25.4 mm, or 1 in), G2 (< 25.4 mm and ≥12.5 mm, approximately 0.49 in), G3 (<12.5 mm and ≥ 5.60 mm, approximately 0.22 in) and G4 (<5.60 mm and ≥2.54 mm or 0.1 in). However, only Root's G1 matches the size classes common in many other experiments, like Stahle and Dunn's and UA's replications, which used fractions of inches (25.4 mm or 1.0 in; 12.7 mm or ½ in; 6.35 mm or ¼ in; 3.175 mm or ⅛ in). The difference is negligible at the second size interval of 12.5 or 12.7 mm, but greater and arguably more significant at smaller classes. These differences are acknowledged but ignored in analysis.

Root's MLR method regressed ordinary (i.e., not cumulative) counts by size class upon "calibration sets" (1992:232) composed of proportions of flakes by count and by size class from experimental reduction modes. I recalculated Root's (1992:Table 6.15) original data to produce calibration sets for the recombined modes described above (Shott 2016:Table 5.53). The y-, or predicted, variable was counted in the mixed experimental or archaeological sample, while the x-, or predictor, variables were proportions in the calibration sets for each experimental reduction mode (i.e., counts are regressed upon proportions). Resulting partial slope coefficients estimated the proportion of each x-variable that contributed to the unknown, mixed y-variable. Given the regression model (Root 1992:239), that is, each x-variable's partial slope coefficient measured mean change in y with unit change in that x, holding constant other x-variables.

Analysis closely followed Root (1992:238–43; see also Kohler and Blinman 1988:17) in all relevant respects. Regression used stepwise entry, and was forced through the origin. When a first solution included negative partial slope coefficients, analysis was repeated after omitting the corresponding x-variable; the iterative process was repeated until all partial-slope values were nonnegative. When two or more x-variables were collinear after iteration, each was omitted separately and analysis repeated once more. The result producing the smallest sum-of-squares regression was used.

CLSR

The second analytical approach follows Stahle and Dunn's CLSR method, applied originally to their experimental dataset described above. Stahle and Dunn justified the preferential use of count or frequency data, so analysis proceeded on counts only. CLSR analyzes cumulative distributions—individual size fraction probabilities summed from 6.35 mm (¼ in) through 25.4 mm (1 in) fractions—not the individual fraction probabilities of MLR. Thus, cumulative probabilities are constrained so as to sum to 1.0, and the method parses any mixture by comparison to the cumulative distribution function (cdf) of the known experimental stages. That is, cdf's of Stahle and Dunn's (1984: Tables 4a–d) separate Stages 1–4 were treated as known or control standards to which mixtures were allocated (Shott 2016:Table 5.54). Using this approach, Stahle and Dunn (1982:Table 1) reported fair success in partitioning of mixtures to their true constituent modes and characteristic proportions.

Stahle and Dunn (1984:39–40) used a CLSR program written for SAS. Dr. Desale Habtzghi of the University of Akron's Department of Statistics wrote a revised CLSR code implemented in R's (R Core Team 2013) *quadprog* package, used here and in summaries of the UA LCAI project (Shott and Habtzghi 2016, 2019). That code was applied to Stahle and Dunn's (1982:Table 1) own hypothetical assemblage mixtures and to a second set of our own devising that involved higher counts in the early Stahle and Dunn reduction stages that probably dominated Modena and Tempiute.

A complementary approach uses the same *quadprog* program but replaces Stahle and Dunn's control standards with the cdf's of UA's three experimental stages described above. That is, UA experimental data for each stage were treated as control standards (Shott 2016:Table 5.54). This approach required modifying *quadprog* to accept only three control standards but otherwise was identical to CLSR analysis using Stahle and Dunn data.

Results of MLR/CSLR Analysis

Both approaches were used first to allocate "pure" or single reduction-mode experimental data, then several combinations of all or parts of experimental reduction modes designed to replicate the mixing that occurs in archaeological deposits. Success was gauged both by identification of known reduction modes and, in the case of hypothetical mixtures, by reasonably accurate proportional allocation.

MLR: Original, Unmixed Experimental Assemblages

Because Root's (1992) data included the 3.175 mm (⅛ in) size class omitted here, values for that class in UA's experimental dataset were estimated by regression. Considering first the size distributions that include the 3.175 mm (⅛ in) fraction, assignments by stage in all datasets sequence correctly, meaning, successively later stages never are classified into earlier reduction modes. In addition, all or nearly all flakes in each experimental stage are assigned to a single Root stage. In other words, the percentage of flakes classified to a mode approaches or reaches 100 (Shott 2016:Table 5.55). Stahle and Dunn Stages 1–2 are assigned to core reduction, Stage 3 to edging, and Stage 4 to thinning. UA Stage 1 is assigned to cobble testing, Stages 2–3 both to thinning. Excluding the 3.175 mm (⅛ in) fraction, again the percentage of flakes classified to a mode approaches or reaches 100. Stahle and Dunn's data now resolve Root's reduction sequence less well, their Stages 1–2 both assigned to core reduction, Stages 3–4 both to thinning. Results for UA data are more satisfactory in general, assigning successive Stages 1–3 of a partial

reduction sequence to cobble testing, core-reduction, and edging modes, respectively.

MLR: Mixed Experimental Assemblages

Permutations of experimental-mode combinations are infinite. A limited set of combinations keeps analysis manageable (Shott 2016:Table 5.56). No theory guided this selection, merely the desire to create a range of combinations. Because archaeological data are from obsidian quarries, for which it is reasonable to assume substantial early reduction, all combinations included the earlier stage or segment of each experimental source. Some involved the entirety of two or more original modes. However, as mixed archaeological assemblages might be expected to include fractions of various reduction modes, other combinations involved Stage 1 and halves or quarters of one or more later segments.

Shott (2016:Table 5.57) reported in detail the results of analysis of mixed datasets, including the 3.175 mm (⅛ in) size class. Again, percentage of flakes classified approaches or reaches 100 in most cases. For Stahle and Dunn's data, the mixture of Stage 1 (to core-reduction) and one-half of Stage 4 (to thinning) produces the expected assignments to Root's modes in approximately the expected percentages. However, mixtures of Stage 1 and various fractions of Stages 3–4 yield unexpected results. When Stage-3–4 flakes comprise more than half of the mixture, one result assigns the mixture solely to Root's cobble testing, which should not include many later-stage flakes, another exclusively to Root's edging and thinning modes. Somewhere between a mixture of 46.5% and 30.3% of Stage-1 flakes the signal for early-stage reduction disappears from Stahle and Dunn's data. The simple mixture of Stahle and Dunn's Stages 1 and 4 assigns the assemblage roughly equally to Root's edging and thinning modes. This is consistent with the result obtained in the mixture of Stage 1 with one-quarter each of Stages 3 and 4, because both yield edging and thinning assignments and the proportional weight of the assignments favors the thinning mode as more of later stages comprise the mixture. Unfortunately, the final Stahle and Dunn mixture, which contains the lowest percentage of Stage-1 flakes, classifies mostly to the early core-reduction mode.

All UA mixtures are assigned to single Root modes. The mixture with the largest percentage of Stage-1 flakes, 1+(½ 3) is assigned to Root's latest reduction mode, thinning. The mixture of Stage-1 and one-quarter each of Stage 2 and 3 flakes contains a lower percentage of Stage-1 yet classifies entirely to the early Root mode of core reduction. Otherwise, most UA mixtures are assigned to Root's thinning mode. Results for both datasets seem equivocal. Stahle and Dunn results seem more reliable, because most of them span and resolve Root's reduction range better. Also, the percentage of Stage-1 flakes in Stahle and Dunn results covers both a wider range and a more intermediate position than does UA data.

In analysis of mixed datasets that exclude the 3.175 mm (⅛ in) size class, again percentage of flakes classified approaches or reaches 100 in most cases. Generally, many mixtures are assigned to more than one original Root mode (Shott 2016:Table 5.58). For Stahle and Dunn's dataset, the mixture of Stage 1 and one-half of Stage 4 yields a reasonable assignment to Root's intermediate edging mode, but does not accurately identify the assemblage as a mixture. The more complex mixture of Stage 1 and one-quarter each of Stages 3–4 does in fact assign the mixture to three Root modes, although they were predominantly assigned to thinning. Root's edging mode emerges in mixtures of progressively lower percentages of Stage-1 flakes, but an early Root stage, core reduction, reemerges at the lowest Stage-1 percentage. This mixture, of Stages 1, 3, and 4, is the sole Stahle and Dunn combination that yields similar results in analysis regardless of the inclusion or exclusion of the 3.175 mm (⅛ in) fraction. Otherwise, results differ considerably between the two flake-size datasets.

For UA's dataset, results differ considerably from those involving the 3.175 mm (⅛ in) fraction. Whereas in the earlier analysis most UA mixtures were assigned to Root's thinning mode, now almost all fall in Root's core-

reduction mode, and the only other Root mode represented is the earliest, cobble testing. UA experimental data represent only early and intermediate segments of the reduction continuum (again, only to Callahan Stage 3); results seem more faithful to this dataset's nature. Yet with percentages of Stage-1 ranging from 12.6–49.6, almost all assignments are to core-reduction, so UA data seem relatively insensitive to degree or complexity of mixture.

CLSR: Mixed Experimental Assemblages

To expedite testing, analysis omitted the 3.175 mm (⅛ in) size class. Again, input data were cdf's while outputs were proportions of flake assemblages assigned to Stahle and Dunn's Stages 1–4, each of which sum to 1. There is no point to estimating each stage's unmixed proportions because it perfectly matches its own known standard. Therefore, for Stahle and Dunn's Stages 1–4 separately, the result always assigns the entire sample to its corresponding stage. Instead, only experimental mixtures are fitted to known standards.

Clearly, analysis of experimental mixtures of Stahle and Dunn's own data closely match actual stage proportions (Shott 2016:Table 5.59). Following Stahle and Dunn (1982:93) the error or distance measure d,

$$d = \sqrt{\Sigma(P_i \text{est} - P_i \text{obs})^2}$$

where $P_i$est is proportion estimated and $P_i$obs is proportion observed for Stage i over i = 1–4 stages, gauges the fit of allocated to observed stage proportions. Like Stahle and Dunn, median value of d is reported. With one slight exception, proportions across stages sum to 1.0 using Stahle and Dunn's known standards. Proportions consistently exceed 1.0 by 1–7% (i.e., 1.01–1.07) using UA known standards, a sufficiently small excess to ignore.

Mixtures from Stahle and Dunn's own experimental data closely match estimated proportions (d = 0.0025; Shott 2016:Table 5.59). However, mixtures from UA experimental data do not fit nearly as well (d = 0.6530). All UA mixtures include substantial proportions of Stage 1, yet $P_i$est only once attains a very small

TABLE 5.15. CLSR Results for UA Mixed Experimental Data Using Stahle and Dunn (upper) and UA (lower) Known Standards. Because Stahle and Dunn's *quadprog* estimates four stages, and UA's *quadprog* three stages, there is no Stage-4 estimate using UA known standards.

Stage Mix	Observed %			Estimated %				
	St1	St2	St3	St1	St2	St3	St4	d
1	1.000	0.000	0.000	1.000	0.000	0.000	0.000	0.0000
2	0.000	1.000	0.000	1.000	0.000	0.000	0.000	1.4142
3	0.000	0.000	1.000	0.467	0.110	0.000	0.423	0.7504
1+3	0.358	0.000	0.642	1.000	0.000	0.000	0.000	0.9083
1+2+3	0.124	0.654	0.222	1.000	0.000	0.000	0.000	1.1161
1+ (1/2 3)	0.527	0.000	0.473	1.000	0.000	0.000	0.000	0.6691
1+(1/4 2)+(1/4 3)	0.361	0.477	0.162	1.000	0.000	0.000	0.000	0.8141
1+(1/2 2)+(1/2 3)	0.220	0.582	0.198	1.000	0.000	0.000	0.000	0.9933

Stage Mix	Observed %			Estimated %				
	St1	St2	St3	St1	St2	St3	St4	d
1	1.000	0.000	0.000					
2	0.000	1.000	0.000					
3	0.000	0.000	1.000					
1+3	0.358	0.000	0.642	0.358	0.000	0.642	–	0.0004
1+2+3	0.124	0.654	0.222	0.102	0.683	0.215	–	0.0365
1+ (1/2 3)	0.527	0.000	0.473	0.526	0.002	0.472	–	0.0025
1+(1/4 2)+(1/4 3)	0.361	0.477	0.162	0.352	0.484	0.165	–	0.0113
1+(1/2 2)+(1/2 3)	0.220	0.582	0.198	0.202	0.603	0.195	–	0.0275

nonzero value. Thus, UA's Stage 1 is poorly estimated by Stahle and Dunn's known standards probably because, as noted above and by Stahle and Dunn themselves (1984:9), their Stage 1 omits the very earliest parts of their reduction episodes. Conversely, mixtures from UA's own data closely match proportions estimated using UA known standards (*d* = 0.0113), but neither unmixed UA known standards or mixtures of them closely match proportions estimated using Stahle and Dunn's known standards (*d* = 0.8612; Table 5.15). For instance, using Stahle and Dunn's standards *quadprog* assigns UA unmixed Stage 3 to Stahle and Dunn's Stages 1, 2, and 4. All mixtures of UA data are assigned entirely to Stahle and Dunn's Stage 1.

Using similar *quadprog* programs to estimate stage proportions, Stahle and Dunn's and UA datasets and methods do not produce similar results. Lacking agreement or convergence upon known stage proportions, analysis of Modena and Tempiute data therefore require comparison to both programs and known standards, followed by careful comparison of results.

Experimental Mixture Analysis: Summary
In general, results of analysis of original unmixed and then mixed assemblages of flakes from other experimental datasets vary with factors like the range of flake-size data used, the complexity of hypothetical mixtures, and the percentage of Stage-1 flakes in those mixtures. Root's MLR method has some tendency to overestimate, that is it assigns nearly 100% of flakes to particular Root modes, and assigns

even mixed assemblages to single modes. Results are not consistent between analyses that either include or exclude the 3.175 mm (⅛ in) flake-size class, nor do they pattern consistently toward later Root stages as the percentage of Stage-1 flakes declines. The *quadprog* approach to CLSR estimation yields generally better results, but clearly the separate Stahle and Dunn and UA known-standard datasets performed much better on their own respective experimental mixtures.

On balance, MLR results are equivocal. In the aggregate, they do not lend great confidence to this analytical method. For unmixed assemblages, results are fairly good in general. In mixed assemblages, results are less consistent. With reservations, analysis of empirical data accordingly is confined to size distributions truncated at the 6.35 mm (¼ in) fraction and mindful of the method's tendency both to overestimate assignment and to sometimes assign mixed assemblages to single Root modes. CLSR results are more encouraging on the whole and merit application to Modena and Tempiute.

As noted above, the likelihood that most empirical archaeological flake assemblages are the mixed results of many different reduction episodes is a major obstacle to the acceptance of mass-analytical methods. Also as discussed above, mixing of a different nature is a problem for other approaches to flake analysis, not somehow a particular shortcoming of one method. Yet the MLR and especially CLSR approaches may be able to apportion such mixed assemblages to their constituent reduction modes, to judge from encouraging but imperfect test results. Mixing of empirical assemblages may become less of an obstacle to analysis as its untangling becomes a goal of analysis.

MLR Analysis of Modena and Tempiute Assemblages

Using Root's calibration set, the original, uncorrected size distribution for the combined Modena assemblage, and for Areas A, B, and 2009-1 separately, all enter only cobble testing in the solution, and account for 85% or more of flakes (Shott 2016:Table 5.61). (Cluster E was omitted for its relatively small assemblage size.) MLR could find no solution for original size distributions for other Modena clusters or major Tempiute ones.

Not surprisingly, size distributions corrected for taphonomic winnowing produced different results. For corrected data, nearly 100% of flakes are assigned. Most Modena assemblages then classified to biface edging, Areas D and E to core reduction. Edging, the third of Root's four successive reduction stages, seems at face value a questionable result for empirical Modena assemblages that probably represent earlier reduction. All major Tempiute clusters are identified with cobble testing, the earliest of Root's modes and therefore a plausible result. Again, all MLR solutions assign assemblages to single reduction modes even though the method is designed to parse mixed assemblages into more than one constituent mode. Unfortunately, then, a method designed to apportion empirical assemblages among two or more reduction modes gives results that assign the entirety of each sample to a single mode only. At face value, MLR applied to Modena and Tempiute suggests no mixing of assemblages, a questionable result.

Although Root (1992) used only his own calibration sets, the method also was applied to Modena and Tempiute by replacing Root's with Stahle and Dunn's (1984:Table 4a–d) data. In this case, the method could resolve no original size distributions. Again, MLR assigned taphonomically corrected Modena data mostly to intermediate or later reduction modes (Shott 2016:Table 5.62), while Tempiute areas remained assigned to the earliest reduction stage. However, the method's failure to resolve any original size distributions raises the question of how well Stahle and Dunn's four successive stages of biface reduction fit archaeological data.

Although Root's and Stahle and Dunn's calibration sets differed somewhat in technology, results are quite similar. Neither calibration set apportioned any Modena or Tempiute assemblage to more than one reduction mode. Mixing seems likely for surface assemblages that accumulated as the result of repeated episodes

TABLE 5.16. MLR Results for Modena and Tempiute Assemblages Using Root's Calibration Set.

Area	N	Original		Counts	
		mode(s)	mode N	%N	%ΣN
All Modena	3,708	cobtest	3,160.4	85.2	85.2
A	1,285	cobtest	1,113.5	86.7	86.7
B	784	cobtest	701.2	89.4	89.4
D	421	no result	—	—	—
F	981	no result	—	—	—
2009-1	115	cobtest	97.9	85.1	85.1
Tempiute N2	173	no result	—	—	—
Tempiute N5	234	no result	—	—	—
Tempiute N6	187	no result	—	—	—
		Corrected		Counts	
All Modena	16,120	edging	15,563.3	96.6	96.6
A	5,707	edging	5,564.5	97.5	97.5
B	3,614	edging	3,572.2	98.8	98.8
D	1,782	core	1,771.9	99.4	99.4
F	4,056	core	3,985.4	98.3	98.3
2009-1	499	edging	481.0	96.4	96.4
Tempiute N2	604	cobtest	619.0	>100	>100
Tempiute N5	763	cobtest	757.2	99.24	99.24
Tempiute N6	638	cobtest	648.0	>100	>100

of quarrying over long periods. Instead, and recalling the MLR method's tendency not to resolve some mixed experimental assemblages into their constituents, this result may be an artifact of the method. Despite this shortcoming, results are consistent between the two calibration sets in the sense that assignments are correlated in all but one case. That is, corrected size distributions assigned to Root's edging stage were assigned to Stahle and Dunn's Stage 3, both of which are the third of four successive modes; those assigned to Root's core reduction were assigned to Stahle and Dunn's Stage 2, both the second of the four modes; and those assigned to Root's cobble testing were assigned to Stahle and Dunn's Stage 1, both obviously the first mode (Table 5.16; Shott 2016:236, Tables 5.61–5.62). Only Modena's 2009-1 produced uncorrelated results, Root's (third-stage) edging versus Stahle and Dunn's Stage 2. Results largely match expected correspondences. Whatever the

MLR method's limitations, at least results are generally consistent between calibration sets.

CLSR Analysis of Modena and Tempiute Assemblages

CLSR analysis was conducted only on taphonomically corrected size distributions. Results are more variable and therefore more satisfactory than are MLR results (Table 5.17). *Quadprog* using Stahle and Dunn's known standards, however, performed poorly for Modena assemblages. Like MLR methods and dataset standards, *quadprog* assigned the entirety of each Modena assemblage to Stahle and Dunn's Stage 1. To this extent, CLSR results resemble MLR results in that they fail to apportion presumably mixed empirical assemblages to more than one reduction mode. However, there is considerable variation in stage assignment for Tempiute assemblages. (The largest assemblages there, N2, N5, and N6, are listed first among Tempiute assemblage for ease of comparison with Modena ones.) As expected, Stahle and Dunn's Stages 3–4 are not well represented in most Tempiute assemblages, as befits quarries where earlier reduction segments should predominate.

Using Root's and especially UA known standards, *quadprog* results are variable, unlike results using Stahle and Dunn standards. As when applied to experimental mixtures, the sum of proportions can slightly exceed 1—by, for instance, 1.2% (i.e., a proportion of 1.012) for Area E—which again is ignored in interpretation. Also, because the cdf for Root's edging and finishing modes were very similar, the resulting collinearity prevented *quadprog* from reaching solutions for all samples. This problem was solved by simply removing Root's most advanced, thinning, mode which, anyway, should be poorly represented in quarry debris assemblages.

Using Root's standards, all Modena areas have high cobble-testing proportions. Using Stahle and Dunn standards, all Modena assemblages classify entirely to cobble testing. For most Modena assemblages, 40% or more of flakes are assigned to UA Stage 1. Root's edging mode and UA Stage 3 are very poorly represented in Modena assemblages, no surprise considering the quarry context of those archaeological samples. There is more variation in UA Stage 2 than in Root's core-reduction assignments, some of which is surprising. Areas A, B, and F are the main quarry deposits where presumably raw cobbles were acquired and initially worked. Using Root's standards, Area B has a slightly larger core-reduction proportion than does Area D. Using UA standards, Area A's Stage-1 assignment is fairly high and Area F's is very high, yet Area B is assigned mostly to Stage 2. These assignments are somewhat surprising, at least for Area B, considering the context of Areas A, B, and F as primary quarry areas. What is more, Areas D, E, and 2009-1, which might be interpreted as workshops dominated possibly by somewhat later reduction segments than are Areas A, B, and F, do not pattern differently. Using Root's standards, Areas E and 2009-1 are

entirely assigned to the first mode, cobble testing, as is Area E to UA Stage 1. Overall the range of variation in Stage 1–2 assignments between the triads A-B-F and D-E-2009-1 nearly overlap. Differences between "outcrop quarries" and "workshops" do not emerge from CLSR analysis any more than they did in other analyses reported above.

As discussed in Chapter 4, Tempiute areas are not as obviously distinguishable by context or prehistoric behavior as, for instance, outcrop quarries versus workshops. Instead, Tempiute probably is a single, very complex palimpsest deposit from which subdivisions emerged post facto as the result of erosion. For all three sets of standards, considerable variation is found among Tempiute assemblages. For Stahle and Dunn's standards, however, again highest proportions by far are assigned to Stage 1. Root's and UA standards produce results roughly evenly distributed across all three modes represented. Like Modena, relatively small portions of most Tempiute assemblages are assigned to Stage 3 using both Root's and UA standards, but proportional assignment to that stage is quite high in several cases. Those two standards produce roughly similar overall results.

Because input data for CLSR analysis was taphonomically corrected, and because that correction was accomplished by rescaling all original assemblages to corrected assemblages of 1,000 flakes, all results reported in Table 5.17 are from assemblages of theoretically equal size. Accordingly, for each site, a simple average of assigned proportions across stages gives an overall mean characterization for the site. Results also appear in Table 5.17. Using Stahle and Dunn's known standards, a strong skew toward Stage 1 is evident at Modena, again to the exclusion of successive stages. But Root's and UA known standards preserve a strong representation for Stage 1 while estimating much greater variation between assemblages and sites. Root's and UA known standards provide more variable results by far than do Stahle and Dunn standards.

CLSR analysis of Modena and Tempiute assemblages is consistent with the expectation

TABLE 5.17. CLSR Assigned Proportions for Modena and Tempiute Assemblages Using Root, Stahle and Dunn, and UA Standards.

Site	Sample	Root				Stahle & Dunn			UA		
		Cobble Test	Core Red'n	Edging	St. 1	St. 2	St. 3	St. 4	St. 1	St. 2	St. 3
Modena	A	0.948	0.062	0.000	1.000	0.000	0.000	0.000	0.425	0.580	0.000
Modena	B	0.729	0.282	0.000	1.000	0.000	0.000	0.000	0.102	0.901	0.000
Modena	D	0.747	0.262	0.000	1.000	0.000	0.000	0.000	0.196	0.750	0.056
Modena	E	1.000	0.000	0.000	1.000	0.000	0.000	0.000	1.012	0.000	0.000
Modena	F	1.000	0.000	0.000	1.000	0.000	0.000	0.000	0.973	0.040	0.000
Modena	2009-1	1.000	0.000	0.000	1.000	0.000	0.000	0.000	0.732	0.277	0.000
Modena	All	0.904	0.101	0.000	1.000	0.000	0.000	0.000	0.573	0.425	0.009
Tempiute	N2	0.000	0.710	0.293	0.629	0.297	0.082	0.000	0.000	0.551	0.459
Tempiute	N5	0.237	0.769	0.000	1.000	0.000	0.000	0.000	0.023	0.982	0.000
Tempiute	N6	0.445	0.563	0.000	1.000	0.000	0.000	0.000	0.358	0.653	0.000
Tempiute	N1	0.000	0.303	0.701	0.315	0.405	0.285	0.000	0.000	0.263	0.747
Tempiute	N3	0.895	0.000	0.105	1.000	0.000	0.000	0.000	0.997	0.015	0.000
Tempiute	N4	0.000	0.000	1.016	0.710	0.000	0.000	0.290	0.152	0.000	0.853
Tempiute	N7	0.000	0.081	0.920	0.241	0.291	0.470	0.000	0.000	0.061	0.946
Tempiute	N8	1.000	0.000	0.000	1.000	0.000	0.000	0.000	0.952	0.063	0.000
Tempiute	N9	0.297	0.000	0.000	1.000	0.000	0.000	0.000	0.188	0.816	0.000
Tempiute	N10	1.017	0.000	0.000	1.000	0.000	0.000	0.000	0.477	0.542	0.000
Tempiute	All	0.389	0.243	0.304	0.790	0.099	0.084	0.029	0.315	0.395	0.301

and high probability of extensive mixing. It documents a method for untangling the mixed assemblages that are common in archaeological context, in the process improving inferences by estimating both kind and amount of various reduction modes that may be present.

Quadprog using UA known standards can be applied to other sources. For instance, Panaca Summit subsurface data (Seddon et al. 2001) described above presumably represent later stages of reduction, as somewhat different analysis of them in Chapter 7 also suggests. Converted to their cdf, the aggregate of Panaca Summit excavated assemblages yielded no proportion assigned to Root's cobble-testing or core-reduction modes or to UA Stages 1–2. Rather, they fell entirely (with proportions of 1.005 and 1.009) within Root's edging and UA Stage 3, respectively. This result is strongly complementary to Modena data, and suggests that early segments of reduction modes were carried out at Modena proper, while successively later ones were performed at workshops to which Modena blanks and preforms were imported. Elsewhere, Beardsall (2013:Table 6) reported excavated flake-size distribution for his Unit 3 at a Manitoba quartz quarry presumably similar to Modena in overall technological characteristics. Converted to a cdf using UA size fractions, this assemblage yielded an estimated Root proportion of 1.0 for cobble testing and UA Stage-1 proportion of 0.508 and a Stage-2 proportion of 0.499, the latter broadly similar to overall Modena results. Beardsall's Unit 11 sample returned a proportion of 1.0 for both Root's cobble testing and UA Stage 1. As at Modena and Tempiute, there is variation in CLSR stage assignment among quarry samples, and the magnitude and location (i.e., at earlier stages) of that variation resembles Modena and Tempiute.

There are good reasons to place greater confidence in UA and, arguably, Root's experimental data as known standards:

1. Root's and Stahle and Dunn's standards in MLR and Stahle and Dunn's standards in CLSR analysis tended to make assignments mostly or entirely to single stages compared to the greater variability found in UA estimates. Empirical deposits that accumulated as the result of perhaps thousands of visits to Modena and Tempiute over millennia are unlikely to yield relatively pure composition by reduction mode. At face value, then, the greater variability of Root and UA CLSR results are one point in their joint favor.

2. Root's and UA standards not only produced somewhat similar results but patterned in more continuous terms than either did with estimated proportions using Stahle and Dunn's standards.

3. *Quadprog* using Root's and UA known standards returned results when applied to Panaca Summit data that suggested predominantly later-stage reduction modes than represented at the Modena quarry itself; UA standards perceived differences in Beardsall's quarry assemblages that escaped Root's standards.

4. Results of CLSR and earlier discriminant analysis were fairly similar for Modena using UA known standards, less so using Root's standards. Discriminant analysis reported above assigned 1,642 flakes (65.3%) to Stage 1, 873 (34.7%) to Stages 2/3. These percentages are fairly similar to the overall Modena proportions by UA stage in Table 5.17.

5. Only UA's experimental dataset is composed of obsidian and thereby most closely matches the mechanical properties of Modena and Tempiute assemblages.

6. A final reason to prefer CLSR analytical results using UA and perhaps Root's standards involves complementary patterning in different variables and datasets. For instance, mean flake-scar density at major Modena clusters patterns clearly with proportions of UA Stage-1 flakes (Figure 5.7) even if attained significance does not reach the conventional threshold value owing to very small sample size ($r = -0.90$; $p = 0.10$). Complementary patterning also is evident between flake and preform datasets, as presented in Chapter 6.

Mixing of reduction modes almost surely is a property of most archaeological flake assemblages (Steffen et al. 1998:141). But rather than

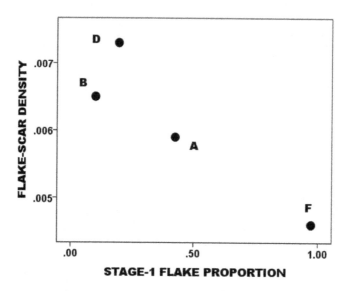

FIGURE 5.7. Flake-scar density versus proportion of UA Stage-1 flakes at four Modena areas.

an obstacle to interpretation, it emerges as a legitimate goal of analysis that assumes its existence and is designed to estimate its nature and magnitude. Emphasizing the likely mixed origin of empirical flake assemblages is a salutary reminder of the nature of archaeological deposits. It is not, however, a counsel of despair invalidating mass analysis or any method that might estimate it rather than assume it represents an insurmountable obstacle to analysis or to pretend that it does not exist. This method is not confined to the current study. Quarries of other toolstones used for other purposes might, of course, have different reduction modes and complex mixtures among them. Their study may require experimental data comparable to each reduction mode and its range. In those situations, CLSR via *quadprog* can be used to disentangle the sites' mixtures as well. Neither is the method confined to quarries. On the contrary, its fullest use will be in joint application to quarry and various habitation assemblages.

Concluding Remarks on Flake Analysis

Analysis of Modena and Tempiute assemblages involved separate attribute and mass analyses. Yet those approaches are complementary in several respects. In attribute analysis of flake

dimensions, on average Modena exceeded Tempiute values in both stages defined by discriminant analysis; Modena flakes were larger in general, a coarse correlate of earlier reduction. (Tempiute's higher incidence of cortex can be explained by the smaller size of cobbles there.) Completeness analysis based on attributes also suggested that reduction at Modena lay earlier on the continuum than most Tempiute samples, as generally did the several predictor equations based upon attributes and/or flake-size distribution. According to Weibull analysis, Modena assemblages also included less advanced segments of the reduction continuum than did Tempiute ones.

MLR and particularly CLSR analysis associated Modena with earlier reduction segments than they did Tempiute. Finally, attribute-based discriminant analysis and aggregate-based CLSR analysis produced broadly similar proportions by reduction stage in Modena assemblages. Anderson and Hodgetts (2007:237) reached similar conclusions in their study of residential sites that involved later reduction stages. Indeed, that study and others cited above are complementary in the sense that they suggest later reduction stages at sites removed from quarry toolstone sources. In Weibull

(Shott 2016:Figure 5.26b) plots, Modena assemblages fall in the same order as they do in CLSR using UA known standards (Table 5.17). That is, the higher the proportion of an assemblage that CLSR assigns to UA Stage 1, the lower its Weibull slope. In this way, patterns evident in Weibull analysis of entire flake assemblages can be explained by CLSR's parsing of those assemblages into distinct reduction modes.

Whatever the merits of technological schemes for flake analysis, attribute analysis and mass analysis were used in this study. Results reported in this chapter, both separately and in comparison, documented their complementarity, lending confidence to the validity and efficacy of the approaches. Attribute and mass analysis have the further virtue that, unlike technological classification, they consider the entirety of flake assemblages and do not place half or more of specimens in "miscellaneous" categories that go unanalyzed.

6

Bifaces

For every million of spear and arrow points, knives, perforators,
and scrapers—and there were many millions used…there are somewhere
in America many times as many millions of broken and malformed failures…
and where are they now but in these quarries and shops?
(Holmes 1892:296).

Flake debris is the great majority of the assemblage at Modena and Tempiute. In most cases, however, flakes were merely by-products, not end products, of the reduction of obsidian cobbles. Flakes were struck mostly in the process of making tools. Besides flakes, Modena in particular contains a substantial assemblage of bifaces. UA research was designed partly to test the Field Processing Model of the pattern and degree of biface reduction at quarries. To that extent, despite the overwhelming numerical preponderance of flake debris, quarry bifaces were equally as important to the accomplishment of project goals.

Bifaces are chipped stone tools that are worked, at least to some extent, on two opposing faces separated by retouched edges. The category "biface" includes both the finished tools, points of various types, and unfinished specimens that span a range of reduction from slightly modified flake blanks to nearly finished tools. In usage that traces back to Muto (1971: 109), a "blank" is an unmodified object, usually a flake, of size and form suitable for producing a tool. A "preform" is a blank that has undergone partial modification toward a finished form. As Crabtree put it, a blank is any piece of stone that can be reduced to a tool such that "the shape or form of the final product is not disclosed in the blank" (1972:42) save in the broadest terms. A preform "is an unfinished, unused form of the proposed artifact. It is larger than, and without the refinement of, the completed tool…thick, with deep bulbar scars, has irregular edges, and no means of hafting" (1972:85). These definitions are somewhat at odds with Thomas's (1983:213–214) terminology. However common his term "roughout" may have been in the literature at the time, it has not persisted as well as "blank" and "preform" have. Thomas also described blanks and preforms as successive stages of reduction. Thus, his approach omits the category "blank" as used here and subdivides the category "preform" into three apparently successive stages (roughout, blank, preform) defined in subjective terms.

Modena and Tempiute yielded surprisingly few finished points. Instead, most bifaces found were production-stage preforms, as initial reconnaissance before UA fieldwork began revealed. This chapter describes the Modena and Tempiute preform and point assemblages, and the coding schemes used to characterize them. Because preforms are much more abundant, it then compares preform assemblages to other, chiefly obsidian, preform assemblages from the Great Basin and selected assemblages elsewhere. Using preforms, the chapter evaluates the popular assumption that reduction is a series of discrete stages. It accomplishes this in part by testing common approaches to preform description and analysis, in particular Callahan's (1979;

see also Newcomer 1971:85–89) stage model of Clovis biface reduction, against continuous models (Shott 2017).

Approaches to Preform Analysis: Stages and Continua

Stone tools are made to desired sizes and forms. Stone being a reductive medium, anyone who wishes to make a tool of a particular size starts with a cobble or blank that is larger and works it down from there. Raw cobbles rarely are thin for their plan area, and flake blanks may only approximate their intended form. To reach tools' desired sizes and forms, the lithic reduction process involves a series of carefully controlled flake removals that disproportionately diminish thickness relative to length and width as it also, in the case of bifaces, creates two opposing faces that converge on first crudely and then finely sinuous edges.

The progress, therefore, from raw cobble or blank to finished product involves simultaneous or successive reduction, thinning, edge-formation, and overall refinement. The study of preform assemblages can reveal details of the production process beginning with blanks and concluding with finished tools, thereby tracing "the evolution of the biface from a raw-material blank to a refined finished product" (Andrefsky 1998:180). Because that process can vary in length, degree, and complexity of modification, preforms can be assigned to progressive degrees or successive stages of the process. Undeniably, then, lithic reduction is a process; arguably, it may have occurred by successive discrete stages. If stages exist, analysis can reveal them, but it should not assume their existence from the start.

Reconstructing reduction sequences—the patterned ways that cores were reduced to tools—is a common goal of lithic analysis. Following Holmes (1894a), who originated the concept, many archaeologists today view reduction as a sequence of essentially discrete stages. Ironically, Holmes himself regarded stages more as descriptive conveniences than empirical states. To him, stages merely revealed the processes of technological evolution (Shott 2003). Against the view of stages as real, discrete entities is the

possibility that reduction is continuous, at least in some respects. The stage concept assumes that stages are valid and replicable, that they are, in other words, defined by legitimate patterns of association between variables, categorical and continuous, and that all archaeologists who contemplate the same specimens would define the same number of stages that possessed the same characteristics and would agree on the stage assignment of each specimen.

Callahan's (1979) Paleoindian reduction sequence is legitimately celebrated both for its great detail and the beauty of its tool drawings. Yet even before Callahan's influential study, Muto could speak of the "blank-preform-product" (1971:109) continuum. Even though he defined and constructed stages, Callahan also described reduction as a continuum (1979:2). As elsewhere, the stage view has deep roots in the Great Basin. Discrete reduction stages may exist, but they must be demonstrated, not assumed.

Callahan's stages were defined by metric and categorical properties of preforms themselves, not the debris struck from them. He reported weight and the basic dimensions of length, width, and thickness of preforms by reduction stages. As in flake debris, Miller and Smallwood (2012) argued that reduction of bifaces can be viewed as a continuum. Thus, the validity of the stage concept also can be tested against Callahan's preform data (Bloomer et al. 1992: 82; Shott 2017). Although he defined from six to nine stages, Callahan reported data only for specimens in Stages 1–4, reasonable since subsequent stages differed little in size from "Stage 4" preforms and more in the details of fluting and haft modification. As stated above, Callahan's Stage 1 is the flake blank. Therefore, the question of stages in biface reduction largely involves Callahan Stages 2–4.

In Callahan's scheme (1979:Table 10), followed fairly closely by Andrefsky (1998:180–181) and Dillian (2002:221–224), Stage 1 is the blank (whether flake or cobble) and Stage 2 is the interval in which initial edging creates the object's perimeter and, broadly, its plan form. In Stage 3, the preform is thinned across most or all of both faces, moderate convex surfaces are formed on both faces and edge sinuosity is reduced, all in the of process removing areas of disproportionate thickness. At this stage failure is fairly common, either by transverse fracture, plunging (*outré passé*) terminations, or abandonment (e.g., remnant crowns defined by step fractures that failed to terminate normally and therefore failed to remove excess thickness). Stage 4 involves secondary thinning, yielding preforms with relatively flat faces, regular cross sections, and moderately sinuous edges. Later stages involve final haft modifications.

In the Mountain West, Sharrock's (1966:43–44, Figures 23–34) scheme for classification and description of mostly quartzite preforms from southwestern Wyoming sites is the most notable and apposite early source. Pedrick's (1985:9–10) system is similar although she recognized a "continuum of activity" (1985:9) in reduction. Other schemes largely followed Sharrock's and then Callahan's lead (e.g., Beck and Jones 2009a:Table 5.22; Beck et al. 2002; Bloomer et al. 1992; Byram et al. 1999:132–133; Cole 2012:430; Dames and Moore 1994:21–35, 21–69; Elston and Juell 1987:29; Estes 2009:63–64; Gilreath and Hildebrandt 1997:34–37; Greubel 2005:235; Hamusek et al. 1997:84–90; Hauer 2005:92–94; Seddon et al. 2001:27; Stoner et al. 2002:88–92; Womack 1977:27–48). Even Dahlstrom and Bieling's (1991:69–70) "morpho-functional" forms, designed in response to perceived deficiencies of stage approaches, essentially reproduced Callahan's (1979) early preform stages.

Shott (2016:Table 6.1; see also Shott 2017) summarized biface-reduction schemes and preform stages drawn from major studies that include Sharrock (1966), Callahan (1979), Pendleton (1979), Andrefsky (1998), and others. (Pendleton's scheme includes both her Great Basin Concave Base series and Stemmed sequences [1979:78–130].) Although there is broad agreement between all schemes and fairly close agreement in some particulars between specific pairs, clearly these heuristic models are not entirely compatible, nor do they present the same set of measures. Some schemes report dimensions by stage and may employ width/thickness ratios, while others report no size dimensions

at all. Some emphasize cross section or scar patterns, while others ignore these attributes. Where it concerns flaking, some schemes refer to amount, others to pattern, still others to whether primary thinning flakes reach midlines or not. Even where specific measures like width/thickness are used, schemes disagree. Andrefsky and Sharrock, for instance, used substantially different width/thickness ratios by stage. Even when following Callahan closely, Sanders (1983: 83,99,111) reported mean length, width, and thickness values for preforms by stage yet did not match Callahan's values for the same stages. In labeling, Beck and colleagues numbered their stages from 0 starting with the blank, while others counted the blank as "Stage 1." Clearly, there is considerable difference in which metric or discrete attributes are important and, in the former's case, what values of them are important. Many agree that there are stages to preform reduction, but they apparently do not agree on the defining criteria of stages nor even, in some cases, on how many stages there are.

What we conclude about the nature and details of reduction processes for biface production depends in part on what we observe about the products of those processes. Any coding scheme that uses only categorical data is apt to regard reduction as a categorical process of passage through discrete stages. Therefore, evaluation of the stage and continuous views of reduction requires coding schemes that are faithful to both possibilities, and that measure relevant variation in ways that allow the data to reveal the processes that formed them.

UA Coding Scheme

Biface preforms were coded for a range of technological and metric attributes (Shott 2016: Table 6.2). Following Beck and others (2002: 494), preforms were assigned to Callahan Stages 0–3 (not the 1–4 common in most sources). For some analytical purposes, preforms were grouped by pairs of Callahan stages (0 and 1 vs. 2 and 3). Although this approach resembles Callahan's system, it does not duplicate it and not only because of the difference in numbering of stages. Callahan's (1979:54–67, Table 10)

Stage 1 clearly refers to unmodified flake blanks. Beck and colleagues' Stage 0 clearly describes modified preforms, albeit minimally formed and thinned, so therefore does not include unmodified blanks. Thus, a strict equivalence of Beck and colleagues' Stage 0 is Callahan's Stage 2, while Beck and colleagues' Stages 0–3 correspond to Callahan's Stages 2–5. (A rougher equivalence is used below.) In Callahan's own view (1979:Table 10), the key technological stages were 2 through 4, so the corresponding Beck and colleagues' stages are 0 through 2.

Assignment of preforms to Callahan's stages may "reflect reduction stage unambiguously" (Elston 1992c:791) or may not (Johnson 1993:159; Miller and Smallwood 2012:31; to Gilreath and Hildebrandt "the distinction between Stage 1 bifaces and bifacial cores is admittedly often arbitrary" [1997:35]). To some degree "stage" is an abstraction of a complex continuous reduction process (Byram et al. 1999:121; Dillian 2002:224; Miller and Smallwood 2012; Muto 1971; Shott 1996b; see also Bloomer et al. 1992:88–90, who even subdivided Callahan Preform Stages 2–4 into early, middle, and late). Yet the detail found in the original source (Callahan 1979) and similarity in keys used (e.g., Beck et al. 2002:494; Cole 2012:Table 11.7; Hauer 2005:92–94) justify the assumption of some consistency in assignment between sources (see also Thomas 1983:422 on this point). UA classification followed Beck and others (2002:494).

Unlike Bloomer and others (1992:86), UA research involved no coding for blank type as, for instance, flake blank versus cobble blank. Preforms having curved longitudinal sections almost certainly were made from flake blanks, but the origin of most preforms is difficult if not impossible to know. Thick preforms of irregular sections could be from cobble blanks but also could be from large flake blanks reduced crudely. Very few of the demonstrably flake-blank preforms and finished tools fairly common in Bonneville basin GBS assemblages (e.g., Arkush and Pitblado 2000:27, Figure 14) occurred at Modena or Tempiute.

For similar consistency in labeling, Callahan-stage assignments were renumbered to follow Beck and colleagues (2002), which means that other sources' Stages 1, 2, 3…were renumbered to 0, 1, 2…. At Gatecliff Shelter, nearly 20% of early-stage preforms and 35% of later-stage ones apparently bore microscopic use-wear evidence (Rowan and Thomas 1982:328). It is no surprise that some preforms might be used as circumstances required, but Modena and Tempiute preforms are analyzed here for evidence of the reduction process, not use as tools.

Discovery mode records how the preform was found. Preforms found within defined areas were listed by area. Many preforms were found outside those areas, so have no entry for that variable. As in most preform assemblages (e.g., Whittaker and Kaldahl 2001:Figure 4.9), most specimens were broken. In flakes, proximal sections are those that retain the platform, while distal sections retain the termination edge. In bifaces like preforms, these distinctions are not so easily made. Broken preforms were identified as proximal if they obviously were from the base of the emerging tool, but also if the fragment's configuration was not clearly distal—bearing a pointed or near-pointed tip. "Proximal" therefore is a default judgment in some cases, whereas specimens were identified as distal only when they clearly bore tips. Medial fragments are midsections that lack both base and tip and therefore have two fracture planes. Some preforms were fractured normal to their longitudinal axis, so may retain base and tip but lack one edge. Any amount of cortex was coded as present. Cross section was observable on virtually all preforms, whether broken or intact. It was coded by geometric form (diamond, triangular, lenticular, plano-convex). Longitudinal section was observable on many preforms but broken ones, especially if small, could not be coded for this variable.

All chipped-stone bifaces bear edges that are sinuous. Stage preforms vary in sinuosity in roughly inverse proportion to the number and size, especially bulb thickness or depth, of the marginal flakes struck from their developing edges. Thus, edges formed by relatively few, large flakes whose bulbs "bit" deeply into the surfaces exhibit few, broad, often irregular, sinuous curves. In contrast, edges formed by relatively many small flakes whose shallow bulbs did not bite deeply into the surface exhibit more, shorter, more regularly spaced, sinuous curves. Edge sinuosity of stage preforms was gauged on a three-point scale taken from McLaren and Smith (2008). Sinuosity should vary from broader to finer as reduction advances (Gilreath and Hildebrandt 1997:34–35).

Most broken preforms bore compression snap or bending fractures caused by "general bending forces applied across a tool axis" (Ahler 1992:44) and the planes formed distinct, relatively sharp edges at the intersection of both faces. Such fractures were coded by orientation, as transverse (Johnson's [1979:25] "lateral snaps") or oblique to the preform's longitudinal axis (e.g., Whittaker and Kaldahl 2001:Figure 4.6). Some preforms bore hinge fractures (Ahler 1992:43; Johnson 1979:25) that feathered onto one surface, plunging (*outré passé*) fractures not uncommon in brittle material like obsidian (Ahler 1992:43; Johnson's [1979:25] "reverse fractures") occasioned by a thinning flake struck from one edge traversing the specimen's width and removing part of the opposing edge, or unrecognizable other fractures. Certain preforms' original flake-blank interior surface was not entirely modified and therefore was observable; this was coded as 1 for the variable "unmodified interior surface." Otherwise, preforms were coded as 0 for this variable.

Continuous-scale metric attributes include maximum length, width, and thickness. Some preforms retained all or part of the flake-blank platform on their interior surfaces. Where present, platform dimensions and angle were also coded. When platforms were present, their location along the preform's (not necessarily the flake blank's) edge was noted, although the bifacially modified and fragmented condition of some specimens precluded this determination. Weight is measured in grams, angle in degrees; all other metric attributes are in millimeters. Interval-scale variables include number of complete sinuous curves per edge, usually from two to five. Scar count was recorded on both faces, including scars only ≥5 mm in length originating on existing edges along with remnant scars no matter their length that no longer extend to the edge of the preform in its final modified condition. Where both faces were so extensively modified as to preclude identification of the flake blank's interior and exterior surfaces, those surfaces were identified arbitrarily.

The Johnson Thinning Index (JTI), a preform-reduction measure devised in earlier quarry studies (Johnson 1981:13), was also calculated for each specimen. Johnson defined JTI as the ratio of weight to plan area:

JTI (gm/cm^2) = weight / plan area

for each preform. Amick (1991:54–60) used the JTI to examine patterns and trajectories of biface-preform reduction at the 26NY4892 obsidian quarry on the Nevada Test Site. JTI declines in value as reduction advances, because weight is removed at a faster rate than plan area in the allometric process of thinning biface preforms to completion. Johnson (1981:18) estimated plan area by a fairly laborious method that involved a two-dimensional scan of each specimen over which he superimposed a polar-coordinate template centered on the preform's longitudinal axis. Polar coordinates of each vector where it intersected the preform's margin were used to determine vector length, which in turn was used to estimate area. Beck and colleagues (2002:495) used two-dimensional scans of each preform, but measured area by overlaying an orthogonal two-dimensional grid graduated in 5 mm increments on the scanned images.

Like Beck and colleagues, I estimated JTI (Johnson 1981:13), but calculated it from area measured differently. The method, following Douglass and colleagues (2008:518, where the expression is marred by a copyediting error) and Thomsen (2004), models preforms as general ellipsoids whose surface areas are given from their main dimensions as:

Surface Area = $[(a^p b^p + a^p c^p + b^p c^p)/3]^{1/p}$

where $p = \ln(3)/\ln(2)$, and a, b, and c are length, width, and thickness, respectively. In Thomsen (2004) the expression above is multiplied by 2π or 4π (both coefficients are given in separate equations that otherwise are identical) to account for the three-dimensional surface area of ellipsoids. Because Johnson used two-dimensional surface area, I omitted these coefficients. As expected, in all datasets analyzed resulting values correlated strongly with a crude measure of plan area obtained as length multiplied by width. Yet the Thomsen measure always was substantially less than the length-width product (because the plan area of irregular ellipsoids like preforms is significantly overestimated by the rectangular plan that this simple product assumes), and the slope of the least-squares regression line of Thomsen upon length × width was <1 (e.g., in Modena data $r =$ 0.98; $p < 0.01$; Thomsen mean = 4.54; length-width product mean = 7.54; regression slope coefficient = 0.63). (See Cadieux [2013:61] for a roughly similar difference in surface area of flakes measured precisely from scans compared to the same length-width product used here.) Weight also correlated very strongly with the Thomsen measure (Shott 2016:Figure 6.4b). When weight was divided by the Thomsen estimate, resulting JTI values scaled similarly to values that J. Johnson (1981:Figure 2.6) reported.

Finally, bifaces were coded for Miller and Smallwood's (2012:Figure 3.2) Flaking Index (FI). This measure was calculated as the number of ≥2 mm flake scars per edge divided by edge length in millimeters. As Miller and Smallwood showed, FI patterns inversely with degree of reduction.

Callahan Stage Typology

When defined by combinations of categorical and continuous variables, Callahan's stages may well be valid. But their distinctiveness and internal integrity in continuous variables is undemonstrated. Mean dimension and weight values by stage certainly differ (Shott 2016:Table 6.4, 2017:Table 2), no surprise since stages were defined partly by size as measured by continuous variables. But differences in mean dimensions grouped by stages that covary with size seem more an artifact of analysis than a property of stages themselves.

If reduction stages are valid, then bifaces should differ among themselves as groups, while specimens within a stage should not. This proposition is easily tested in Callahan's data. Stages were subdivided into two equal or approximately equal halves by weight. (Substages of Callahan's Stages 1 [n = 4 in first substage, n = 5 in second] and 3 [n = 10 in first substage, n = 8 in second because of tied cases at the boundary value between substages] were slightly unequal.) Of course, weight differed between substages which, like the larger stages, arbitrarily divide a continuum of variation. However, width differed significantly between each stage's substages, length in all cases except Stage 1, and thickness in Stage 3. As with "types" of height, metric differences *within* Callahan's stages were as great as those *between* them. Similarly, Sanders found "varying degrees of Stage IV reduction" of preforms (1983:111) at the Adams quarry/workshop, suggesting considerable variation within this "stage."

Consider a view of size variation in Callahan's preforms by stage that does not assume sequential variation. Principal-components analysis using length, width, thickness, and weight yielded a single significant component that explained 74% of variance in the data. The component (PC1) clearly is a measure of size because all variables loaded highly on it. Among stages, weight always correlated most strongly with component score, width usually being second; length and thickness yielded weaker correlations and were not always significant. (Preform width-thickness ratio, a shape measure that Callahan considered important in distinguishing stages, correlated with the component only in Stages 3 and 4, suggesting that shape and size covary best at advanced reduction stages.) This seems reasonable on technological grounds because reduction begins with cores that naturally vary a good deal, continues with flake blanks that vary considerably, and culminates in finished tools that, owing to size, technological, and functional constraints, vary less. Weight is perhaps the best summary measure of size among original variables, which further demonstrates that the component measures size because weight is a summary size measure.

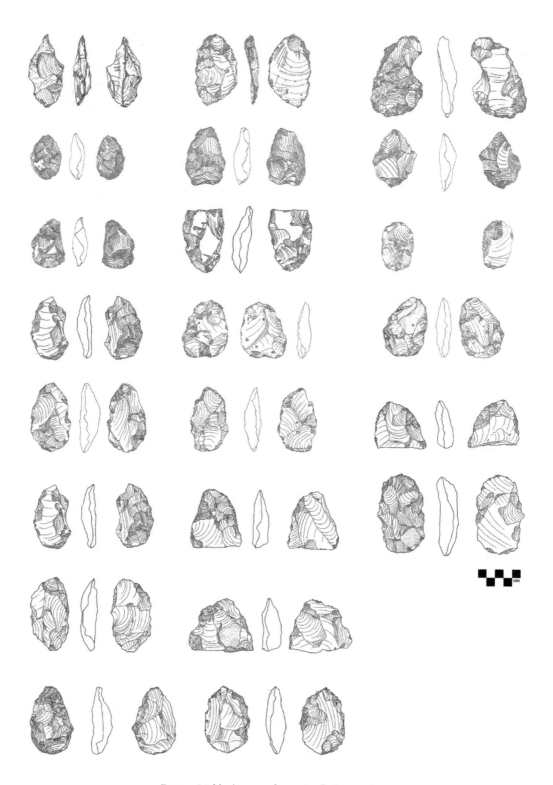

FIGURE 6.1. Modena preforms by Callahan stage.

Mean component scores by Callahan stage are about equally spaced, each separated from its stage neighbors by values of about 0.60.

Shott (2017:Figure 4) plotted weight against PC1 for Callahan specimens. Of course the variables are highly correlated, because weight contributed greatly to the component's definition. The plot's importance is to demonstrate first the continuous relationship between the variables and the considerable overlap in range between specimens of different defined "stages." Size, measured either by weight or the principal component, varies continuously, not by discrete stages. Stages do not separate in the plot. A very similar pattern emerged in analysis of a different, mostly Paleoindian, sample of preforms (Shott 2017). Stages lack integrity because each overlaps considerably with the one(s) preceding and following it. For instance, some "Stage 1" specimens have lower values on both variables (i.e., are smaller) than many "Stage 2" and even some "Stage 3" specimens. Quadratic regression describes the relationship well ($r^2 = 0.98$), linear regression only slightly less so ($r^2 = 0.94$). Regression is a continuous model of variation and relationship. In metric dimensions and weight, Callahan's biface stages arbitrarily parse a continuum of variation.

None of this is to criticize Callahan, nor does it prove that reduction is understood only as a continuous process. Callahan's (1979:Table 10) model includes categorical as well as continuous variables, but most of the former are difficult to replicate or are of unknown relevance (e.g., regularity of outline, "nature of reduction emphasis," "degree of concentration during fabrication," degree of trim) and some that seem more replicable are included in the coding system used here (e.g., cross section form). Perhaps some categorical variables sort strictly or associate significantly by stage. In the fine details of fluting, which occurred after Callahan's Stage 4, sequence may better describe the process than does continuous variation. Despite Callahan's and others' emphasis upon categorical attributes, many of his (1979:Table 10) variables are in fact continuous-scale quantitative ones.

Perhaps such variables sort or associate by stage in other experiments. Yet in Callahan's experiments, which rightly influenced two generations of archaeologists, much variation described as sequential is continuous.

As useful as biface-stage typologies may be, they may not accommodate all significant patterns of variation. In their Mammoth Lakes study area, Skinner and Ainsworth (1991) recovered obsidian preforms in various stages of production that bore little or no faceting on interior faces. They described a specialized flake-blank production method (1991:162–163) and subsequent working of first exterior and then interior faces, the latter sometimes to only limited degree. Such "unifacial bifaces" also are reported near the Wild Horse Canyon obsidian quarry (Dames and Moore 1994:21–70), at Yosemite (Humphreys 1994:Figure 6), and at Stockhoff (Sharrock 1966:43). Preforms that match Skinner and Ainsworth's description occur at Modena (e.g., Figure 6.1) and Tempiute. Skinner and Ainsworth's (1991:161) scheme only partially corresponded to Callahan's, both because of the nature of the reduction sequence they describe and because their description did not include some of the details provided in other sources. Among other things, it is very difficult to establish correspondence with the Callahan scheme beyond Skinner and Ainsworth's Stage 4.

Preceding analysis suggests that stages are constructs, not revealed reality. In strictest terms, the biface production process is continuous (Muto 1971; Pendleton 1979:107; Shott 1996b, 2017), and can usefully be understood and modeled as such. Indeed, some analysis in this chapter exploits the complex variation in preform size and form by using multivariate analysis to identify continuous dimensions of variation that, at least arguably, crosscut stages. But stage typologies are a firmly embedded habit of thought in lithic analysis. They are useful when their limitations are understood, although archaeologists must resist the temptation to reify biface preform stages; they are constructs only, useful for certain purposes and revealing important dimensions of variation, not empirical units that exist independently of our analytical approaches.

Modena and Tempiute
Preform Assemblages

UA investigations recovered over 270 preforms at Modena (Figure 6.1). The dataset for this analysis appears in Shott (2016:Appendix A). Mean values of size and faceting variables for this assemblage are 62.3 mm for length, 41.3 m for width, 13.6 mm for thickness, 38.8 g for weight, interior- and exterior-surface scar count 10.5 and 11.3, respectively. (Length and weight values are for intact specimens only.) In the Great Basin alone, data on preform metric and non-metric attributes is nearly voluminous and prohibitive to synthesize for comparison. (Greubel [2005:Table 3-17], for instance, presented basic metric data on nearly 500 mostly obsidian production-stage preforms at Hunchback Shelter.) Yet brief, selective review of major assemblages is worthwhile.

Quarry and associated workshop assemblages at Newberry Crater have shorter, thinner, and considerably narrower preforms on average (Connolly et al. 1999:Table 6.4) than does Modena. Modena's mean length is less than the means of all stages in Coso's Early Period and Little Lake preform assemblages and near the Stage 3 mean in Early and Middle Newberry ones; mean width and thickness are nearest Coso's Early Period Stage 4, Little Lake Stage 3, and Early Newberry Stage 2 preforms while Modena widths are nearest Stage 3 at Middle Newberry with thickness approximating Middle Newberry Stage 2 preforms and Stage 3 Late Newberry preforms (Gilreath and Hildebrandt 1997:Tables 22, 29, 35, 40, 45). All stages of Haiwee Period quarry preforms considerably exceed Modena mean values (Gilreath and Hildebrandt 1997:Table 52). Compared to the Stockhoff basalt quarry, Modena values most closely resemble Stage 3 preforms in length and width although thickness is higher than Stockhoff Stage 3 preforms (Womack 1977: 31, 36, 39, 40). When compared as well to the Tosawishi chert quarry, Modena values are nearest Stage 4 preforms in length, width, and

weight but nearest Stage 3 ones in thickness (Bloomer et al. 1992:Table 7). Not surprisingly, preforms in Panaca Summit assemblages, most of which probably were exported from Modena, have generally lower ranges of values for length and width than does the Modena assemblage (Elston and Juell 1987:Table 5). Obsidian and other preforms at Sunshine exceed Modena preforms in average length and weight, but are narrower and thinner on average (Beck and Jones 2009a:Table 5.16). Estes (2009:Appendix E) shows mean values of obsidian preforms consistently lower than Modena values, particularly in weight. Dames and Moore (1994:21-33, 21-69) described a similar range and pattern of variation in biface preforms at Wild Horse Canyon and vicinity but did not report metric values or assign specimens to Callahan stages.

Modena platform variables occur too rarely to be considered in analysis. By condition, 59 preforms are intact, 120 proximal, 28 medial, and 40 distal; four bear longitudinal fractures. The Modena preform assemblage mostly is broken, consistent with reports from other quarries and workshops (e.g. Beck and Jones 2009a:Table 5.15; Bloomer et al. 1992:97, Tables 7, 8; Bucy 1974:9; Connolly et al. 1999:61, Table 6.4; Dillian 2002:225, 223; Doelman 2008:142; Elston 2005:106; Greubel 2005:Table 3-10; Holmes 1892, 1984b:15; Knell 2014:218; Rego 2010:174; Sanders 1983:78, 82–98; Womack 1977: 31, 36, 39, 40). Some may be complete elements of composite tools like "mescal cleavers" (Smith and Pond 1994), but this possibility seems remote given the location of Modena and Tempiute relative to agave stands, and the fact that obsidian and other toolstone quarries elsewhere in North America very distant from agave also include many broken preforms. Most fragments are identified as proximal, recalling that this is a default judgment for many specimens especially at early reduction segments where distinct base and tip were not yet formed or could not be distinguished. Most preforms have lenticular (biconvex) cross sections (n = 93), most of the rest plano-convex ones (n = 34) and, where observable, longitudinal sections are straight in 72 of 149 cases. Edge sinuosity follows a descending trend from wide (n = 206) to intermediate (n = 153) to fine (n = 52) on both margins. Most fractures are either transverse (n = 113) or oblique (n = 88), both probably the result of load application in reduction that exceeded tensile or compression thresholds of Modena obsidian (Luedtke 1992:83). All but seven of 41 distal fractures on medial fragments are transverse or oblique. Fifty-nine preforms bore at least a partly unmodified interior surface. This figure comprises 22% of all preforms, but nearly 44% of the 136 preforms for which an interior surface was clearly recognizable. Finally, 74 of 266 (28%) recordable preforms bear cortex.

Among Modena preforms, condition is associated with cortex (χ^2 = 16.9; p = 0.01). Proximal fragments pattern independently of cortex, medial and distal fragments disproportionately lack cortex, and intact ones disproportionately possess it. This pattern probably owes to an intervening condition, degree of reduction, because more extensively reduced preforms are both unlikely to bear cortex and are at high risk of failure. Condition patterns weakly with fracture type (χ^2 = 9.00; p = 0.17), with hinge fractures slightly positively associated with medial fragments. Condition and sinuosity also pattern (for edge 1 χ^2 = 32.9; p < 0.01; for edge 2 χ^2 = 20.3; p < 0.01). On edge 1, intermediate sinuosity is overrepresented among proximal fragments, fine sinuosity among medial fragments, and both among distal fragments. Those same sinuosity states are underrepresented among intact preforms; broad sinuosity is underrepresented among distal fragments and overrepresented among intact preforms. On edge 2, intermediate sinuosity is independent of condition. The fine state is overrepresented among medial and distal fragments but underrepresented among intact preforms, while broadly sinuous edges are underrepresented among medial fragments and overrepresented among intact specimens.

Cortex is associated with cross section (χ^2 = 18.6; p < 0.01) such that irregular sections are likelier to bear cortex and lenticular ones to lack it; plano-convex cross sections are independent of cortex cover. Cortex also patterns with sinuosity on edge 1 (χ^2 = 14.2; p < 0.01), where the broad state is more common among cortex-bearing preforms, the fine state more common among preforms that lack cortex; the intermediate sinuosity state shows a negative association with presence of cortex. Cortex and fracture type are independent of each other (χ^2 = 0.30; p = 0.86).

Sections are associated (χ^2 = 36.3, p < 0.01). Irregular cross sections co-occur with curved or irregular longitudinal sections but not straight ones; lenticular cross sections show the opposite pattern, while plano-convex cross section and longitudinal section are independent. Cross section also patterns with sinuosity, strongly on edge 1 (χ^2 = 58.0; p < 0.01) and weakly on edge 2 (χ^2 = 6.39; p = 0.17). On edge 1, broad sinuosity is associated with irregular sections while being underrepresented with lenticular ones, while intermediate and fine sinuosity exhibit the opposite pattern. Some of this patterning also is evident on edge 2. Overall results do not reach conventional significance, but fine sinuosity is underrepresented among lenticular cross sections and overrepresented among irregular ones, directly the opposite of its patterning on edge 1. Again, there is patterning with variables associated with reduction but it is complex and not universal. Sinuosity and fracture type are independent (on edge 1 χ^2 = 5.70; p = 0.22; on edge 2 χ^2 = 2.70; p = 0.61), as are fracture types among medial preform fragments (χ^2 = 0.85; p = 0.66).

In sum, intact preforms are likelier to resist fracture, retain cortex, and have irregular cross and longitudinal sections. They also tend to possess broader edge sinuosity, probably a consequence of their disposal in the early segments of the reduction continuum, or Callahan Stage 0. Conversely, more broken preforms lack cortex, bear lenticular cross sections and straight longitudinal sections, and exhibit finer sinuosity. These properties in part reflect broken preforms' more advanced production, where risk of failure rises. Hinging is common among medial fragments or, put differently, perhaps hinging is associated with multiple fractures that yield medial fragments. All of these patterns of association are explained to some extent as the natural consequence of different degrees of

TABLE 6.1. Modena and Tempiute Preform Size and Faceting Variables Mean and Standard Deviation by Callahan Stage. Intact specimens only for length, weight, sinuosity, and faceting variables. No Stage-3 preforms were found at Tempiute.

Variable	CS	n	mean	s	Variable	CS	n	mean	s
Modena									
length (mm)	0	40	64.0	9.3	interior	0	40	10.3	4.8
	1	14	58.6	7.4	scars	1	14	11.0	4.0
	2	4	62.8	10.3		2	4	10.3	6.5
	3	0	–	–		3	0	–	–
width (mm)	0	88	43.2	7.4	exterior	0	40	10.9	3.9
	1	96	42.6	8.1	scars	1	14	12.2	3.2
	2	47	38.4	8.9		2	4	13.5	6.6
	3	14	29.5	5.3		3	0	–	–
thickness (mm)	0	91	16.5	4.2	sinuous	0	33	2.4	0.9
	1	102	13.5	3.7	cycles	1	13	2.6	1.1
	2	51	10.5	3.5	edge 1	2	2	2.0	1.4
	3	14	8.1	2.1		3	0	–	–
weight (g)	0	40	42.5	17.3	sinuous	0	21	3.1	1.3
	1	14	31.0	11.8	cycles	1	6	3.8	1.0
	2	4	32.5	22.4	edge 2	2	2	6.0	1.4
	3	0	–	–		3	0	–	–
Tempiute									
length (mm)	0	5	50	2.9	interior	0	5	8.2	2.8
	1	3	57	18.1	scars	1	3	12.0	2.6
	2	1	41	–		2	1	14.0	–
width (mm)	0	14	34.9	5.1	exterior	0	5	9.4	3.5
	1	4	33.5	10.0	scars	1	3	7.3	4.9
	2	3	37.3	18.8		2	1	13.0	–
thickness (mm)	0	14	14.5	3.2	sinuous	0	4	2.2	0.5
	1	5	14.4	5.8	cycles	1	3	2.0	1.0
	2	3	12.0	7.0	edge 1	2	0	–	–
weight (g)	0	5	17.7	3.8	sinuous	0	3	1.7	0.7
	1	3	29.0	26.5	cycles	1	0	–	–
	2	1	10.0	–	edge 2	2	0	–	–

reduction experienced by preforms. Fracture type is largely independent of other categorical variables.

Analysis by Callahan Stage: Modena

If Callahan (or any) stages are valid, preform variables should pattern with them, as Modena data do to some extent. Table 6.1 summarizes Modena preforms by size, faceting, and sinuosity, subdivided by Callahan stage. Maximum length and weight (intact specimens only) are overall size variables. Although they vary by Callahan stage (for length $F = 1.9$; $p = 0.17$; for weight $F = 2.8$; $p = 0.07$) neither variable patterns consistently with stage, probably owing to low Stage-2 sample size. Maximum width and thickness also covary by Callahan stage (for width $F = 15.1$; $p < 0.01$; for thickness $F = 39.2$; $p < 0.01$) and pattern consistently with stage. Sinuosity and faceting variables (also confined to intact specimens, where n is low) pattern differently. Sinuosity does not pattern significantly on the first edge ($F = 0.5$; $p = 0.64$) but does on the second ($F = 5.2$; $p = 0.01$). This result is ambiguous because edges were designated arbitrarily. Certainly this result does not strongly indicate patterning consistent with the stage model. Neither faceting variable varies significantly with Callahan stage (for the interior face $F = 0.1$; $p = 0.98$; for the exterior face $F = 1.3$; $p = 0.29$) although faceting on exterior faces increases by stage as expected. The incidence of quasi-unifacial preforms may help explain the lack of patterning for interior faces.

To minimize expected cell counts <5, association between Callahan stage and categorical variables was confined to variable levels of high frequency only. Also, association was calculated for paired Callahan stages 0–1 and 2–3, both to minimize the sparse-cell problem and to clarify what sometimes was complex patterning by the four original stages. As in other chapters, association is measured by χ^2 and results interpreted by treating standardized residuals of $|>1|$ as significant.

Cortex patterns strongly but complexly by stage ($\chi^2 = 32.7$; $p < 0.01$). It is not a simple matter of cortex presence steadily declining in frequency by stage as its absence correspondingly rises. Instead cortex is overrepresented in Stage 0 and underrepresented in Stages 2–3, while its absence is underrepresented in Stage 0 and overrepresented in Stage 2 only. Patterning is clarified somewhat in paired Callahan stages ($\chi^2 = 17.6$; $p < 0.01$) because cortex presence is overrepresented in Stages 0–1 and underrepresented in Stages 2–3, directly opposite the pattern for preforms without cortex. Preform condition is associated with Callahan stage ($\chi^2 = 60.1$; $p < 0.01$) because intact preforms are overrepresented in Stage 0 and underrepresented in subsequent ones, opposite the pattern for broken preforms, especially medial and distal fragments. Risk of breakage increases after Stage 0, a pattern seen at quarries or workshops elsewhere (e.g., Rego 2010:176). Significance and patterning persist in paired Callahan stages ($\chi^2 = 30.6$; $p < 0.01$). Stage 0 preforms were dif-

ficult to break, probably because they were thick and because their limited reduction subjected them to fewer risks of failure in knapping. Yet even intact preforms in this stage probably were rejected because of the inability to satisfactorily reduce thickness relative to width, indicated in some cases by the presence of step fractures that defined remnant crowns. As preforms were progressively thinned to later Callahan stages, their risk of fracture increased but their relative scarcity at these stages probably owes as much to the high export rate of successfully thinned ones. In effect, what was left to recover at Modena were broken fragments, of course, and the relatively few intact preforms that either were overlooked or failed to satisfy design requirements.

Cross section also patterns by stage ($\chi^2 = 114.9$; $p < 0.01$), where Stage 0 is overrepresented among irregular cross sections and Stages 2–3 overrepresented among lenticular cross sections; the fewer plano-convex preforms are underrepresented at all stages except 1, where they are overrepresented. Thus, most preforms originally bore irregular cross sections, only to have them later transformed to the lenticular form, with a significant number transiting in effect through plano-convex form before becoming lenticular. Again, significance and patterning persist in paired Callahan stages ($\chi^2 = 80.5$; $p < 0.01$). Longitudinal sections are disproportionately curved or irregular at Stage 0, pattern independently with Stage 1, and become disproportionately straight in Stages 2–3 ($\chi^2 = 54.0$; $p < 0.01$; by paired Callahan stages $\chi^2 = 42.4$; $p < 0.01$). Curved sections at Stage 0 implicate flake blanks, irregular ones cobble blanks. In both cases, longitudinal sections become straight only by Stage 2. Callahan stage and fracture type do not covary ($\chi^2 = 9.0$; $p = 0.17$; by paired stage $\chi^2 = 0.4$; $p = 0.84$), although hinge fractures are slightly overrepresented in Stage 0 and underrepresented in Stage 1, and oblique fractures are underrepresented in Stage 0 while overrepresented in Stage 3. The most common fracture type, transverse, patterns independently of Callahan stage. On both edges, sinuosity patterns with stage (for edge 1 $\chi^2 = 102.0$; $p < 0.01$; for edge 2 $\chi^2 = 78.8$; $p < 0.01$) because broad

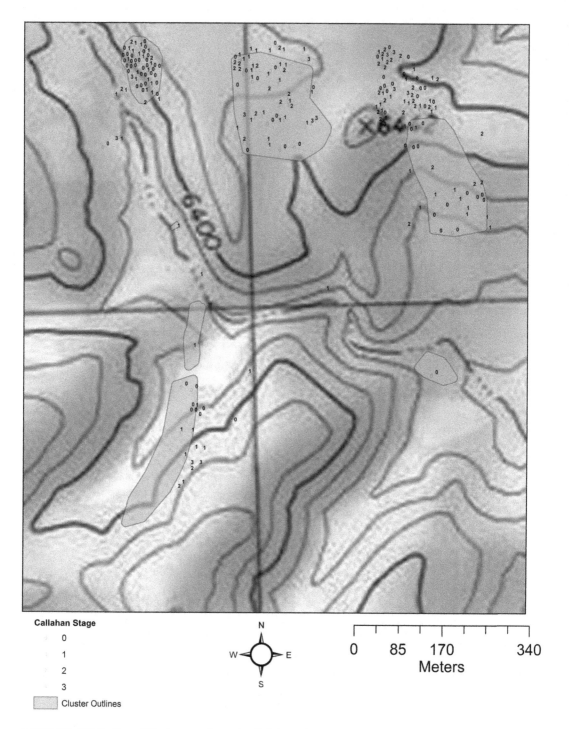

FIGURE 6.2. Distribution of Modena preforms by Callahan stage.

sinuosity is overrepresented at Stage 0 and underrepresented in Stages 2–3, opposing the pattern for the intermediate and especially the fine variant (the latter of which steadily progresses from underrepresented to heavily overrepresented from Stages 0–3 on both edges). This pattern also persists in paired Callahan stages (for edge 1 χ^2 = 57.5; p < 0.01; for edge 2 χ^2 = 41.6; p < 0.01). Finally, where interior and exterior surfaces are distinguishable, unmodified interior surfaces are overrepresented in Stage 0 and underrepresented within Stages 2–3, opposite the pattern for modified interior surfaces (χ^2 = 16.2; p = 0.001). This variable does not pattern with Stage 1. Paired Callahan stages also pattern with modification of interior surfaces (χ^2 = 11.5; p = 0.001).

Altogether, size, edge, and faceting variables pattern inconsistently with Callahan stages. It is no surprise that nominal- or ordinal-scale variables pattern better with ordinal-scale stages. In general, as preforms progress by stage, cortex rapidly disappears, risk of failure increases, cross section grows more symmetrical and lenticular, longitudinal sections straighten, and sinuosity of edges becomes more refined. Unmodified interior surfaces can be common in Stage 0 but are much underrepresented in subsequent stages. Fracture type does not pattern by Callahan stage. Yet patterning sometimes is complex, and, in many cases, there is no consistent trend to rising or falling standardized residuals by Callahan stage. The stage concept captures and represents to some degree the major patterns of variation through the reduction process, but the complex covariation and inconsistent results in size, edge, and faceting variables counsel a broader approach that also considers continuous dimensions of variation.

Spatial Association by Area

Spatial distribution of preforms by Callahan stage is shown in Figure 6.2. Because of low preform counts in Areas E and 2009-1, analysis is confined to Areas A, B, D, and F. Area F has an unusually many Stage 0 preforms, Areas B and D unusually few (χ^2 = 27.6; p < 0.01). Area F also has more Stage-1 preforms and fewer Stage-2

TABLE 6.2. Modena Preforms by Callahan Stage and Area.

Callahan Stage	Condition			
	Proximal	Medial	Distal	Intact
0	38	4	4	40
1	55	9	16	14
2	22	9	13	4
3	4	4	6	0

Callahan Stage	Area			
	A	B	D	F
0	17	12	6	34
1	19	22	11	17
2	6	15	5	3
3	0	4	2	1
Paired Stage	**A**	**B**	**D**	**F**
0+1	36	34	17	51
2+3	6	19	7	4

preforms than expected, while Area B has more Stage-2 preforms than expected. Areas B and D have unusually many Stage 3 specimens, Area A unusually few. Thus, Area F is skewed toward earlier stages, Area A slightly toward the latest stage. Areas B and D pattern similarly, being underrepresented in Stage 0 and largely overrepresented in Stages 2–3. Callahan-stage pairs largely repeat this pattern (χ^2 = 15.6; p < 0.01). By paired stages, Area B skews toward the later stage, Area F toward the earlier one. Areas A and D do not pattern by paired stage. Taken together, Area A largely bears a typical preform assemblage that resembles overall stage proportions across the Modena quarry. Areas B and F exhibit antagonistic patterning, B skewing modestly toward later stages and F strongly toward earlier ones. Somewhat equivocally, Area D resembles B.

Chapter 5 reported strong complementarity in results of attribute and flake-size distribution analyses. Comparison of Table 6.2 data to Table 5.17 suggests complementarity at a different scale: between flake and preform assemblages. In converting Table 6.2 counts to proportions for comparison to Table 5.17, a strong pattern emerges in the admittedly limited data from the four Modena areas with largest preform assemblages. Proportion of Stage-1 flakes correlates strongly and positively ($r = 0.99$; $p = 0.01$) with proportion of Callahan-Stage 0 (CS0) preforms and strongly and negatively ($r = -0.95$; $p = 0.05$) with proportion of CS2 preforms (Shott 2016:Figure 6.12). CS1 preforms pattern similarly to CS2 specimens. Area B has both the highest proportion of CS1–2 preforms and, correspondingly, the lowest proportion of UA Stage-1 flakes, while Area F has both the highest proportion of CS0 preforms and, correspondingly, the lowest proportion of UA Stage-2 and -3 flakes. Separate variation in flake and preform assemblages is better understood in light of such joint variation between them.

As described in Chapter 4, UA investigations included selective transects laid out to seek preforms within and near Areas A, B, and F (but not D or smaller areas). Adding preforms from the vicinity of areas creates area groups. Data organized this way show spatial patterning, which largely reproduces results reported above ($\chi^2 = 23.1$; $p < 0.01$). Area Group B is strongly underrepresented in Callahan Stage 0 and in paired stages 0–1, and overrepresented in Stages 2 and 3 and paired stages 2–3; Area Group F shows the opposite pattern. In area groups, however, A and D possess stage preforms in similar proportions to the Modena quarry in general.

Quantification of the Modena Preform Assemblage

As above, UA investigations recovered over 270 preforms at Modena. Although many are broken fragments, not unexpected at a quarry where successful reductions were exported for completion and use elsewhere and most failures were left behind, rates and patterns of breakage can vary between assemblages in ways that complicate comparison of their sizes. Thus, three hypothetical assemblages each of, say, 100 preforms may represent different numbers of original specimens and therefore assemblage sizes if one of them consisted entirely of intact preforms and the other two entirely of fragments. In the first case, the number of original preforms is 100. In the second, it could be 100 if each fragment is unique and refits no other frag-

ment, or as few as 50, if each fragment refitted to one other, or even 34 if the set consisted of 33 each of proximal, medial, and distal fragments that all (but one) refit. In the conceivable but improbable third case, the 100 pieces all could derive from a single badly fragmented original biface. Size—number of specimens present—is a fundamental characteristic of any stone-tool assemblage, but to establish comparable figures for assemblages that have experienced different degrees or patterns of breakage requires methods to control for such potential double-counting (Nelson 2000:109) as source of variation.

UA attempted no systematic refitting of broken Modena preforms. Most specimens were found in isolation from others (but not from flake debris, obviously). Preforms found near one another were examined for refits, none of which were found. Refitting also would have been complicated by opportunistic reworking of fragments, as commonly occurred, in an attempt to thin or at least to remove flakes from fracture planes.

Z. Nelson (2000) used several methods to estimate original numbers of notched Ramec points at an obsidian workshop at Teotihuacán. Among them, most relevant here, is "estimated tool counts" (Shott 2000), found by subtracting the mean length of end products from the mean length of production-stage preforms as, essentially, critical differences (Nelson 2000:109–111). Preform fragments were assigned to stages, and those fragments greater than the critical difference measures were counted as single failures; smaller fragments were ignored. Nelson estimated number of preforms for successive preform stages and summed estimates across the stages.

This method is difficult to apply to the Modena assemblage, because it requires knowing the dimensions of intact specimens, none of which exist for Callahan stage 3. In addition, mean length dimensions from Callahan stage 0 through 2 do not pattern consistently. Nelson used length, whose mean by Callahan stage varies: 64 mm at Stage 0, 58.6 at Stage 1, 62.8 in Stage 2 (Table 6.1). The low sample size attributed to Stage 2 partly explains the reversal in trend of mean length, but also makes it difficult to calculate Nelson's critical differences by stage. To follow Nelson, assuming a critical difference of 5 mm between Stages 0 and 1 should allow for estimating a minimum number of Stage-1 preforms. Unfortunately, all Stage-1 preforms exceed that critical difference, so Nelson's method fails to control for the possibility of double-counting.

Nelson's approach resembles the use of diagnostic elements to define "estimated tool equivalents" (ETE) and resulting "tool information equivalents" (TIE; Shott 2000). These are used to estimate total number of original intact specimens represented in assemblages that include fragments (Shott 2000). Preforms, however, possess relatively few diagnostic elements, such as notches, shoulders, and haft elements. In production-stage preforms, a crude approximation can be applied by coding specimens as intact or as proximal, medial, or distal fragments. This approach defines intact tools as 100% and proximal, medial, and distal segments as 33% each of one ETE. TIE is then calculated from ETE (Shott 2000:729). For the Modena preform assemblage of 59 intact and 188 proximal, medial, or distal fragments (remaining Modena specimens were lateral fractures or so extensively fragmented that diagnostic element could not be determined) the resulting TIE estimate is 183.7 (≈184).

This result is not as esoteric as it may seem to be. Systematic quantification methods, if used consistently, control for variation between assemblages or other datasets in pattern and degree of fragmentation. Tools are fragile, but variously so, with fragmentation varying by patterns of original use, degree of curation, rates of site reoccupation, depositional context, and postdepositional taphonomy. Raw counts do not remotely control for these sources of variation; on the contrary, uncritical use of raw counts practically ignores them. Only quantification methods control for so diverse a set of complicating factors. Valid comparison between assemblages that may differ in any complicating factor requires their use.

Reduction Analysis
Johnson Thinning Index (JTI)

Dissatisfaction with the ambiguity of stage approaches like Callahan's led J. Johnson to devise JTI from dissatisfaction with the ambiguity of stage approaches like Callahan's, using it as a way to characterize "biface trajectory" models (1981:21–25) of continuous reduction. Amick (1985) used Johnson's index in his analysis of Fort Payne workshops in central Tennessee. He noted that, as a ratio-scale quantity, JTI "allows placement of…bifaces along a production continuum" (1985:140) that moots the need for "subjective, qualitative" (1985:140) stage assignment, thus complementing a stage approach. Amick, using a different method than Johnson's to calculate plan area (1985:140–142), found a clear inverse relationship between JTI and presence-absence of cortex, and significantly lower index values in flake than in core blanks. Amick used a different method than Johnson's to calculate plan area (1985:140–142). JTI was defined and measured above for UA preforms.

Amick (1985:142) used JTI not just descriptively, but also to compare preform assemblages by, for instance, plotting frequency distributions of the range of JTI values. Thus, he (1985:145) compared his assemblages to Johnson's (1981) workshop data to identify continuous degree of difference in range and distribution of JTI values that corresponded to site type and degree of advancement of the reduction continuum. Johnson's (1981:23, Figure 2-5) comparison of two workshop sites in his Mississippi study area showed clear differences in range and mode (and probably mean) of JTI values in assemblages dominated by early-stage and later-stage biface reduction (Figure 6.3a). Amick's (1985:Figure 4) "Grade-1" bifaces generally resembled the former distribution, his "Grade-2" bifaces the latter.

Using the plan-area estimate described above, JTI values were computed for Modena and Tempiute preforms. Surprisingly, the overall Modena distribution is much narrower than Johnson's assemblages with its range and mode closely resembling the 22Ts818, "late stage" (Johnson 1981:23) distribution. Amick (1991:

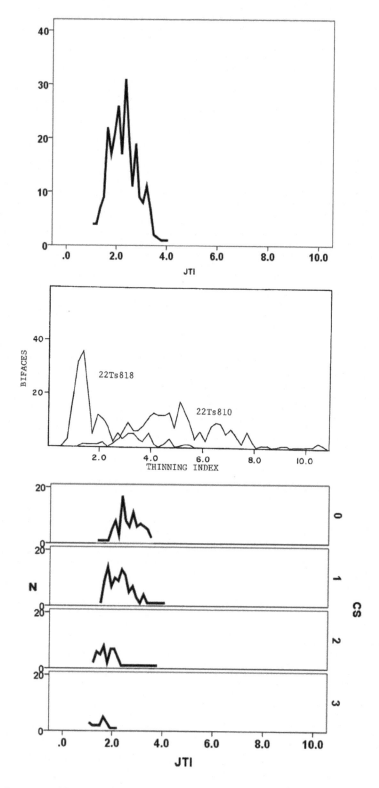

FIGURE 6.3. Modena preform JTI by Callahan stage: a. overall (Johnson's Figure 2-5 shown for comparison); b. by Callahan stage.

Table 6-15) found similar results at the Buck-board Mesa obsidian quarry, suggesting that obsidian and chert JTI distributions may not be comparable, although different methods for measuring JTI may help explain the difference. Figure 6.3b plots the distribution of JTI at Modena by Callahan stage where, not surprisingly, both range and median tend to decline with stage.

Despite favoring a view of reduction as a continuum, Johnson's (1981:23–24) careful study of his JTI distributions led him to identify "breakpoints" that he used to define ranges of values. Johnson-like "breakpoints" are not easily detected in Figure 6.3. Reformatting the same variable into intervals of 0.1, possible JTI "breakpoints" in Modena data lie at Johnson's value of 1.7 and 2.9, the latter near Johnson's "breakpoint" at 3.1. Admittedly, it also reveals possible "breakpoints" at 2.3 and 2.6 which Johnson did not find in his data. On balance, the Modena JTI distribution reasonably approximates Johnson's (1981) own data in the location of critical values.

Johnson defined the following tripartite division:

JTI	≥3.1	stage 1
JTI	1.7–3.0	stage 2
JTI	<1.7	stage 3

Using this scheme, of the 247 Modena preforms for which JTI could be computed, 24 (9.7%) are assigned to Johnson's stage 1, 177 (71.6%) to his stage 2, and 46 (18.6%) to his stage 3. These JTI stage assignments correspond well with Callahan stage ($\chi^2 = 86.1$; $p < 0.01$) and Callahan paired stage ($\chi^2 = 68.8$; $p < 0.01$), so ranges of JTI values largely capture the range and complex patterns of variation encoded in Callahan stages.

In his Mississippi quarry-preform assemblage, Johnson (1979) tested for association between fracture type and his JTI "breakpoint" at 1.7. Hinge and crenated fractures among others occurred more often in earlier production stages (1979:26). Modena data, however, reveal no association between fracture type and a two-part division at JTI's 1.7 breakpoint ($\chi^2 = 3.9$; $p = 0.27$). Use of the three-part JTI groupings listed above also fails to indicate association ($\chi^2 = 4.2$; $p = 0.38$). Modena preforms do not pattern jointly by JTI and fracture type.

Flaking Index (FI)

Like JTI, Flaking Index (FI) is a measure of degree of reduction or finishing of preforms (Miller and Smallwood 2012). As a brief example of complementarity between flake and preform assemblages—the tendency for variables in those separate datasets to covary—FI was plotted against UA Stage-1 flake proportion as estimated using CLSR. Although correlation does not attain conventional threshold values ($r_s = -0.80$; $p = 0.20$), patterning in the data seems clear. As FI rises from Area F to Area B, indicating somewhat more advanced stages of preform production at the latter, it is matched by a corresponding decline in the proportion of UA Stage-1 flakes in overall flake assemblages. Similar to other examples discussed above and in Chapter 5, this result indicates that patterning in flake and preform data, independent in concept and measurement, are not independent statistically. Using different measures applied to different data, both flake and preform assemblages register patterning in degree of reduction.

Preform Cache Data

Although no known caches of Modena obsidian preforms exist, a number of obsidian preform caches are documented for the Great Basin and Mountain West. Modena data can be compared to caches for which basic dimensions and/or weight are reported. Comparisons were made to identified obsidian preform caches from sources that reported data in sufficient detail, making no claim to exhaustiveness. Comparative sources included nine preforms identified as early Holocene from 42TO2622 (Young et al. 2006:68, Appendix A) and Daron Duke (personal communication, 14 March 2014), six from Koompin cache (Pavesic 1966:53) found about 35 km from the source, 11 Parman/Great-Basin Stemmed

TABLE 6.3. Mean Length, Width, Thickness, and Weight of Modena and Cache Preforms.

		N	mean	sd	Student's t	p
Length (mm)	Modena	59	62.3	13.4		
	Cache	129	68.9	27.1	2.46	0.02
Width (mm)	Modena	249	41.3	8.6		
	Cache	129	40.2	11.2	0.30	0.76
Thickness (mm)	Modena	265	13.6	4.5		
	Cache	129	9.8	2.8	9.35	<0.01
Weight (g)	Modena	59	38.8	17.2		
	Cache	87	42.4	38.1	0.76	0.45

Length and weight are for intact specimens only.

preforms from McNine (Amick 2004:Table 1) found 25–50 km from the source, 15 (including five unifacial) preforms from Warner Valley (Weide and Weide 1969:Table 1), Hafted Bifaces 1, 5, and 6 from Nicolarsen (Barnes 2000:92–96), 45 from the Smith cache "nearby" an obsidian source and dated to 1200 BP (Lohse et al. 2008), 32 from Rock Creek found <50 km from the source, and 9 from Cedar Draw found 70 km from the source (Kohntopp 2001:38, 45). Other obsidian cache data did not include specimen weight, essential in the analysis to follow (e.g., Connolly et al. 2015:182–185; Humphreys 1994:Figures 7–8; Marschall 2004:Appendix B), or did not describe cache specimens in sufficient detail for consideration here (e.g., Stoffle et al. 2011:38–39). Benson (1980:25, Figure 17e) reported one obsidian preform from a well-preserved cache in southwestern Utah, not included in this study. Other data on obsidian cache preforms (e.g., McGuire et al. [2012:134] on eight biface caches in the Yosemite vicinity) could not be located. Caches of bifaces made from chert or other toolstone are not uncommon in the Great Basin and environs (e.g., Davis et al. 2014) but are not considered.

In an initial principal-components analysis of linear dimensions that included them, preforms from Loa (Janetski et al. 1988) accounted for more than half of the range of size-related PC1 scores; 63 "Great Blade Cache" preforms (Rick and Jackson 1992) formed a conspicuous lower outlier widely separated from other data. Conversely, Caballo Blanco preforms (Gary and McLear-Gary 1990) were nearly an order of magnitude heavier than most other obsidian preforms. These sources were omitted as anomalous. Relevant data were not available for other regional sources on obsidian preform caches (e.g., Butler 1980:123; Cressman 1937; Garfinkel et al. 2004; Scott et al. 1986).

Mean values of major dimensions and weight show that Modena preforms are shorter but thicker than those found in caches, about the same width, and slightly lighter (Table 6.3). The decreased length and increased thickness over exported specimens suggest the unsuitability of Modena preforms for refinement to completed bifaces. The similarity between the datasets in width suggests that this dimension was key; once Modena preforms reached a width approaching 40 mm, they were adjudged either ready for export or were rejected and discarded.

As Chapter 7 discusses in detail, a further approach to analysis distinguishes degree of reduction between preform assemblages in complexly patterned multivariate metric data. It involves principal-components analysis (PCA) of length, width, and thickness, extracted from a matrix of correlation coefficients to account for the different ranges of variation in dimensions. Following the approach, separate PCA was conducted for the Modena and cache assemblages.

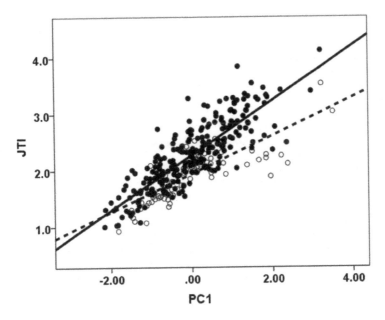

FIGURE 6.4. Modena (solid circles and line) and Cache (open circles and dashed line) preform JTI versus PC1.

In both, the result is a single component whose eigenvalue >1, which explains 58.0% of variance in the Modena assemblage and 70.4% in the cache sample. Length, width, and thickness all have high positive loadings with principal component 1 (PC1), making it a reflection of general size in both datasets.

The reduction measure JTI plotted against PC1 score separately for each dataset distinguishes the assemblages. Least-squares regression analysis yielded the following results:

For Modena: $JTI = 2.27 + 0.49{*}PC1$
            (0.02)   (0.02)
For cache data: $JTI = 1.83 + 0.32{*}PC1$
              (0.03)   (0.03)

where parenthetical figures are 95% confidence limits of coefficients. The regression slope coefficient is significantly higher for the Modena than the cache assemblage ($t = 4.38$; $p < 0.01$; Figure 6.4). As discussed in Chapter 7, a higher slope in the relationship between reduction measures like JTI and size measures like PC1 indicates earlier stages or segments of the reduction process. Because the reduction measure JTI declines at a faster rate with size in Modena pre-

forms than among cache specimens, Modena's preform assemblage as a unit occupies a somewhat earlier reduction range.

Yet compared with experimental and other archaeological data presented in Chapter 7, the difference in this case is modest, and the overlap between the point scatters is considerable. In effect, in their position in the reduction continuum these cache data closely follow the Modena quarry assemblage; they are only slightly more advanced in reduction, so may be considered representative of the degree of reduction experienced by most preforms at the point of export from the Modena quarry.

Some preform caches are dated by association. McNine and 42TO2622 are early prehistoric deposits associated with WST/GBSS bifaces, while Warner, Smith, Rock Creek, and Cedar Draw are middle to late prehistoric in age. Most other caches are not dated, although, for Oregon, Marschall (2004) posited a chronological difference between caches of lanceolate and ovate bifaces. It simplifies somewhat to argue that earlier prehistoric occupation of the Great Basin involved more extensive land use, certainly in mobility magnitude if not

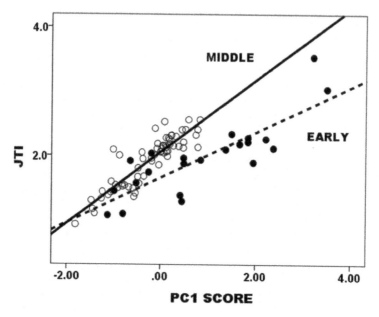

FIGURE 6.5. JTI versus PC1 score for Early (solid circles and dashed line)
and Middle Prehistoric (open circles and solid line) cache preforms.

necessarily in mobility frequency (*sensu* Shott 1986), than middle and later prehistory. But analysis following subdivision of the cache data by early and middle prehistoric groups suggests further differences of degree, in this case within the cache dataset. JTI plotted against PC1 score shows a significantly lower slope for early versus middle prehistoric caches ($t = 4.15$; $p < 0.01$; Figure 6.5). Regression results are:

For early preforms: JTI = 1.64 + 0.31*PC1
                          (0.09)   (0.05)
For late preforms: JTI = 1.89 + 0.53*PC1
                          (0.02)   (0.03)

Although sample sizes are low, results at least suggest that in earlier Great Basin prehistory obsidian preforms were somewhat more advanced in reduction than they were in middle prehistory. Broadly, this is consistent with the assumption of greater land-use scale in earlier prehistory.

Analysis continues by defining four approximate quartiles of the range of PC1 scores. There is a clear gap circa 1.50 that defines a group of large preforms at high positive values (1.75–3.98) of PC1. A smaller gap exists circa 0, which defines a second group (0.06–1.25), and a third can

be defined not by a gap but by a trough between two modes of negative values (−0.69 − −0.05, and <−0.72; Shott 2016:Figure 6.21). These divisions form four subgroups of preforms, equal to the number of Callahan stages defined in UA data. Because PC1 is a size component, those subgroups are numbered from 1–4 in descending series, again to approximate the Callahan scheme.

Because cache preform subgroups are defined by mutually exclusive ranges of scores on size-related PC1, of course all major dimensions and weight differ by subgroups. All ANOVA F values are significant, and all pair-wise LSD comparisons are significant except those between Subgroups 1 and 2 in thickness and Subgroups 3 and 4 in weight. Cache preforms compared to Modena values by Callahan stage show that the lowest Modena mean length value (62.8 mm) and mean weight value (31–32 g) are reached between cache subgroups 2 and 3, and the lowest Modena thickness value (about 8 mm) is reached between cache subgroups 3 and 4. The lowest Modena mean width (about 30 mm) is slightly below the mean for cache subgroup 4. Therefore, acceptable preforms made at Modena were likely exported when

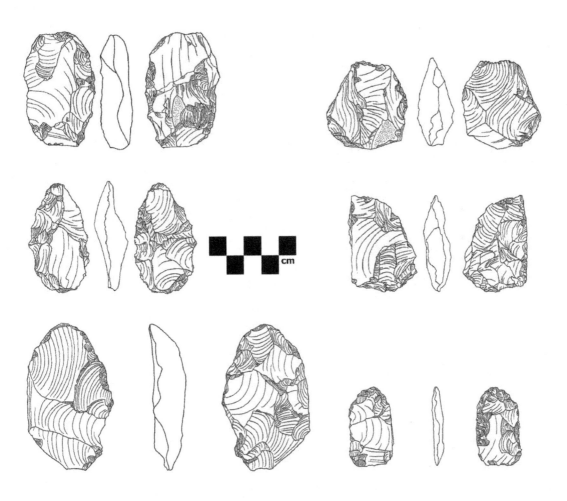

FIGURE 6.6. Tempiute preforms by Callahan stage.

they reached the vicinity of mean values found broadly around cache subgroup 3.

Preform Analysis: Tempiute

Despite fairly intensive UA investigations, only 22 preforms were found at Tempiute (Figure 6.6). As noted in Chapter 4, that effort included transect survey across the entire site specifically in search of preforms and finished diagnostic points.

Detailed data on Tempiute preforms appears in Shott (2016:Appendix F). Mean length is 51.3 mm, mean width 35.0 mm (again, both are for intact preforms only), mean thickness 14.1 mm, mean weight 20.6 g, and mean interior- and exterior-surface scar count 10.1 and 9.1, respectively. In an earlier section, mean metric

attributes of Modena preforms were compared to a selective regional sample. Tempiute's much smaller assemblage warrants comparison only to Modena. Tempiute preforms are significantly shorter, narrower, and lighter ($t = 3.3$; $p < 0.01$; $t = 3.2$; $p < 0.01$; and $t = 3.04$; $p < 0.01$, respectively) but not significantly thinner ($t = 0.6$; $p = 0.58$) than are Modena ones. (For length and weight, comparison is confined to intact preforms.) The smaller original nodules at Tempiute probably explain most of these differences. This comparison is not strictly of like to like, as the Tempiute assemblage is heavily skewed to Callahan Stage-0 preforms, (nearly two-thirds at Tempiute versus the slightly more than one-third at Modena). Correspondingly, Tempiute has proportionally fewer Stage-1 bifaces and slightly fewer Stage-2-ones. No Tempiute pre-form is assigned to Callahan Stage 3.

Nine of 22 Tempiute preforms are intact, most of the rest proximal (n = 7). Most are irregular in cross section (n = 11; 6 are plano-convex) and straight (n = 12) in longitudinal section. Seven Tempiute preforms bear trans-verse fractures, three oblique ones. Only two preforms bore platforms, so the sample size for relevant variables is far too small for analysis. The Tempiute assemblage includes no medial fragments, so there are no data to report for fracture plane 2. As at Modena, most Tempiute preforms are broken, but a higher proportion are intact than at Modena; proximal fragments are about half as common at Tempiute as at Modena. While only about 28% of Modena pre-forms bear cortex, more than half of Tempiute ones do (n = 12). Together, these findings sug-gest a higher frequency of cobble blanks com-pared to flake blanks at Tempiute, no surprise considering the small size of Tempiute cobbles would have made it difficult to remove flakes of suitable length and overall size to serve as blanks. Transverse fractures are somewhat more common at Tempiute and oblique ones corre-spondingly less common compared to Modena.

At Tempiute, mean dimensions and weight do not pattern consistently by Callahan stage. This may owe in part to the extremely low sam-ple sizes, which also make it difficult to obtain significant differences by stage. In fact, there are no significant differences in mean values by Callahan stage in any variable (Shott 2016:Table 6.26). The very low incidence of preforms in Callahan Stages 1 and higher complicates at-tempts to interpret the structure of the Tempiute assemblage or to compare it to Modena.

UA investigations found no preforms in most Tempiute areas. Five were found in N5, four more near that area, two in N2, and one in N6. Other Tempiute preforms could not be associated with an area. The small sample size and the clear predominance of N5 makes formal analysis moot. Clearly, N5 is the center of pre-form production, or at least preform discard, at Tempiute.

Using the same quantification method ap-plied to Modena, the 22 preforms or preform fragments at Tempiute yield a TIE value of 16.2. The few Tempiute specimens in Callahan Stages 1 and higher make it impossible to plot JTI by stage. It pushes this very small dataset too far to seek "breakpoints" in it (Johnson 1981:23).

Biface Technology Profiles

Thomas (1983:419–425) used "bifacial technol-ogy profiles" to graphically compare and con-trast the composition of biface-preform assem-blages at quarries and other sites. He defined different hypothetical or idealized profiles or cumulative-frequency curves for quarries, what amount to workshops or places where pre-form reduction spanned the range of "stages" in equal proportions, and occupation sites whose "repair curve" represents maintenance of already-finished tools. This is a useful heuristic and popular form of preform analysis in Great Basin studies (e.g., Estes [2009:177, Figure 5.8] identified his late Pleistocene biface assemblages with biface reduction and maintenance curves; Pedrick considered the Lake Range Quarry's preform assemblage to be near the "ideal quarry curve" [1985:26]), yet one that elides a great deal of complex variation in preform assemblages. Because of its popularity, it is worth applying to preform assemblages. As noted above, Thomas's definitions of preforms and their stages differ from those used here; for broad comparison, his Stages I–IV are equated with Beck and col-leagues' Callahan Stages 0–4. Thomas's Stage V representing finished points are consistent with few Modena and Tempiute specimens, not nec-essarily composed of local obsidian.

Figure 6.7 shows the resulting Modena and Tempiute technology profiles or cumulative-frequency curves, omitting Thomas's Stage V. It is no surprise that both assemblages are closest to Thomas's idealized quarry curve, Tempiute slightly more so than Modena. How-ever, Thomas's profile reaches 100% at his Stage I, equivalent to Callahan Stage 0 here whereas Modena and Tempiute profiles reach only roughly 40–60% by this stage. In effect, Thomas's idealized curve assumes that reduc-tion at quarries is confined to only the earliest preform stage, with subsequent stages occurring elsewhere. In contrast, prehistoric knappers at

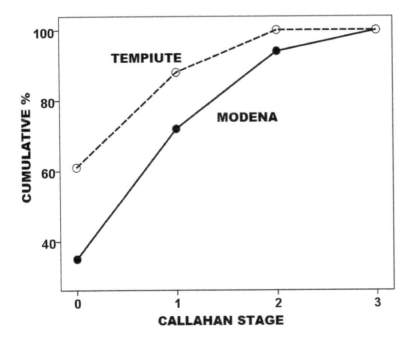

FIGURE 6.7. Modena and Tempiute technology profiles.

Modena and Tempiute worked many preforms to intermediate stages (see also Knell 2014:219), revealing more complex behavior that requires more detailed analysis and more advanced models like the Field Processing Model for its explanation. There also are differences, at least of degree, between Modena and Tempiute curves, but both the complexity of quarry assemblage formation and the small size of the Tempiute sample argue against simplistic interpretation of those differences.

Rank Plots

Throughout, this chapter has evaluated stage versus continuous models of the reduction and biface-production processes. One final way to evaluate these somewhat competing views is by rank plots of continuous variables thought to measure degree of advancement of reduction. As discussed above, preform weight, PC1 score, and JTI are such continuous measures.

If stages exist, then preforms belonging to the same stage should have very similar values for each of these variables; rank plots should group specimens by stage—all Stage-0 specimens together, then all Stage-1 specimens, and

so on. They also should yield nearly horizontal patterns of rank order within stages—because stage members will differ little in value across a considerable rank-order range—separated by abrupt drops that mark the boundary between stages. Plots should yield, that is, step-like patterns of progressive decline with rank.

Figure 6.8 shows no such pattern in the Modena preform assemblage nor, after removal of one exceptionally large specimen, in the Tempiute assemblage. In both cases, a rather free pattern of interspersing of preforms by stage appears, not strict succession by stage. Nor are horizontal segments separated by distinct steps found; instead there exists a relatively smooth decline in values with rank order. Distinct biface-preform stages are no more apparent in Figure 6.8 than they were in other analyses and data patterns reported above.

Conclusion to Preform Analysis

Modena preforms mostly were broken, no surprise considering that most successfully reduced preforms probably were exported for finishing and use elsewhere. Breakage that varies by type and frequency between assemblages

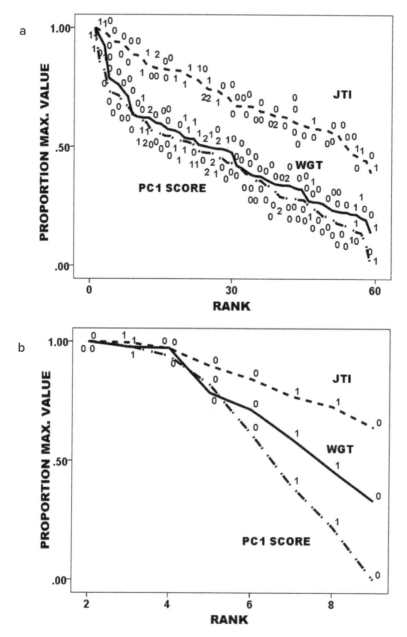

FIGURE 6.8. Rank plot of weight, PC1 score, and JTI: a. Modena; b. Tempiute.

complicates their comparison by size unless systematic quantification methods are used, as they were here and could be in other quarry studies. The production process for biface preforms can be modeled as successive stages, but in many respects is continuous. Both continuous and staged approaches are valid, for different purposes. Variables like weight and JTI vary continuously, not by stage, with size measures, and rank plots suggest similar continuous variation; patterning even in technological variables like cortex and sinuosity is complex and equivocal when viewed by stage.

Analysis of flake debris (Chapter 5) is complementary to preform analysis in some respects, notably the correlations found between proportion of Stage-1 flake debris and proportion of CS0 and CS2 preforms by Modena area. Differences by Modena area in proportion to Callahan-stage preforms is explained, as is joint variation in flake and preform assemblages across the site. A critical export threshold circa 40 mm may have existed. Compared to preforms from obsidian caches distributed across the Great Basin, Modena specimens are slightly less advanced or reduced. Most Modena and Tempiute preforms fall in CS0, progressively fewer into CS1 and CS2 and very few into CS3. This observation, not uncommon at Great Basin toolstone quarries, demands explanation. Great Basin archaeologists have proposed some explanations, which are explored and evaluated at some length in Chapter 7.

Points

Completed diagnostic projectile points were neither a major focus of UA's research design nor particularly abundant on the ground. UA field crews collected all points encountered but made no specific efforts to seek them. It is a truism that formal tools like diagnostic points brought into quarries often were discarded there because the abundance of toolstone made them superfluous (e.g., Gramly 1984). Such imported tools are expected to be made mostly of toolstones exotic to the source, and to be in a range of states of use, reduction, and reuse potential. Call this the replenishment hypothesis. The logic is that when a quarry is visited, whatever tools were imported are discarded, in a range of states of reuse, because they are easily replaced. That may be true as a generalization, but it does not apply particularly to Modena or Tempiute nor, evidently, to dacite quarries elsewhere in the Great Basin (Duke 2013:343). The abundant evidence of quarrying attests to considerable prehistoric use, but it is not matched by a sizeable assemblage of discarded imports. Selective uncontrolled collection may partly explain the paucity of diagnostic points at Modena and Tempiute, but Modena at any rate is not well known or easily accessed.

However true the replenishment thesis may be is a matter for separate study. A review of the Great Basin quarry literature at best partially supports it. However, the replenishment hypothesis assumes that imported formal tools like points are replaced immediately by equally formal, finished tools made at the source. Analyses in Chapters 5 and 7 suggest instead that the goal of on-site reduction was not finished tools to replace used imports, as the replenishment hypothesis assumes, but production-stage biface preforms for export and finishing elsewhere. If so, then replenishment may not have been common. No doubt some replenishment of some points and toolkits occurred, but neither the size of the finished-point assemblage nor the results of detailed analysis suggest that replenishment was common. Alternatively, at least some of the diagnostic-point assemblage at Modena and Tempiute may be palimpsests, the accumulation over long periods of traversal of the sites by hunting parties that used, sometimes broke, and sometimes lost the points they brought with them. To that extent, the assemblage of diagnostic points at Tempiute and Modena may not be entirely related to the sites' roles as toolstone sources.

Not surprisingly, the relatively small assemblage of finished points has a high proportion of broken specimens. Many Great Basin point types are lanceolate or stemmed, and specimens of different types may have different time-space distributions. These points tend to be fractured at the juncture of haft and blade. Haft elements typically required close tolerances for hafting, so often underwent grinding, thinning, and other methods of secondary treatment in order to attach newly finished tools to shafts and foreshafts. The aggregate effect of such extensive treatment is that the haft elements of specimens of a single type might have been modified in ways that suggest they belonged to different types (e.g., Beck and Jones [2009b:185–187] discussed several repair or resharpening trajectories that could, for instance, transform Parman into Silver Lake points). This can lead archaeologists to identify several types in lanceolate/stemmed-point assemblages that actually are, in

FIGURE 6.9. Points: a. Modena; b. Tempiute.

fact, a single type. The classification of broken haft elements should not be taken too far (Musil 2004).

Modena

We found only seven points or point fragments, including one chert specimen that itself probably is a broken preform (Figure 6.9a.d). Scattered across the site in such low numbers, the point assemblage supports little analysis. Metric, technological, and use attributes appear in Shott (2016:Table 6.27), largely following Beck and Jones's (2009b:124–126) coding scheme, itself based in part on Thomas (1981). One notable attribute of the small Modena point assemblage is that three of seven artifacts are not composed of obsidian. Because of the small number of obsidian points, and again, our research design's focus on other artifact categories, no obsidian point was sourced or measured for OHD. Rather than analyzing data from this small assemblage, this section describes each point.

Figure 6.9a.a. This proximal or stem fragment bears a snap fracture just below (distal of) the blade:stem juncture. Cross section is lenticular, with slightly expanding, probably soft-hammer facets forming a well-defined longitudinal ridge. Fine retouch along stem margins probably also was accomplished by soft-hammer, possibly even hard-hammer; many of these scars terminate in steps. Stem margins are lightly ground. One corner of the original base probably was damaged or broken. The corner was repaired by beveled retouch while the opposite corner was not altered, making the base edge slightly oblique to the longitudinal axis. It lacks evidence of haft abrasion on either face (Beck and Jones 2009b:189). Some crushing and stepping on the fracture plane at one edge suggests slight opportunistic use after breakage. Point fragments of this specimen's general size, form, fracture type, and location are abundant in a Late Pleistocene/Early Holocene assemblage at the Sunshine Locality (Beck and Jones 2009b:- Figures 6.18, 6.28–6.29). Lafayette and Smith (2012:Figure 5) associated this fracture type and location with projectile use.

Figure 6.9a.b. This is a finished stemmed point, with straight to slightly contracting stem margins. Cross section on the stem is lenticular. Stem and remnant central segments of the blade bear fine, shallow, nearly collateral flaking that suggests finishing by pressure. The blade is very short relative to the stem, and is steeply beveled in an alternate pattern. Retouch facets there are deep and parallel to expanding, probably from use of a soft hammer. The specimen is a heavily reworked WST/GBSS point. Whatever its original size and form, it may exemplify one of the rejuvenation trajectories by which Cougar Mountain points become other defined types in the series (Beck and Jones 2009b:Figures 6.13, 6.25). It lacks the "abrasion on the surface of the stem and the portion of the blade…confined within the socket" (Beck and Jones 2009b:189) that some such points exhibit.

Figure 6.9a.c. One base corner is reworked, perhaps after an oblique fracture, which makes the remaining base slightly asymmetric and slightly oblique to the tool's longitudinal axis. The center of one face bears what may be a remnant of the flake blank from which the point was made. Both edges are retouched by removal of fairly wide, deep subparallel facets, probably from soft-hammer percussion. One blade edge is beveled to just below (i.e., distal to), but not reaching, the shoulder. The tip is slightly asymmetrical and probably was reworked. In Thomas's (1981:Figure 11) key this probably is an Elko Corner-Notched point, although the identification is qualified by the slight basal reworking.

Figure 6.9a.d. Nearly square in outline, this artifact probably is the remnant of an unfinished preform rather than a finished point. Cross section is lenticular to plano-convex. Thinning and forming on both faces was accomplished by wide, parallel, probably soft-hammer flakes. The base is only partly finished; one segment of it may be the remnant of the flake blank from which the preform was made. The specimen bears a snap fracture perpendicular to what probably is its longitudinal axis. The fracture plane is slightly reworked at one edge from the slightly convex face. The same face on the op-posite end of the fracture plane bears several in-vasive but very thin or shallow facets, probably from pressure flaking. The tool was used or at least retouched in two different areas at least briefly after fracture. Toolstone is an irregularly banded grey-white chert.

Figure 6.9a.e. This is a finely made leaf-shaped biface finished by parallel collateral flaking. Two very shallow indentations, not directly opposite one another, may mark a blade-stem juncture asymmetric to the tool's longitudinal axis, but those indentations may be fortuitous and may also postdate the specimen's comple-tion. Otherwise, there is no visible distinction between stem and blade. In longitudinal section, the blade is noticeably thinner than the most proximal region, the probable stem. Edges are slightly beveled in an alternate pattern. Material is a variegated grey to light blue chert; toward the tip the matrix is tinged pink and may have been heat-treated. Superficially resembling the Cottonwood Leaf-shaped (Thomas 1981:Figure 11) or Ovate types, this point is unlikely to match either type; its point of maximum width is much nearer the base (i.e., more proximal) and its flaking pattern is expanding and overlapping, unlike the subparallel flaking of many Ovate specimens (Beck and Jones 2009b:Figure 6.15).

Figure 6.9a.f. Whatever its original size and form, this point probably was broken and re-configured. Although the point in its current condition bears no visible fracture plane that ex-tends to both faces, it has well-defined shoulders on both margins that are not symmetrical. Also, one face of the stem bears an oblique fracture plane or deep step-termination flake that orig-inated from base corner. Stem margins both contract, but at different angles toward the base. The slightly concave base is lightly abraded. One stem face bears two parallel thinning facets (length approx. 10 mm) that originate from the base; although these may be remnants of an original stem that was multiply fluted, rework-ing of the stem precludes certainty. The blade is finely retouched, probably by pressure-flaking,

and is very slightly beveled in alternate pattern. The toolstone is a red-brown chert that may be the product of heat-treatment. This is an ex-tensively reworked point that *may* have been a Paleoindian fluted biface, a possibility suggested by the complex rejuvenation patterns and tra-jectories among Paleoarchaic lanceolate and stemmed points (Beck and Jones 2009b:183–187).

An unillustrated obsidian tool remnant had a hard but probably exciting life. It was broken at least once and is so extensively worked on both faces that it is impossible to determine if the remnant is stem or blade. It bears a snap fracture that is extensively reworked, almost forming a unifacial bit edge, along one corner of the fracture plane. One edge bears a broad, shallow notch near the fracture plane, notching accomplished by one or two removals forming very steep facets. Nearly from the fracture plane, across the notch, and almost reaching the distal or proximal extremity, that edge is beveled and bears many fine pressure-retouch facets. The opposing edge is irregularly faceted and, despite extensive retouch, irregularly sinuous, a config-uration that suggests opportunistic use.

Tempiute

The Tempiute point assemblage is even smaller than Modena's (Figure 6.9; Shott 2016:Table 6.27). Again, it is far too small to support analy-sis in any detail.

Figure 6.9b.a. This obsidian tool, found by Bob Hafey, is a heavily reworked WST/GBSS point. What was the stem at its time of discard may originally have been the blade. Whatever the case, what now is the stem bears wide, expand-ing flake scars indicative of soft-hammer finish-ing. The stem's face is much more extensively faceted on one face than on the other. The base and one margin on its proximal-most segment were removed by a plunging overshot flake struck from the opposing margin. The opposite stem margin is mostly intact and contracting; because the damaged and partly removed stem margin is roughly symmetrical to the intact margin, probably the point originally had a con-tracting stem. What now is the blade is, on one face, merely a slightly reworked oblique fracture plane that may represent a failed attempt to resharpen or repair the edge just distal of the shoulder, resulting in a massive plunging overshot flake. This massive scar originates at what was the thickest segment of the point in longitudinal section, and the same location on the opposite margin bears several invasive scars from application of relatively massive force. Despite the oblique fracture that probably detached most of the original blade, the fracture plane was itself slightly retouched on the opposite face before the artifact was abandoned. There is no clear evidence of abrasion on the stem face that would be consistent. The cross section is irregular, whether from original design or the artifact's extensive reworking. As above, it illustrates the sometimes extensive rejuvenation efforts to which large lanceolate WST/GBSS points sometimes were subjected.

Figure 6.b.b. This is a WST/GBSS specimen with rounded base and heavily reworked blade. Toolstone is a variegated chert whose red-brown hues may owe to heat treatment. The longitudinal section along the stem is uniformly thin, but thickens noticeably on the blade. The stem's cross section is lenticular almost to the point of plano-convexity, but this owes to the extremely flat aspect of one fully-faceted face, possibly the interior surface of the original flake blank. The opposing face bears subparallel collateral flaking that forms a well-defined but shallow central ridge. Stem margins and base are abraded, but there is no clear evidence of facial abrasion from socket-hafting. Shoulders are rounded,

either by design or from reworking over their original locations on what is a heavily reduced blade. One blade edge is beveled. The point's tip appears to have been deliberately reworked to a chisel form, although not by burination (cf., Lafayette and Smith 2012:Figure 14). Because the toolstone is relatively coarse-grained, whether or not the chiseled tip "exhibits striations running perpendicular to its squared-off end" (Beck and Jones 2009b:191) cannot be determined. Among WST/GBSS points, chisel-tipping often is associated with alternate beveling (Beck and Jones 2009b:Table 6.21), as this point exhibits. This set of attributes suggests either use as knife or utility tool in place of or in addition to use as dart point (Beck and Jones 2009b:192; Lafayette and Smith 2012).

Figure 6.9b.c. This point has an expanding stem with originally well-defined shoulders. The base is slightly concave. One shoulder was broken and slightly reworked. Both blade margins are inflected in a pattern consistent with retouch/resharpening from the tip only part of the distance to the shoulder. One face bears what may be a caliche deposit. Although for measurement purposes the point is complete, it does bear a slight burin scar that extends from the tip for a distance of approximately 15 mm along one edge. Material is a translucent blue-white chert. The artifact may be an Elko Corner-Notched point that was sufficiently reworked to remove the original shoulders, although its PSA is slightly low compared to the range for that type (Thomas 1981:Figure 11).

7

Testing the Field-Processing Model
in Biface-Preform Data

*The weaknesses of quarry and mine studies have been directly
caused by the overemphasis on description for its own sake,
in the absence of an explicit theoretical perspective*

(Torrence 1986:165).

Ancient hunters did not eat stone, but formal models start from the commonplace observation that toolstone and other goods are, like food, resources for consumption. Just as foods like deer or acorns might be gathered from around the landscape and then processed, similar to how toolstone occurs as raw cobbles outcropping at places distant from locations of subsequent use and must be processed into tools of usable size and shape. Where hunters and food collectors had to separate needed materials from the rest, ancient knappers had to separate the useless from the useful, tools and flakes from cobbles in this case.

Knappers processed toolstone by systematic reduction (e.g., Holmes 1894a, Shott 2003) producing one or more useful tools like points from each cobble. Like butchering, the reduction process proceeded as a continuum sometimes divided into "stages" (Callahan 1979; Shott 1996b). Depending on circumstances, all segments or "stages" can be carried out at toolstone quarries in order to reduce carried material to the minimum (e.g., the long-haul scenario above), only some can occur there while other stages are completed elsewhere (shorter-haul scenarios), or little can occur there (the shortest-haul scenario). Ancient people probably visited quarries to supply themselves for considerable periods

of time. Doing so required making many tools from many cobbles. Anyone who has carried more than a handful of raw cobbles over any distance soon appreciates the wisdom of taking only the absolutely necessary material and leaving the rest behind.

Thus, the production and use process can be modeled in ways that admittedly simplify contextualized human behavior, but that identify its constraints and may explain its modalities. What goes for deer hunting and plant gathering then—hauling distance affects degree of field processing—may go for toolstone as well: the farther you expected to carry the finished or partly finished products, the more processing you may do at the quarry. Deer butchering, plant collecting, and quarry reduction all involve field processing.

Although formal models of toolstone acquisition, processing, and use are comparatively recent, archaeologists have long appreciated their underlying logic. In their studies of prehistoric quarries and lithic production, generally archaeologists recognized the importance of transport of products from quarries and the constraints that transport imposes on quarry production. To a pioneering lithic analyst, for instance, an Oklahoma chert quarry was a "factory wherein the raw material was prepared for market, and the shapes were carried only far enough to make transportation easy and profitable" (Holmes 1894b:15). For Ohio's Flint Ridge quarry, Mills reasoned similarly, because it was "uneconomical to transport blocks of material of which nine-tenths would be thrown away as useless" (1921:92; see also Smith 1885:868–869). These statements captured the essence of the later formal models tested in this chapter.

Similarly, at an obsidian quarry in northern California, "Indians roughed out blanks on the spot, rather than transport unworked chunks of obsidian from which so much wastage would be derived" (Heizer and Treganza 1944:304). Ericson interpreted the debris at California obsidian quarries as the result of efforts to reduce transport of waste flakes" (1984:6; see also Cobb 2000:94). Toolstone acquisition research on the northeastern margin of the Great Basin suggested that "A group planning to visit a source would take the time at or near the source to reduce and prepare the material for transport. This would be even more important the farther the group had traveled to procure the resource" (Loosle 2000:283). Elsewhere, early-stage bifaces were more common at quarries and later-stage bifaces at more distant workshops in the Knife River Flint region of the Dakotas, a pattern that Ahler (1986:94) linked to processing and transport cost. Although not framed in the context of formal behavioral modeling, Wilson's study of quarry production concluded that "bulky goods of little value have steeper gradients [i.e., shorter transport distances] than do lighter, more valuable goods" (2007:393). Rare ethnographic accounts of lithic quarry use also support such expectations applied to toolstone processing and use (Binford and O'Connell 1984:415; Gould 1980:126; Nelson 1987:140).

The Field-Processing Model

Like the schlepp effect in zooarchaeology, such qualitative reasoning is useful but limited. It recognizes the imperatives of transport costs, but formal modeling and its virtues—explicit definition of variables and their relationships, fairly precise measurement of costs and benefits, finer parsing of causality among contributing factors—is a more powerful explanation of behavior. In zooarchaeology and elsewhere, the costs of handling, processing, and transport are encompassed in the field processing model (FPM) applied to animal (Bettinger 2009) and plant foods (Bettinger et al. 1997; Bird and Bliege Bird 1997; Metcalfe and Barlow 1992).

The FPM itself is drawn from central-place foraging theory (e.g., Bettinger et al. 1997; Bird and O'Connell 2006; Charnov 1976), which assumes that people move regularly, obtain food and other goods at places distant from their residences, and that resources occur in packages that combine both useful and not-useful parts. The central-place model explains foraging behavior by linking return to foraging time via a (usually) logarithmic utility function. The greater the travel time (or other cost) to other foraging patches, the longer the time that optimal foragers will remain in the current one, tolerating lower return rates in the process.

Surovell (2009:192, Figure 7.4; see also Miller 2018; Torrence 1989) applied the model to stone tools by linking work performed to tool use life via a function that expressed tool effectiveness and, by extension, return as a logarithmically decreasing function of use life. In this context, use life is a variable under the user's control that may be manipulated in response to time or other costs of replacing the tool. Taking into account resharpening and the often nonlinear utility curves characterizing the life histories of lithic implements, Kuhn and Miller (2015; see also Andrefsky 2008, Miller 2018 modeled tools as resource patches, and their declining rate of return as a utility function. They predicted a tool's discard to occur when its declining utility reached the average for its type, and for type longevity to vary positively with its replacement time or cost and inversely with its average return rate. Several of their predictions were supported by limited analysis of large sets of southeastern Pleistocene and early Holocene point data (2015:186–189). Clearly, the FPM is one variant of a general model that relates effort to return via nonlinear functions and expresses optimal effort as a function of external costs. It can be applied to any problem or activity whose terms can be reduced to the model.

Metcalfe and Barlow's (1992) FPM example was piñon nuts, which contain both useful nutmeats and useless shells. Traditionally, processing and transport costs did not attract as much attention by lithic analysts, but that situation changed in the past two decades, as formal mathematical models of processing and transport came to the field. In this context, Elston (1992a) and Beck and colleagues (2002; see also Beck 2008; Smith 2015) demonstrated the FPM's relevance to toolstone acquisition, Barton (2001), Clarkson (2007:136), and Marwick (2013) to flake-tool use, and Surovell (2009) to formal-tool use. At the same time, experiments demonstrated the substantial costs to transport chert (e.g., Hollenbach 2009:92–93), further suggesting the FPM's relevance to quarrying.

The FPM applies to hunter-gatherers largely as a consequence of their mobility. Most practice large-scale land use, acquiring resources across the landscape and processing and transporting them from place of occurrence to place of consumption. Options include transporting the entirety of the resource or partly processing it in the field. Transport obviously has its costs in time and effort, and useless parts of resource packages incur transport costs without providing benefits; their transport is pure loss. To avoid this loss, one option simply is to process the resource package completely in the field, such that only useful parts of it are transported. But field-processing incurs its own costs in time and effort, both of which are proportional to the distance transported, the time and effort required in processing, and the opportunity costs of the time invested in processing. The increased transport time and effort entailed in lack of processing also has opportunity costs, but these rarely are modeled (but see Elston 1992a:33, 37, 1992b).

The constraint that activates the FPM, accordingly, is the quality of labor. As Elston put it, "Because human load carrying capacity is strictly limited…resources usually are processed at or near their source to reduce bulk and

weight" (1992a:44; see also Hollenbach 2009:93). The FPM predicts that cores and flake blanks are quarry-processed to more advanced reduction stages in proportion to the distance over which the product is to be transported. The underlying logic is that degree of processing at the source, which removes some proportion of waste material whose utility is 0, is a variable under knapper control, and that s/he will process more extensively there with greater anticipated transport distance in order to minimize both the cost of transport (i.e., more reduced cores/preforms/tools are both smaller and lighter) and the risk of lost effort and material from material flaws and production failure (e.g., Binford and O'Connell 1984:415). Flaw and failure risks—venture or opportunity costs in Elston's (1992a) sense—both increase with stage of reduction, so are minimized by processing to an optimal extent at the source, where failure is easily redressed by the abundance of raw cobbles, rather than elsewhere, where the opportunity to resupply is precluded (e.g., Turner and Bonica 1994:28).

Utility and the FPM

Mathematically, the FPM is given as:

$$z_{x-1 \leftrightarrow x} = p_x(u_{x-1}/[u_x - u_{x-1}])$$

where $z_{x-1 \leftrightarrow x}$ is critical round-trip travel time for any two successive processing stages $x-1$ and x, p_x is processing time to stage x, and u_x and u_{x-1} are resource utility at stages x and $x-1$, respectively (Bettinger 2009:91, 94). Figure 7.1 graphically depicts the basic model, plotting utility on the ordinate against processing cost on the abscissa. Key is the slope and form of the utility function U, which defines the optimal solution as a function of cost and increased utility. Because the terms for utility cancel out each other in the mathematical expression of the FPM, "we can calculate utility in any scale we choose" (Bettinger 2009:94). Metcalfe and Barlow (1992:354) scaled utility from 0–1.

Utility rises with processing time. Slope of the utility curve predicts the travel time or distance, z_i, at which processing is cost-effective. Amount or degree of optimal field-processing rises with required transport distance between

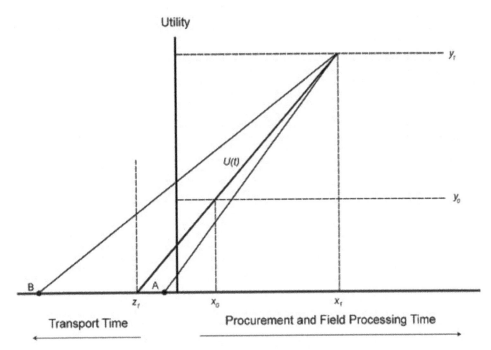

FIGURE 7.1. Central place foraging field-processing model ("FPM"). Source: Beck et al. 2002:Figure 4.

source and destination. As the distance between the ordinate and the destination rises (e.g., from A to B in Figure 7.1), more field processing at point-of-acquisition should occur. Bird and Bliege-Bird (1997) tested and confirmed this model ethnographically in hunter-gatherer food procurement (see Houston 2011 for other ethnographic tests). The form of the utility curve—linear in Figure 7.1 but probably logarithmic in empirical application, utility rising with processing effort at a constantly declining rate—is not arbitrary, certainly with respect to toolstone. Considerable experimental and archaeological evidence suggests that mass is a measure of toolstone utility (e.g., Beck et al. 2002:490; Elston 1992a:40; Kuhn 1994; Shott 1996b) and that as core reduction advances the amount of mass removed declines exponentially (Shott 2016:Figure 7.2).

An important extension of the FPM to toolstone (Beck et al. 2002:489; see also Elston 1992a) assimilated the stage typologies of biface reduction (e.g., Callahan 1979; Muto 1971) to a continuous, "differentiable" nonlinear utility function (Shott 2016:Figure 7.3). This idea iden-

tified the reduction process in the production of bifaces from preforms as a variety of field processing (see also Loosle 2000:283). Beck and colleagues' logic lacked a measure or currency of utility in processed toolstone (Houston 2011:529). Elston (1992a, 1992b) bridged this gap by devising: (1) a utility measure, the amount of use or value extracted from tools, either in time or amount of work performed (Elston 1992a; see also Barton 2001:296; Shott 1996a); and (2) a utility function $U(t)$ that expresses the relationship between the cost of tool production, again in time or work, and the value realized in the reduced cost of transporting unfinished tools to eventual places of use in the terrane. Beck and colleagues' and Elston's models also assumed that different toolstones are comparable in quality, although Earl's (2010) less detailed model nevertheless considered differences in toolstone quality.

Strictly, the entity that quarriers maximize is Elston's (1992a:41) "proportional utility," each resource unit's value scaled to vary, as in Metcalfe and Barlow (1992), between 0–1 depending on its state. Applied to toolstone, waste has

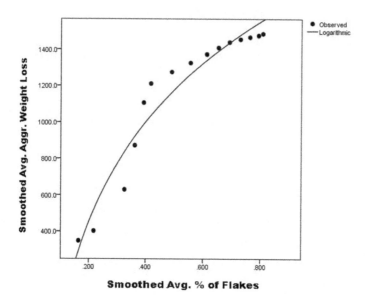

FIGURE 7.2. UA experimental utility data fitted to a logistic model.

a proportional utility of 0, and finished, serviceable tools a proportional utility of 1. Thus, a raw cobble possesses a proportional utility somewhere between those values, and its utility approaches 1 as it is reduced to remove useless mass and progressively approximate its final, useful form.

All else equal, the FPM predicts that the greater the transport distance from the quarry, the more advanced the stage of reduction, *qua* processing, that preforms should undergo at the quarry (Beck et al. 2002:492; Elston 1992a). Greubel and Andrews (2008:53) recognized this logic but linked staged production to craft specialization, not transport costs. This possibility raises the specter of equifinality, acknowledged but not otherwise considered here except to point out that Greubel and Andrews (2008:53, 57) conceded the uncertain evidence for their alternative explanation and that craft specialization is unlikely in the cultures that occupied most of Great Basin prehistory. The FPM can tell us a good deal about how ancient hunter-gatherers husbanded raw and partly worked materials at toolstone quarries and how they used them across the larger areas they occupied.

Following Elston (1992a), use life utility can

be measured by weight loss between raw cobble or flake blank and finished product. A utility function therefore plots weight loss against time or effort invested in reduction, measured in this case by the cumulative proportion of weight of flakes detached in successive time intervals during reduction. Experimental reduction of Glass Butte, Oregon, toolstone as part of the larger UA project corroborates Beck and colleagues' asymptotic utility function. Reduction of five obsidian cobbles to late-stage biface preforms yielded a smoothed aggregate weight-loss (and therefore utility) curve that clearly is asymptotic (Figure 7.2); it fits exponential and logistic distributions (r^2 = 0.76) but a logarithmic distribution (r^2 = 0.94) more closely, and is a reasonable approximation to logarithmic utility curves (e.g., Shott 2016:Figure 7.30). UA experimental data fit a cubic function slightly better, which with three parameters is less robust than one-parameter distributions like the logarithmic. Marwick (2013:Figure 9) used a cubic function, also possessing multiple parameters, to model multiple adaptive optima for Pleistocene and Holocene Thai foragers. As noted above, the central-place foraging model that subsumes the FPM typically assumes logarithmic utility functions (Charnov 1976), so the logarithmic function defined by UA data seems suitable for its few parameters and consequent robusticity.

> *Very few weapons, as compared with the great amount of flint used, were ever fully completed here. The great number of roughly finished specimens found here...and the great quantities of similarly shaped pieces from this locality occurring at places quite distant, show that the majority of the pieces worked here were brought nearly to the required shape and that it was left with the final owner to give each one such degree of fine finish and symmetry as suited him*
>
> (C. Smith 1885:868).

Testing the FPM Model in UA Data

In sum, and as adumbrated to some degree by C. Smith and others, the FPM predicts that how far you must transport processed goods influences how much processing you do at the point of acquisition. To use this insight, archaeologists must reverse the logic or at least the perspective. We cannot watch what ancient people did to animals killed or toolstone acquired. We can, however, observe the consequences of those actions in the material record. By looking both at places of acquisition and at the distribution of goods processed to different degrees at different distances across the terrane, we can reconstruct prehistoric actions and reveal the imperatives that underlay them.

The ideal test is of the FPM's nonlinear utility model (Figure 7.1). A reasonable approximation of that test assimilates the possibly staged nature of biface reduction. Yet the data requirements for testing such versions of the FPM are fairly high, including precise data on procurement, processing, and transport costs, the utilities of unprocessed and processed packages, *qua* cores (Beck et al. 2002:490), and the scale of the lithic terrane. What is more, not all flake debris removed from cores in the process of making tools lacks value because some may be used as tools; cobbles of different size and

form deliver varying utility in finished tools; the functional requirements, design, and performance of different tool types may vary; and toolstone may vary in knapping and functional qualities.

Few if any of these factors can be measured or controlled in most archaeological contexts, a common problem in the testing of detailed behavioral-ecology models in coarse, time-averaged data (Bird and O'Connell 2006:155; Elston 1992a:32–33; Houston 2011; Marwick 2013; Surovell 2009). Accordingly, C. Beck and colleagues adopted a qualitative (2002:490) approach to testing the FPM. Their test involved comparison of "directional trends" (2002:492), meaning they explored variation in transport distance between dacite, not obsidian, assemblages from quarries and residential sites in two central Great Basin datasets. Where transport distance was lower, less processing at the source was expected and earlier-"stage" products and by-products were expected at residential sites. Cowboy Rest Creek Quarry (CRCQ) and the Knudtsen residential site lie about 9 km apart in Grass Valley; Little Smoky Quarry (LSQ) is located in Little Smoky Valley, with the residential site LPL1 60 km to the east in Jakes Valley (Beck et al. 2002:492–493). For some analyses, Butte Valley residential sites CCL3 and CCL9, about 90 km northeast of LSQ, were included for comparison to that quarry; Kessler and colleagues (2009:150) considered the sites similar in assemblage character to LPL1. All of these sites are located about 150–200 km northwest of Modena. Although Modena obsidian is reported from at least CCL3 (Beck and Jones 1994:Table 4.3), most material from all sites is dacite.

The FPM predicts greater quarry processing with greater transport distance, but direct observation of processing time and transport distance is impossible archaeologically, as is direct measurement of processing and transport cost. Instead, Beck and colleagues examined variation jointly in degree of processing exhibited in assemblages and distance from their sources. The logic is that greater observed distance implicates greater transport distance. For instance, the greater distance between LSQ and its residential sites suggests greater degree of advancement of processing at the latter compared to CRCQ and its associated sites. That logic applies here as well.

C. Beck and others tested the FPM in both preform and flake data. They classified preforms by Callahan reduction stage (2002:494). Although for many purposes it is preferable to regard the biface-production process in continuous terms (e.g., Miller and Smallwood 2012; Shott 1996b; Wilson and Andrefsky 2008:94–94), in the literature most data are reported by stage; as a practical matter, therefore, stages must be used in analysis. Beck and others also calculated JTI for each specimen. As discussed in Chapter 6, JTI declines in value as reduction advances, because weight is removed at a faster rate than plan area in the process of thinning biface preforms to completion. Beck and colleagues expected proportionally more early-stage preforms and higher JTI values for preforms at quarries than at residences. Results (2002:496–498) supported these expectations. Although not a formal test of the FPM, preforms of different toolstones were imported to Paiute Creek Shelter in the northern Great Basin in more advanced stages from sources, including obsidian, more distant from the site (LaValley 2011:42, Figure 5). These results also were consistent with the FPM.

Kessler and others (2009) tested the FPM in flake debris. They used all platform-bearing flakes, whether broken or intact, and structured their analysis largely as a comparison of two quarry sites to their respective residential sites. Analysis showed flakes at quarry sites to be larger in most dimensions, and the distribution of flakes by cortex cover, exterior-surface scars, and platform scars to differ between quarry and residential sites, quarry flakes exhibiting more cortex cover and fewer surface and platform scars (Kessler et al. 2009:152–156, Tables 10.6–10.9).

Elsewhere, R. Beck (2008) tested the FPM in toolstones in two western Utah datasets. His test was structured around composition of flake assemblages, defined as differences in richness,

evenness, and heterogeneity (joint variation in richness and evenness or proportional differences between types). R. Beck's types were technologically defined flake types whose replicability between observers and datasets is of uncertain validity (Prentiss 1998; Railey and Gonzales 2015; Shott 1994:77–78); in any event, similar data were not collected for this study. Smith (2015:117–120) extended the model to finished tools by comparing mean dimensions and qualitative indicators of resharpening in obsidian diagnostic points between the Great Basin's "chert core" and "obsidian rim." Results supported the model because generally obsidian points found at a distance from their sources were more heavily resharpened.

Thus, the FPM has been examined in several Great Basin studies. Overall, results support the model and encourage further efforts, attempted here. This chapter tests FPM predictions mostly in Modena quarry data. Like that of C. Beck and colleagues', the analysis involves limited comparison between quarry and other sites across terranes, yet extends testing by defining relevant continuous data. Furthermore, the chapter's focus upon quarries holds toolstone quality constant for many purposes, although some comparative data are not necessarily from study sources. The strong emphasis on bifacial reduction in earlier research and this text largely holds utility variation constant by gross reduction mode and tool type.

Extended Test Case
Preform Analysis: Callahan Stages by Distance from Source

Testing of the FPM in the data involves first preforms and then flakes. The distribution of preforms by Callahan stage differs slightly between Modena Areas A, B, and F, but not between those areas combined and adjacent workshops (Areas D, E, 2009-1; $\chi^2 = 3.23$; $p = 0.36$, 1 E<5; in paired Callahan stages [0–1, 2–3], $\chi^2 = 0.18$; $p = 0.70$, 0 E<5; Shott 2016:Table 7.1a, b). All Modena areas contain similar distributions of preforms by Callahan stage, so the site can be treated as a unit in analysis. R. Jackson and colleagues (2009: 123, Appendix B) classified preforms by Callahan stage in their sample survey a short distance from the quarry itself. This area contains no known primary deposits of Modena cobbles but may include some float or secondary cobbles and bears considerable evidence of cobble reduction.

The aggregate distributions of preforms by Callahan stage at Modena and in Jackson and colleagues' sample differ (χ^2 = 17.4; p < 0.01, 1 E<5; Shott 2016:Table 7.2a), chiefly because the latter includes none in Stage 0. Preform distributions by paired Callahan stage (again, 0–1, 2–3) are not different between the samples (χ^2 = 1.91; p = 0.17; Shott 2016:Table 7.2b). On balance, preforms are not distributed differently by Callahan stage within the Modena quarry, and Jackson and colleagues' near-site distributions differ only equivocally from Modena's. Therefore, preform samples from all Modena areas can be combined for comparative analysis to other parts of the Modena terrane, and over very short distances there are minimal differences in the population of preforms by Callahan stage.

Differences are greater between Modena and obsidian preforms found farther afield in the Modena terrane, for instance in Cole's (2012: Table 11.11) survey of Meadow Valley Wash. Survey units in that study were located from near Modena to as far as 60 km away. The Meadow Valley Wash preform sample clearly differs from Modena's (χ^2 = 319.7; p < 0.01, 0 E<5; Shott 2016:Table 7.3a). Standardized residuals indicate that the Modena sample includes significantly more specimens in Stages 0 and 1 and the Meadow Valley Wash sample significantly more in Stages 3 and 4. Paired Callahan stages (in this case 0–1, 2–4) produce similar results (χ^2 = 255.9; p < 0.01, 0 E<5; Shott 2016:Table 7.3b), in which all standardized residuals are significant and Modena's are positive for early Callahan stages and negative for later ones while Meadow Valley Wash's are the opposite. Cole also reported that only "late-stage [pre]forms are present" (2012:577) at Sand Dune in Meadow Valley Wash. Other assemblages in Modena's terrane pattern similarly (Lawrence et al. 2005:Table 25.8; McKee et al. 2013:Table 35; Schweitzer et al. 2005a:Table 25.18; Schweitzer et al. 2005b:Table

17.24; see also Shott 2016:324). So too at Tosawihi, where "stage at which [preforms] were exported…probably varied from early Stage 3 to Late Stage 4, with most pertaining to middle and late Stage 3" (Bloomer et al. 1992:95; see also Bloomer and Ingbar 1992:246).

To this point, results are clear. Consistent with the FPM, there are significant differences in the distribution of preforms by Callahan stage between Modena and distant assemblages, with Modena specimens skewed toward earlier stages.

Seddon's (2005a; see also Andrews 2005) study of obsidian preforms and debris in Utah also supported the FPM. His data were from the entire Kern River project that traversed Utah from its southwest corner to Salt Lake City (Reed et al. 2005b). Along its length, this project area transited several obsidian terranes, including Modena's. In Seddon's analysis obsidian from these sites was not separated by source, and dominance of Modena cannot be assumed. Seddon examined patterns of variation in preform stages and flake sizes according to a set of ordinal distances from the nearest obsidian source—<5, 6–25, 26–50, and >50 km—without knowing if preforms and flakes originated from that source.

Considering the comparative abundance of obsidian sources and supply in the region, Seddon first expressed skepticism of processing requirements at quarries, reasoning that "there was little need to prepare staged or export bifaces at a quarry for use" (2005a:687) elsewhere. Yet his own data indicated otherwise (2005a:689). Seddon went on to demonstrate that obsidian preforms fell progressively into higher Callahan stages (i.e., were more extensively reduced and therefore processed) with distance from nearest obsidian source (2005a:Table 35-3). From preform-stage data Seddon inferred preparation at quarries to "reduce the risk of raw material failure" (2005a:695), another conclusion consistent with the FPM.

Although preforms in Seddon's study cannot be sourced to Modena (surely some were but many probably originated at other obsidian sources), it is worth comparing that dataset to Modena. The assemblages show a marked difference in preform distribution by Callahan stage. The Kern River sample, for instance, included no Stage-0 preforms, 15 Stage-1 specimens, and 303 of 318 classified as Stage 4 (Shott 2016:Table 7.5). The difference is highly significant (χ^2 = 347.2; p < 0.01, 0 E<5), as it is when stage categories are combined (χ^2 = 304.5; p < 0.01, 0 E<5).

Seddon's (2005c) Modena obsidian-hydration calibration identifies specimens with band readings >4.0 μ as "confidently Archaic." Most preforms from Modena itself fall in this range, as do many of Seddon's Kern River specimens. Accordingly, data can be used to test the FPM in this one chronological subdivision of Great Basin prehistory. Distribution of Modena and Kern River Archaic preforms, recalling that the latter includes a number of obsidian sources, again show a marked difference in preform distribution by Callahan stage, the Kern River sample including none in Stage-0 and a single Stage-1 specimen, and 57 of 69 classified as Stage 4 (Shott 2016:Table 7.6). Unsurprisingly, results are highly significant (χ^2 = 88.7; p < 0.01, 0 E<5), even when stages are pooled (χ^2 = 68.3; p < 0.01, 0 E<5), also consistent with the FPM.

Although not formal tests, other preform data are consistent with the FPM. Farther afield in the Great Basin, "obsidian bifaces were arriving in the [Shasta] valley in pre-reduced forms, being transported into Shasta Valley directly from the quarry and/or some intermediate location" (Hamusek et al. 1997:90) while more locally available chert preforms were found in roughly equal proportions across reduction stages. Earl (2010) expressed toolstone proportions in northern Utah assemblages as a joint function of distance but also obsidian quality. Preforms were knapped and then reduced to intermediate stages at the Soda Lake source area, then exported to residential sites elsewhere in the Mojave Desert (Knell 2014). Preforms of different toolstones, including obsidian, were imported to Paiute Creek Shelter in the northern Great Basin in more advanced stages from sources more distant from the site (LaValley 2011:42, Figure 5). At the Mt. Hicks quarry, later-stage preforms tended to occur only in late

prehistory when inferred transport time and distance were low (Martinez 1999:158–159).

For a study area in east-central Nevada approximately 250 km northwest of Modena, where the outer range of Modena's and perhaps Tempiute's terranes overlap with that of other toolstones, Hauer's (2005:92–94) preform stages followed Callahan and closely resembled C. Beck and colleagues' (2002:Table 2) scheme. Hauer (2005:106, Table 7) reported three preforms of Modena obsidian, one at Stage 2 and two at Stage 4 (converted from Hauer's report of Stages 3 and 5). Most preforms were imported to the Sunshine Locality in Long Valley, about 250 km northwest of Modena, in an advanced production stage (Beck and Jones 2009a:Table 5.23), although most specimens there were chert, not obsidian. Estes's (2009:64) preform stages seem similar but are not identical to the Callahan scheme; he (2009: Appendix E) reported two Modena preforms from Jakes Valley, about 220 km northwest of the source, one each of middle and late stage. The large obsidian preform assemblage at Hunchback Shelter, about 70 km northeast of Modena, where its terrane gives way to Wild Horse Canyon obsidian, is dominated by mid- to late-stages (Greubel 2005:Table 3-204; see also Greubel and Andrews 2008), matching Hunchback's interpretation as an intermediate workshop between quarry source and places of finishing and use of tools. Similarly, Talbot and others (2000: 340–341) inferred transport of prepared blanks of Wild Horse Canyon obsidian to explain the technological character of debris assemblages at Five Fingers Ridge, about 80 km east-northeast of that source, that were scarce in cores and dominated by what they identified as late-stage reduction flakes. However, Griffin's (2013) test of the FPM in obsidian and other toolstones in the Tahoe region did not support most model predictions and Hocking's (2013:42, 54) study of dacite and chert sources in southern British Columbia provided only partial support for FPM expectations.

Beyond the Great Basin, a similar pattern of larger, less advanced preforms at the source and smaller, more advanced ones elsewhere was observed in the terrane of basalt adze quarries in New Zealand (Turner and Bonica 1994:28) and quartzite quarries in Quebec (Burke 2007: 68). In flake tools, Clarkson (2007) found support for the FPM in Australian data where, for instance, weight of lancet cores varied inversely with transport distance from quarries (2007:148, Figure 7.12). In Modena's and Tempiute's terranes and elsewhere, on balance, quarries and outlying sites differ in assemblage composition by preform stages or degrees of finishing, often in proportion to distance. This too supports the FPM.

Preform Analysis: Continuous Variation

In Callahan's (1979) experimental data, preform weight and JTI correlated with a principal component 1 (PC1) of preform dimensions. At successive reduction "stages," the variables declined with PC1 at an ever-accelerating rate (Shott 2015:557–560; 2016:329–334).

Weight and JTI are sufficiently closely correlated that analysis of both may seem redundant. But most Modena preforms are broken. There, the size dimension represented by PC1 and differently by weight is the size of broken and intact preforms freely mixed together. Neither weight nor PC1 score is a direct measure of original size in broken specimens, although both capture the pattern of covariation between relevant variables. However, JTI is a valid measure of both intact and broken tools (Amick 1991:55; Johnson 1981:18; see also Miller and Smallwood 2012:31 for their similar thinning index). JTI scales weight to the plan area of a specimen. For instance, an intact preform that weighs, say, 10 g and measures, say, 5 cm^2 gives a JTI of 10/5 = 2.0. If the preform were broken into two equal halves, each fragment's JTI would be the same, 5/2.5 = 2.0. Weight and JTI both must be taken into account in analysis of the Modena assemblage.

Continuous Variation in Preform Assemblages: Modena

It is worth using the same approach in comparing obsidian preforms from the quarries to elsewhere in Modena's and Tempiute's terranes. At Modena, weight and JTI are correlated (r_s =

0.90; $p < 0.01$). Preform weight varies inversely by Callahan stage (for weight, $F = 24.1$; $p < 0.01$; for JTI, $F = 34.3$; $p < 0.01$; Shott 2016:Figure 7.7). PCA yields one component whose eigenvalue >1, again interpreted as size, that accounts for 58.0% of variation. (In this case, a second component [eigenvalue = 0.97] explains 32.3% of variation, with a high negative loading for length and high positive one for width, with thickness near 0.) Weight ($r = 0.94$; $p < 0.01$) and JTI ($r = 0.90$; $p < 0.01$) covary strongly with PC1, and Callahan stages roughly partition the continuum with considerable admixture.

Separate PCA on paired Callahan stages (in this case, following Beck et al., 0–1 and 2–3) shows significant difference in slope of regression of weight upon PC1, despite the modest visual difference (Figure 7.3). Difference in slope coefficients is nearly significant in JTI, but the pattern is unexpected because the more advanced staged pair has a slightly higher coefficient (Shott 2016:Figure 7.8b). Respective slope coefficients in regression of weight upon separate PC1 by Callahan paired stage are 14.86 and 12.75 ($t = 2.2$; $p = 0.03$); of JTI they are 0.37 and 0.46, respectively ($t = 1.9$; $p = 0.06$).

To this degree, Modena preform data pattern similarly but not identically to Callahan's. To extend analysis, they can be compared to metric data on obsidian preforms from Panaca Summit (Elston and Juell 1987:Tables 5–6, who did not report Callahan stage assignments), assuming that the great majority of obsidian deposited there originated at Modena as sourcing data indicates (Seddon et al. 2001:Table 4.3). Modena was discovered only recently, but its geochemical profile was defined earlier. Uncertainty about its exact location invited its identification with Panaca Summit (e.g., Elston and Juell 1987) at which a concentration of sites attracted archaeological work (Elston and Juell 1987; Seddon et al. 2001). Following Schiffer (1975:266), Panaca Summit, located about 20 km from the Modena quarry, is a "founding curate set." As described in Chapter 2, "rare obsidian cobbles" (Hull 2010:33) may occur at Panaca Summit, but the most parsimonious assumption is that most or all of the worked obsidian found there originated at Modena.

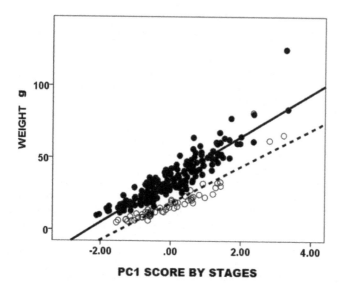

FIGURE 7.3. Modena preform weight against PC1 score by grouped stages. (CS0–1 solid circles and line, CS2–3 open circles and dashed line.)

PCA of Panaca Summit preforms alone also yields a single eigenvalue >1 on which length, width, and thickness all load strongly. There is also a significant correlation of weight with PC1 ($r = 0.89$; $p < 0.01$). A common plot of weight against each assemblage's separate PC1 score shows a considerably lower regression slope for Panaca Summit's than Modena's assemblage (Figure 7.4):

Modena: weight = 30.5 + 16.3 * PC1
    ($r = 0.94$; $p < 0.01$)
Panaca Summit: weight = 5.1 + 3.9 * PC1
    ($r = 0.89$; $p < 0.01$).

The difference in slope is significant ($t = 16.2$; $p < 0.01$). This result does not reflect merely the dominance of early-stage preforms at Modena. Even the more advanced pair of Callahan Stage 2–3 preforms at Modena differs in slope from Panaca Summit preforms, where respective slope coefficients are 15.2 and 3.9 ($t = 12.9$; $p < 0.01$).

The common plot of JTI upon each assemblage's PC1 score also shows a considerably lower regression slope for Panaca Summit compared to Modena:

Modena: JTI = 2.8 + 0.49 * PC1
    ($r = 0.84$; $p < 0.01$)

Panaca Summit: JTI = 1.1 + 0.25 * PC1
    ($r = 0.67$; $p < 0.01$).

Again, the difference in slope is significant ($t = 5.4$; $p < 0.01$). And again, even the more advanced pair of Callahan Stage 2–3 preforms at Modena differ in slope from Panaca Summit preforms, where respective slope coefficients are 0.54 and 0.25 ($t = 5.3$; $p < 0.01$).

This pattern of declining slope of regression of weight and JTI upon PC1 implicates more advanced reduction at Panaca Summit. The area's distance from Modena further supports FPM predictions. Besides the distribution of preforms by Callahan stage, significant differences between assemblages or subsets of them emerge in the slope of the regression of weight upon size component PC1, a continuous variable. This not only corroborates the FPM but adds continuous patterns of variation to its testing and suggests the possibility of further testing in comparable data acquired from other assemblages.

Continuous Variation in Preform Assemblages by Modena Area

Assemblage-wide patterns can be broken down by area at Modena. For this purpose, only Areas A, B, D, and F and their vicinities as defined above have sufficient assemblage sizes for

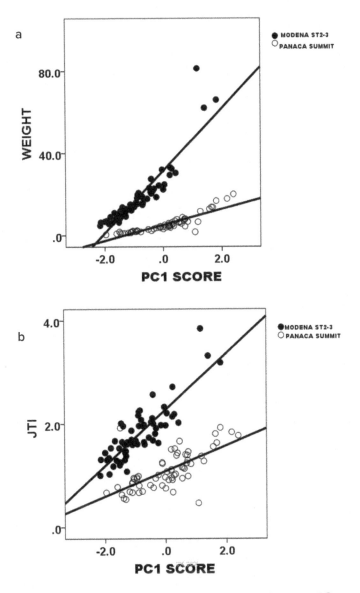

FIGURE 7.4. Modena and Panaca summit preform weight and JTI against PC1 score.

separate treatment. Table 7.1 presents descriptive data for weight and JTI. Areas pattern as does the entire quarry assemblage in most cases, because both weight and JTI correlate inversely with Callahan stage. In Area A, however, there are extreme outliers at CS 2 for both variables. In Area D, CS 1 exceeds neighboring stages in both measures, and CS 0 and CS 2 are nearly identical in mean weight. The anomalous CS 2 means for weight and JTI are not owing to small sample size; CS 2 is the most common preform

stage in Area D, and values for both measures there are the highest among all Modena areas and stages. Although n = 1 for CS 3 in Area F, both weight and JTI pattern consistently in that area.

Both variables differ by Callahan stage in Areas A, B, and F; differences in neither variable are significant by Callahan stages in Area D. Yet pairwise LSD *p* values between successive Callahan stages are not significant in Area A (or, of course, in Area D), while most are significant

TABLE 7.1. Preform Weight and JTI by Area at Modena. ANOVA *F* and associated *p* value calculated across Callahan stages within each area, and Tukey's LSD *p* calculated for successive Callahan stages.

CS	n	Mean	sd	F	p	LSD	n	Mean	sd	F	p	LSD
		Weight (g)						JTI				
		Area A						Area A				
0	33	32.4	11.5	5.5	<0.01		31	4.3	1.4	6.1	<0.01	
1	40	27.9	13.7			0.19	38	3.6	1.7			0.12
2	25	21.3	19.6			0.08	25	2.8	2.4			0.08
3	5	8.7	4.4			0.80	5	1.2	0.6			0.79
		Area B						Area B				
0	12	34.7	12.1	9.9	<0.01		10	4.5	1.5	8.9	<0.01	
1	26	26.0	9.8			<0.05	26	3.4	1.2			<0.05
2	16	19.1	7.6			<0.05	13	2.5	1.0			<0.05
3	4	9.4	2.8			0.07	4	1.3	0.4			0.08
		Area D						Area D				
0	6	34.9	13.6	1.4	0.28		6	4.5	1.7	1.9	0.18	
1	10	51.0	30.6			0.22	8	6.4	3.8			0.23
2	4	34.2	22.8			0.26	3	3.0	0.3			0.09
3	2	16.9	4.1			0.43	2	2.3	0.5			0.78
		Area F						Area F				
0	33	46.4	14.2	10.2	<0.01		33	5.9	1.7	10.2	<0.01	
1	18	31.8	9.9			<0.05	16	4.2	1.2			<0.05
2	5	22.5	9.0			0.15	5	2.9	1.1			0.12
3	1	11.0	–			<0.05	1	1.6	–			<0.05

in Areas B and F. LSD p is nearly significant between Callahan Stages 2 and 3 in Area B, and the somewhat more significant difference between stages 1 and 2 in Area F may owe to small sample size. In sum, differences in both weight and JTI are significant across all four Callahan stages in all areas examined, but are significant between successive stages only in Areas B and F.

Similar analysis can be conducted by area within Modena. As at the assemblage level, for clarity and brevity analysis is confined to preforms distinguished by paired Callahan stages (CSpair, where CSpair 0 spans Callahan Stage 0 and Stage 1, CSpair 2 the more advanced stages), not single stages (CS), although the pattern in all four Callahan stages is similar (Shott 2016:Table 7.9). Most regression results pattern as expected, CSpair 0 showing higher slope, although Area A does not conform (see Figure 7.5 for weight, where Areas A–F are represented by progressively lighter circles and progressively sparser regression lines). Whether CSpair 0 and 2 regression slopes differ significantly in Area A is irrelevant, since CSpair 2's slope is higher, not lower as expected. Differences in slope coefficient are significant for both variables except in Area D, whose CSpair 2 sample size is small (in Area B for weight, $t = 2.92$; 1-tailed $p = 0.01$, for JTI $t = 2.38$; 1-tailed $p = 0.04$; in Area D for weight, $t = 1.66$; 1-tailed $p = 0.24$, for JTI $t = 1.58$; 1-tailed $p = 0.28$; in Area F for weight, $t = 2.61$; 1-tailed $p = 0.02$, for JTI $t = 2.45$; 1-tailed $p = 0.04$), although the small sample sizes for CSpair 2 in Areas D and F qualify results.

Data can be interrogated further. For CSpair 0, Areas A and B have nearly identical slopes, Areas F and D higher ones. Areas A and F differ significantly in slope ($t = 2.41$; $p = 0.02$), as do Areas F and D ($t = 2.11$; $p = 0.04$). Among source areas, early-stage preforms were somewhat less extensively reduced at F compared to A and B. Area D shows a higher, not lower, slope for early-stage preforms, contrary to expectations for a workshop area. For CSpair 2, Areas B and F have nearly identical slopes that lie between Area A's high and Area D's low ones. Areas A and B slopes differ significantly ($t = 2.61$; $p = 0.01$), but Areas F and D slopes do not ($t = 0.57$,

$p = 0.60$). For CSpair 2 preforms, Area A's slope significantly exceeds that of other areas, indicating less extensive reduction of CSpair 2 preforms there compared to other areas. Although its slope is not significantly lower than Area F's, Area D patterns as expected because it exhibits a lower slope than any of the source areas.

Results are similar in plots of JTI upon PC1 separately by CSpair. For CSpair 0 preforms, again Areas A and B have nearly identical slopes; A's is significantly lower than F's ($t = 2.42$; $p = 0.02$) while F's in turn is significantly lower than D's ($t = 2.11$; $p = 0.04$). For later-stage preforms, again areas pattern from A to D. Areas A and B differ significantly in slope ($t = 2.61$; $p = 0.01$) but Areas F and D do not ($t = 0.56$; $p = 0.60$). Therefore, Area D patterns as expected among later-stage preforms by exhibiting the lowest slope, but against expectation among early-stage ones.

Tempiute's Preform Assemblage

Tempiute's much smaller preform assemblage precludes similar treatment. Overall, however, weight in both Modena and Tempiute preform assemblages patterns directly with PC1 (Shott 2016:346–349). The two assemblages differ significantly in the slope coefficient that describes the rate of decline in weight versus size (Modena = 16.3, Tempiute = 7.6; $t = 5.41$; $p < 0.01$). Despite this difference, the overall slope for the Tempiute assemblage also is significantly higher than is found for Panaca Summit sites ($t = 2.88$; $p < 0.01$). If the Tempiute assemblage's reduction slope is lower than Modena's, it remains higher than that of founding-curate assemblages like that of Panaca Summit.

Flake Analysis

Flake debris is much more abundant than are stage preforms, and the FPM must be tested in flakes as well. Kessler and others (2009) did so for the assemblages studied by C. Beck and colleagues (2002), concluding that CRCQ was indeed the source of Knudtsen's toolstone, and that much of the material from its outliers originated at LSQ (2009:147–148). Like Modena and Tempiute, C. Beck and colleagues' flake

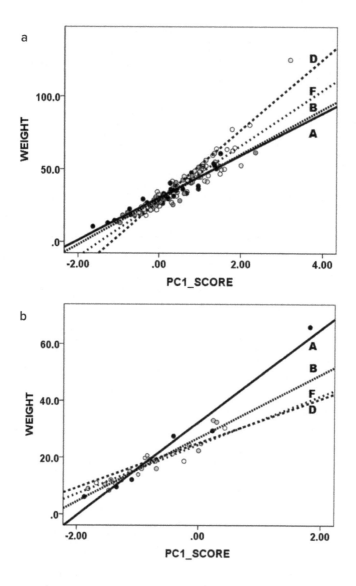

FIGURE 7.5. Weight against PC1 for Modena Areas A, B, D, and F by CSpair:
a. CSpair 0–1; b. CSpair 2–3. (Areas A–F represented by progressively
lighter circles and progressively sparser regression lines.)

assemblages were obtained by controlled surface collection (2002:492–493).

Kessler and others compared quarries and
habitation sites by flake mean metric attributes,
incidence and distribution of cortex, and mean
dorsal and platform faceting. They obtained
results consistent with the FPM's expectations.
Specifically, quarry flakes were larger and
heavier, showed higher incidences of exterior

cortex, fewer exterior facets and less extensive
platform preparation than did flakes from supplied sites. Also, CRCQ and LSQ differed by
degree in their ranges of flake-size distribution
and incidence of exterior cortex, in ways consistent with FPM expectations and the greater
distance between LSQ and its supply range
(Kessler et al. 2009:152, 156).

Kessler and colleagues' analytical protocol

(2009:151–153) differed somewhat from UA's research design. Among flake attributes, thickness was omitted in UA data. Kessler and others (2009:Table 10.7) divided exterior-surface cortex cover into ordinal categories, whereas UA data were coded merely for presence or absence, a practice considered more valid (Shott 1994:74–75). Kessler and colleagues' (2009:Table 10.9) platform-preparation categories distinguished cortical from faceted platforms, although even platforms bearing a single facet can retain cortex, and distinguished abraded platforms as a separate category, although such platforms can bear single or multiple facets. Finally, Kessler and colleagues' (2009:Figure 10.4, Table 10.10) size categories are not equivalent to the intervals used here and elsewhere (e.g., Ahler 1989b). Assuming square, not rectangular, dimensions from their Figure 10.4, Kessler and colleagues' categories 1 and 2 approximate the <6.35 mm (<¼ in) interval, their categories 3–5 the 6.35 mm (¼ in) interval, category 6 the 12.7 mm (½ in) interval, categories 7–8 the 19.05 mm (¾ in) interval, and categories 9+ the 25.7 mm (1 in) interval.

Flake Analysis at Modena

Tables 7.2 and 7.3 compare Modena to CRCQ and LSQ and sites in their terranes, assuming that the considerable difference in sample sizes, particularly the low numbers for CCL3 and CCL9, does not affect results; at any rate, in certain analyses, data from residential sites were pooled. Incidence of cortex and platform-scar distribution also pattern consistently with the FPM (Shott 2015:562; 2016:352–355). Because reduction at quarries often starts with cortex-bearing cobbles, all else equal quarry debris should exhibit higher incidence of exterior-surface cortex than debris from other assemblages. One thing that may not be equal is mean and range of cobble size, their lower surface: volume ratio leaving larger cobbles with less cortex to retain on detached flakes (Bradbury and Franklin 2000). Size of CRCQ and LSQ cobbles being unknown, analysis assumes no difference from Modena in this important respect.

Modena and CRCQ are similar in distribution of exterior-surface faceting, especially in the 0- and 1-scar categories, although they diverge slightly at higher categories. LSQ is strongly skewed to higher degrees of faceting similar to residential sites, though the sample is admittedly small. Modena and CRCQ again are similar in platform faceting, LSQ again skewed toward higher values, although in this case residential sites have significantly higher percentages of platforms bearing 2+ scars (Shott 2015:Table 7).

Modena flakes are lighter than CRCQ ($t = 3.94$; $p < 0.01$) but not LSQ ($t = 1.0$; $p = 0.34$) flakes, possibly an effect of difference in density between obsidian and dacite. However, Modena obsidian flakes are much heavier than dacite flakes from residential sites (in all t tests between Modena and residential sites all p values <0.01. Note also the high variation in flake weight at LSQ.) Modena flakes are shorter than CRCQ ($t = 3.03$; $p < 0.01$) but not LSQ ($t = 1.0$; $p = 0.35$) flakes, and again are much longer than flakes from residential sites (all p values <0.01). Modena flakes are narrower than CRCQ ($t = 8.1$; $p < 0.01$) and LSQ ($t = 4.6$; $p < 0.01$) flakes, but wider than those from residential sites (all p values <0.01). Altogether, in flake size Modena specimens are much more similar to CRCQ and LSQ than to residential sites, although somewhat smaller on average than those from the central Nevada quarries.

Analysis of debitage assemblages from contexts much nearer Modena, at Meadow Valley Wash and Panaca Summit, mostly involved size-sorting and technological flake classification. Unfortunately, few individual flake-metric or other attribute data were recorded (Cole 2012: 466–471; Seddon et al. 2001:28–29), which limits comparison between Modena and neighboring locales. Again, the FPM would predict that Modena flakes should be larger and that more of them should bear cortex compared to nearby sites dominated by Modena obsidian.

The Meadow Valley Wash sample (by omitting several survey units in the Modena vicinity that contained "astronomical" [Cole 2012:268] numbers of obsidian flakes and presumably

TABLE 7.2. Exterior-Surface Scar Distribution and Mean (and Standard Deviation) of Flakes at UA and C. Beck et al. sites. Source: C. Beck et al. (2002).

Site	0 scars ct (%)	1 scar ct (%)	2 scars ct (%)	3+ scars ct (%)	Total
Modena	201 (8.0)	294(11.7)	400 (15.9)	1,617 (64.4)	2,513
Tempiute	143 (15.1)	131(13.9)	177 (18.7)	494 (52.3)	945
CRCQ	13 (7.1)	24 (13.1)	42 (23.0)	104 (56.8)	183
LSQ	1 (1.6)	1 (1.6)	6 (9.4)	56 (87.5)	64
Knudtsen	0 (0.0)	2 (0.8)	23 (9.3)	222 (89.9)	247
LPL1	0 (0.0)	1 (3.0)	5 (15.0)	27 (81.8)	33
CCL3	0 (0.0)	1 (14.3)	0 (0.0)	6 (85.7)	7
CCL9	0 (0.0)	0 (0.0)	1 (4.8)	20 (95.2)	21

	Modena	Tempiute	CRCQ	LSQ	Knudtsen	LPL1	CCL3	CCL9
weight (g)	14.8 (18.2)	8.3 (8.9)	35.2 (69.9)	18.2 (28.0)	1.2 (2.2)	1.0 (1.1)	1.3 (1.3)	1.1 (0.6)
length(mm)	33.4 (14.6)	29.2 (11.0)	38.4 (21.9)	35.5 (17.5)	13.9 (7.6)	13.4 (6.0)	16.5 (6.2)	14.9 (4.4)
width (mm)	30.5 (12.7)	25.5 (10.3)	47.7 (28.7)	40.7 (17.5)	16.0 (8.6)	13.5 (7.3)	16.0 (6.5)	17.5 (4.1)
n	2,514	945	183	64	247	64	8	21

represented workshops on the source's periphery) included 3,297 flakes; mean weight of proximal flakes was 1.9 g, of nonproximal flakes 1.3 g (Cole 2012:Table 11.18). At Modena, mean flake weight is 10.0 g in the Stage-1 sample and 8.5 g in the Stage-2 sample. Meadow Valley Wash and Modena means cannot be tested for difference, because Modena figures are means of means (i.e., calculated from each collection unit's flake count and aggregate weight). Mean weight of intact flakes at Modena was 14.8 g, not strictly comparable to all flakes from Meadow Valley Wash. Nevertheless, the great difference in mean values suggests statistical significance. For Panaca Summit sites, Elston and Juell (1987: Tables 39, 45, 50, 55, 65) reported incidence of cortical and noncortical flakes, of which more than 80% were noncortical. About 53% of the sample of measured and coded Modena flakes are noncortical, a significant difference ($\chi^2 = 701.4$; $p < 0.01$, o E<5). In these limited data, flake weight and incidence of cortex cover pattern as the FPM predicts.

Flake Analysis at Tempiute

As discussed above, quarry debris should show higher incidence of exterior-surface cortex, but cobble size complicates this expectation. Tempiute cobble size probably was small, yet Tempiute shows the highest incidence of cortex (Shott 2016:Table 7.11).

Like Modena, incidence of cortex is higher at Tempiute than at CRCQ ($\chi^2 = 265.1$; $p < 0.01$, o E<5). LSQ has substantially fewer cortical flakes ($\chi^2 = 287.3$; $p < 0.01$, o E<5; for both CRCQ and LSQ compared to Tempiute, all standardized residuals exceed |1| in all cells). Central Nevada residential sites with founding-curate assemblages have markedly lower incidence of cortex for which statistical belaboring is unnecessary. Distribution of cortex patterns significantly between Tempiute and the combined quarry sites CRCQ and LSQ ($\chi^2 = 265.2$; $p < 0.01$, o E<5), and standardized residuals exceed |1| in all cells. Unlike Modena, Tempiute differs significantly from CRCQ in distribution of exterior-surface faceting ($\chi^2 = 9.23$; $p = 0.03$, o E<5), Tempiute being more skewed toward

o counts than is CRCQ. Compared to Tempiute, LSQ is strongly skewed to higher degrees of exterior faceting similar to residential sites, though the sample is admittedly small ($\chi^2 = 31.2$; $p < 0.01$, o E<5; Table 7.2). Again, differences between Tempiute and central Nevada founding-curate assemblages require no statistical belaboring. Also unlike Modena, Tempiute differs from CRCQ ($\chi^2 = 72.2$; $p < 0.01$, o E<5) and greatly from LSQ ($\chi^2 = 156.7$; $p < 0.01$, o E<5) in platform faceting because it exhibits many more unfaceted platforms. As before, LSQ skewed toward higher values, although in this case residential sites have significantly higher percentages of platforms bearing 2+ scars (Shott 2016:Table 7.13).

If Modena flakes were lighter than CRCQ but not LSQ flakes, Tempiute flakes are lighter than flakes at both dacite sources (for CRCQ, $t = 5.20$; $p < 0.01$; for LSQ, $t = 2.82$; $p < 0.01$). As at Modena, this difference possibly is an effect of difference in toolstone density but also perhaps cobble size. Indeed many of the results of comparisons between Tempiute and CRCQ and LSQ are consistent with those from Modena. Tempiute flakes are much heavier than dacite flakes from residential sites (at Modena, in all t tests between Tempiute and residential sites all p values <0.01). Tempiute's flakes are shorter than CRCQ ($t = 5.50$, $p < 0.01$) but again also LSQ ($t = 2.84$, $p < 0.10$) flakes, and much longer than flakes from residential sites (all p values <0.01). Tempiute's flakes are narrower than CRCQ ($t = 10.36$; $p < 0.01$) and LSQ ($t = 6.87$; $p < 0.01$) flakes, but wider than those from residential sites (all p values <0.01).

In size Tempiute specimens are much more similar to CRCQ and LSQ—and to Modena— than to residential sites, although they are somewhat smaller on average than those from the central Nevada quarries. Tempiute does differ from those two quarries, however, in lower incidence of exterior-surface and platform faceting, contrary to Modena. Despite the modest differences in their mean values, the large Modena and Tempiute assemblages make significant the differences in their weight ($t = 14.00$; $p < 0.01$), length ($t = 9.10$; $p < 0.10$), and width ($t = 11.90$;

TABLE 7.3. Flake-Size Distribution at UA and C. Beck et al. Sites. Modena data for measured and coded intact flakes only.

Site	ct (%)	ct (%)	ct (%)	ct (%)	Total
Modena	488 (19.4)	751 (29.9)	629 (25.0)	647 (25.7)	2,515
Tempiute	239 (25.1)	380 (39.9)	235 (24.7)	91 (9.6)	945
LSQ	12 (4.8)	12 (4.8)	75 (29.8)	153 (60.7)	252
LPL1	60 (48.4)	32 (25.8)	25 (20.2)	7 (5.6)	124
CCL3	9 (56.3)	4 (25.0)	3 (18.8)	0 (0.0)	16
CCL9	11 (27.5)	19 (47.5)	10 (25.0)	0 (0.0)	40

Kessler et al. (2009:Figure 10.4, Table 10.10) size classes 9–10, 7–8, 6, 3–5 approximated to Modena size classes 25.4 mm (1 in), 19.05 mm (¾ in), 12.7 mm (½ in), and 6.25 mm (¼ in), respectively.
Modena data for measured and coded intact flakes only.

$p < 0.01$) when compared to one another, Tempiute flakes being smaller in all dimensions.

Flake-Size Distribution Data

Kessler and others (2009) analyzed flake attributes and briefly reported flake-size distributions. A complementary approach involves more detailed analysis of Modena and Tempiute size distributions. Following Ahler (e.g., 1989b; see also Shott 1994), different experimental modes, including several that vary along the reduction continuum, can be distinguished in multivariate analysis. Size distributions or cumulative size distributions also can be compared to mathematical models that describe fracture mechanics. For instance, Stahle and Dunn (1982; see also Ingbar et al. 1992 and Shott 1997b:117) fitted flake-size distributions from experimental biface production to the Weibull model, and showed that progressive reduction segments or stages had higher slopes in regression of measures of flake quantity upon measures of flake size. In other experimental data, slope of the regression line of ln-cumulative percentage by size class against size class itself rose as reduction proceeded (Shott 1994:Figure 2). That is, progressive segments of other biface-production experiments patterned by slope in plots of ln-cumulative proportions upon flake size (Shott 1994:93). Ingbar and colleagues (1992:64–67) took a similar approach, plotting Weibull stage models against empirical data from Tosawihi Locality 36. Thus, regression-line slope is a mea-

sure of degree or stage of reduction, and has the added virtue of measuring continuous variation between flake assemblages.

Modena

The size distribution of Modena flakes coded for attribute analysis can be compared to size-distribution data from LSQ and its terrane (Table 7.3). Results are reported in Shott (2016: 375–377), where regression lines of the aggregate Modena log-cumulative percentage flake size by count upon flake size, and the similar distribution of flakes from LSQ and its associated residential sites are compared to regression lines for stages 1, 5, and 9 of Behm's (1983; see also Shott 1994:Figure 2) experimental biface-production data. Lines for both Modena and LSQ lay well above, not near or even below, Behm's Stage 1. Recalling that regression-line slope rises as reduction progresses, Modena and LSQ slopes are considerably lower even than Behm's earliest stage. However, Modena data were not corrected for taphonomic winnowing as discussed in Chapter 5. Presumably, taphonomically corrected Modena and LSQ slopes would fall closer to Behm Stage 1. In contrast, the line for LPL1 and other residential sites closely resemble that for Behm's Stage 5, suggesting middle-stage reduction, although taphonomic correction might move that line toward Behm's Stage 9. Thus, flake-size distribution data from Modena, LSQ, and the latter's terrane also seem consistent with FPM predictions.

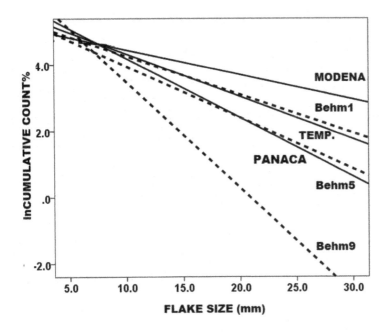

FIGURE 7.6. Regression slope of Modena, Tempiute (Areas N2, N5, and N6 only), and Panaca Summit (surface contexts only) flake-size distributions.

The size distribution of flakes from excavations at Panaca Summit sites includes considerably more specimens in the 6.35 mm (¼ in) fraction than either the Panaca Summit or Modena surface assemblages, possibly because smaller flakes on the surface were winnowed by sheet wash. (Using different size classes, McKee et al. [2013:Table 36] reported broadly similar patterns from UNEV pipeline sites, such that smaller flakes were progressively more common with distance from obsidian sources.) Therefore, the most direct comparison between Modena and Panaca Summit sites is with flakes collected from the surface of the latter rather than their excavation samples, since all Modena data are from the surface. As discussed above, analysis assumes that most if not all obsidian discarded at Panaca Summit originated at Modena.

Figure 7.6 plots the regression lines of the aggregate Modena log-cumulative percentage flake-size distribution and the similar distribution of flakes from Seddon and colleagues' (2001:Tables 4.11, 4.32, 4.48, 4.55, 4.65, 4.73, 4.81, 4.82) Panaca Summit surface contexts. (Size distributions are truncated at 6.35 mm, but Figure

7.6's x-axis is extended to <5 mm. Lines nearly converge owing to the constraint that cumulative percentage cannot exceed 100 and its log-transform of 4.61; lines converge around but do not reach that 100% value at the flake-size limit of 6.35 mm because they are least-square regression lines, not interpolations of data points. Data points are omitted for clarity.) Again, these data are not corrected for taphonomic winnowing. For comparison, Figure 7.6 also plots Behm's stages 1, 5, and 9. Again, the Modena line's slope is lower even than Behm's earliest stage, indicating very early stages or degrees of reduction, and Behm's later stages have progressively higher slopes. The Panaca Summit line has a considerably higher slope than Modena's, similar to Behm's Stage 5, which indicates more advanced stages of reduction with distance from the source. Thus, ratio-scale flake-size distribution data from Modena and nearby sites also are consistent with FPM predictions.

Overall, the Modena flake-size distribution patterns clearly and consistently as expected for a quarry, where early reduction segments should dominate. The pattern remains generally clear when Modena areas are plotted separately, with only Area D showing a somewhat lower slope than other areas (Shott 2016:Figure 7.26). The difference in slope between Area D and the main quarry areas, indicating slightly more advanced degrees of reduction at the former, is consistent with its interpretation as the largest Modena workshop area.

Tempiute

In aggregate flake-size distribution Tempiute falls below Modena and the LSQ quarry, very near Behm 1 and above later Behm stages and the founding-curate assemblages of central Nevada (Figure 7.6). Tempiute clearly is an early-reduction assemblage like Modena, and its lower placement in Figure 7.6 may owe as much to small cobble size as to any technological difference from Modena. There is no point in comparing Tempiute flake-size distributions directly to Panaca Summit assemblages, because the latter are not near Tempiute nor probably dominated by Tempiute obsidian. Nevertheless, Tempiute's placement near Behm 1 suggests that, like Modena, its flake-size distribution comprises earlier-stage reduction than do founding-curate sets at Panaca Summit. The major Tempiute areas N2, N5, and N6 pattern similarly to the entire quarry assemblage (Shott 2016:Figure 7.27). Both separately and in the aggregate, flake-size distributions of debris assemblages at Tempiute suggest early reduction segments.

Discussion

As with other variables used in this study, most other flake-size data also support the FPM. Seddon's (2005a:693) Kern River data, for instance, showed that obsidian debris became smaller in general with distance from several sources, including Modena, although intermediate distances suggested greater processing than either shorter or longer ones. Significantly, he linked lithic processing needs to mobility type more than scale (i.e., mobility frequency [MF] more than mobility magnitude [MM] *sensu* Shott [1986]), arguing that high MF, usually associated

with only modest MM, imposed the greatest constraint and therefore adaptive value to field-processing. This is because high MF prevented knappers from visiting toolstone sources regularly, whereas the lower MF and higher MM associated with logistic mobility permitted more regular access to quarries (Seddon 2005a:695). Seddon's test, assuming that MF was higher in the Archaic than the Formative, supported this argument because Archaic assemblages at similar distances from quarry sources as Formative ones contained higher proportions of smaller flakes and later-stage preforms that indicate later processing/reduction stages (2005a:697). In general, Seddon's results were consistent with "a relatively high degree of planning for raw material exploitation...across all time periods" (2005a:689). Finally, qualitative interpretation of the debris assemblage from 42WS1630, near St. George, Utah, about 70 km southeast of Modena, from which the only two analyzed flakes were sourced to Modena, suggested almost entirely later-stage reduction, such that "primary reduction of an unaltered piece of raw material to produce cores/blanks, or usable primary flakes, did not occur at the site" (Westfall et al. 1987:128).

Future Data Needs and Tests

As encouraging as were earlier tests and results reported here, they concern only the most robust predictions of the FPM. Contrary to optimization models like the FPM, Brantingham (2003) proposed a neutral model that assumed no risk-reduction or other constraints on toolstone economics. Brantingham's formal model yielded expectations for distance-to-source distributions, assemblage diversity, and technological composition (e.g., degree of core reduction) that resembled expectations of optimization models like the FPM. Greubel and Andrews (2008) related similar patterning in their data to the existence of craft specialization. Cultural and historical context and competing adaptive needs can subordinate toolstone acquisition to other needs, and archaeological behavioral-ecology models do not directly measure costs, benefits, or behaviors in time-averaged assemblages (Joseph 2002; Marwick 2013:560–561). Combined, these factors create an equifinality problem—different causes producing similar results—that is common in archaeology. We cannot change how the archaeological record formed, but we can devise model tests that are as congruent as possible with available data.

Such tests must be commensurate with the continuous nature of lithic reduction and the FPM's "continuous and differentiable" (Metcalfe and Barlow 1992:348) utility functions, only partly achieved in this study. A suitable research design approaches this goal in three ways. First, its focus on one major source would control for toolstone quality and core size/form, hence confine analysis to a single-source utility function. Second, data would be continuous, including proportions of Callahan-stage preforms and reduction measures like JTI, flake dimensions and percentage variation in their categorical attributes, and flake-size distributions. (Another approach, used here to some degree, involves size-distribution data to identify flake assemblages to interval- or ratio-scale segments of reduction continua [e.g., Root 1992]). Third, such variables would be measured across many sample locations, preferably in a probabilistic regional sample, not the opportunistic comparison between relatively few studies that chance to report comparable data. In this way, distance would be treated as a true continuous variable, not a categorical one. More variables that are more fine-grained and measured at more locations are better to distinguish between the neutral model and optimization models like the FPM.

Another challenge is time control. A mid- to late-Holocene span showed no time differences in the import of nearly-finished obsidian and other preforms into a northern Great Basin consumer site (LaValley 2011:42, Figure 4), but variation in land-use scale and associated toolstone processing imperatives may have varied over time. Large sites like Modena surely are time-averaged accumulations that freely mix cultural material of different ages. In arid landscapes like

the Great Basin, many parts of whose surface were stable throughout prehistory, even small open sites like those used to test the FPM in this and earlier studies probably are accumulations as well. One form of chronological control is hydration dating which, at least for Modena obsidian, resolves past time coarsely and unevenly (Seddon 2005c). This study involved those data in a very limited way, but more extensive testing requires better chronological control.

Transport distance and associated costs are central to the FPM, yet nowhere in this or similar studies was it possible directly to estimate this quantity. Although results are clearly consistent with the FPM, until land-use scale can be estimated or measured directly and differences in it by time period can be identified, more direct tests of the FPM are impossible. Probably land-use scale was larger in pre-Fremont times than later, but this remains an assumption; it also is possible that land-use scale increased again in late prehistory.

Accordingly, as important to progress as are this and previous studies, even more important would be carefully designed regional research to permit more precise testing of the FPM in the continuous terms commensurate with the model. For instance, Cole's (2012) obsidian preform data could be compiled by survey unit and examined for possible patterns of variation in Callahan stage distributions as a function of distance from Modena. This assumes, of course, that all obsidian preforms in that study area are from Modena. The assumption can be avoided in existing preform data and in new regional fieldwork in the Modena terrane that uses portable XRF technology (e.g., Frahm 2016) to source preforms and flakes, including the abundant small ones, in the field. XRF would be particularly useful in Meadow Valley Wash to the north and west, where secondary sources of Modena are unlikely because drainage at the source itself runs southeast, and therefore should not complicate the measurement of transport distance. Hydration measurement of both Modena preforms and flakes also should be part of such a research design. Assuming shorter transport distances later in prehistory (as above, land-use scale may have varied cyclically or erratically, not monotonically), the FPM predicts that later preforms would be processed at the quarry less extensively than earlier ones.

The result would be a test of the FPM model against dozens to hundreds of observations of flakes, preforms, and points, not the few sets of data used in this and previous studies. Among other things, it could seek patterning in ratio-scale regression slope of weight upon PC1 in subsets of preform data and in plots of ln-cumulative flake counts by size class at successive distances from Modena, subdivided by definable time periods when possible, varieties of continuous analysis used here but not yet applied systematically to other data. Such a test would document not merely presence and direction but also more precise *degree* of data's fit to model predictions and possibly variation through time in that degree of fit. Its focus on one source and adjoining terrane would control substantially for the independent effects of toolstone quality and core size/form.

Conclusion

Based on assumptions of risk-reduction and minimization of transport costs, the field-processing model (FPM) applied to stone-tool quarries predicts that degree of completion of the production process relates directly to transport distance; the greater the transport distance the nearer to completion of the production process at the quarry. The FPM was tested and supported in earlier Great Basin lithic studies (C. Beck et al. 2002; R. Beck 2008; Elston 1992a, 1992b; Kessler et al. 2009). Modena and Tempiute data further support the model. Specifically, preforms by Callahan stage are skewed toward earlier stages at Modena and Tempiute compared to neighboring sites, and distributions tend toward later stages with greater distance from the source. Particularly significant is the difference in the ratio-scale measure of reduction of preforms, not previously documented, in which Modena quarry preforms show less advanced degree of reduction than do assemblages from Panaca Summit. Also, the size and attributes of flakes at Modena and Tempiute resemble those from central Nevada dacite quarries and differ significantly from dacite assemblages at residential sites in central Nevada and obsidian assemblages near Tempiute and Modena.

This and earlier studies encourage serious engagement with the FPM. To date, however, model predictions have been tested in data acquired either for other purposes or from only limited portions of larger lithic terranes. Most model predictions are coarse and therefore vulnerable to equifinality. More robust FPM predictions require finer-grained data. The challenge in future testing of the FPM in stone tools, and all behavioral-ecology models applied to lithic and other archaeological data, is to design and complete research that uses the fullest range of finest-grained evidence to test the most robust predictions of the model.

8

Estimating Scale of Quarry Production

A glance at the Modena and Tempiute quarries is enough to appreciate that a great deal of reduction occurred at each of them. No less is true of many other obsidian sources in the Great Basin, and toolstone quarries around the world. But how much is a "great deal"? No exact answer is possible because of the many factors that contribute to the relationship between reduction and its by-products. Archaeologists often speak of the intensity of reduction at quarries and elsewhere, signifying some combination of type, amount, and rate of production. Because "intensity" conflates these factors, it may be wiser to speak of reduction scale.

Around the world, quarries are characterized by copious quantities of flake debris. Such abundance, especially when concentrated as at Tempiute and Modena, may overwhelm common archaeological expectations and make estimation of quantity seem futile, the numbers of artifacts beyond counting. Yet no matter how much flake debris, and how many cores and tools may be at quarries, their numbers are finite, and so capable of estimation. No exact answer may be possible, but estimation is justified both for its own sake as well as for comparison. Modena, for example, contains what seem staggering numbers of flakes but is much smaller than obsidian quarries like Bodie Hills and the Coso Fields. The sheer scale of quarry debris may be daunting, yet careful research design and data collection can produce samples from which estimation of original quantity is possible. Fortunately, UA's research design involved probabilistic sampling from which estimation of quantity is possible.

Whatever the amount and character of debris at quarries, it relates only obliquely to scale of sociopolitical complexity in the prehistoric cultures that created it. Kinds, amounts, and volumes of debris were generated by societies of different scale and political complexity, and the activities that produced debris themselves could be organized at different scales. Large debris scatters across areas measuring from hectares to km² were produced by state-level societies (e.g., Shafer and Hester 1983), complex chiefdoms (e.g., Cobb 2000; Torrence 1986), tribes (e.g., Ahler 1986; Burton 1984), and band-level societies like those in the prehistoric Great Basin (e.g., Gilreath and Hildebrandt 1997; Singer and Ericson 1977) and elsewhere (e.g., Hiscock and Mitchell 1993).

Even large quantities must be scaled to the span of accumulation and the volume of debris generated in typical reduction episodes. Cobb (2000:159–173) systematically sampled Dillow's Ridge, one part of the larger Mill Creek complex extensively exploited in late prehistoric Illinois. Cobb's sample produced an estimated 86,000 kg of debris, a superficially impressive figure that, nevertheless, combined with reasonable estimates of debris generated in the manufacture of each hoe (the main object of production there) and of length of site use, yielded an estimate of 432 hoes/year. Workshops (not even quarries) at Neolithic Çatalhöyük contained as much as 132 metric tons of debris, even though obsidian was imported from nearly 200 km away mostly in the form of partly finished preforms. Yet over the span of accumulation, this volume amounts to approximately 100–300 kg/year, or 10–30 trips assuming 10 kg/person/trip (Cessford and Carter 2005). Using samples of different design and precision, European archaeologists have estimated much higher rates of Neolithic stone-axe production (Bosch 1979:130; Le Roux 1979:55).

Accordingly, large volumes of debris and the scale of production they implicated could be produced not only by centralized polities but also by small-scale societies (Burton 1984:244; Schyle 2007:97–105). Certainly as much as anywhere else, Great Basin quarries have been the subjects of major studies (e.g., Buck et al. 1994; Connolly 1999; Gilreath and Hildebrandt 1997; Singer and Ericson 1977). There is no reason to doubt that the small-scale prehistoric polities of the Great Basin could have produced debris of the scale and distribution found at Modena and Tempiute. Even the abundance of flake debris in the enormous Coso Fields could have been produced by intermittent visits by small work groups organized by small-scale societies (Gilreath and Hildebrandt 1997:182).

The purpose of this chapter simply is to estimate relevant quantities—of flakes, preforms, and analytical core units (Carr and Bradbury 2001)—present in the extensive quarry deposits at Modena and Tempiute. It follows the natural progression of the reduction sequence that begins with flakes and cores, then proceeds to the (partially) finished products in the form of stage preforms. In the process, it exploits the probabilistic nature of the samples at Modena and Tempiute as the basis for valid estimation, and introduces several methods for estimating quantities of original products and debris both from samples and from the fragmentary remains that are common at quarries. Shott and Olson (2015) reported some of these data and analysis.

Estimating Number of Flakes

Possibly the most salient characteristic of obsidian quarries is their abundance of flake debris. Despite this abundance, flake debris may seem uninformative about details of production scale and nature. Yet many tools themselves were exported from quarries, and many remaining ones are rejects or failures, so may not be representative of all aspects of scale or technology of production. In this circumstance, flake debris may provide better estimates of scale if their abundance can be calibrated to biface preform production rates. Accordingly, this chapter follows Gilreath and Hildebrandt's logic, because "in determining the magnitude and range of stone-tool working that occurred at a location, debitage resulting from both failed and successful reduction events is superior to [or at least complementary to] the artifact assemblage as a basis for study" (1997:20).

Owing to the density or extent of their debris fields, estimates of flake quantity at some European quarries involved limited sampling of debris itself to estimate deposit depth, which then was multiplied by field size (e.g., Bosch 1979:130; Le Roux 1979:55; Torrence 1986:203–204). As an alternative to this reasonable but indirect method, UA's sample was designed to yield direct estimates of flake quantity.

As described in Chapter 4, UA fieldwork involved two probabilistic random samples, Stage 1 and Stage 2, from clusters at Modena and Tempiute. At Modena, we collected more than 8,500 flakes in Stage-1 samples, and counted and weighed almost 5,900 flakes in Stage-2 samples. In the absence of prior knowledge, we used simple random sampling. Stage-1 and Stage-2 samples were independent, and designed in part to test the replicability of sample results. Estimates derived from the two samples cannot be combined.

Many sample units at both Modena and Tempiute measured less than 1 m². In those units, the number of flakes was converted to count/m². For instance, count in a ¼ m² sample unit would be multiplied by four. The average count/m² for each cluster was then multiplied by the area of the cluster to obtain estimates of total flakes for the cluster, along with ±1 standard error (s.e.) boundaries. Table 8.1 reports estimates of total flakes for Modena and, for reasons set forth below, of all intact flakes as well as intact flakes in 12.7 mm (½ in) and 6.35 mm (¼ in) fractions from Stage-1 sample units. (The table includes estimates for Modena's small Area U, not otherwise analyzed.) Because Stage-2 sample units were not collected they yielded only aggregate count and weight of flakes, not separate estimates of intact flakes in any size classes. There is a considerable difference in estimates between Stage-1 and Stage-2 samples. Roughly splitting the difference, sampling suggests that investigated areas of Modena contain about 26 million flakes. To place this figure in context, much more limited and possibly not probabilistic sampling at Mount Edziza in British Columbia led to an estimate of 48 million pieces of obsidian there (Fladmark 1984:145). Elsewhere, limited testing at the Game Hut obsidian quarry at Newberry Crater produced estimates of >15,000 flakes/m³ (Connolly 1999:36) which, unless that site is very small, probably mean that the size of the Game Hut flake assemblage exceeds Modena estimates. Systematic sampling at two Aegean obsidian quarries intensively exploited during the Bronze Age yielded estimates of flake quantity that ranged from 30 to 50 million (Torrence 1986:Table 31). Table 8.1 also gives estimated counts for Tempiute. In this case, the Stage-1 estimate significantly exceeds the Stage-2 one. Together, they suggest that approximately 2 million flakes occur at the site, less than one-tenth the estimate for Modena.

Table 8.1 reports estimates of total flake weight for Stage-1 and -2 samples at Modena and Tempiute. Point estimates for flake weight at Modena range from approximately 222 million to 276 million grams. Dividing these figures by the estimated number of flakes yields mean weight per flake of 9–10 g. Actual mean weight of intact Modena flakes is 14.8 g. Point estimates for flake weight at Tempiute range from approximately 7 million to 15 million grams. Dividing these figures by the estimated number of flakes in the comparable samples (Table 8.1) yield mean weight per flake of 5.5–6.8 g. Actual mean weight of intact Tempiute flakes is 8.3 g. For both quarry assemblages, not surprisingly, mean weight of intact flakes slightly exceeds estimated mean weight of the entire sample, but figures are similar and therefore validate estimates of flake quantity by count and weight.

Approaches to Estimating Scale of Production

Estimating the total number of flakes at Modena areas is a straightforward, if necessarily approximate, exercise grounded in probability theory. The number of flakes at quarries like Modena and Tempiute is good to know for its own sake and for broad comparison with other quarries. But alone, this quantity is merely a number that reveals little about the nature and scale of prehistoric activity at the quarries. Mere numbers must be calibrated to relevant measures of past action like cobbles worked and tools or preforms manufactured. That is, numbers must be converted to estimates of prehistoric quarry production.

One way to measure this quantity is, as above, simply by counting the number of flake by-products and spent cores, or to measure the aggregate weight of these artifacts. Yet all else being equal, larger cobbles produce more debris, as do different kinds of reduction or efficiencies of reduction of equivalent cobbles. Count and weight are valid but to measure production scale and to compare between loci of a site or between sites, it is useful to have a common measure of scale. All toolstone production involved cobbles, so number of cobbles worked is a legitimate measure of production scale.

Arriving at such estimates requires several assumptions or analytical steps. First, the goal of all production is assumed to be bifaces and all flakes therefore assumed to be generated in biface production, or analysis may allocate varying fractions of the debris to biface and other production modes. Second, the stage(s) to which bifaces or other products were processed must be assumed or inferred from some combination of the recovered tool assemblage and the debris assemblage. Third, the quantity or quality of flake debris necessary to complete each biface to each recognized stage must be assumed or known experimentally.

Assumptions furnish the simplest route to estimation, and may be reasonable depending

TABLE 8.1. Estimated Number and Weight of Flakes at Modena and Tempiute.

COUNT

Modena Stage 1

| Area | Total Flakes (n) | | | Intact Flakes | Intact 12.7 & 6.35 mm² Flakes |
	-1 s.e.	Estimate	+1 s.e.	Estimate	Estimate
A	8,663,292	10,611,180	12,559,068	1,244,319	1,560,114
B	7,171,101	9,156,606	11,142,111	1,113,969	1,567,007
D	635,801	755,589	875,378	159,614	272,749
E	76,982.2	91,183	105,383	37,168	19,806
F	1,181,844	1,401,057	1,620,270	540,998	309,440
U	3,577	4,471	5,365	5,523	2,893
2009-1	59,416	72,101	84,785	17,266	13,686
Σ	17,792,013	22,092,187	26,392,360	3,118,855	3,745,695

Stage 2

| Area | Total Flakes (n) | | |
	-1 s.e.	Estimate	+1 s.e.
A	9,329,121	10,729,917	12,130,713
B	14,558,374	16,993,843	19,429,311
D	659,942	798,160	936,377
E	84,494	107,289	130,085
F	1,355,499	1,443,184	1,530,869
U	16,111	21,792	27,473

Tempiute Stage 1

Area	Total Flakes (n)			Σ 12.7 & 6.35 mm^a Flakes
	-1 s.e.	Estimate	+1 s.e.	Estimate
N1	513,500	669,738	825,976	134,970
N2	842,217	947,769	1,053,321	255,084
N3	17,373	25,376	33,379	11,126
N4	6,635	9,576	12,517	3,101
N5	265,379	310,206	355,034	109,379
N6	267,680	304,964	342,248	95,600
N7	8,991	14,079	19,168	6,970
N8	46,764	54,306	61,849	18,964
N9	42,574	54,821	67,068	19,246
N10	13,114	25,954	38,794	13,797
S5	759	1,352	1,945	1,144
Σ	2,024,984	2,418,141	2,811,298	669,381

Stage 2

Area	-1 s.e.	Estimate	+1 s.e.
N1	218,610	258,079	297,548
N2	655,302	707,345	759,388
N3	21,667	24,986	28,304
N4	2,519	3,648	4,777
N5	194,253	212,781	231,310
N6	—	—	—
N7	5,297	7,528	9,758
N8	—	—	—
N9	30,764	39,512	48,260
N10	56,279	64,475	72,671
S5	2,392	3,432	4,472
Σ	1,187,084	1,321,785	1,456,487

TABLE 8.1. (cont'd.) Estimated Number and Weight of Flakes at Modena and Tempiute.

Flake Weight (g)

Modena Area	Stage 1 -1 s.e.	Stage 1 Estimate	Stage 1 +1 s.e.
A	63,435,618	113,861,268	164,286,918
B	45,619,407	82,777,606	119,932,659
D	4,657,008	6,888,760	9,118,669
E	841,199	1,180,145	1,519,091
F	11,533,781	16,301,822	21,070,499
U	16,569	139,127	261,659
2009-1	462,313	769,473	1,076,839
Σ	126,565,895	221,918,471	317,266,334

Tempiute Area	Stage 1 -1 s.e.	Stage 1 Estimate	Stage 1 +1 s.e.	Stage 2 -1 s.e.	Stage 2 Estimate	Stage 2 +1 s.e.
N1	1,368,105	3,052,981	4,737,652	882,213	1,449,087	2,015,757
N2	4,254,332	6,311,863	8,369,394	3,212,006	3,759,557	4,307,841
N3	237,168	490,538	744,102	108,531	168,262	227,798
N4	2,679	60,990	119,301	0	33,436	102,657
N5	1,412,963	1,946,709	2,480,455	1,022,665	1,286,250	1,549,836
N6	1,808,752	2,548,696	3,288,640	—	—	—
N7	0	61,824	128,248	0	71,443	148,879
N8	298,252	559,869	821,486	—	—	—
N9	138,583	519,121	899,659	104,539	223,584	342,557
N10	27,320	194,928	362,400	242,328	362,946	483,564
S5	0	19,167	47,694	5,980	24,960	43,940
Σ	9,548,154	15,766,686	21,999,031	5,578,262	7,379,525	9,222,829

Modena Area	Stage 2 -1 s.e.	Stage 2 Estimate	Stage 2 +1 s.e.
A	79,851,384	114,672,888	149,494,392
B	91,471,662	133,205,018	174,941,520
D	5,292,809	8,586,071	11,877,491
E	639,774	998,153	1,356,157
F	14,408,330	17,108,145	19,807,324
U	41,449	180,339	319,229
2009-1	767,406	1,128,244	1,488,748
Σ	192,472,814	275,878,858	359,284,861

a 12.7 mm = ½ in; 6.35 mm = ¼ in

on the quality of the arguments or experiments that ground them. However, many arguments and experimental data can justify similar assumptions. Critical in this respect is to ground the assumptions as broadly and deeply as possible in available evidence, both empirical and experimental. This study follows the methodology set forth below, although alternative approaches also exist (e.g., Allard and Burnez-Lanotte 2008; Kotcho 2009:288–292; Schyle 2007:93–97).

Analytical Core Units

A simple count of spent cores is one measure of reduction scale, but cores can be reduced to splinters at quarries or exported and therefore escape detection. In any event, UA fieldwork yielded far too few cores at Modena and Tempiute to account for the vast amounts of flake debris found at the quarries. As discussed in Chapter 5, cores were not a focus of investigation so were not specifically sought at Modena, nor were they ordinarily collected when encountered except in Stage-1 sample units. Only Areas A and B there produced significant samples of cores from Stage-1 or Stage-2 units, where the clustering of cores in relatively few, small sample units yielded very high estimates of the total core assemblage. For other Modena areas and for Tempiute, probabilistic samples of cores were far too small for valid estimation. The smaller Tempiute quarry justified collection of cores as encountered. Simple counts of flakes may not account for differences in cobble size and the sampling challenges of finding cores make them poor estimates of production scale.

Instead, two different experimental datasets were consulted. Although they used different subsets of flakes and somewhat different measures of cobble frequency, they yielded similar estimates of number of cobbles reduced. This result suggests a robust relationship between number of cobbles and amount of flake debris justifying use of experimental data to estimate reduction scale at Modena and Tempiute.

Carr and Bradbury Method

Carr and Bradbury proposed a "standardized measure of reduction" (2001:142) that they called the *analytical core unit* (ACU). In experimental

data, they found a statistically significant correlation between number of platform-bearing flakes in the 12.7 mm (½ in) and 6.35 mm (¼ in) fractions (subsequent discussion in this section is confined to flakes in these fractions) and the weight loss experienced by cobbles during the reduction process. Because the relationship was log-linear, Carr and Bradbury (2001:143) computed the natural log, ln, of weight loss, which they used in a regression equation to estimate number of platform-bearing flakes. Both variables being ln-transformed, relationships discussed here are ln-ln in scale.

ACU is a statistical abstraction that is not strictly equivalent to the actual number of cobbles x worked to produce any y platform flakes. Instead, it converts platform-bearing flakes to an estimate of number of worked cobbles, derived from the statistical relationship expressed in the regression between flakes and weight loss experienced by cobbles. ACU, expressed as cobble weight loss, thus serves as the standardized reduction measure that Carr and Bradbury sought, a measure that converts flake counts to estimates of cobbles reduced. In this way, it enables comparison of production scale between assemblages, within or between sites.

Carr and Bradbury's data were derived from 20 of their own experiments using Dover chert from Tennessee. In their original data, kindly made available (A. Bradbury, per. comm. 16 November 2010), mean number of platform-bearing flakes per cobble was 39.7 and mean weight loss experienced by cobbles was 452.8 g (mean ln-weight loss = 5.81). Carr and Bradbury's (2001) dataset included an outlier, experiment DR14 (Shott 2016:Figure 8.1a). That case removed, linear regression models the relationship between variables (Figure 8.1). The result is ($r = 0.89$, $p < 0.01$):

Number of platform flakes = −58.5 + 16.55 *
     ln(weight loss)

(This expression differs from what Carr and Bradbury [2001:143] reported. Part of the difference owes to exclusion of their outlier, but some may owe to datasets; they reported 26 experiments yet their Figure 8.4 plotted only 20 cases.) However, regressions that contain

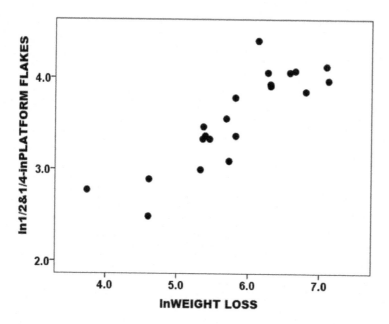

FIGURE 8.1. Log-log plot of 12.7 and 6.35 mm (½ and ¼ in)
platform flakes against weight loss, without DR14.

nonzero constants assume either a quantity of flakes already in existence before reduction begins (when Bo>0) or a certain deficit of flakes that must be made up before flakes accumulate with weight loss (when Bo<0). Following Ingbar and colleagues (1989) and Carr and Bradbury (2001), therefore, it seems wiser to force regression through the origin, so that weight loss and number of detached flakes both start from zero, and that the number of flakes detached rises with weight loss. To linearize the relationship, both variables were logged.

In these data, regression through the origin yields the following ($r = 0.99$; $p < 0.01$) model relating flake products to cobble-weight loss (Figure 8.1):

ln(Number of platform flakes) = 0.61 *
    ln(weight loss)

In archaeological data, number of platform flakes is known and weight loss or ACU is sought. ACU can be estimated from flake count by inverting the axes and terms of Figure 8.1 and regressing ln-weight loss upon flake count, which yields:

Ln-weight loss = 4.01 + 0.05 * (platform flakes)

Again, by forcing regression through the origin the following was obtained ($r = 0.99$; $p < 0.01$):

Ln-weight loss = 1.63 * (ln-platform flakes)

UA experiments involved seven Obsidian Butte cobbles worked down to one or more Callahan Stage-3 preforms. In these data, mean number of platform-bearing flakes was 282.3 and mean weight loss experienced by cobbles was 1,883.3 g (mean ln-weight loss = 7.54). Compared to Carr and Bradbury's data, UA's larger cobbles produced considerably more platform flakes in more extensive reduction, as well as a more modest correlation ($r = 0.57$; $p = 0.33$). Within the UA dataset, the relationship between variables is somewhat weaker.

Combining Carr and Bradbury's and UA data (confining the latter to platform flakes in the 12.7 mm [½ in] and 6.35 mm [¼ in] fractions) produces statistically better results ($r = 0.70$; $p < 0.01$) but a conspicuously nonlinear scatter plot (Shott 2016:Figure 8.4a). Compared to Carr and Bradbury's data, UA's show much more variation in number of platform flakes than in ln-weight loss. Again, the log-log relationship yields a more nearly linear relationship

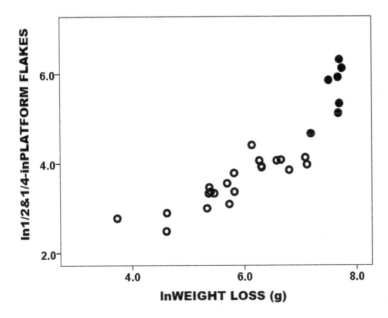

FIGURE 8.2. 12.7 and 6.35 mm (½ and ¼ in) platform flakes (in-count) against in-weight loss in combined Carr and Bradbury (open circle) and UA (solid circle) data.

(Figure 8.2; $r = 0.89$, $p < 0.01$), and the following equation:

ln-platform flake count =   Eq. 8.1
    0.66 * (ln-weight loss)

Yet, half of the cases fall outside the 95% confidence limits. Nevertheless, this value is used to calculate "ACU1." Inverting the regression gives:

ln-weight loss = 1.62 *   Eq. 8.2
    (ln-platform flake count).

This value is used to calculate "ACU2."

On balance, these are somewhat noisy data, but they span a considerable range of cobble sizes and involve fine-grained chert along with obsidian. They represent statistical tendencies in relatively high-quality toolstones that can serve this study's objectives.

Carr and Bradbury (2001:143) suggested that their regression of platform flakes y upon ln-weight loss x be solved for y by empirically estimating mean weight loss of cobbles and inserting that value into the equation. Solved for y, the equation estimates the number of platform-bearing flakes per ACU. The total number of such flakes in an assemblage divided by that average in turn yields estimated number of ACU.

Empirical Weight Loss Estimates

Empirical estimation of weight loss of Modena and Tempiute cobbles requires estimates of original cobble weight and values for mean weight of exhausted or abandoned cores. Starting with Modena, Hull (1994:Table 7-2) reported weights for about 10 cobbles from the vicinity of the Modena quarry. Most, like the cobbles illustrated by R. Jackson and colleagues (2009:Figure C-18) from several kilometers east of the quarry, are small, and may reflect the intensive use and resulting depletion of more workable cobbles there (Rowley et al. 2002). Other sources cited in Chapter 3 referred anecdotally to the size of Modena cobbles, which obviously varied. Lacking better data, Hull's three Modena cobbles that exceeded 1,000 g in weight were used to crudely estimate size of workable cobbles; their mean weight is 1,513 g (somewhat smaller than but comparable to the mean weight of our Obsidian Butte cobbles, 1,883 g).

The few cores found at Modena average 93 g. The difference between this figure and 1,513 is 1,420 g (ln weight loss = 7.26), taken as an empirical estimate of the weight loss experienced by Modena cobbles in toolstone production. Weight of discarded cores amounts to little more

TABLE 8.2. Stage-1 and Stage-2 Sample ACU Estimates.

Modena	Stage-1 ACU1			Stage-1 ACU2			Stage-2 ACU3		
Area	Lower 95%	Mean	Upper 95%	Lower 95%	Mean	Upper 95%	Lower 95%	Mean	Upper 95%
A	5,375	12,974	16,506	10,615	16,580	22,545	11,364	15,272	19,179
B	5,914	13,004	16,064	8,227	14,307	20,388	17,393	24,187	30,981
D	982	2,263	2,843	814	1,181	1,547	750	1,136	1,522
E	66	164	212	99	142	186	89	153	216
F	1,555	2,568	2,785	1,518	2,189	2,860	1,809	2,054	2,299
2009-1	0	114	171	74	113	152	77	100	124
Σ	13,892	31,060	38,580	21,346	34,512	47,678	31,483	42,902	54,321
Tempiute									
N1	1,294	2,284	3,274	1,486	2,737	3,988	739	1,055	1,371
N2	3,319	4,316	5,313	3,028	3,873	4,719	2,474	2,891	3,308
N3	85	188	292	40	104	168	76	102	129
N4	0	52	116	16	39	63	6	15	24
N5	919	1,851	2,782	909	1,268	1,627	721	870	1,018
N6	1,174	1,618	2,061	948	1,246	1,545	0	0	0
N7	0	118	247	17	58	98	13	31	49
N8	135	321	507	162	222	282	0	0	0
N9	98	326	553	126	224	322	91	161	232
N10	111	233	356	3	106	209	198	263	329
Σ	7,135	11,307	15,501	6,732	9,876	13,021	4,317	5,388	6,459

than 6% of original cobble weight. This closely resembles the figure of 6.9% of original weight retained in UA experiments, but other experimental data described below vary from about 24–54% of original weight retained. Taken together, then, the use of only large Modena cobbles and their comparison to the small sample of Modena cores, themselves quite small, maximizes the estimated amount or degree of reduction per cobble and the number of flakes per cobble, and thereby minimizes the estimated number of cobbles. Using these data, therefore, ACU estimates are conservative.

For Tempiute, Hafey (2003:6) reported cobbles as large as 100 mm in maximum dimension, although the largest of the few unmodified cobbles found during fieldwork measured approximately 65 mm in maximum dimension. Obviously, unmodified cobbles on the surface there may have remained in that state only because they were considered too small to work. Hughes (a reported field visit in L. Johnson and Wagner [2005:34]) reported a cobble of up to 80×100 mm. Tempiute fieldwork recovered six cores averaging 42.5 mm in maximum dimension (maximum value = 48 mm) and 21.4 g in weight (approximately one-quarter the mean weight of Modena cores). Estimation assumes that unmodified Tempiute cobbles measured 90 $\times$ 70 mm. Regressing weight upon the product of length and width in UA's sample of Obsidian Butte experimental cobbles yields:

Weight (g) = −0.46 + 0.08 * (length * width).

Inserting the postulated product of length and width at Tempiute (6,300) into this regression yields an estimate of 503.4 g per unmodified cobble. Subtracting the mean weight of expended Tempiute cores, 21.4 g, from this figure yields 482 g (ln = 6.18) of weight loss. As in the case of Modena, this figure assumes fairly large original cobbles and highly extensive reduction of cores (>95% reduction by weight), so again is a conservative estimate of ACU.

ACU Calculations

For Modena, inserting the natural log of estimated cobble weight loss, 7.26, into Equation 8.1 and solving for y yields 4.79. The inverse natural

log of this value is 120.5, which becomes Equation 8.1's estimate of number of 12.7 mm (½ in) and 6.35 mm (¼ in) platform-bearing flakes per ACU. This figure is used as the denominator to estimate ACU1 from estimated count of relevant flakes. Inserting 7.26 in Equation 8.2 and then solving for x yields 4.45. The inverse natural log of this value is 86.0, which is Equation 8.2's estimate of 12.7 mm (½ in) and 6.35 mm (¼ in) platform-bearing flakes per ACU2. The two results are not identical, of course, but are encouragingly similar considering the range of variation in original data. Together, they suggest that somewhere near 100 flakes in the 12.7 mm (½ in) and 6.35 mm (¼ in) fractions are detached per ACU. For comparison, this figure is much higher than the 7 flakes per macrocore assumed for the Sta Nychia and Demenegaki obsidian quarries in Greece, and the estimated number of macrocores reduced there is correspondingly much higher than Modena ACU estimates (Torrence 1986:Table 32). Yet estimates from Levantine Neolithic chert quarries are closer to those used here (Schyle 2007:97–98).

For Tempiute, inserting the natural log of estimated cobble weight loss, 6.18, into Equation 8.1 and solving for y yields 4.08, whose antilog is 59.1. This value is used as the denominator to estimate Tempiute ACU1 from flake count. Following the same procedure as for Modena, solving for x in Equation 8.2 yields a value of 49.4, which is then used as the denominator for estimating ACU2. Again, values for ACU1–2 estimation are close, suggesting that approximately 50–60 flakes were struck in the processing of each Tempiute ACU. The significant difference between flakes per ACU at Modena and Tempiute owes to the much larger size of the former's cobbles. Table 8.2 shows ACU1 and ACU2 estimates from Stage-1 samples, and ACU3 estimates from Stage-2 samples, for both sites.

Extending the ACU Concept: Additional Experimental Data

Carr and Bradbury's analysis was confined to platform-bearing flakes in the 12.7 mm (½ in) and 6.35 mm (¼ in) size fractions. Our own experimental data include all flakes generated per cobble and weight loss experienced by that cobble. Similar data were found in Lothrop (1988:Tables 7.19 and 7.21), Baumler and Downum (1989:Table 1), J. D. Rogers (1982:Tables 9, 48), and Morrow (1997:Tables 1, 3). Lothrop's experiments involved five large shale cobbles (1988:410) reduced from raw form to flake blanks and preforms, Baumler and Downum's three small cobbles, two of chert and one of obsidian, reduced to blanks, Rogers's 27 cobbles of Boone and other chert reduced either to produce flakes or arrow-point preforms, and Morrow's three successive stages in the reduction of a Burlington chert bifacial core to a Callahan-Stage "2–2.5" preform. Lothrop's, Baumler and Downum's, and Morrow's experimental data represent similar types or modes of reduction to Modena and Tempiute, but Lothrop's involve larger cobbles, Baumler and Downum's data smaller ones, and Morrow's are intermediate in both cobble or objective-piece size so are perhaps comparable to Modena reduction modes. J. D. Rogers's data represent somewhat different reduction modes and, like Baumler and Downum's, smaller cobbles.

On balance, experimental sources provide similar but not identical reduction modes across a considerable range of original cobble sizes, with the exception of Lothrop's work on fine-grained chert or obsidian. Thus, the combined dataset spans a considerable range of original cobble size and degree of reduction. All but Rogers (who reported only total flakes) also reported resulting flakes by the same or similar size classes used by Carr and Bradbury and in this study, but none distinguished platform-bearing or intact flakes from others. As a result, only total number of flakes can be used, and there is no need to confine use to flakes in the 12.7 mm (½ in) and 6.35 mm (¼ in) size classes.

Total flakes pattern when plotted against original-depleted core weight (i.e., weight loss). Baumler and Downum's and Rogers's cases appear as a tight cluster at low values on both axes, but they distribute satisfactorily along the least-squares regression line in the ln-ln plot (Figure 8.3). Correlation ($r = 0.99$; $p < 0.01$) and rank-correlation are nearly the same using original or log-transformed variables. For consistency with estimation of ACU1 and ACU2, analysis here is of ln-ln data, and again is regression through the origin. The result:

ln-total flakes = 0.89 * (ln-weight loss).   Eq. 8.3

A similar inversion of variables, as in the previous case, produced very similar estimates to ACU2 so is not reported. As above, estimated ln-weight loss per Modena cobble is 7.26 g. Inserting that value into Equation 8.3 yields an estimate of 640.0 flakes per ACU, called "ACU3." For Tempiute, ln-weight loss is 6.18, so ACU3's denominator is 244.7. Obviously, the number of flakes generated per cobble by the ACU3 expression significantly exceeds comparable ACU1 figures, because ACU3 values refer to all flakes, not just 12.7 mm (½ in) and 6.35 mm (¼ in) platform-bearing flakes. Table 8.2 shows ACU estimates and 95% lower-upper estimates (mean ± 1 s.e. × 1.96) for each Modena cluster. Although 95% confidence ranges may seem wide, they are consistent with UA's economical sampling strategy. Sample fraction in square meters is very low across areas, and even the number of sample units, equally as important as sheer fraction if not more so (Nance 1983), is modest. Probabilistic samples would need to be much larger to significantly reduce 95% confidence limits, but the robust results lend confidence to the quality of the estimates.

In general, ACU1 and ACU3 estimates are broadly consistent. Also, separate estimates derived from Stage-1 and Stage-2 samples agree in most cases. Note, for instance, the very similar point estimates and 95% ranges for Areas A and B in ACU1–2. That is, these independent samples are somewhat redundant, a conclusion useful for reference in future research designs for obsidian quarries. Yet even similar point estimates can be associated with somewhat different 95% confidence ranges. For instance, ACU3 values for Area F are similar in the point estimate but the Stage-2 sample's 95% confidence range is considerably narrower than Stage 1's. More significant is the difference between Area B ranges in ACU3–3 between stage samples. Stage-2 point estimates are nearly twice as high

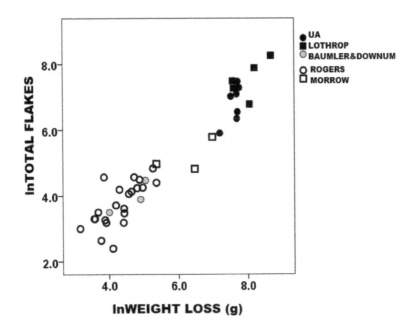

FIGURE 8.3. All flakes against cobble weight loss in additional experimental sources.

as Stage-1 estimates, because the mean number of flakes per 1 m² was significantly higher in the Stage-2 than Stage-1 sample. Although stage sampling mostly was redundant, in some respects they therefore yielded different estimates or error ranges.

Finally, whether ACUs were calculated from estimates of number of platform-bearing flakes in two size classes or from total number of flakes, it is no surprise that ACU estimates for Areas A and B are highest, followed by Area F. These three areas are the densest deposits of flake debris at Modena, and thereby yield the highest estimates for number and density of flakes. Areas D, E, and 2009-1 may be workshops. This inference is supported by their considerably lower estimates of all flakes and platform-bearing flakes in the 12.7 mm (½ in) and 6.35 mm (¼ in) fractions and, by extension, lower ACU estimates.

Unfortunately, the coarse, uneven time resolution of the Modena OHD curve complicates calculation of annual rates of ACU production. Despite the difficulty, these estimates may seem less impressive considering the time span over which they occurred. As Chapter 9

reports, most Modena hydration values fall in the long "confidently Archaic" interval, and even calibrated results show mostly Archaic and Formative occupation. The span of the Archaic interval is perhaps 9,000 years. If so, sampled regions of Modena account for about four ACU/year distributed across this interval. The form of the Modena OHD curve suggests peak use during the Archaic, broadly perhaps from 8000–3000 BP. Even this five-millennium interval accounts for seven to eight ACU/year. Therefore, anywhere from roughly four to eight ACU accounts for the needs of two to four persons/year assuming Ericson's (1982:145) estimate of five to 20 dart points/person/year in the Great Basin. Tempiute lacking a calibrated OHD curve, no similar calculation can be done for this quarry.

Recalling the conservative nature of ACU estimates, results suggest that the sampled sections represent 35,000 or more cobble reductions of typical size and degree of reduction at Modena, equivalent to reduction of original cobbles from approximately 1,500 g to approximately 100 g. Tempiute saw roughly 10,000 cobble reductions, equivalent to reduction of original cobbles from approximately 500 g to approximately 20 g. Until similar estimates are made for other Great Basin quarries, there are no comparative data for these figures. Even at face value, Tempiute seems a modest obsidian source by regional standards, Modena a larger but still not exceptional one. Bodie Hills, the Coso Field, and other obsidian sources are much larger.

Specific values used to calculate ACU_{1-3} are described above. Results are gratifyingly robust, because the several ACU equations yield similar estimates and 95% confidence-limit ranges. Yet ACU also could be calculated using various other data and analysis permutations. These include a regression constant, original rather than log-transformed data, and various combinations of experimental datasets. Resulting ACU estimates, of course, vary with these permutations, but all results obtained fell within 25% of reported values. The consistency with which further analyses resembled initial values provides support that the method used to estimate ACU is robust. In fact, the estimation method seems relatively insensitive to such permutations, and may be more sensitive to input values for original cobble size and amount of cobble weight loss, or degree of core reduction.

Preform-Stage Bifaces

As described in Chapter 4, most Modena and Tempiute preforms were found by chance, as crews traversed the quarries during sampling or in the vicinity of collection units as they were sampled. Such discoveries cannot be the basis for statistical estimation, because these samples are uncontrolled for bias and largely reflect the routes and patterns of crew activities at the sites. Other preforms at Modena were found in transect surveys conducted for that specific purpose, and similar transect surveys were conducted across the entirety of the Tempiute debris field. Transect surveys for preforms were conducted at Modena using judgmental, not probabilistic, methods so cannot be used for site-scale estimation. Zones adjacent to and overlapping small sections of Areas A and B were rather intensively transect-sampled for points and pre-

forms in 2005, but transects were not confined to the concentration areas so cannot be treated as valid samples just of those areas. At Modena, however, a number of preforms were found in either Stage-1 and Stage-2 units. Because these units were drawn probabilistically, such data are suitable for estimation. Because Tempiute was entirely traversed by transects surveyed to seek preforms, that sample could in theory be used for estimation. Unfortunately, very few preforms were found in Tempiute transect or unit sampling, precluding estimation there.

Accordingly, to estimate the overall number of preform-stage bifaces, analysis is confined to Stage-1 and Stage-2 data from Modena. UA fieldwork at Modena recovered more than 250 biface preforms, of which the 26 found in Stage-1 sample units and 12 in Stage-2 units serve this purpose. Tempiute yielded only about 25 preforms; only one was found in a Stage-2 sample unit, none in Stage-1 units, prohibiting further analysis. Table 8.3 lists Stage-1 sample preforms by area at Modena, along with preform density per square meter and spatial extent in meters squared. (Stage-2 estimates are unreliable, owing to its very small sample. Density/m² was found using corrected preform counts per sample unit. For example, a unit measuring 0.25 m² that contained one preform is recorded as a density of four preforms/m².) These probabilistic samples serve as the source for estimating the size of the Modena preform population. Multiplying estimated density by area yields point estimates of preform-stage bifaces by cluster. Results suggest that about 42,000 preform-stage bifaces exist in sampled areas of the site. (Recall Chapter 6's quantification exercise, which estimated that the 59 + 188 = 247 preforms equated to a preform TIE of about 184. That is, accounting for breakage reduces preform TIE, *qua* count, of original specimens by roughly 25%. If so, then the estimate of 42,000 preform fragments and intact specimens reduces to approximately 31,500 preform TIEs.)

Areas A, B, and F yielded higher density and preform estimates than did other areas (for preform count per area, $t = 4.84$; $p = 0.005$; for density per area, $t = 7.60$; $p = 0.001$, both for

TABLE 8.3. Estimated Number of Modena Stage Preforms from Stage-1 and Stage-2 Samples.

Area	Σ area m²	Stage 1			Stage 2		
		# preform	preform/m²	Estimate (n)	# preform	preform/m²	Estimate (n)
A	30,060	10	0.7339	22,062	2	0.1468	4,412
B	31,466	5	0.4598	14,467	4	0.3678	11,574
D	18,429	2	0.0339	625	0	0	0
E	3,737	1	0.1081	404	0	0	0
F	6,354	7	0.6667	4,236	6	0.5714	3,631
2009-1	3,338	1	0.0690	230	0	0	0
Σ				42,024			19,617

comparison of means of the two groups listed). Obviously, preforms exist in considerably higher numbers in primary areas, and much lower numbers elsewhere. Because UA sampling of primary clusters was complete (i.e., our probabilistic Stage-1 and Stage-2 samples sampled the entireties of A, B, and F) and extensive but not complete of other areas, Table 8.3 figures should be treated as minimum ones for the entire quarry.

Even such minimum figures may seem large. Yet calibrated to Modena's span of use, annual production rates are modest. Assuming the 11,000-year span suggested above, this estimate of preform-stage bifaces amounts to fewer than four per year. Even the shorter 7,000-year span that encompasses most of Modena's calibrated occupation span (see Chapter 9) produces 42,000 bifaces at the rate of about six per year (or if, as above, total preform TIE is about 31,500, fewer than five per year).

Estimating the Scale
of Biface Production

Having estimated the quantity of flakes and cobbles, ACUs, and stage preforms remaining on site, it remains to estimate the total number of preforms or other bifaces produced at Modena and Tempiute. By extension, the difference between that estimate and the number of stage preforms left at quarries becomes the corresponding estimate of exported products. We found few finished, diagnostic bifaces and an abundance of stage preforms, and the Field Processing Model suggests that preforms, but not finished points, were the intended product at quarries for subsequent export and completion elsewhere. Therefore, the method used to estimate the original quantity of bifaces assumes that only Stage 2 or 3 bifaces (*sensu* Beck et al. 2002) were the intended product at Modena and Tempiute.

Experimental sources report the quantity and character of flakes resulting from various kinds of lithic reduction (e.g., Allard and Burnez-Lanotte 2008:35–36; Newcomer 1971; Pelegrin and Chauchat 1993; Sundström and Apel 1998; Tarasov and Stafeev 2014; Torrence 1986:205). For instance, Pelegrin and Chauchat (1993:377–378) reported an average of 350 g of flake debris >20 mm in the production of the large foliate preforms that were the object of their reduction experiments. They also calibrated debris mass to preform length (1993:Figure 9), but the range of preform length was unusually high (100–220 mm). Great Basin obsidian preform caches suggest length ranging from about 70–150 mm (Amick 2004:Table 1; Garfinkel et al. 2004; Pavesic 1966). Sources on the mean length of obsidian preforms at other sites are too numerous to synthesize, but selective review suggests that most ranged between 70–110 mm (e.g., Beck and Jones 2009a:Table 5.16, 5.30; Connolly, ed. 1999:Tables 6.4, 7.5, 8.5, 9.9, 9.16; Gilreath and Hildebrandt 1997:Tables 22, 29, 35, 40, 45, 52, 58) toward the lower end of Pelegrin and Chauchat's range.

Mean length of intact Modena preforms is approximately 48 mm, well below that range but similar to the length reported for Gatecliff

Shelter (Thomas 1983:Tables 52–54), admittedly not all of which were obsidian. (Given the smaller size of cobbles there, preforms at Tempiute probably were even shorter than Modena ones. We found only nine intact preforms at Tempiute, which average 41.6 mm in length.) For this approximation, I use Pelegrin and Chauchat's mean figure of 350 g/biface and equate their threshold value of 20 mm with the 19.05 mm (¾ in) fraction in UA data. Using the Pelegrin-Chauchat's approach, total weight of flakes ≥19.05 mm (¾ in) divided by 350 gives an estimate of preforms produced:

# of preform-stage bifaces =   Eq. 8.4
      # of ≥19.05 mm flakes / 350.

Hanson and Madsen (1983:48–51) also reported experimental data, theirs on number of flakes produced in the course of knapping large bifaces to various stages of completion of Scandinavian Neolithic axe replicas. Their Experiment IA and IIA data involved six chert cobbles that on average exceeded the starting weight of our experimental data by a factor of approximately three, and probably exceeded the starting weight of Modena and certainly Tempiute cobbles by comparable amounts. Hanson and Madsen's data, therefore, can be used for general comparison but probably are not a good model for the reduction trajectories that produced most flake debris at Modena and Tempiute. Shafer and Hester (1983:529) estimated the number of a particular biface type at the Maya chert quarry of Colha, Belize, from the number of a specific flake type, tranchet flakes, which do not occur in Great Basin quarries. Tarasov and Stafeev (2014:253–254) used a similar approach, but for a very different subject, large metatuff adzes in Russia.

This literature is difficult to synthesize, owing in part to normal variation in toolstones, end products, and reduction modes. And no matter how useful it may be, much of the literature does not report original or exhausted size (in weight or dimensions) of cobbles or other worked materials. Some of it reports only number, omitting weight, size distribution, and technological character, of flake assemblages. Lacking data on cobble size it is impossible to

calibrate debris quantity or character to amount or scale of reduction.

Yet several studies are particularly detailed and systematic, so deserve close study. At Bodie Hills, Singer and Ericson (1977:183–185) first used their archaeological sample to produce a point estimate of 479 million pieces of worked obsidian. Then they assumed that either 90% or 100% of obsidian debris was produced in processing cobbles and flake blanks to semifinished preforms. Then-available experimental data were more limited; citing Newcomer (1971) they assumed an average of 50 ≥2 cm flakes per biface, although their own data included counts of flakes down to 1 cm in maximum dimension. Singer and Ericson's (1977:185) expression was:

$$B = d(D) / F \qquad\qquad \text{Eq. 8.5}$$

where B = the estimated number of bifaces, d = the proportion of flakes generated in biface production, D = the total number of flakes, and F = the number of flakes generated per biface. Expressing d as a range between 0.50 and 0.90, Singer and Ericson (1977:185) estimated 4.8–8.6 million bifaces produced at Bodie Hills.

It is easy to criticize this method. It is unclear if Singer and Ericson's sample was probabilistic and therefore a valid basis for estimation. They assumed rates or proportions of biface production but did not generate empirical estimates for comparison. Their estimate of F, from Newcomer's 50 flakes per biface, either refers ambiguously to production, to completion, or to some intermediate stage and, as above, is not calibrated to original and depleted size of the objective piece. Nor does it specify the reduction mode, apart from the broad description of handaxe manufacture. Different F values would yield significantly different results. For example, Magne and Pokotylo's (1981:35) 87 would reduce the estimated number of bifaces by nearly half, Sundström and Apel's (1998:177) exactly by half, and Tarasov and Stafeev's (2014:254) by a factor of more than seven. Similarly, Schyle's (2007:96, Table 5.1) empirical analysis estimated 70–80% weight reduction of raw cobbles in the process of producing large preforms; although Schyle did not estimate the number of flakes, when converted to count by any reasonable method his estimate of aggregate flake weight greatly exceeds Newcomer's value. Other sources reported even a wider range of figures (e.g., Ahler 1975:Table 6; Jones and White 1988:73; Magne and Pokotylo 1981:35; Morrow 1997:Table 3; Root 1992:Table 6.14). But criticism is less important than the fact that Singer and Ericson took an explicit, systematic approach. One small candle is better than cursing the darkness.

Z. Nelson (2000:70–73) used a similar approach to estimate original number of Ramec points, a notched finished biface, from an obsidian workshop at Teotihuacán in the Valley of Mexico. His "preform weight-change estimate" (see also Schyle 2007:93–97) was computed as the difference in mean weight between the Ramec intended end products and successive blank and preform stages. For each reduction stage from blank to finished tool, Nelson calculated the difference between the mean weight of specimens found in that stage and Ramec points, identified the associated production debris with specific debris size ranges (not the size classes used by Ahler [1989a] or here), and divided the aggregate weight of debris in his archaeological assemblage by the difference in weight. Nelson performed such calculations for each successive preform stage, associating debris at each stage with overlapping ranges of size classes in his data.

Ahler (1975:86–135) compiled a large set of experimental data that involved several toolstones and a very wide range of reduction modes described in some detail (1975:Table 5). From repeated performance of the same reduction mode on cobbles of roughly the same size and form and of the same toolstone, he calculated mean number and weight of size-sorted flakes per reduction mode (1975:Table 17). Ahler's modes included several core reductions to produce flake blanks suitable for finishing into bifaces, which approximate the inferred object of reduction at Modena and Tempiute and so may have particular relevance. Ahler then multiplied the frequency of semifinished and finished tools of various types by the mean number and weight of flakes generated in comparable experimental reductions (1975:130–135). The quantity of flake debris not accounted for

by recovered tools was used as an estimate of export.

The strength of Ahler's study (see also Tarasov and Stafeev 2014:254) is its experimental derivation of average or expected number, type, and size distribution of flakes resulting from repeated replications of various reduction modes. But no more than Singer and Ericson did Ahler report original or depleted size of cores for calibration of flake assemblages. Applying his experimental data to archaeological samples, Ahler also ignored the probability that the latter were mixtures of various segments of various reduction modes. Yet this approach, along with Ahler's later studies (e.g., 1986, 1989a, 1989b), comprehended a range of reduction modes and avoided the practice of assuming any one or other, therefore arbitrary, value (e.g., Newcomer's 50 per biface) of flakes generated in reduction episodes. In its place, Ahler grounded his estimates of quantity and character of flakes in repeated experiments.

Root (1997), a student of Ahler, used a large set of experimental data that encompassed a fairly wide range of reduction modes. Root's and Ahler's experimental datasets may overlap. Root's data produced estimates of number and weight of flakes per cobble, and he used experimental size-sorted "calibration sets" (1997:38) with multiple linear regression to allocate flakes to various reduction modes (e.g., cobble testing, biface edging, biface thinning, bipolar reduction). Experimental data and analysis apportioned total flake assemblages, or subdivisions by size or technological class. For biface production, flake counts were subdivided by edging-stage and thinning-stage, which does not correspond precisely to the Callahan preform stages used by many archaeologists. Nevertheless, in this way quantity of flakes can be converted to estimates of bifaces or stage preforms.

Root's method has its own limitations. Its experimental data are confined to Knife River Flint, a fairly fine-grained chert that nevertheless may differ from obsidian in flaking properties. Although a range of reduction modes was replicated, they are not necessarily comprehensive (although more so than virtually any other experimental dataset known) so there is no guarantee that all empirical reduction modes are represented in experimental data. Strictly, Root's method requires the size classes that he used (1997:Table 2; see also Ahler 1989a, 1989b), although interpolation can reconcile differences in size classes used (e.g., Shott 1997b). Finally, like Ahler and others, Root did not calibrate products and flake by-products to size of original cobbles or amount of reduction they experienced.

Limitations acknowledged, Root's method is grounded in a large experimental dataset. Significantly, it considers to some extent the staging of biface preforms and the amount and character of debris produced by stage, and its estimate of flakes generated per biface are experimentally grounded. (Those figures also are substantially higher in roughly the same flake-size range than the 50 flakes per biface that Singer and Ericson used; all else equal, Root's method will produce more conservative estimates of number of bifaces or preforms produced.) Perhaps most important of all, the method acknowledges, not ignores, the mixing problem (i.e., the likelihood that empirical archaeological flake assemblages are the joint product of various reduction episodes and modes) and develops a procedure for allocating flakes to various modes. It has been applied with satisfactory results to other datasets (e.g., Shott 1997b).

One other important detail of Ahler's and Root's experimental data deserves note. Both labeled the size classes used to sort flake debris "G1–G4," from largest to smallest. Ahler (1975:Table 6) listed size classes that correspond exactly to UA values of 25.4 mm (1 in; "G1"), 12.7 mm (½ in; "G2"), 6.35 mm (¼ in; "G3"), but did not sort by the 19.05 mm (¾ in) interval also used here. (This is a small matter easily handled by simply pooling our 19.05 and 12.7 mm [¾ and ½ in] fractions for direct comparison to these sources.) However, Ahler (1986:46) listed G1 and G2 as above, but then placed G3 at 5.66 mm (0.22 in) and G4 at 2.54 mm (0.10 in). Root's (1997:Table 2) size classes also were called G1–G4, where G1 = 25.4 mm, G2 = 12.7 mm, G3 = 5.60 mm, and G4 = 2.54 mm. Despite the slight

discrepancy reported, Root's size thresholds probably are identical to Ahler's. As described in Chapter 5, UA analysis involved size sorting that differed slightly. We also used 25.4 and 12.7 mm classes, (1 in and ½ in, respectively), but then 6.35 mm (¼ in) and, by interpolation for some purposes, 3.175 mm (⅛ in) classes. Uncertainty about exactly which size thresholds Ahler used, and the lack of strict comparability between some Ahler variants, Root's system, and the UA protocol, may introduce error, acknowledged here but impossible to control.

Estimation Equations

These approaches are worth applying at Modena and Tempiute. Pelegrin and Chauchat's method simply divides the aggregate weight of flakes ≥19.05 mm (¾ in) by 350 g. Singer and Ericson's approach, via Newcomer, assumes the removal of 50 flakes in the production of each biface. Using it, any point estimate of number of flakes divided by 50 gives an estimate of the number of bifaces produced. Other approaches require more detail and involve more nuanced relationships between production scale, reduction modes, and flake quantity.

To use Ahler's method requires deciding which of his reduction modes (1975:Table 5's "Technological Variants") and products (1975: Table 8's "Technological Products") are most relevant to the data at hand. Although Ahler used the tool assemblages found at various occupational sites as guides to the reduction modes carried out there, this approach is poorly suited to Modena and Tempiute. Tools probably were exported from quarries at much higher rates than at occupational sites, thereby leaving little evidence of reduction modes in semifinished or finished specimens. This explains why comparatively few finished tools were found at Modena and other quarries.

Instead, assuming that quarries were the site of primary reduction of raw cobbles, three of Ahler's (1975:Table 8) reduction modes were considered the likeliest to be represented at Modena and Tempiute: "small, crude bifacial" (no. 3), "thick, bifacial core tools" (no. 6) and "non-bipolar core" (no. 7). Obviously, products are not numbered in technological order since nonbipolar core reduction (no. 7) must precede production of core- or flake-blank bifaces and other tools (nos. 3, 6). Mode 3 yielded very few flakes (Ahler 1975:Table 8), so is omitted from analysis.

Ahler's (1975:120–122) own application of the approach to archaeological assemblages from occupation sites found no. 7 unsuitable for its high concentration of weight in the 25.4 mm (1 in) class. He therefore substituted results of another experiment (1975:Table 19), called "7, variant" here. Yet the two mode-7 datasets seem equally plausible candidates for occurrence in UA data, so Ahler's approach offers the flexibility of using either, singly or in combination with mode 6. For instance, assuming nonbipolar core as the sole reduction mode, the total number of >6.35 mm (¼ in) flakes divided by 170.3 (19.3 + 44.1 + 106.9) gives an estimate of number of cores reduced. Similarly, assuming nonbipolar core reduction followed by production of large, thick bifaces as the only two reduction modes, the total number of flakes >6.35 mm (¼ in) divided by 292.6 (24.8 + 75.9 + 191.9) gives an estimate for the combination of these modes. Separate production estimates also can be generated for separate flake-size classes, although analysis at that level of detail is not attempted.

It is not clear from Ahler's (1975) description if he viewed reduction modes like 7 and 6 to be successive, such that their combination models amount (and to some degree kind) of flake debris generated from initial core reduction followed by biface-preform production from flake blanks or the reduced core. Analysis here assumes that such reduction modes are in fact successive and that the combination of either variant of mode 7 with mode 6 is legitimate. The following expressions give their corresponding estimates:

Ahler 6 + 7: # of preform-stage   Eq. 8.6
    bifaces = ≥6.35 mm flakes / 292.6

Ahler 6 + var. 7: # of preform-   Eq. 8.7
    stage bifaces = ≥6.35 mm flakes / 189.3.

Ahler (1975:Table 17) reported mean count and weight of flakes by size class (G1 = 25.4 mm

[1 in], G2 = 12.7 mm [½ in], G3 = 6.35 mm [¼ in or .223 in, given here as ¼ in only]; see also Root 1997:Table 2) for combinations of reduction modes and intended products. For analysis here and following from the assumptions above, the most relevant products are from modes 6 and 7 (Ahler 1975:Table 17). Ahler's figures broadly agree with those reported by Tarasov and Stafeev (2014:254) for large, bifacially worked axe preforms.

Ahler (1975:133) also used experimental data to express biface preforms produced as a function of aggregate weight in the 12.7 and 6.35 mm (½ and ¼ in) size fractions. Specifically, the equation relates large, thick bifaces in a coarse silicified sandstone to weight as:

$$((\text{wgt(g) } 12.7 + 6.35 \text{ mm})*0.69) / 136 \qquad \text{Eq. 8.8}$$

The toolstone used to derive this expression is much coarser than obsidian, and the description of preforms as "large, thick" is quite broad. Relevance to obsidian quarries is uncertain. Nevertheless, it is worth estimating biface production scale at Modena and Tempiute using this method as well.

Root's approach is at once more analytically sophisticated than Ahler's but simpler to apply. Root (1992:Tables 6.1–6.2) reported mean count and weight by size class for several reduction modes, in most cases including variants of modes (e.g., skilled edging and also expert edging). Assuming that most Modena and Tempiute reduction involved core reduction and early-stage preform production, Root's most relevant modes include cobble testing, unprepared and prepared core reduction, and biface edging. Root (1992:Tables 6.1–6.2) reported relevant data for three variants of biface edging, but neither separately nor combined do the variants match summary data reported in Root (1997:Table 6); the latter is used here. Accordingly, the following expressions give separate estimates of preform-stage bifaces using Root's experimental data:

core reduction + biface edging: Eq. 8.9
    # of preform-stage bifaces =
    ≥6.35 mm flakes / 307.9

cobble testing + core reduction +   Eq. 8.10
    biface edging: # of preform-stage
    bifaces = ≥6.35 mm flakes / 527.2.

In Root's approach (1997:Table 6), "unprepared core" reduction generates 71.0 >19.05 mm (¾ in) flakes per cobble, and "skilled edging" of biface preforms to Callahan Stage 2 generates 154.6 >6.35 mm (¼ in) flakes. Root (1992:97) explicitly linked his edging and thinning modes. Otherwise, as in Ahler's experiments, it is not clear if others among his modes are successive such that, for instance, cobble testing precedes core reduction, which precedes biface edging. From Root's (1992:91–98) description, I assume that they are. Accordingly, these modes were combined for some analyses. Significantly, Root (1997:Table 6) also reported rates of production of products (e.g., cores, edged bifaces) per reduction mode.

These data make it possible to estimate not just preforms but also spent cores per reduction episode. For this purpose, however, it is invalid to sum the products by modes, as though cobble-testing flake count corresponds to x cobbles, and core-reduction flake count to y separate cobbles, and biface-edging flake count to again separate z cobbles. Treating these modes as successive, it is the core products generated by the earliest mode that matter, other products themselves being reduced to preforms. Accordingly, the sum of cobbles tested across relevant modes from Root (1997:Table 6) is used to estimate core products.

Admittedly, there is some ambiguity in Root's data, because it is unclear if his (1997: Table 6) "biface edging" corresponds to his (1997: Table 1) "skilled biface edging" or "expert biface edging" or both combined. Despite this, the additional strength of Root's approach is that his MLR method assigns mixed empirical assemblages to various reduction modes (as ambiguous as results reported in Chapter 5 were), avoiding the assumption of reduction modes represented in assemblages required by Ahler's approach. Therefore, mixed empirical assemblages first can be submitted to MLR analysis to allocate them into constituent reduction modes,

then the number of instances of such modes can be estimated using Root's production figures. For analysis, however, I assume that all reduction was to produce biface preforms.

A final method to estimate production scale uses UA experimental data. In five analyzed cobble reductions, 4,443 ≥6.35 mm (¼ in) flakes were struck to produce 17 Stage-2 preforms (*sensu* Beck et al. 2002). The result is an average of 261.4 flakes/preform, yielding the expression:

UA experiment: # of preform-   Eq. 8.11
    stage bifaces = ≥6.35 mm flakes / 261.4.

The result is an estimate of the number of preform-stage bifaces produced at Modena and Tempiute. Furthermore, the preform estimate can be divided by 17/5 to estimate the number of cobbles required to produce that number of bifaces (from 17 preforms generated by five analyzed cobbles), as:

UA experiment: # of biface cobbles =   Eq. 8.12
    # of preform-stage bifaces / (17/5).

(This figure for bifaces per cobble is much lower than what Flenniken and Ozbun [1988:98] reported for undescribed experiments with Newberry Crater obsidians.) UA experimental data furnish a final independent estimate of cobbles reduced, by dividing the 4,443 flakes by the number of cobbles, five. Then dividing the point estimate of number of ≥6.35 mm (¼ in) flakes by 888.6 (4,443 / 5) gives an estimate of cobbles worked, or:

UA experiment: # of biface cobbles =   Eq. 8.13
    ≥6.35 mm flakes / 888.6.

Neither these latter estimates of cobbles worked nor those from Root's (1992, 1997) experimental data are obtained using Carr and Bradbury's (2001) ACU method, so are not strictly comparable to results of that method. Yet if such independent estimates converge, they are mutually reinforcing and therefore lend confidence to analytical results. Moreover, UA experimental data are more suitable models of quarry reduction at Modena than at Tempiute, because experimental cobbles were roughly the size of Modena cobbles and much greater than

Tempiute ones. It is unlikely, for instance, that three or more preforms could be knapped from a typical Tempiute cobble or that 888 ≥6.35 mm (¼ in) flakes could be struck to produce one Stage-2 preform from such a cobble. Therefore, UA experimental data probably underestimate the number of Tempiute cobbles worked.

Results

Table 8.4 reports the various estimates for preform-stage production at Modena. Pelegrin-Chauchat and Newcomer (via Singer and Ericson) estimates of stage preforms at Modena are very high, and differ between themselves nearly as much as, together, they diverge from other estimates. Because of this divergence and the somewhat simplistic assumptions of their equations, I discount these results. Estimates from Ahler's combined core-reduction and preform-production experiments are lower and, although somewhat different, between them suggest that 75,000–115,000 stage preforms can account for the quantity of flake debris at Modena. From Root's experimental data, the combination of core reduction and biface edging yields an estimate slightly less than 100,000, while the more conservative (because it requires more flakes for each preform produced) and arguably more realistic combination of cobble testing, core reduction, and biface edging suggests about 72,000 reduction episodes at Modena. Because this combination of reduction modes generated an average of 1.14 stage preforms in Root's (1997: Table 6) experiments, Table 8.4 adjusts these figures accordingly, yielding an overall estimate of nearly 82,000 stage preforms. UA experimental data give an estimate of more than 84,000 stage preforms. Finally, preform-stage production estimates from Ahler's (1975:133) expression (Eq. 8.8) are quite high, nearer the range of Pelegrin-Chauchat's and Newcomer's figures but still considerably different from them in absolute value. (In fact, the difference between these three higher estimates and the larger number of more consistent lower ones exceeds the value of most lower ones.)

Where relevant, estimates from Stage-2 sample data are even higher, reflecting the higher flake-count estimates of that sample. The Pelegrin-Chauchat and Ahler weight method require data that UA Stage-2 samples could not collect, and UA experimental data did not require estimates of flake quantity from field sampling. Conservative estimates of stage-preform production scale at Modena and Tempiute are found using Stage-1 sample data, but Stage-2 data suggest considerably higher figures.

Of course, independent estimates do not correspond in detail. However, excluding Pelegrin-Chauchat's and Newcomer's figures, they are fairly consistent and approach the mutual reinforcement sought. On balance, then, and excluding high figures, estimates of the quantity of flake debris at Modena yield conservative estimates of approximately 80,000–100,000 stage preforms. These are impressive figures that compare to biface preform estimates for the Tosawihi quarry complex (Bloomer and Ingbar 1992:246), but are surprisingly modest in broader perspective. If the quarry was used regularly for perhaps 7,000 years, these estimates convert to roughly 11–15 preforms per year, scarcely enough to account for one user (Ericson 1982; Luedtke 1984) and still a modest production rate despite the magnitude of the estimates. Similarly large estimated figures converted to similarly modest production rates in Tarasov and Stafeev's (2014:255) quarry analysis.

Cobbles Reduced

As above, Root's (1992, 1997) and UA's own experimental data also permit estimation of cobbles reduced. In the sequence of cobble testing, core reduction, and biface edging, each reduction episode accounts for 0.29 worked cobbles (Root 1997:Table 6). Multiplying episodes estimated from Stage-1 sample data by this figure gives an estimate of 23,721 cobbles worked. UA experimental data provide two separate but remarkably similar estimates. One is found by dividing the estimated number of stage preforms, 81,796, by 17/5 (3.4), the number of stage preforms per cobble in those experiments. The result is 24,857 cobbles. The second is found by dividing flake count by 888.6, the number of flakes per reduced cobble

TABLE 8.4. Estimated Preform Production from Modena and Tempiute Stage-1 and Stage-2 Samples.

Modena Stage 1

Source	Pelegrin	Newcomer	Ahler	Ahler	Ahler	Root	Root	Root	UA
Equation			8.8	8.6	8.7	8.9	8.10	8.10[d]	8.11
Cluster			wgt.	6&7	6&7(var.)	core red.[b]	cobble[c]		
A	126,354	212,224	156,164	36,265	56,055	46,952	34,463	39,288	40,594
B	86,852	183,132	125,864	31,294	48,371	40,516	29,739	33,902	35,029
D	7,336	15,112	7,184	2,582	3,991	3,343	2,454	2,798	2,891
E	2,623	1,824	2,060	312	482	403	296	338	349
F	38,378	28,021	33,949	4,788	7,401	6,199	4,550	5,187	5,360
U	346	89	316	15	24	20	15	17	17
2009-1	1,338	1,442	1,174	246	381	319	234	267	276
Σ	263,228	441,844	326,710	75,503	116,705	97,753	71,751	81,796	84,515

Stage 2

Source	Pelegrin[1]	Newcomer	Ahler	Ahler	Ahler	Root	Root	Root	UA
Equation			8.8	8.6	8.7	8.9	8.10	8.10[d]	8.11
Cluster			wgt.[a]	6&7	6&7(var.)	core red.[b]	cobble[c]		
A		214,598		36,671	56,682	47,478	34,849	39,728	
B		339,877		58,079	89,772	75,194	55,193	62,920	
D		15,963		2,728	4,216	3,532	2,592	2,955	
E		2,146		367	567	475	348	397	
F		28,864		4,932	7,624	6,386	4,687	5,343	
U		436		74	115	96	71	81	
2009-1		1,412		241	373	312	229	261	
Σ		603,296		103,092	159,349	133,472	97,969	111,685	

Tempiute Stage 1

Source	Pelegrin[1]	Newcomer	Ahler	Ahler	Ahler	Root	Root	Root
Equation	8.4		8.8	8.6	8.7	8.9	8.10	8.10[d]
Cluster			wgt.	6&7	6&7 var.	core red.[b]	cobble[c]	cobble[c]
N1	3,489	13,395	11,448	2,289	3,538	2,963	2,175	2,480
N2	8,932	18,955	22,113	3,239	5,007	4,194	3,078	3,509
N3	1,008	508	980	87	134	112	82	94
N4	125	192	226	33	51	42	31	35
N5	3,164	6,204	6,547	1,060	1,639	1,373	1,007	1,149
N6	3,133	6,099	5,767	1,042	1,611	1,349	990	1,129
N7	105	282	237	48	74	62	46	52
N8	925	1,086	1,131	186	287	240	176	201
N9	1,142	1,096	1,590	187	290	243	178	203
N10	175	519	595	89	137	115	84	96
S5	34	27	87	5	7	6	4	5
Σ	22,234	48,363	50,720	8,264	12,774	10,700	7,854	8,953

Stage 2

Source	Pelegrin[1]	Newcomer	Ahler	Ahler	Ahler	Root	Root	Root
Equation			Eq. 8.8	Eq. 8.6	Eq. 8.7	Eq. 8.9	Eq. 8.10	Eq. 8.10[d]
Cluster			wgt.[a]	6&7	6&7 var.	core red.[b]	cobble[c]	cobble[c]
N1		5,162		882	1,363	1,142	838	956
N2		14,147		2,417	3,737	3,130	2,297	2,619
N3		500		85	132	111	81	93
N4		73		12	19	16	12	14
N5		4,256		727	1,124	942	691	788
N6		0		0	0	0	0	0
N7		151		26	40	33	24	28
N8		0		0	0	0	0	0
N9		790		135	209	175	128	146
N10		1,290		220	341	285	209	239
S5		69		12	18	15	11	13
Σ		26,436		4,517	6,982	5,849	4,293	4,894

[a] Data unavailable from Stage-2 sample.
[b] Core reduction & biface edging.
[c] Cobble testing, core reduction, and biface edging.
[d] (Cobble testing, core reduction, biface edging) * 1.14.

in UA experiments. The result is 24,682 cobbles. These two very similar results also resemble the estimate from Root's experimental data. Taken together, these estimates are about 25% below ACU figures reported above. Given the uncertainty and imprecision inherent in these methods, ACU and cobble estimates are at least broadly consistent.

Tempiute
The same methods and equations were used to estimate original quantities at Tempiute. Results appear in Shott (2016:Table 8.10). As at Modena, there is variation among estimates; Pelegrin-Chauchat, Newcomer, and Ahler weight estimates considerably exceed other Ahler, Root, and UA estimates. In Stage-1 sample data, as at Modena the latter estimates converge, here in the range of roughly 8,000–13,000 stage-preforms produced.

Cobbles Reduced
Again, similar to Modena, Root's (1992, 1997) and UA's own experimental data also permit estimation of cobbles reduced. Using the same methods described above, Root's (1997:Table 6) method gives an estimate of 2,596 cobbles. UA experimental data provide two separate but, in this case, identical estimates of 2,721 cobbles. Consistent with Modena, this figure resembles the estimate from Root's experimental data. Unlike Modena's, these estimates are about 75% below Tempiute ACU figures reported above. As noted above, however, UA experimental data probably underestimate the number of Tempiute cobbles worked; these figures must be viewed with caution.

Preform Production Efficiency
The high incidence of broken preforms at Modena and Tempiute is not unusual compared to other obsidian quarries in and near the Great Basin (e.g., Gilreath and Hildebrandt 1997). Elsewhere, 96% of the preforms found at Knife River Flint quarries were broken (Root 1997:41). The reason is obvious: broken stage preforms were discarded on the spot, and successfully reduced ones mostly exported for continued reduction and/or use elsewhere.

Root (1997:41–42) exploited this fact to estimate "production efficiency" at parts of the Knife River source. He defined efficiency as the ratio of successfully reduced and exported tools, based on estimates of production scale, to the total number of preforms attempted. The latter quantity was defined essentially as the (exported and therefore uncountable) number of successful reductions plus the broken and discarded failures present at the quarries. The expression thus is:

Production efficiency =   Eq. 8.14
successful exports / (successful exports + reduction failures).

Root (1997:41) defined the numerator of Eq. 8.14 as the product of production estimates, thus assuming that all quarry flake debris derived from successfully reduced and exported specimens. Obviously, reduction failures also generated considerable debris. For comparability, I follow Root's method, thus using production-scale estimates at Modena and Tempiute as the numerator and adding estimated of failed preform reductions found as the estimate of the total preform population at the sites to that figure to form the denominator. Nevertheless, this method ignores the substantial fraction of the quarries' overall flake populations that were struck from failed preforms.

Root (1997:41) also noted the obvious fact that failed preforms generated two or more fragments. In experimental data, production efficiency is successful products divided by total attempts, the latter a lower figure than broken preforms. In archaeological data it is virtually impossible to determine the number of original preforms from the number of fragmentary ones found, although methods to estimate the former from the latter (Shott 2000) were used in Chapter 6 to quantify the recovered Modena assemblage. As useful as they are, Table 8.4 estimates are derived from quantity and type of flake debris, not actual preforms recovered.

For Modena, Equation 8.14 uses stage preform production-scale estimates (Table 8.5) as the numerator, and those figures plus estimated number of preforms still present at the site (Table 8.3) as the denominator. For the latter, the estimate is from Stage-1 or Stage-2 samples, and assumes that all remaining preforms are broken. Yet 22.3% of the overall Modena preform assemblage is intact, as are 18.5% of those in the Stage-1 sample, suggesting that approximately one-fifth of bifaces still present there are intact. (The Stage-2 sample is unusual in containing 42.6% intact preforms.) Again, correcting for fragmentation, the original estimate of 42,000 preforms produced at Modena would be reduced to about 31,500, affecting the estimates reported in Table 8.5. This much acknowledged, the figure of 42,000 is retained for calculation.

Conservative estimates of the total number of stage-preforms produced at Modena range from 80,000–100,000 (Table 8.4), and the Stage-1 sample estimate of preforms remaining at the site is 42,024 (Table 8.3). Using Eq. 8.14 to estimate production efficiency, successful exports are the difference between the total produced and the figure remaining (e.g., 80,000−42,024 or 100,000−42,024 for the ends of the production-scale range). Successful exports divided by total product (e.g., [80,000−42,024] / 80,000) thus measures production efficiency. Accordingly, for the entire quarry, production efficiency is roughly calculated from the extremes of the conservative range of total stage preforms as:

(80,000-42,024) / 80,000 = 0.475 or 47.5%;

and:

(100,000-42,024) / 100,000 = 0.580 or 58.0%.

As an example, Table 8.5 provides estimates of efficiency rate by Modena area from one set of production-scale estimates: UA experimental data entered into Eq. 8.11 above. (Other conservative production-scale estimates using Ahler or Root data would produce slightly different efficiency values.) For Area E the estimate of remaining (i.e., failed) preforms exceeds the production-scale estimate.

For the entire Modena quarry and for the detailed estimates for Areas A and B from Eq. 8.11, estimates of production efficiency are near 50%. Yet Table 8.5 also suggests that efficiency varied considerably across the quarry. Nor do rate estimates pattern neatly between the source areas of A, B, and F and workshop areas

TABLE 8.5. Preform Production Efficiency at Modena Using Total-Production Estimate from UA Experimental Data.

Area	Estimated Production Eq. 8.11	Estimated Remaining Table 8.6	Production Efficiency Eq. 8.14
A	40,594	22,062	0.457
B	35,029	14,467	0.587
D	2,891	625	0.784
E	349	404	>1.000
F	5,360	4,236	0.210
2009-1	276	230	0.167
Σ	84,515	42,024	0.503

D, E, and 2009-1. Among the former, A and B give fairly high estimates, but F's efficiency rate is low. Among workshop areas, D has a high efficiency rate, but 2009-1's is quite low.

Production-efficiency estimates for Tempiute are problematic because of the very small size (n = 1) of the sample of preforms in probabilistic (in this case, Stage-2) samples. Advisedly, using the estimate of 426 stage preforms remaining there and the conservatively estimated 8,000–13,000 preforms produced there, production efficiency is estimated as:

(8,000-426) / 8,000 = 0.947 or 94.7%;

and:

(13,000-426) / 13,000 = 0.967 or 96.5%.

These remarkably high figures, well above most Modena estimates and most but not all of Root's (1997:Table 7) estimates for one Knife River Flint workshop, should not be taken at face value. Nevertheless, they suggest that production efficiency at Tempiute was much higher in general than at Modena, despite or perhaps because of its much smaller overall production scale.

Modena-Tempiute Comparison

Modena and Tempiute both are major quarries and both served as important sources of toolstone for prehistoric peoples of the southern and central Great Basin. Yet the quarries differ considerably in scale of production as estimated using methods described in this chapter.

TABLE 8.6. Ratio Comparisons of Preform-Stage Bifaces at Modena and Tempiute.

					Stage 1				
	Eq. 8.4 Pelegrin[a]	Newcomer	Ahler Eq. 8.8 Wgt.	Ahler Eq. 8.6 6&7	Ahler Eq. 8.7 6&7 var.	Root Eq. 8.9 core red.[b]	Root Eq. 8.10 Cobble[c]	Root Eq. 8.10 Cobble[c]	UA Eq. 8.11
Modena Σ	263,228	441,844	326,710	75,503	116,705	97,753	71,751	81,796	84,515
Tempiute Σ	22,234	48,363	50,720	8,264	12,774	10,700	7,854	8,953	9,251
M/T	11.84	9.14	6.44	9.14	9.14	9.14	9.14	9.14	9.14
T/M	0.08	0.11	0.16	0.11	0.11	0.11	0.11	0.11	0.11
					Stage 2				
Modena Σ		603,296		103,092	159,349	133,472	97,969	111,685	
Tempiute Σ		26,436		4,517	6,982	5,849	4,293	4,894	
M/T		22.82		22.82	22.82	22.82	22.82	22.82	
T/M		0.04		0.04	0.04	0.04	0.04	0.04	

Source: Table 8.5.
[a] Data unavailable from Stage-2 sample.
[b] Core reduction & biface edging.
[c] Cobble testing, core reduction, and biface edging.
[d] (Cobble testing, core reduction, biface edging) * 1.14.

Estimated ACU at Modena exceeds Tempiute figures by factors of three to nearly four (Table 8.2). However, proportions differ in estimates of cobbles reduced using Root and UA experimental data, where Modena exceeds Tempiute by a factor of more than nine. For preform-stage bifaces, Table 8.6 compares summary estimates for Modena and Tempiute. As above, the most reliable, certainly the most convergent, estimates are Ahler's using Equation 8.6, Root's using Equations 8.9 and 8.10, and UA's using Equation 8.11. In Stage-1 sample data, Modena estimates exceed Tempiute ones by a factor exceeding nine (in fact, given the identical estimation methods, by exactly the same ratio of 9.14 as for estimates of cobbles worked). In Stage-2 data, that ratio is more than doubled, to a factor of nearly 23.

Despite the impressive abundance of debris on Tempiute's surface, that quarry witnessed the reduction of an estimated one-third to one-quarter of Modena's ACU and possibly even lower estimates of actual cobbles worked. (Yet those latter estimates probably are low, for reasons given above.) Tempiute also produced somewhere between roughly one-tenth and one-twentieth of the estimated preform-stage bifaces that Modena did.

Sourcing data described in Chapter 10 broadly agrees with these results. There, an opportunistic rather than probabilistic sample of regional sites from which Modena or Tempiute obsidian were sourced identified 584 finished projectile points of Modena obsidian versus 80 of Tempiute obsidian, a difference of a factor of roughly seven. Similarly, 52 Modena preforms versus six Tempiute ones suggests a difference of a factor of nearly nine.

Modena-Tempiute
Production Scale in Context

However approximate estimates of bifaces produced at Modena and Tempiute may be, and whatever the disagreement among estimation methods, results nevertheless place production scale at Modena and Tempiute in perspective. One small Late Preclassic Mayan workshop at Colha, for example, may have generated 75,000 bifaces, which lies in the range of total produc-

tion at Modena (Shafer and Hester 1983:529). The impressive quantity of material found at Modena notwithstanding, its highest estimates of bifaces produced are an order of magnitude less than Singer and Ericson's (1977) estimates for Bodie Hills, and low compared to estimates for chert quarries outside of the Great Basin like Knife River (Ahler 1986). They are much lower than European Neolithic production estimates, including Bosch's (1979:130) for the Rijckholt mine in Holland, Le Roux's (1979:55–56) for Breton axe quarries, and Torrence's (1986:205) for Aegean obsidian quarries.

Estimating Toolstone
Demand and Consumption

To this point in analysis, focus has been on estimating supply or outputs. But supply and demand are equally important when modeling the economics of prehistoric toolstone acquisition. Unfortunately, there is very little information about the scale of demand or the factors that determined it in prehistoric cultures that used stone. Of course prehistoric Great Basin residents needed toolstone, but how much? Did they require toolstone cobbles of particular sizes or shapes? Were different kinds or qualities of toolstone required for different purposes? The answers to these and other questions are both important to know and probably vary over the span of Great Basin prehistory. The only option is to use the little information that is available. Focus here is on demand for toolstone.

Luedtke (1984:66) modeled annual toolstone demand as:

$$L = \Sigma\ T_i/D_i\ (S_i + M_i + R_i)$$

where L is demand (g) per household, T_i is amount of task i that requires stone tools "of a specific type" in performances or uses, D_i is each type i's discard rate in the same units at T_i, S_i is the mean weight of specimens of each tool type at discard, M_i is the amount of unused manufacturing debris generated in producing each specimen in type i, and R_i is the amount of unused resharpening debris generated in maintaining each specimen in type i. Obviously, L and the size of the tool inventory depend ultimately upon diet, labor organization, climate because of lesser or greater need for clothing and shelter, and lithic technology itself. For instance, where ground stone tools were used for a wide range of tasks as in New Guinea, the need for chipped stone flakes and tools was correspondingly reduced (Luedtke 1984:73). These factors in turn determine the range, number, and complexity of tasks for which stone tools were used.

Luedtke (1984:Tables 6.1–6.3) summarized toolstone demand for three ethnographic cases. Possibly the most relevant on ecological grounds were two interior Australian hunter-gatherers groups, the Ngatatjara and the Pintupi (approximately 20,600 g/yr and 37,100 g/yr, respectively. Also for the Western Desert region of the Ngatatjara, Gould [1980:130] provided estimates similar to Luedtke's, but only a small fraction of total L was from quarry sources, a distinction otherwise ignored here. Perhaps by partly considering nonquarry sources or because of different cultural contexts, Hayden [1977] estimated considerably higher rates of toolstone consumption for desert Australia.) Luedtke (1984:Table 6.4) also modeled toolstone demand and estimated L for temperate-climate Late Woodland Great Lakes horticultural cultures (approximately 57,200 g/yr). The Great Basin is a colder desert climate than interior Australia, but neither as seasonal or possibly as environmentally diverse as the American Midwest. What's more, the Australian groups used industries that featured flake tools more than bifaces, a common emphasis in North America and certainly at Modena. Foley and Mirazón Lahr's (2015:12) estimates for very broadly comparable African flake-tool industries ranged from 10–100 flakes/person-year (although the lower figure may pertain to premodern hominids), with similar estimates for debris generated in the production of those tools. Even this source's higher figure seems extremely conservative. In technology, the North American Late Woodland case may be somewhat more comparable to the Great Basin. As a result, none of Luedtke's estimates of L are strictly applicable for any particular Great Basin group or time period. Yet the range in values suggests that estimates of L in the vicinity of 30,000–40,000 g/yr

are reasonable, at least as approximations for the purpose of comparison and interpretation.

Relevance to this study is qualified in at least two respects. First, Luedtke's toolstone estimates were for chert. To the extent that brittle obsidian breaks in use more readily than does chert or wears more rapidly on its edges, then all else equal the discard rate D for obsidian may be higher than for chert. This possibility is acknowledged but cannot be measured. Second, L is measured in grams. For a fixed volume of toolstone, chert may be somewhat heavier than obsidian. Luedtke (1992:Table 6.2) reported a fairly narrow range and a mean of approximately 2.60 g/cc in chert. Yet C. Skinner (1983:39) reported values for obsidian density only about 10% lower than chert. Luedtke's estimates might be reduced by this factor, yielding a range for L of approximately 27,000–36,000 g/yr.

Taking that figure at face value, it can be used with knowledge of preform and flake-debris weight to convert toolstone demand to quantity of material found at quarries like Modena and Tempiute. Luedtke's estimate of L takes account of weight of production debris as M_i, which at Modena and Tempiute is assumed to extend through Callahan preform Stage 3. I assume further that flake debris generated in completing preforms to tools comprises 10% of total production debris weight (i.e., that 90% of M_i is found at quarries), and ignore weight of resharpening flakes, R_i, as minimal. Given the broad range of these estimates, that is, I make no allowance for later-stage reduction or resharpening of tools during use.

UA reduction experiments produced 11 Stage-3 preforms that weighed an average of 58.2 g (≈60 g), and resulted in the accumulation of a total of 7,830 g of flake debris (average = 7,830 g / 11 preforms ≈ 712 g/preform). Intact Modena preforms (n = 59) weighed an average of 38.9 g (≈40 g), intact Tempiute ones (n = 10) an average of 19.3 g (≈20 g). Modena and Tempiute averages are for all intact preforms, including those not yet reduced to Stage 3, so are maximal figures for preforms at that stage. Given the range in average preform weight from approximately 20 g at Tempiute to 60 g in UA

TABLE 8.7. Estimated *hhyd* (Minimum and Maximum) and Reductions to Stage-3 Preform (Minimum and Maximum) at Modena.

	Stage-1			Stage-2		
	Lower 95% wt	Total wt	Upper 95% wt	Lower 95% wt	Total wt	Upper 95% wt
Max. *hhyd*	4,688	8,219	11,751	7,129	10,218	13,307
Min. *hhyd*	3,516	6,164	8,813	5,346	7,663	9,980
Min. redns. to St. 3	147,660	258,905	370,144	224,552	321,859	419,166
Max. redns. to St.3	196,880	345,207	493,525	299,402	429,145	558,888

hhyd = g/household/year. Weights are in grams.

experimental data, Modena's average of approximately 40 g seems a reasonable middle figure. Accordingly, I assume that each reduction to a Stage-3 preform consumed 40 g of actual preform and 712 g of flake debris, for a total of 752 g (≈750 g) of obsidian. This seems a generous estimate, because it adds Modena's mid-range estimate of preform weight to UA experimental data's average flake-debris weight for the production of larger Stage-3 preforms. If, as above, *L* ranges from 27,000 to 36,000 g/household-year, then these figures divided by 750 g yield estimates of 36–48 reductions to Stage-3 preforms/household-year.

Toolstone demand from such distant, if somewhat ecologically comparable, ethnographic cases combined with a chain of inference that involves rough estimates at each step recommend this estimate as a crude heuristic, not a precise calibration rate. Still, it can be used to at least broadly calibrate the volume of flake debris, estimated directly from UA's probabilistic sampling, and number of preforms produced, to regional consumption via Luedtke's equation.

Ericson (1982:145) estimated that Great Basin men required 5–20 dart points and 50–100 arrow points per year. For several reasons these figures are not comparable to Luedtke's. First, they apply to individuals, not households, although it is arguable that only men used points and that each household contained one man. Second, dart and arrow points may have been used concurrently, not successively in time. Third, the figures are for one tool type only,

not the complete range of stone tools, and are expressed in number of finished products, not mass of material required to manufacture those products. Fourth, the technology and reduction sequences for dart and arrow points may have been different, particularly because the latter might be made from relatively small flake blanks that could be struck either from recycled abandoned preforms or by poorly controlled core reduction. Chapter 9 documents a pronounced decline in Modena's production curve before the introduction of bow-and-arrow technology, so Ericson's estimate for dart-point demand seems most relevant to this question. Because they pertain to individuals, not households, and to points, but not other tools, they should be regarded as minimal figures for purposes of estimating toolstone demand and consumption.

Household-years of Demand

As above, Luedtke's (1984:66) model of toolstone demand suggests, broadly, a consumption rate of 27,000–36,000 g/household/year. Call these "household-years of demand" (*hhyd*). The Stage-1 and -2 sample estimates of toolstone weight at Modena are approximately 222 million g and 276 million g, respectively (Table 8.7). Dividing these estimates by the extremes of Luedtke's range suggest that Modena accounts for 6,164 to 8,219 (Stage-1 sample) or 7,663 to 10,218 (Stage-2 sample) *hhyd*. Corresponding figures for Tempiute are much lower, 438 to 584 (Stage-1 sample) or 205 to 273 (Stage-2 sample) *hhyd*. Tempiute figures are unreliable because Stage-2 sampling there was more limited than at Modena and therefore probably substantially underestimate actual quantity. Accordingly, treatment in this section is confined to Modena.

Again assuming 7,000 years of regular exploitation of Modena, these *hhyd* estimates account for only one to at most two households' annual demand for toolstone, found by dividing total-weight estimates by 7,000. Like the estimates of preforms reported above, initially impressive figures become modest when calibrated for the span of use of the quarry. Also as above, the Luedtke model's *hhyd* estimate itself accounts for 36–48 cobble or blank reductions to Callahan Stage-3 preform. Multiplying the minimum *hhyd* estimate by the lower figure and then by the upper figure give minimum reductions to Stage-3 preforms (Table 8.7). One last time assuming 7,000 years of use, point estimates of maximum reductions to Stage-3 preforms convert to roughly 80 such episodes per year.

Modena quarry debris is estimated to represent approximately 40,000 ACU and 80,000–100,000 Stage-3 preforms. Table 8.7's considerably higher estimates of reductions to Stage-3 preforms are difficult to square with those estimates. Depending upon reduction technology and cobble size, one cobble can yield a number of flake blanks and, ultimately, Stage-3 preforms; ACU estimates may not be all that inconsistent with Table 8.7's estimates of reductions. But the estimated number of Stage-3 preforms produced at Modena is less than half the estimated number of reductions to Stage-3 preform. All estimates made here are approximate, based as they are on limited experimental and ethnographic data that may not be directly comparable to Modena's cobble sizes and the region's ethnographic conditions. Luedtke's figures may overestimate Great Basin lithic demand, and UA and other experimental datasets used to generate estimates may not be faithful to prehistoric technology in all salient respects. There is much latitude for error in data of this nature. Despite the lack of agreement, all esti-

mates are consistent with modest rates of quarry use for roughly seven millennia or proportionally heavier use over shorter spans.

Conclusion

In analytical perspective, the impressive scale of obsidian deposits at Tempiute and especially Modena are qualified somewhat by demand or usage estimates. Whatever the spatial extent of the debris fields at Modena, particularly at Areas A, B, and F, in the aggregate they account for relatively modest rates of toolstone consumption over the postulated approximately 5,000–7,000 years of chief use of the source; again, the span and intensity of Tempiute's exploitation is unknown. If demand estimates are reasonably accurate, as rough as they admittedly are, it would not take many people very long, in archaeological terms, to deplete Modena nor, presumably, Tempiute considering its much smaller production estimates.

As discussed in Chapter 3, prehistoric depletion is the inferred fate of several Great Basin obsidian quarries. These include not just ones significantly smaller than Modena or even Tempiute (e.g., Buckboard Mesa [Amick 1991:80–81]; the Highland chert quarry [Reno and Pippin 1986:126]) but larger ones as well (e.g., the Coso Field [Hartwell et al. 1996:57]). Rowley and colleagues (2002) suggested that Modena was depleted during prehistory. Of course depletion is not absolute; even now, by careful searching useful nodules can be found at Modena. But a toolstone quarry need not be absolutely exhausted to lose much of its value. Once a point of diminishing return is reached between time available for search and toolstone acquired, a quarry ceases to be a reliable source of supply. It passes from destination to place of opportunity if one's travels take them to the neighborhood for other reasons. That transformation may have been the fate of Modena and almost certainly of Tempiute well before the end of Great Basin prehistory.

9

Obsidian Hydration Dating

Archaeologists have long known that obsidian hydrates at its surface in a time-dependent process. This knowledge led naturally to the development of obsidian hydration dating (OHD) as a way directly to date artifacts made of obsidian, like chipped stone tools. Obsidian being common in the Great Basin, it appealed to archaeologists' desire for time measurement and control. As a result, the Great Basin is a major center of obsidian studies, including those exploring the potential of hydration dating.

Unfortunately, several factors besides time affect the rate of obsidian hydration, including depositional context—because buried as opposed to surface-exposed artifacts may hydrate at different rates (e.g., Beck 1999; Beck and Jones 1994)—local differences in elevation and climate, and particularly humidity, intrinsic water content of obsidians, variation in climate during the Holocene, possible recycling and reuse at widely different times during the late Pleistocene or Holocene, and obsidian materials themselves (e.g., Duke 2008:73; Hull 2010; Liritzis and Laskaris 2011; Rogers 2008; Seddon 2005b:501).

In addition, traditional optical methods of rim definition and measurement are imprecise; as Seddon put it, "The observed, sharp hydration front or band edge may be a result of optical properties rather than hydration properties" (2005a:501). Specifically, comparison of instrumental and optical methods suggests that "the depth of water diffusion extends well beyond the optically defined diffusion front" (Liritzis and Laskaris 2011:2016 and Figure 1). Instru-mental methods like secondary ion mass spectrometry (SIMS) almost certainly are superior (Riciputi et al. 2002) and can produce results at odds with optical methods (e.g., Stevenson et al. 2004:564–565). But they also are more expensive, and few laboratories conduct OHD using SIMS.

Induced hydration curves for different obsidian toolstones largely controls for the different hydration rates of obsidians; in effect, hydration rate can be calibrated to material, although this method failed to produce satisfactory results for Modena or Tempiute (Rogers and Duke 2014:14–15). Reuse can be difficult to detect, but sometimes is evident or suspected from visible differences in degree of surface weathering, extensive modification of tools, particularly their haft elements, or from multiple hydration bands visible on the artifact. Amick (2007:235–238) used similar reasoning to infer considerable prehistoric reuse or recycling of older obsidian cores, flakes, and tools at the Nevada Test Site. Assuming relatively short use life between production and discard, and relatively modest elevation range occupied during that use life, elevation at the location of an obsidian artifact's discovery is a valid measure by which to control for that factor. Broad patterns of climatic variation in the late Pleistocene and through the Holocene are known, but they apply unevenly across such a large and physiographically diverse region as the Great Basin; for areas that lack local paleoenvironmental data, long-term climatic variation can be difficult to measure. Effective hydration temperature (EHT) measures local climatic effects upon hydration rate. Temperature and humidity measurement at only three sites in Butte Valley demonstrated considerable variation in temperature at the surface but less at depth, and similar variation in humidity as a function of depth (Beck and Jones 1994:Table 4.2). Generally, subsurface humidity was fairly constant but differed substantially from surface values, leading to the conclusion that "low humidity at the surface should significantly affect hydration rates" (Beck and Jones 1994:59). Elsewhere, EHT has been shown to vary greatly with depth in ways that compromise the accuracy of OHD dating (King 2004; Ridings 1996), although this source of variation can be partly controlled (Rogers 2007; Rogers and Duke 2014:6–9).

Yet surface-subsurface context itself is a variable over archaeological time. Whether artifacts were buried or exposed upon discovery is a simple matter of recording, but context at discovery is not necessarily original or long-term context. All obsidian artifacts were exposed at least for brief use and possibly for considerable times after discard; conversely, what is exposed on the surface at discovery may have been buried previously. Finally, surface-exposed obsidian can be altered, either by wind or other weathering agents whose effects Duke (2008: 76–77) minimized by measuring hydration rims on unweathered step fractures, or by intense natural fires (Buenger 2003:18, 27–28; Solomon 2002; Steffen 2005:86–89). Unfortunately, fire effects do not correlate closely with visible alternations like crazing and vesiculation (Steffen 2005:119), nor in Buenger's experiment did obsidian specimens exhibit any "significant form of thermal alteration" (2003:225) except for expansion of preexisting radial fractures.

On balance, time affects hydration rate but only among a set of factors whose interactions and effects can be complex. What is more, traditional optical methods of defining and measuring diffusion fronts and therefore hydration rims are coarse and questionable. Consequently, OHD registers time but other factors as well in ways complex and difficult to disentangle. It is a dating method in a qualified sense, or alter-

natively "a secondary source of chronological data" (Liritzis and Laskaris 2011:2015). Holding constant several manifestly important complicating factors, differences in OHD rims measure time. But optical OHD often is the chief or sole dating method available, which justifies its use with care.

OHD in the Great Basin

Despite its intrinsic limitations, particularly of chronological resolution (e.g., Rogers 2008), OHD has yielded quite good results in some places. For instance, the abundance of Topaz Mountain and Browns Bench obsidians in the western Bonneville basin (Arkush and Pitblado 2000) allowed Duke (2008:Table 15) to construct a fairly reliable and well-resolved local chronology there. Unfortunately, typological cross-dating of OHD data from that study and Seddon (2005a, 2005b) suggested that Modena hydrated more slowly than many other obsidians, so offered poorer prospects for time resolution (Duke 2008:83, Figure 32). More recent attempts to produce induced-hydration curves for Modena and other Lincoln County sources were unsuccessful (Rogers and Duke 2014). Similar cross-dating of Butte Valley sites suggested that Modena hydration values resolved time less consistently than did Tempiute ("Source B" in Beck and Jones [1994:Figure 4.6]) as well. Yet in Rogers and Duke's (2014:Table 8.7) study, Modena hydrated at a considerably higher rate than did Tempiute. Modena's hydration response may explain how Jakes Valley fluted and WST points yielded statistically indistinguishable results in Modena but statistically different results in Browns Bench obsidian (Estes 2009:173–174), although mean rim thickness was higher for WST than for fluted points, implying greater age. On the other hand, Modena patterned reasonably well compared to the Brown's Bench standard in Hauer's (2005:Figure 8) White Pine County study area.

Modena is among common OHD subjects owing in part to its regional abundance (Hull 1994; Seddon 2005a). The comparative scarcity of OHD analysis of Tempiute samples (e.g., Beck and Jones 1994) justifies emphasis here upon Modena, although A. Rogers and Duke (2014; see also McGuire et al. 2014:64–69) recently derived empirical hydration rates for Tempiute as well.

Hull (1994) conducted the earliest systematic OHD research on Modena, continuing that work recently (2010). Modena and other study sources have been identified often in sourcing and OHD studies in the past twenty years. Among recent studies, Stevenson (2008) and McGuire and colleagues (2014) are noteworthy, but along with Hull (1994), Seddon (2001a, 2005a) and A. Rogers and Duke (2014) are the most significant efforts. Hull (2010:90) criticized Seddon (2001a) for ignoring both depositional context and EHT as sources of variation; King (2004) documented the independent effect of EHT on hydration results, a factor that A. Rogers and Duke's (2014:6–8) method attempted to control. Seddon (2005a) expanded the Modena database, and used explicit statistical criteria to define chronological intervals that corresponded to ranges of OHD values. Time range and time-stage definition was based on the known time ranges of the diagnostic points that were the chief subject of analysis (Reed et al. 2005b:Table 29-1), although more recent research suggests that some types' age ranges are subject to revision (Smith et al. 2013:Figure 3). However, variation in values and overlap between artifacts of different type or associated date produced different degrees of confidence in the intervals defined. The resulting sequence (Seddon 2005a:Table 24-14) then was blind-tested against additional Modena obsidian specimens closely associated with radiocarbon dates, "thereby demonstrating the utility of the relative sequence for Modena obsidian" (Hull 2010:90).

Seddon's work, particularly the 2005 chronology, is commendable but inherently limited. It resolves past time unequally, being considerably more precise in the late Holocene than earlier. (Approximate time spans listed in Shott's [2016:Table 9.1] are from Reed et al. [2005b:Table 29-1], presumably Seddon's chronological source.) Of course, any geochemical variation within obsidian sourced to

Modena, as elsewhere (e.g., Eerkens and Rosenthal 2004; Gilreath and Hildebrandt 1997), may account for some part of the current database's imperfect ability to resolve past time, although Wills (2013) found little difference in hydration rate among Bodie Hills variants. In that case, future detailed characterization studies may refine the Modena OHD curve by resolving it into two or more separate, more homogeneous subsources. Also, Hull (2010:91–92) noted that the diffusion fronts of several measured Modena artifacts were broad. Whatever the explanation for the documented limitations of Modena hydration as a means of dating, Seddon's study and the data he compiled is an important source worth using.

Seddon's OHD chronology was based upon rim values measured on diagnostic points of known type ages, although the wide chronological distribution of types like Elko Corner-Notched introduces uncertainty. Data collected in the course of this study included rim values for some additional points, most of which are high values that fall in Seddon's Archaic and earlier intervals. Overall, they seem consistent with his calibration, and suggest that results are robust.

McGuire and colleagues (2014:64–70; see also Slaughter and Winslow 2004:55–56) took a similar approach, cross-referencing OHD rim values to documented ranges of diagnostic point types and/or associated radiocarbon dates. Interestingly, McGuire and colleagues (2014:65) suggested hydration rates so similar between Modena and the Kane Springs sources as to form a single calibration curve; Beck and Jones (1994) also noted similar hydration rates to Topaz Mountain and Butte Mountain obsidians. McGuire and colleagues also found little difference in hydration rate between surface and buried specimens, except from one north-facing high-elevation rockshelter whose rate was much lower (2014:68–69).

After concluding that induced hydration was not possible for Lincoln County obsidian sources, A. Rogers and Duke (2014), like Seddon, used rim values from diagnostic points of known chronological range to estimate hydration rate of Modena and Tempiute obsidians. They expanded Seddon's and McGuire and colleagues' datasets, confining treatment to several fairly common point taxa, and weighted OHD values inversely to the time range of taxa. They combined their dataset (2014:Tables 8.1, 8.5) with Seddon's (2005a) based on similarity in mean rim value of 10 Rosegate points from Seddon and two of their own (2014:Table 8.3), relatively small samples of a type that spanned less than a millennium of recent prehistory. Like Seddon, A. Rogers and Duke (2014:23–25, Table 8.5) then cross-referenced OHD rim values of diagnostic points as well as flake debris with radiocarbon results from the Gold Butte project area in Clark County (McGuire et al. 2014). Seddon's (2005a) Modena dataset and their own produced similar results, which justified their combination (Rogers and Duke 2014:25). They then fitted EHT-corrected OHD rim values to radiocarbon age by linear regression. A. Rogers and Duke's (2014:Table 8.7) results from 99 Modena specimens suggest a mean hydration rate there of 15.22 µ/1000 cal yr @ EHT 20°C ($s = 1.99$), from merely four Tempiute specimens of 6.51 µ/1000 cal yr @ EHT 20° ($s = 1.81$).

These results are somewhat limited by the relatively small datasets used, particularly for Tempiute. Also, that source's hydration rate is based entirely on inferred ages of diagnostic specimens, and is not anchored to a radiocarbon chronology (Rogers and Duke 2014:25). For Modena the larger dataset that combined A. Rogers and Duke's with Seddon's (2005a) data inspires more confidence. Limited Tempiute OHD results and calibration are not considered here.

Production-Rate Curves

One major goal of UA research being to test the Field Processing Model of quarry use, a corollary required a program of obsidian-hydration dating of Modena and Tempiute preforms. Therefore, 88 of the 267 Modena preforms were selected for OHD analysis. Four did not yield measurable hydration rims, and five had two rims. The preform sample was not drawn randomly, but instead in roughly equal pro-

portion by Callahan reduction stage and by cluster within Modena. As discussed below, the Modena results also include eight preforms recorded by Lytle (2010). Obviously, reduction of specimens that bore two rims dated two different events. Strictly, analysis and interpretation here is for all measurable hydration rims, a slightly larger number than specimens, on the logic that the source's production curve and chronology include minor rates of reuse or further reduction of older preforms. Fifteen of 26 preforms found at Tempiute were submitted for analysis, all of which had one measurable rim. OHD analysis was conducted at the Northwest Research Obsidian Laboratory. Results appear in Shott (2016:Appendix N).

Neither Modena nor Tempiute preforms were sourced, both as an economy measure owing to the samples' large size and on the assumption that most if not all derived from their respective source. I assume that any error introduced into analysis of OHD data is insignificant.

Modena

Singer and Ericson (1977:Figure 8) published among the first "production-rate curves" for Bodie Hills, essentially a smoothed curve of the frequency of OHD rim values. They argued that the curve revealed the range and pattern of the timing of prehistoric use of the quarry. Although Jackson (1984:117–119) questioned the adequacy of their sampling, arguing that use of Bodie Hills continued later than the circa 1500 BP decline that Singer and Ericson's curve suggested, similar curves and patterns are found at other obsidian quarries (e.g., Bloomer and Jaffke 2008:Figure 5 for the Tahoe region, Gilreath and Hildebrandt 2011:171, 178 for the Coso Field, King et al. 2011:152 and Halford 2008:18 for the Bodie Hills region; Martinez 1999:Figure 6.1 for Mt. Hicks). Typological cross-dating from diagnostic points suggest similar occupation patterns at other toolstone sources in the Great Basin (e.g., Bettinger 2015; Hockett 2009; R. Jones et al. 2003). Post-Mazama obsidians at Newberry Crater, a geochemically complex group, also have well defined modes and roughly normal distributions that naturally peak more

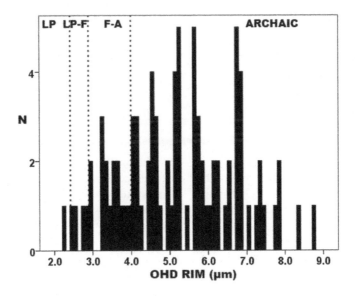

FIGURE 9.1. Composite distribution of obsidian hydration rim values at Modena. (LP = Late Prehistoric; F = Formative; A/Archaic = Archaic)

recently because of their younger age (Connolly and Byram 1999:Figure 14.1). Generally similar patterns were observed at the Mt. Edziza quarry in British Columbia (Fladmark 1984:154).

There are differences, however. Each of the several curves from the Coso Field peaks at OHD values that correspond to approximately 1400 BP, similar to Bodie Hill's (Gilreath and Hildebrandt 1997:172; cf., Rogers 2003, whose corrections increased the estimated age of many samples) and composite distributions from the Casa Diablo area (Mone and Adams 1988:Figure 2) but considerably later than the Modena distribution. Also, Gilreath and Hildebrandt (2011:180) and Halford (2001:Figure 2) reported more complex, bimodal curves for parts of some California obsidians' terranes.

Whatever the case at Bodie Hills or elsewhere in the Sierra and western Great Basin, the distribution of hydration-rim values of Modena specimens is roughly symmetrical and centered between 5–7 microns. As noted above, Lytle (2010) recovered eight preforms at Modena. The mean hydration-rim value for the larger Modena sample (mean = 5.2 μ) and Lytle specimens (mean = 4.5 μ) are statistically indistinguishable (t = 1.405; df = 99; p = 0.17).

Therefore, Lytle specimens are combined with the UA assemblage for analysis here. Figure 9.1 shows the composite distribution of OHD values for Modena preforms.

Figure 9.1 also shows Seddon's (2005a) OHD chronological intervals. Clearly, most Modena specimens fall in the Archaic interval. The relatively wide range of values in that interval, from 4.1 to nearly 9.0, suggests that use of the Modena quarry began relatively early in Great Basin prehistory. Although it persisted into the Late Prehistoric-Formative, only three preforms have hydration-rim values in the Late Prehistoric interval. To judge from the distribution of values, use of the Modena quarry rose steadily from earliest prehistory, peaked during the Archaic, and gradually declined thereafter. It seems approximately normally distributed. As above, production curves at many other western North American obsidian quarries take broadly similar forms.

Hydration-rim values for points assigned to types were found in several sources. Major ones included Hull (1994:Tables 7-6 to 7-9), who listed values by point type, and Reed and colleagues (2005: Vol. IV, Appendix G), who reported rim values by obsidian type and artifact, according to a unique field-specimen number. Other sources consulted are listed in Appendix B.

OHD Distributions by Modena Area

The overall Modena distribution can be subdivided meaningfully in several ways. Debris clusters, particularly Areas A, B, and F, were the subject of intensive, probabilistic sampling, forming natural subunits of the quarry zone. Nearly 20 preforms were recovered from Area D, but only six were submitted for OHD analysis. None were found in Area E and only one in Area 2009-1, neither of which was submitted for OHD. OHD rim histograms differ little among Areas A, B, and F (Shott 2016:Figure 9.4). Because many preforms were found outside of areas, sample sizes by area are somewhat lower than in the entire assemblage. Area A's curve is slightly broader and more discontinuous than are others'. No distribution is clearly normal, but neither are they conspicuously skewed or bimodal. Mean OHD rim values differ significantly among areas ($F = 3.20$; $df = 3$; $p = 0.03$). LSD tests identify Area A's mean value as significantly higher than others, which do not differ from one another. All means and distribution modes fall comfortably within Seddon's Archaic interval.

Chapter 4 described transect sampling for preforms conducted near or within several Modena areas. When preforms found near areas are included with those area samples, the distribution of OHD rim values slightly changes. Notably, vicinity-Area A's larger sample becomes more nearly normal in distribution and somewhat lower in mean value. Vicinity-Area B's sample size and distribution differs slightly from B alone, vicinity-Area F's sample size only increases by one from F alone. These subsamples do not differ significantly in mean OHD value ($F = 1.11$; $df = 3$; $p = 0.35$). LSD tests reveal no significant differences between any pairs of clusters.

Altogether, there is a slight tendency for Area A to exhibit higher OHD values and, by extension, occupation age. That tendency is somewhat obscured when cluster-vicinity preforms are included in analysis. All Modena clusters possess OHD means that fall in Seddon's Archaic period, and all have OHD distributions that largely fall in that period. To judge from OHD analysis of preforms, at least, most use of the Modena quarry occurred from late Pleistocene through middle Holocene. Cluster A appears to have been the first area of Modena used extensively, at least in preform production, but exploitation extended to other areas of dense natural occurrence of cobbles soon thereafter. Dames and Moore (1994:21-40, 21-50, 21-73) reported OHD results for the Wild Horse Canyon quarry (42BE88) and nearby quarry/workshop 42BE52 that suggested most use of that source in Archaic times and little evidence of late prehistoric use, broadly consistent with Modena data.

OHD Distributions by Callahan Stage

Another way to examine patterning in OHD results is by Callahan reduction stage. Results show little variation by range (that is not correlated with sample size) or in central tendency ($F = 1.00$; $p = 0.40$; Shott 2016:Figure 9.5). No LSD $p \leq 0.05$. When Callahan stages are paired, again mean differences are not significant ($t = 0.31$; $df = 91$; $p = 0.76$). Nor is there significant association between Callahan stage and Seddon interval (Shott 2016:Table 9.7); pooling intervals 2–4 to minimize low counts, the distribution of preforms by Callahan stage and Seddon interval are independent ($\chi^2 = 1.92$; $df = 3$; $p = 0.53$).

Viewed from the quarry itself, there is little variation by which to test the FPM in preform data. At the same time, Modena's occupation span as measured by its OHD rim curve suggests that most occupation occurred during the Archaic period, when land-use scale and mobility parameters presumably were high. If there was little variation in these organizational properties of Great Basin cultural systems during the Archaic, then there should be little variation in the chronological distribution of Modena preforms, which is the pattern revealed. Yet the length of the Archaic interval and the adaptive flexibility of hunter-gatherer land use make it unlikely that Archaic mobility was constant or unchanging.

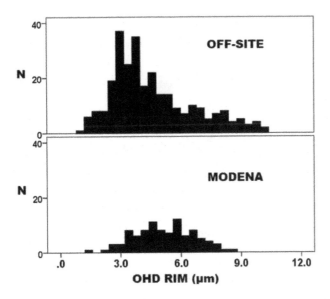

FIGURE 9.2. Modena and terrane ("off-site") OHD distributions at the same scale.

Production Curves in Modena's Terrane

Besides the quarry itself, Modena obsidian is fairly abundant and widely distributed in its southern Great Basin terrane. A number of sources document the presence, and in some cases the abundance and composition of Modena obsidian assemblages at occupational sites. Modena obsidian is common in archaeological sites from east-central Nevada to southwestern Utah, and is distributed even more widely, in at least small quantities, as far as Chaco Canyon (Duff et al. 2012).

Data on Modena's occurrence across its terrane is compiled in Appendix B.1. (Some sources reported relevant details by site, others only by project area.) This section compiles these values for analysis, called "terrane" data, and compares them to the hydration distribution from Modena itself. R. Jones and colleagues (2003; see also Beck and Jones 1994) obtained rim-thickness for Butte Valley and other sites in their east-central Nevada study area. Because they reported data either as means over several specimens or graphically within ranges of values, their data could not be used here. Similarly, Wells (1993:89, Figure 3.11) reported and graphed Modena band measurements but did

not tabulate exact values, so that source likewise, could not be used.

Curves for individual sites in Modena's terrane vary considerably. Some resemble the Modena curve (e.g., from HPL5 in Butte Valley [Beck and Jones 1994:Figure 4.3]), but many do not. For instance, the Modena distribution in the Gold Butte project area roughly 70 km south of the quarry is nearly uniform, and lacks the well-defined mid-Holocene mode evident in the quarry distribution (McGuire et al. 2014:Figure 5.8). Neither is that mode clearly defined in the composite Modena curve compiled by Bernatchez and others (2013:Figure 5) from UNEV, Kern River, and other surveys in southwestern Utah. Instead, that curve is broad and diffuse, with most values ≤4 µ, corresponding to Seddon's Formative-Archaic and later intervals. In Butte Valley, HPL2's distribution seems skewed to later dates (Beck and Jones 1994:Figure 4.3).

The Modena terrane's overall hydration-rim distribution (Figure 9.2) also differs significantly from the quarry itself (Figure 9.1). Drawn from a number of sites and sources, it is a considerably larger dataset than the quarry's. Accordingly, Figure 9.2 shows Modena and terrane curves using the same ordinate scale. The

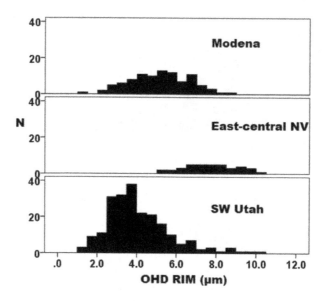

FIGURE 9.3. Distribution of obsidian hydration rim values by region.

terrane distribution is right-skewed and peaks at lower, later values corresponding to younger ages than does the Modena distribution. The two distributions differ significantly in mean value ($t = 2.71$; $df = 123.8$; $p < 0.01$). (In contrast, several habitat zones surrounding the Mt. Hicks source yielded production curves similar to the source curve; there the greatest, if still modest, difference was found with the lacustrine zone [Martinez 1999:Figure 6.5].)

Differences between curves at the Modena quarry and elsewhere in its terrane may owe partly to differences in EHT (King 2004), even though elevation differences and the geographic scale of Modena distribution are modest. The difference in location of modes and general forms of the distributions also may reflect partly the vagaries of uncontrolled sampling. The terrane distribution is dominated by east-central Nevada data—chiefly from Jakes and Butte Valleys—that are largely early Holocene in age (data from Duke's [2008, 2011] project area in adjacent western Utah are similar), and by a host of specimens from a considerable number of sites in southwestern Utah, mostly of Formative and Late Prehistoric age. (But the sample also includes data from sites in the Modena environs itself and other regions such as Clark County, Nevada, so the sum of east-central Nevada and southwestern Utah cases is slightly less than the entire terrane sample.) These include Fremont sites in central Utah and Fremont and Virgin Anasazi sites in the vicinity of St. George, Utah, and in the Gold Butte project area in Nevada. Some east-central Nevada data sources are from studies oriented to late Pleistocene and early Holocene occupations (e.g., Beck and Jones 2009a, 2009b; Estes 2009; Jones et al. 2012; R. Jones et al. 2003). Many of these originated in scholarly, not compliance, research, although east-central Nevada data are not strictly confined to those periods or projects. In comparison, most southwestern Utah data sources are compliance projects, and that area's archaeological record may have been dominated by its late prehistoric occupation.

In sum, terrane data are not systematic or probabilistic samples of the chronological or spatial distribution of Modena obsidian. Yet they suggest significant patterns of variation. Broadly, the Modena distribution overlaps extensively in range of values and, by extension, time with both east-central Nevada and southwestern Utah distributions (Figure 9.3), but is statistically different from both of them ($F = 90.5$; $df = 2$; $p < 0.01$; Shott 2016:Table 9.8). All pair-wise t-tests also yielded significant results, so the east-central Nevada Modena OHD curve is significantly earlier than Modena's itself, which is, in turn, significantly earlier than the southwestern Utah curve.

The east-central Nevada distribution extends farther back in time than does the quarry distribution itself. Quarry and southwestern Utah ranges overlap more extensively, but despite the latter's clear later mode it too extends back farther in time than does the quarry distribution. Clearly, Modena obsidian was used from nearly the start of Great Basin prehistory and quarry data do not completely sample the site's chronological span of use. Also, Modena obsidian remained a major source—in fact, increased markedly in occurrence—in southwestern Utah into later prehistory, even as the quarry production curve fell off.

Variation in Terrane Curves

Like data from Modena itself, terrane curves can be subdivided in useful ways. For instance, Stevenson (2008:Figure 6) documented somewhat cyclical trends in the proportion of Modena obsidian in his southwestern Utah study area. Modena's popularity peaked in Stevenson's Middle Archaic period, then declined later in the Archaic before rising to a secondary Formative peak before its final late-prehistoric decline; in most time periods, however, Modena was the most common obsidian sourced. Wells's (1993: 89, Figure 3.11) data from in and near Great Basin National Park showed a clear peak in Modena OHD rim values circa 5 µ and a long, low tail corresponding to later ages, a distribution that resembles the site's more than the overall terrane curve. Beck and Jones (1994:67) reported Modena rim values from their Butte Valley study area suggesting peak use in early prehistory followed by later decline.

Haarklau and colleagues (2005:Appendix C) reported OHD rim values for obsidian samples at the stratified Conaway and O'Malley rockshelters south of Modena in Lincoln County (D. Fowler et al. 1973). Modena's proportion among all sourced obsidian at Conaway shows a general rising trend through time (Shott

2016:Table 9.9), although sample sizes are small. O'Malley's considerably larger assemblage show some, but only limited, variation in smoothed proportions; throughout O'Malley's extensive occupation span, Modena was the most common obsidian used. On balance, these data are more consistent with overall terrane data than with the source production curve itself.

Few if any preforms were measured for OHD rim values in southwestern Utah, although many were in east-central Nevada. However, a number of flakes were measured in both regions. The resulting production curves somewhat resemble the overall distributions from the two regions, although in this subset of data modes and right tails are more similar (Shott 2016:Figure 9.9); again, however, mean values differ (for east-central Nevada, mean = 8.1; for southwest Utah, mean = 3.9; t = 8.48; df = 72; $p < 0.01$).

Most Great Basin archaeologists consider the appearance of relatively small Cottonwood, Desert Side-Notched, Rose Springs/Rosegate points to mark the adoption of the arrow (e.g., Garfinkel 2007), while Elko and earlier types are considered dart points. The production curves for arrow versus dart points in the terrane sample show clear differences between the inferred point types (Shott 2016:Figure 9.10); again, mean values differ (t = 9.26; df = 103.9; $p < 0.01$). Yet the presumed dart-point distribution considerably overlaps the arrow-point one, suggesting either that smaller dart points were reused and therefore resharpened, which would have removed or truncated an earlier hydration rim, or that darts persisted in secondary use well after the adoption of arrows.

Several sources (e.g., Hull 1994; Reed et al. 2005b) reported OHD rim values for finished points assigned to various Great Basin types. Figure 9.4 shows the distribution for each defined type, taking type assignment from various sources at face value. Not surprisingly, type distributions overlap somewhat in time, as might be expected from imprecision in dating, typological amibiguity, and the likelihood that at least some types truly did overlap in time. Results are broadly consistent with Seddon's

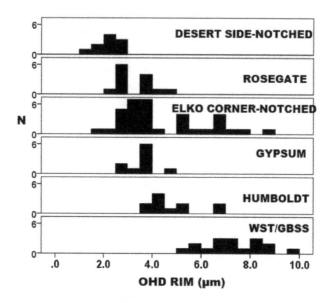

FIGURE 9.4. Distribution of obsidian hydration rim values by point types.
(WST/GBSS = Western Stemmed Tradition/Great Basin Stemmed Series)

(2005a) Modena calibration—as they should be, because many specimens from which Figure 9.4 was compiled came from that study—since type distributions occupy ranges consistent with the general understanding of the sequence and age of types (see Klimowicz 1991:Figure 9-1 for similar pattern in diagnostic points from Nevada Test Site obsidians). Results also corroborate the wide chronological distribution of the Elko Corner-Notched type. Somewhat surprisingly, they indicate a broad range for Western Stemmed Tradition points, perhaps partly a function of reuse.

Reconciling the Modena
and Terrane Curves

As above, the Modena source production curve suggests greatest use in the early and middle Holocene, followed by late prehistoric decline. The evidence for a later prehistoric peak in Modena use, particularly in southwestern Utah data, may be explained by limited OHD samples at the source; the southwestern Utah sample size is much higher than the source's. Alternatively, it might be explained by any of five other possibilities:

1. The quarry proper may have been depleted during the Archaic period, and later pre-

historic use of Modena obsidian limited to cobbles in gravel trains downstream—toward southwestern Utah—or other secondary sources. (Extensive use of secondary cobble sources is documented or inferred elsewhere in the Great Basin [e.g., Amick 2007:233–234; Halford 2001, 2008:18–19; T. Jackson 1984:1170] and West [e.g., Church 2000]). This possibility is consistent with the scarcity of sometimes ambiguous rock circles at Modena. If such features truly are chiefly late prehistoric Numic in origin (Cole 2012:241), their rarity suggests limited Modena use in late prehistory. Yet the high incidence of later prehistoric use of Modena obsidian documented in the terrane data runs counter to this scenario, although admittedly much of that use may have been by Fremont cultures that predated the Numic expansion. Furthermore, the Modena pattern is broadly consistent with OHD results reported for Wild Horse Canyon, where quarry and associated workshops showed mostly Archaic and Formative occupation (Dames and Moore 1994:21-40, 21-73; Reed et al. 2005b:166–173). A regional sample of points showed more Formative use and a regional sample of flakes showed widely varying results that included rim values suggesting late prehistoric use (Seddon 2005a:458–472). Connolly and Byram (1999:122, Figure 14.3) found a somewhat similar pattern at Newberry Crater. The Buckboard Mesa obsidian source's production curve also indicates earlier Holocene peaks (Amick 2007:235), complementary to the production curves from nearby smaller obsidian sources which themselves were noticeably skewed to the late Holocene (Klimowicz 1991:Figure 9-4). For that region encompassing the smaller sources on the Nevada Test Site, "local obsidian production occurred relatively recently and probably represents extensive exploitation since the last 3,000 years" (Klimowicz 1991:105), suggesting that smaller sources were used only after the main local source, Buckboard Mesa, was exhausted. The Wild Horse Canyon and Buckboard Mesa patterns are not identical to Modena's, but do exhibit significant differences in age profiles between quarry and terrane samples that suggests the most intensive industrial use in earlier prehistory.

2. Use of the quarry may have continued into the Formative and Late Prehistoric in different ways than earlier. Perhaps, for instance, the earlier emphasis upon biface production from cobble or large-flake blanks was replaced later by small-blank production for small tools like arrow points. Bellifemine (1992:5) suggested as much for the earlier pattern of quarry and terrane use rates in the Borax Lake terrane, Giambastini (2004: 399–413) for the terranes of several eastern California obsidians, and Dames and Moore (1994:21-40, 21-50, 21-73) for Wild Horse Canyon and its associated workshop compared to later regional occurrences of those obsidians. Ericson (1982:145; cf., Halford 2008:18) also favored this scenario to explain a similar decline in the incidence of late prehistoric preforms at Bodie Hills and other California quarries, which he linked to the adoption of bow-and-arrow technology, as did Elston (2005:106–107) for Camels Back Cave, where he suggested that

Desert series arrow points were made directly from thin flake blanks, and Bettinger (2015:47–48) and Hockett (2009:Table 2) for the Great Basin in general. Finally, Connolly and others (2015:186–187) likewise argued that the bow-and-arrow's introduction made smaller secondary cobbles of Oregon obsidians useful for producing small points whereas earlier dart points required larger blanks and, by extension, cobbles; Noll (2012:237) linked a similar technological shift in the Northwest Plateau to changing technological organization.

3. Yet the Little Lake cache documents staged biface production in the region as late as AD 1300 (Garfinkel et al. 2004). At Hunchback Shelter, flake-blank arrow points were fairly common at the Archaic-Formative transition, although admittedly arrow points made from formal bifacial blanks were more common in Fremont contexts (Greubel and Andrews 2008:54). Amick (2007:239) linked the adoption of bow-and-arrow and the smaller blanks required to produce arrow points to increased recycling of debris and discarded tools near Buckboard Mesa.

4. Any shift to flake-blank production may have rendered unnecessary both preforms and extensive staging of reduction. Although OHD rim values do not convert directly to past time, in Ericson's data, elsewhere in eastern California (e.g., Giambastini 2004:400), and at Modena the production curve's drop-off broadly coincides with the traditionally inferred timing of the introduction of arrow technology in western North America (e.g., Blitz 1988), although Ames and colleagues (2010) and Geib and Bungart (1989) suggested a considerably earlier introduction. Arrow points, considerably smaller than dart points, presumably could be produced from small raw cobbles or relatively small flake blanks, a scenario that Giambastini (2004:400) suggested for eastern California obsidian sources, as did Dahlstrom and Bieling (1991:68) for the vicinity of the Bodie Hills quarry in California, although their own data were equivocal (1991:71). At Camels Back Cave, between

1420–790 BP small points were produced "directly from small, thin flakes...probably on their way to becoming points in the Fremont/Desert series" (Elston 2005:106–107). A complementary or alternative possibility is that by Formative times most large cobbles at Modena had been reduced, leaving only flaked debris and small cobbles as toolstone sources. Small cobbles at other Great Basin obsidian sources may have been exported for reduction elsewhere (Sappington 1984:25, 31), so may have been at Modena as well.

5. The emphasis upon biface preform and finished-tool production may have persisted into late prehistory, but in a context of higher regional population and therefore regional packing and reduced land-use scale. In this scenario, land-use and organizational context changed, such that Modena was exploited only by nearby populations whose relatively short transport distance favored reduction to completion at the source and/or the export of raw cobbles for reduction elsewhere—the extreme options in the FPM. This is the scenario that Gilreath and Hildebrandt (1997:181) favored for obsidian sources and workshops in the Coso Volcanic Field, that Giambastini (2004:405) suggested to partly explain changing patterns of obsidian use elsewhere in eastern California, that Greubel and Andrews (2008:57) suggested for the Mineral Mountains vicinity, and Duke and Young (2007:135) espoused for central Utah. Regional packing also figured in Bettinger's (2015:46–48) scenario.

6. Whatever the technological emphasis in quarry exploitation, the noticeable peaks found in many production curves toward the end of the broadly defined Archaic period may reflect craft specialization and large-scale production for exchange (Gilreath and Hildebrandt 2011; King et al. 2011). In this scenario, whether or not involving higher regional population and territorial packing, production peaks reflect the increased volume of production for exchange.

7. Time's arrow moves in one direction only. This truism suggests that, all else equal, older sites should preserve more poorly and therefore be less abundant than younger ones, and that the degree of this taphonomic effect should be a function of time. Such taphonomic bias has been formally modeled (e.g., Surovell et al. 2009:1717) in studies of long-term population trends and for other purposes. Using Surovell and colleagues' regression model, the passage of 5,000 years destroys approximately half of original sites, the passage of 10,000 years about 91% of them. Site destruction occurs by combinations of organic decomposition and geological processes like deep burial (which does not destroy sites but greatly reduces their discovery probability, with similar effects) or erosion. The effects of such processes are minimal upon preforms at quarries which, after all, do not decompose (although they can be recycled and further reduced centuries or millennia after first use). Thus, taphonomic bias upon the population of Modena preforms is minimal. But these processes can degrade significantly the archaeological record of occupation sites across the landscape, in other words the population from which this chapter's terrane sample is drawn. Such taphonomic bias might go far to explain the late-prehistoric skew in the Modena terrane's southwestern Utah OHD curve, but not the east-central Nevada one. Thus, taphonomic bias could be only a partial explanation for observed data.

On existing data, these alternative explanations are difficult to distinguish but at least suggest several lines of future research. First, intensive survey downstream of the Modena source might identify either substantial numbers of raw obsidian cobbles or small workshops accumulated around concentrations of secondary cobbles, thus suggesting considerable use of secondary sources that might be shown to date to later prehistory. Second, more intensive sampling of preforms or even flakes from the source itself might alter Modena's production curve. If Ericson's (1982:145) arrow-adoption explanation is correct, and if arrow-point production occurred there without involving the staging of preforms, then fairly intensive sampling of Modena's flake assemblage might indicate continued use of the source well into late prehistoric times. Third, Gilreath and Hildebrandt's (2011) alternative actually is consistent with the FPM. If it is correct, again OHD of the Modena flake assemblage should indicate continued late-prehistoric use. Occupational data from surveys of Modena's lithic terrane should document rising population, greater regional packing, and reduced land-use scale and mobility parameters, because the regional packing and the use of small flakes on which it is premised would have reduced transport costs to the quarry's users and thereby moot the need for staged production.

OHD Calibration

Rogers and Duke (2014) produced a calibration of Modena OHD. Using their spreadsheet tool, OHD values for all Modena preforms (including Lytle's eight specimens) were calibrated to the radiocarbon time scale. In A. Rogers and Duke's calibration, the uncertainty associated with each date—its standard deviation—is directly proportional to estimated age, and increases monotonically with it. The calibration, therefore, does not permit differential weighting of estimated date by associated error or uncertainty.

The somewhat surprising result of calibration is summarized in the calibrated OHD production curve. Figure 9.5a shows this curve using 1,000-year intervals, Figure 9.5b the same data using 500-year intervals. Although the general pattern is similar—a rising trend from the late Pleistocene to the relatively late Holocene, followed by a precipitous late prehistoric decline—the two histograms differ in detail. It is tempting to favor the higher resolution of Figure 9.5b, which suggests considerable erratic variation that includes sporadic late Pleistocene use of Modena and short-term spikes (e.g., around 6500–7500 BP, 6000–6500 BP, and a somewhat more sustained one between 2500–4000 BP) followed by equally short-term declines amidst

the general rise in occupation dates from late Pleistocene to circa 2000 BP. But this detailed view rests on 90 calibrated OHD dates across a 12,000-year span and 24 500-year intervals, an average of fewer than four dates per interval. The sample size of 90 from a single site is fairly large, but the time span is great.

Accordingly, it seems more prudent to favor the millennium-interval curve of Figure 9.5a. On balance, the calibration curve reveals a steady rise from 11,000 BP to a peak at 3000–4000 BP (a mode 500–1,000 years earlier than Figure 9.5b's) followed by first modest then steep decline in the last millennium of prehistory. In these admittedly more limited data, there is no Fremont/Anasazi lull followed by the modest latest-prehistoric Numic spike found in the Gold Butte study (McGuire et al. 2014:199) or in Duke and Byerly's (2014:78) project area.

The calibrated curve differs considerably from the raw OHD curve (Figure 9.1), which is much more symmetrical and therefore normal in distribution. At face value, the raw curve suggests peak use and production at Modena in the middle Holocene. In contrast, the calibrated curve is noticeably right-skewed, its mode shifted to more recent age. Both curves have relatively well defined single modes located well before the Fremont/Anasazi and late prehistoric periods, although the calibrated curve suggests a considerably more recent peak. Span of peak Modena occupation is difficult to determine from Figure 9.1's raw OHD distribution. The calibrated curve indicates use of the quarry throughout Great Basin prehistory, with most occurring between approximately 8,000–1,000 years ago. As stated, Modena's raw OHD curve generally resembles that from other major Great Basin obsidian quarries. Until comparable calibrations are available for those sources, how similar their calibrated distributions are to Modena's will remain unknown.

It is plausible to accommodate Modena's calibrated OHD curve to any of the explanations listed above for its raw curve. The first scenario involved depletion of the quarry cobble supply; the calibrated OHD curve would merely alter the timing, not the effect, of this process. The

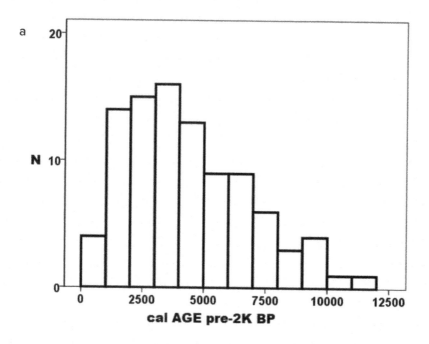

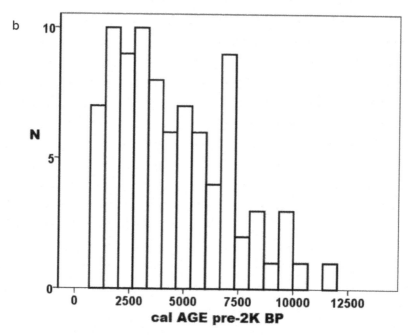

FIGURE 9.5. Frequency distribution of Modena calibrated OHD dates: a. by 1,000-yr intervals; b. by 500-yr intervals.

second scenario involved a shift from biface to blade production, possibly linked to the introduction of the bow-and-arrow. Although the calibrated curve begins its decline well before the introduction of the bow-and-arrow, its precipitous drop occurs not long after that event. The third scenario involves regional population increase and resulting packing and decline in group range, with concomitant changes in the conditions of the FPM that explain the decline in overall biface production, including the knapping of preforms. This too remains a possibility, again however with its inception occurring later in time. Finally, the fourth scenario, which is not incompatible with the third, requires a change in procurement mode that favored restricted access, specialized quarrying and production, and exchange of finished or semi-finished products. Like the second and third scenario, the calibrated OHD distribution accommodates this one by a shift toward the recent in the timing of the process.

The above discussion described how the raw OHD curve from the Modena quarry differs in form and location from both the aggregate and regional terrane datasets. Direct comparison of calibrated OHD distributions is possible only with calibration of the various terrane locations within Modena's terrane, which itself requires compilation of site elevations and surface-subsurface data. Until then nothing is certain, but the apparent difference between Modena and its southern terrane distributions (mostly but not entirely southwestern Utah) may be reduced or eliminated in calibration. If so, there will remain no reason to believe that latest prehistoric use of Modena obsidian was confined to secondary sources.

Calibrated Results by Area

Like the raw OHD distribution, calibrated OHD values differ in mean between defined areas at Modena (Table 9.1; $F = 2.8$; $p = 0.02$). Again, however, the large number of such areas makes a significant result likelier. Also, as in the raw OHD curve, there are no significant differences when areas and their vicinities are compared ($F = 1.4$; $p = 0.24$), nor in LSD tests do any pair-

TABLE 9.1. Mean Calibrated OHD Age by Modena Area and Callahan Stage.

Area	n	mean	Grouped Area	n	mean
A	14	6399.8	A/vic. A	33	5145.8
B	19	4098.1	B/vic. B	23	4337.7
D	7	3254.6	D	7	3254.6
F	20	3936.1	F/vic. F	21	4182.8
vic. A	19	4221.7			
vic. B	4	5476.0			
vic. F	1	2702.1			

Callahan Stage			Grouped Stages		
0	27	4548.2	0-1	59	4463.0
1	32	4391.1	2-3	28	4563.8
2	20	4995.5			
3	8	3484.8			

wise comparisons reach 0.05. Nevertheless, and leaving aside the very small sample from Area D, Area A and vicinity seem particularly older than does Area F and its vicinity.

Similarly, there are no significant differences in mean calibrated OHD age by Callahan stage (Shott 2016:Table 9.1; $F = 0.7$; $p = 0.55$). Again, in LSD tests no pair-wise comparison reaches a significance value of ≤0.05. Only Stage 3 seems younger on average than other stages, a possible difference whose small sample size (n = 7) precludes significance. When preforms are combined into paired Callahan Stages 0–1 and 2–3, again the difference is not significance ($t = 0.2$; $p = 0.86$). As in the OHD values, calibrated OHD ages do not pattern significantly by area within Modena or by Callahan stage.

Summary

More than 80 biface preforms found in UA investigations at Modena were submitted for obsidian hydration dating. Like many other quarries' OHD curves, the Modena distribution is roughly normal, and indicates peak use before the late Holocene. Most Modena values fall in Seddon's (2005b) Archaic range, and there are no major differences between clusters or Callahan reduction stages in mean OHD value. Yet a dataset of Modena OHD values from sites in its terrane, compiled from Hull (2010), Seddon (2005a) and various other sources, differs considerably from the quarry curve. In east-central Nevada (and probably in adjacent west-central Utah), where several studies focused on late Pleistocene to early Holocene occupation have occurred in recent decades, the OHD curve has a significantly higher mean value than does Modena's; in general, that region's curve is offset somewhat to older time intervals compared to Modena. Southwestern Utah data also are offset but toward more recent intervals. OHD curves for flakes somewhat repeat the pattern found in points.

It is unclear if these differences reflect prehistoric patterns of occupation or vagaries of sampling, archaeological research interests, and the comparative abundance of prehistoric deposits of different age. Modena OHD curves by defined point type conform to regional expectations, and also further demonstrate, if need be, the unusually wide chronological span of the Elko Corner-Notched type. Differences in OHD distributions between Modena and different parts of its terrane owe to some combination of changing proportional use through time of quarry versus secondary Modena toolstone, changing technology of biface and other tool production, and changes in regional settlement range that altered the terms of the Field Processing Model by promoting export of raw cobbles rather than stage preforms.

10

Modena and Tempiute Terranes

Inferring Scale and Pattern of Prehistoric Land Use

This report has described the obsidian sources of Modena and Tempiute, and UA fieldwork undertaken there. It also described the flake, preform, and finished-biface assemblages found at the quarries, inferred scale and nature of production at two of the sources, and implicated export and, by extension, transport of semi-finished obsidian tools from them. Trivially, quarries were sources of toolstone, and most products of quarry reduction were exported for use, maintenance, and eventual discard.

In archaeological context, Elston (1990a, 1992a:35) defined a quarry's terrane as the region over which a toolstone is common to dominant. Any balanced consideration of Modena and Tempiute must consider not only what happened at the quarries and what was left there, but also what was exported, how far, and where. That is, a source's terrane must be mapped and characterized. Terranes of fairly abundant obsidians like these are apt to be extensive. This chapter makes an initial attempt at mapping the terranes of Modena and Tempiute. Doing so requires engaging the theoretical literature on modes of toolstone acquisition and distribution, how those modes might be distinguished in archaeological data, and how Great Basin archaeologists have approached this matter. Then it requires the compilation of sourcing data from a considerable sample of regional archaeological sites, and the interpretation of those data and the maps generated from them.

Prehistoric Hunter-Gatherer Land Use and Toolstone Acquisition

Hunter-gatherers tend to be mobile and prehistoric hunter-gatherers commonly used stone tools. Accordingly, archaeologists compile data on the abundance and distribution of toolstones at archaeological sites and interpret them to infer scale and pattern of hunter-gatherer land use. Even in the crudest sense, toolstone distributions reflect some aspects of ancient land use. Knife River chert, for instance, is distributed across millions of square kilometers of central North America, and even its more limited region of highest abundance encompasses an area as large as the entire Great Basin (Ahler 1986:4–5, Figure 1). Whether Knife River Flint's distribution registers land-use scale, annual or longer-term, of the cultures that used it or instead the complex composite of embedded acquisition within home ranges, purposeful long-distance trips, and exchange remains unclear.

Renfrew's (1984:119–153) study was an early systematic effort to explain the scale and pattern of obsidian toolstone distribution. In his Aegean study area, materials from relatively few available sources were widely distributed and circulated among chiefdom-scale societies. Given the many obsidian sources present in the Great Basin, sometimes in close proximity, and the domination of the area throughout its prehistory by hunter-gatherers along with late prehistoric horticulturalists, Renfrew's various models and the large spatial scale they encompass may not all be relevant there. For the Great Basin, "Monotonic Decrement" arguably is most relevant, yet this deliberately simplified model must be modified to account for number and density of distinct sources, broader distribution of secondary sources, size and form of obsidian cobbles, knapping and wear properties of various toolstones, and rates of toolstone consumption at settlements of different function (Skinner 1983:88–90; Torrence 1986:16). It is no surprise that sedentary groups organized into chiefdom-scale polities would establish systems for long-distance exchange (Renfrew 1984:124), and no less surprising that hunter-gatherers whose mobility magnitude might be high would rely more heavily upon direct, "embedded" (*sensu* Binford 1979), procurement. What is somewhat surprising is that, at least in the southern Great Basin, many toolstones like Modena and Tempiute fall off in frequency—monotonically or asymptotically (Renfrew's graphical model [1984:138] may have assumed asymptotic decline because its x-axis is logarithmic, but his text referred consistently to arithmetic distance)—at relatively short distances of <100 km from their sources (e.g., Seddon 2005a; Smith 2010, 2011). Yet even for the European Paleolithic, where home ranges might be expected to be large, toolstone data reflect surprisingly modest distribution scales (e.g., Féblot-Augustins 2009; Geneste 1988; Moutsiou 2014), an observation corroborated by limited ethnographic observation (e.g., Gould 1980:124).

The logic behind distributional studies like Renfrew's is straightforward. If obsidian toolstones can be identified with particular geochemical sources, particularly those possessing a small, well-defined geographic natural distribution, then the distance between natural and cultural occurrence somehow registers scale of land use. The logic underlies the common practice of sourcing obsidian and other toolstones and decades of studies that attempt to infer pattern and degree of land use from the archaeological distribution of toolstones, whether as distribution zones (e.g., G. T. Jones et al. 2003; Jones et al. 2012) or for what they reveal of

changing organizational dynamics over time (e.g., Duke 2011). Ideally, source information combined with data on the pattern and degree of reduction that points and other tools underwent "allows archaeological sites to be read like a travel diary" (Grayson 2011:297).

However clear and direct the logic, the actual prehistoric patterns of land use and toolstone exploitation that produced empirical distributions are apt to be complex, and their archaeological correlates can be difficult to distinguish. This complexity in both prehistoric behavior and archaeological formation processes creates the specter of equifinality in toolstone distributional studies, a problem identified even in Renfrew's pioneering work. After attempting to distinguish the separate distributions resulting from random-walk and down-the-line acquisition modes, Renfrew (1984:122, 146, 152; see also Féblot-Augustins 2009; Torrence 1986:21–22) acknowledged that their archaeological signatures were very similar. Among other things, we must appreciate the complexities of prehistoric land use and its relationship to distance and toolstone acquisition.

Distance between natural occurrence of toolstones and their archaeological occurrences ("transport distance") is a common measure of hunter-gatherer mobility in Great Basin archaeology. Strictly, it is a common measure of mobility *magnitude* (MM; *sensu* Kelly 1983; Shott 1986:21), the distances covered in typical annual rounds, an important mobility property or dimension but not the only one. There is also mobility *frequency* (MF), how often residential moves occur in typical annual rounds (Shott 1986:23). In these terms, the common study of mobility in the Great Basin and elsewhere concerns MM, not MF.

Madsen (2007:15–16) distinguished the presumably greater logistic mobility of presumably male task groups and the presumably lesser residential mobility of entire populations. Premo's (2012) foraging model also compared residential and logistic mobility (*sensu* Binford 1979); because logistic mobility involved fewer moves per year (i.e., lower MF), he questioned the common assumption, invoked by Madsen and others, "that LMS [logistic mobility strategy] foragers tend to move over a greater geographic extent than RMS [residential mobility strategy] foragers" (2012:648). In the process, Premo highlighted the vital importance of distinguishing between MM and MF. Perreault and Brantingham's (2011:65) similar model yielded right-skewed transport distances that approximated foraging radii of 75 km but whose right tail exceeded 250 km.

Absent long-distance exchange of goods like toolstone and assuming that toolstone acquisition was embedded, Madsen's contrast between maximum land-use scale and residential-group mobility is a distinction without a difference. It implicates merely a different mode of action and movement that nevertheless falls within a group's land-use scale. Yet it usefully distinguishes between a complete group's mobility magnitude and the presumably greater magnitude of smaller task groups. Because obsidian from Brown's Bench, Modena, and Tempiute were transported to Butte Valley, for instance, does not necessarily mean that entire residential groups regularly traversed the complete breadth of "conveyance zones."

Measuring such land-use scale is a common practice in part because of the ubiquity of XRF and other sourcing methods and the suitability of Great Basin toolstones—fine-grained volcanics as well as obsidian, but cherts less so—to those methods. But transport distance equals MM only in the broadest sense and, as above, transport-distance data are noisy products of many factors in complex interaction. Small quantities of toolstone can be transported great distances under circumstances that reflect only unusual or rare events, not necessarily common or normative ones. Gauging ordinary MM from maximum toolstone distance is like estimating a person's commuting distance to work from the exit stamps in his or her passport; it may confuse ordinary with unusual movement. Only if maximum transport distance approximates foraging radius, the maximum map distance covered in ordinary residential moves over reasonably short intervals, is transport distance a valid measure of MM (Brantingham 2003:289).

Distribution of source material in distant archaeological sites may comprise a prehistoric Great Basin "travel diary" (Grayson 2011:297) but one that owes to complex underlying processes that make it problematic to read and difficult to interpret.

Simulations of hunter-gatherer mobility also suggest considerable complexity in the relationship between scale and pattern of land use and the distribution of toolstones. On the one hand, Ingbar's (1994) deterministic simulation showed that toolstone distribution and the number of toolstones in site assemblages varied as much with MF, toolkit size, and tool use life as with MM or overall land-use scale. His simulations tended to *under*estimate land-use scale because people could regularly use toolstones from sources that were not represented in all of the places they occupied. Ingbar concluded that "understanding how a technology is or was organized, beyond the use of particular raw material sources, is a prerequisite to interpreting variation in source proportions" (1994:50). On the other hand, even modest rates of mobility frequency and magnitude can transport toolstones over considerable distances that sometimes exceed normal foraging radius or scale.

Brantingham (2003) modeled toolstone procurement as a neutral process that assumed the equivalence of toolstone sources in abundance and technical quality, randomness of their distribution, and neither selection for particular sources nor logistic trips to acquire material. Under deliberately simplified conditions, his simulation showed modest modal transport distances (Brantingham 2003:499). This is consistent with the common observation, already noted, that most obsidian distribution in the Great Basin (e.g., Hughes and Bennyhoff 1986:246, 250, 252; McKee et al. 2010; Stevenson 2008) and California (Heizer and Treganza 1944:299) was local. However, maximum transport distances can significantly exceed ordinary foraging radius (Brantingham 2003:498; see also White 2012:275), such that residential-group MM was seriously *over*estimated from maximum transport distance. (This directly counters Ingbar's [1994] conclusion, noted above, that distance-to-source data can *under-estimate* land-use scale. Toolstone distribution studies are notoriously ambiguous.)

Surovell (2009) also described simplified formal models that computed the relative cost of direct versus embedded procurement. For his embeddedness option, the salient cost measure was not simple distance from a foraging location to sources but the mean logistic trip distance (2009:131). Surovell's formal model and simulation indicated that embedded procurement almost always was more efficient (i.e., had a lower cost than direct procurement [2009:132–133]). It also suggested that the number and distribution of sources bore upon search and travel costs but, like Ingbar, that the intricacies of hunter-gatherer land use generated instability in the economics of procurement and that distance to the closest available source was disproportionately influential. Surovell's results suggest unappreciated complexities in the relationship between distance-to-source and procurement mode. Among other things, it counsels the importance of distinguishing between the distribution of finished tools and flake debris.

In this connection, Basgall (1990) argued that points and other tools generally were transported greater distances than was the debris from their production and possibly their resharpening. The legitimate distinction that Basgall made between artifact categories and their origin, meaning, and interpretation is complicated in sourcing studies if the category "flake" is not technologically subdivided. Although flake "types" are ambiguous in definition and interpretation, as discussed in Chapter 5, meaningful characteristics of sourced flakes like presence/absence of cortex, overall size, and exterior-surface faceting would support legitimate distinctions between, for instance, production and resharpening debris. Absent the description of such characteristics, Basgall's suggestion about the difference between distributions of points and flakes is valid but difficult to apply.

A. White's (2012) detailed agent-based models more closely approximated a range of hunter-gatherer mobility regimes. He too found that, despite broad correlations between land-use scale and transport distance, significantly different mobility parameters produced highly overlapping ranges for transport distance, in other words, equifinality among the factors that determine the latter. All model results produced familiar negative-exponential fall-off curves for transport distance (2012:Figure 8.8), which varied somewhat in scale and skewness. A. White (2012:273–280) also concluded that mean transport distance correlated better with land-use scale than did maximum transport distance, which was highly sensitive to factors like year-to-year fluctuations in range, groups fusion, and intergroup recruitment.

Formal models possess deliberately simplifying assumptions that do not always approximate prehistoric realities. Yet even with such assumptions they suggest a complex relationship between toolstone acquisition, use and discard on the one hand, and land-use practices on the other, resulting in uncommon but influential events for the transport of toolstone over distances considerably exceeding ordinary MM. Such complexity is revealed in, for instance, right-skewed distributions of transport distance (e.g., Féblot-Augustins 2009:Table 3.2, Figure 3.7; Geneste 1988:Figures 3–5; A. White 2012: Figure 8.8), suggesting that occasional, very long transport distances may be poor reflections of land-use scale. Clearly, hunter-gatherer mobility patterns are multifaceted, as are their relationship to the economics of toolstone procurement. On balance, different plausible assumptions about toolkit mobility frequency, inventory size, technological organization, and mobility parameters can accommodate empirical distance-to-source data to a wide range of land-use scales and practices. Simple distance-to-source data reflect many practices and processes (Thatcher 2000:32–34), not just MM and land-use scale.

Besides the complexity of prehistoric land use is the deceptive complexity of the quantity "distance." Distance is an abstract concept in formal models, most simply measured as a straight line between source and discard location. Topography seemed not to alter or impede toolstone distribution patterns in European Paleolithic data (Féblot-Augustins 2009:39; Geneste 1988). Browne and Wilson's simulations concluded that "a straight-line route is a more appropriate measure for the path from lithic source to site than a least-cost route" (2013:3961; see also Putzi et al. 2015:346, Figures 12, 14, where a straight-line distance measure performed nearly as well as a least-cost measure), a finding largely independent of map scale. However, even this result was qualified by rerouting transport paths to avoid high slopes, obviously common in the basin-and-range topography of the Great Basin.

Great Basin Obsidian Sourcing Studies

In North America, natural occurrences of obsidian are confined to the Mountain West. The Great Basin alone contains dozens of known obsidian source (Grayson 2011:Figure 9.5) and more remain to be discovered. Prehistoric distribution of obsidians is documented as far east as the Ohio Valley in Early Woodland times (Stoltman and Hughes 2004) as the likely result of exchange for social aggrandizement (Hatch et al. 1990; Stevenson et al. 2004), as well as during the Middle Woodland and "throughout the Late Prehistoric period" (Anderson et al. 1986:848; see also Hughes 1984:369; Johnson et al. 1995:6). Obsidian artifacts from sources as near the project area as Utah's Mineral Mountains may have reached the mid-Atlantic coast (Dillian et al. 2007), although unresolved questions of context in similar cases make the claims difficult to evaluate (Boulanger et al. 2007). They certainly reached northwestern Louisiana, apparently during Paleoindian times (Boulanger et al. 2013:5). Norton (2008) reported occurrences of several obsidians—including sources in Nevada and California, west of the Lincoln County project area—in primarily Archaic contexts, while White and Weinstein (2008) noted the material in later contexts in the southeast. Assuming the contextual validity, especially of the few artifacts reported from the northeast, these occurrences testify to the broad prehistoric distribution of western North American obsidians. Yet such discoveries seem to be exceptions that prove the rule that most obsidian-source distributions are relatively limited.

Great Basin
Toolstone Acquisition Modes

In the Great Basin, inference to scale of mobility and land use usually involves geochemical sourcing of toolstones, most often obsidian and fine-grained volcanics, and the measurement of distance from site of archaeological occurrence to natural source. This practice became commonplace once the validity of instrumental methods like XRF was established in the 1970s. As elsewhere, the equifinality in archaeological pattern arising from the different procurement modes noted above emerges as a possibility; Basgall (1990:118) interpreted occupation site assemblages in the Mono Lake vicinity as the product of embedded procurement but acknowledged the alternative possibilities of exchange and of selection of different obsidian sources for different functional tool types, a possibility that Faull (2006) advocated for Red Rock Canyon near the Coso fields.

Like Basgall, most Great Basin studies assume direct procurement rather than exchange (e.g., Smith 2011:462), and usually "embedded" procurement (*sensu* Binford 1979:259) rather than travel to a source specifically to acquire toolstone. Heizer and Treganza, for instance, argued for obsidian procurement by prehistoric peoples "while hunting, gathering food, or moving across country" (1944:298) rather than by purposive expeditions to sources. Yet Great Basin archaeological data indicate long-distance exchange for *Olivella* beads, for example at Hidden Cave (Thomas 1985:238–239) where considerable numbers of obsidian tools also were found (Thomas 1985:Tables 51 and 53; see also Faull 2006; Hughes and Bennyhoff 1986). Although most obsidian at Hidden Cave was traced to sources within 200 km, its association with *Olivella* beads at least suggests the potential for long-distance obsidian exchange, and complex exchange systems may have included transportation of *Olivella* with different obsidians (Hughes 1984:372). Ericson (1977, 1982) also saw evidence for relatively long-distance utilitarian exchange of obsidian in California, Connolly and colleagues (2015) the same in the Pacific Northwest, and Cottrell (1985) for either exchange or direct procurement of jasper over distances of 175 km. Considering obsidian's superiority to other toolstones in many respects (Elston 1990b:Table 42), it may have been exchanged rather than directly acquired, particularly in obsidian-poor areas like the Great Basin's "chert core" (Thomas 2014).

Great Basin and Plateau ethnography suggests the possibility of such exchange. Sappington (1984:24–25; see also Heizer and Treganza 1944:299; Thatcher 2000:116), for instance, cited sources both on production for exchange and on expeditions mounted for direct procurement of obsidian in the northern Great Basin, California, and the Plateau. The Washo directly acquired or traded for obsidian from California sources well west of their local ranges, and perhaps as far south as San Diego (Downs 1966: 37; Hughes and Bennyhoff 1986:241), as did some Pomo groups (Heizer and Treganza 1944: 299–300). Owens Valley Paiute engaged in long-distance exchange across the Sierra Nevada for commodities that included obsidian (Steward 1933:257), Ball (1941:52) cited sources on long-distance expeditions specifically to acquire obsidian, one Northern Paiute account described direct procurement involving travel over 200 km negotiated across another group's range (Fowler 1989:71), and Shoshone people of eastern Idaho traveled to trade fairs to acquire obsidian from sources perhaps as distant as Glass Buttes in central Oregon (Liljeblad 1957:88–89). The Nez Percé practiced direct procurement ("Parties were sent out to collect" obsidian [Spinden 1908:184]), and northern California groups traded over considerable distance in Oregon obsidians, sometimes involving transport of raw cobbles (Gould 1966; cited in Skinner 1983:109). Hughes and Bennyhoff (1986:Figure 2) mapped fairly extensive obsidian exchange networks, including one that linked Modena to occupation sites in west-central Utah. Of course such distant sources may have been acquired in finished or near-finished form as small amounts, but ethnographic sources attest to circulation of obsidian by modes and at scales that the concept of embedded procurement cannot easily accommodate.

Farther afield, Fladmark (1984:154) questioned the universality of embedded procurement, arguing that sources of abundant obsidian from a British Columbia quarry may have drawn knappers from great distance and, by extension, from numerous bands. Root (1997) inferred large-scale production for exchange at the Knife River Flint quarries on the northern Plains for groups of comparable sociopolitical complexity to the Great Basin, which might help explain the wide distribution of that material (Ahler 1986:1). Even farther afield, Gould and Saggers (1985; see also Gould 1980:124) argued that physical properties of different toolstones like edge resistance to wear can justify either embedded acquisition or exchange for preferred materials, and also that social and ideological practices must be considered when gauging groups' territorial range. Yet Gould's own (1980:141–159) fairly elaborate social explanation for Western Desert Australian toolstone distributions did not account for extensive tool resharpening and high curation rates (Davidson 1988) which, by implicating long use life and extensive land use, supported instead the more parsimonious perspective of embedded procurement. Hunter-gatherer toolstone use and distributions are more complex than either simple utilitarian, social, or ideological models can accommodate (Barbarena et al. 2018; Féblot-Augustins 2009; Newlander 2012, 2018).

Distinguishing Embedded and Indirect Procurement in the Great Basin

In the same way that the FPM, tested in this study and elsewhere, need not explain all aspects of quarry behavior and toolstone transport (e.g., Jackson 1988), embedded procurement of toolstone may not have been the sole prehistoric acquisition mode. Embedded procurement is a reasonable baseline assumption, but other modes of distribution may have contributed as well to the aggregate pattern and distribution of toolstone from sources.

Basgall (1990:124) proposed that procurement by exchange would register in occupation-site assemblages as "equitable representation" of finished tools and flake debris, namely, finished tools and substantial amounts and wide technological ranges of debris from the same, presumably distant, sources. If procurement were embedded, spatial "disjunction" in source materials would occur (i.e., tools from a source occurring in sites farther from the source while debris from their production or maintenance in sites nearer the source), the scale of that disjunction reflecting the scale of land use.

Perhaps the best known Great Basin example of sourcing data to infer land-use scale is G. T. Jones and colleagues' (2003; Jones et al. 2012; see also B. Fowler 2014) research on the natural origin of various obsidian toolstones in their Jakes and Butte Valley research areas in east-central Nevada. Their data for this area, situated in Thomas's (2014:Figure 15.2) "chert core" and relatively distant from major sources of the Great Basin's "obsidian rim," revealed a pattern of extensive reliance upon one source well to the north, Browns Bench, and two to the south, Tempiute (originally identified as "Unknown B" [G. T. Jones et al. 2003:15, 38]) and Modena, along with considerable contributions from other sources. G. T. Jones and colleagues (2003:19) defined "obsidian conveyance zones" by the pattern of predominant toolstone source distributions in their study area and elsewhere in the Great Basin. Their eastern conveyance zone (2003:Figure 13) encompassed a region that ranged from the Browns Bench to Tempiute and Modena sources. Later work corroborated the general pattern, even if it divided the large eastern conveyance zone (Jones et al. 2012:Figure 1), in part by documenting dominance of Tempiute and Modena obsidian in Coal Valley and the definition of a southern subsection (Jones et al. 2012:Table 1, 361–363). Hauer (2005:139–154) documented even larger obsidian toolstone distributions and, by extension, conveyance zones for another central Nevada study area.

G. T. Jones and colleagues (2003) proposed that their eastern conveyance zone corresponded to the annual range of Paleoarchaic hunter-gatherer groups of the eastern Great Basin. Such zones were notable both for their large size and generally north-south elongated form, corresponding largely to the region's basin-and-range topography. G. T. Jones and colleagues for instance, saw little evidence for regular movement across drainages, concluding that "Paleoarchaic mobility in the central Great Basin appears to have emphasized a territory whose principal axis ran north to south and covered more than 450 km" (2003:23). Yet G. Smith (2010, 2011) saw considerably smaller "conveyance zones" in the northwestern Great Basin than G. T. Jones and colleagues (2003) found for that area, although Smith (2010:873) reported Kane Springs obsidian more than 600 km northwest of its source. Elsewhere in the Mountain West, local obsidian dominates in eastern Idaho but artifacts from Arizona sources 650 km away also occur, and Wild Horse Canyon obsidian, whose source lies not far northeast of Modena, occurs in considerable quantity as far away as southwestern Wyoming (e.g., Lee and Metcalf 2011:14–15). Yet European Paleolithic chert-distribution patterns suggest movement mostly across, not along, major topographic features (Féblot-Augustins 2009:39).

The difference in inferred size of "conveyance zones" may owe partly to differences in distribution and density of toolstone sources primary and secondary (Jones et al. 2012:356), which are plentiful in G. Smith's area but nonexistent in Jones and colleagues'. G. Smith (2011:467; see also Basgall 1990; Duke and Young 2007:132; Smith and Harvey 2018) suggested that points, particularly obsidian ones, may register the largest land-use scale while other tools and toolstones may reflect annual movements. (The relatively limited spatial distribution of the abundant, high-quality Tosawihi chert—most of which is distributed within only 60 km of the source [Elston 1992b:1]—supports this view; cf., Cottrell [1985:833] who reported chert transport of 175+ km on a sustained basis.)

Based on Elston and Zeanah's (2002; see also Elston et al. 2014) model of sexual division of labor among Great Basin hunter-gatherers, Madsen (2007) suggested that the scale of such conveyance zones indicated not annual ranges of residential groups, but instead the broader range of male task groups. In A. White's (2012) agent-based simulations of toolstone distributions under various mobility regimes, maximum distance-to-source usually exceeded residential groups' mean annual ranges. White (2012:280), however, suggested that this owed partly to groups' shifts of annual range within larger territories. Applying this logic, Simms (2008:Figure 3.8) resolved merely the southern half of Jones and colleagues' largest zone into a series of separate annual ranges each of 5–10 years' duration of a local band's lifetime range. For a major Oregon source, several "overlapping prehistoric procurement ranges" (Thatcher 2000:107), not a single one, may have contributed to the overall distribution.

On both empirical and theoretical grounds, Newlander (2012, 2018) placed the debate in a different perspective, in the process reinforcing the point made above about distinguishing daily or short-term MM from longer-term or periodic land-use scale. First, he noted that G. T. Jones and colleagues' (2003) conveyance zones greatly exceeded the annual ranges of even the most dispersed, mobile groups in a global ethnographic hunter-gatherer sample and of ethnographic Great Basin groups as well (Newlander 2012:60–64; see also Park 2010:66 for the Yellowstone region of Wyoming and Montana and Shackley 2002:61–63 for hunter-gatherers in the Southwest). Then he questioned the need for such extensive logistic mobility to explain this degree of dispersion, as Madsen (2007) suggested for the eastern Great Basin Paleoarchaic foragers who exploited productive marshes (Newlander 2012:65–66). (Using limited and selective ethnographic data, Moutsiou [2014:20–28] echoed Newlander's argument for the Old World Paleolithic.) Citing models of hunter-gatherer population density, distribution, and social connections (e.g., Wobst 1976), Newlander argued for long-distance "nonutilitarian" mobility for information, spouses, and general social connectedness (2012:70–72; see also Féblot-Augustins 2009; Thatcher 2000: 34, 40, 107) and suggested that the scale of distribution of obsidian reflected such social mobility rather than daily or subsistence ("utilitarian")

mobility. (Unsourced obsidian found in an apparent dedicatory cache in the Escalante Desert [Stoffle et al. 2011:38–39] may be an example of symbolic mobility of toolstone.) By implication, "conveyance zones" need not reflect the scale of land use or MM so much as the scale over which social relations are maintained, a conclusion echoed by Park (2010) for northwestern Wyoming. In the process, Newlander complemented obsidian with chert sourcing (2012:176–240; see also Duke and Young 2007, and, for a similar example from the Southwest, Zeigler et al. 2011) and demonstrated their equal value, merely in different respects, in registering land-use scale and pattern. In summary, Newlander suggested that "the annual or territorial ranges utilized by Paleoarchaic populations may be better reflected by chert or FGV provenance than by obsidian provenance" (2012:10–11).

The conveyance-zone approach assumes that toolstone acquisition is embedded and that its distribution and abundance at discard is the exclusive function of the acquiring group's scale and pattern of land use. For both ethnographic and environmental reasons, aboriginal California differed significantly from the Great Basin, but Ericson (1977) modeled late prehistoric obsidian toolstone distribution and abundance there as a function of travel routes, topography, population density, and distance to main and secondary (in the sense of cultural choice, not geology) sources. Results implicated topography and trail systems (1977:115) more than population density and distance to secondary sources (1977:123). Accordingly, Ericson suggested that intergroup exchange accounted for a considerable portion of the scale over which obsidian moved. (Yet distance to secondary sources may be important in obsidian-poor landscapes like G. T. Jones et al.'s [2003; Jones et al. 2012] Butte Valley study area or other toolstone-poor habitats.) In Ericson's scenario at least, embedded procurement and discard reflecting local-group movement patterns did not completely explain obsidian toolstone distributions; instead, some degree of down-the-line exchange (1977:113) mediated and complicated local-group land-use.

On balance, the myriad processes that distribute toolstone across the landscape—MM at various demographic and geographic scales, generation-scale population movements, the possibility of at least occasional direct procurement, and intergroup exchange of toolstones—make it difficult to disentangle their separate effects. In the face of this complexity and the analytical morass it creates, the concept of conveyance zones is best understood as a general empirical pattern that is the aggregate of various causes and sources and that does not necessarily reflect utilitarian land-use scale.

Modena and Tempiute Terranes

However ambiguous source-distributional data are in light of the complexities of prehistoric land use and how the archaeological record formed, at some point analysis must confront them. Raw data on the occurrence of Modena and Tempiute obsidians is found in many southern Great Basin site reports. Unfortunately, given the variation in detail in consulted sources, available data are uneven. This chapter attempts a first assay, and considers the amount and especially quality of the better data needed to evaluate competing interpretations of toolstone distributions.

Whatever explains the scale and pattern of prehistoric Great Basin toolstone distribution, each source's empirical distribution can be described along several dimensions. These include the greatest geographic extent of distribution, the direction(s) in which material was transported from the source, the shape of the overall distribution zone, and variation within that zone in gross abundance or abundance subdivided by technological categories like cores, debris, preforms, and various finished tools. Depending on the amount and quality of dating evidence, chronological variation in these dimensions can be gauged. Finally, depending on the quality of inference, typical or predominant distribution modes (e.g., direct vs. embedded), and forms (e.g., "down the line" [distance-decay] or more complex, staged, variants) also can be gauged.

Whatever explains it, the general Great Basin pattern in obsidian toolstone distribution is surprisingly limited. Although some transport covered long distances (e.g., Connolly et al. 2015:Figure 11-5; Hughes 1984:368–370; Sap-

pington 1984:Tables 3.1–3.2; Smith 2010:873), most sources are well represented in archaeological assemblages within approximately 50–75 km radii, becoming less common beyond that distance (e.g., R. Beck 2008:768; Duke 2011; Haarklau 2001: Table 12; Heizer and Treganza 1944:Map 1; Hull 1994:7-35, 7-36; McKee 2009; McKee et al. 2013:Table 37; McKee et al. 2010; Panich et al. 2015; Reed et al. 2005b:Appendix G; Smith 2010; Stevenson 2008; Yoder et al. 2012; see Zeigler et al. [2011] for a similar pattern in southwestern New Mexico and Elston [1992b:1] for a similar pattern in chert; Moutsiou [2014:Tables 7.4–7.5] reported similar distribution scales for obsidian in Old World Paleolithic sites, Putzi et al. [2015] for Hawaiian obsidian). Archaeologists generally attribute such limited distribution to scale of land use, but Bettinger (1982:121) inferred territoriality and source control in the Owens Valley; symbolic or ceremonial factors also may contribute to source distributions (Dillian 2002; Thatcher 2000:34).

Yet not surprisingly, finished tools like points and debris from their resharpening can be more widely distributed than cores and core-reduction debris from obsidian sources like Modena (e.g., Eerkens et al. 2007; McKee 2009; again, Moutsiou's [2014:114, 117] Paleolithic data are similar; see also Geneste 1988:Figure 4). Variation in natural distribution of obsidian affects this pattern as well because obsidian-poor regions often have material from comparatively distant sources (e.g., Johnson and McQueen 2012; G. T. Jones et al. 2003; Jones et al. 2012; Sappington 1984:31; Skinner 1983:88). Key to distinguishing the separate effects of scale of prehistoric land-use and source distributions is to both calibrate obsidian quantity—not just presence/absence—to distance and to gauge the technological character of obsidian assemblages as a function of distance.

Data Sources

As above, XRF and other obsidian-sourcing methods have become popular in Great Basin archaeology in recent decades. For the southern Great Basin that includes the Modena and Tempiute terranes, Haarklau and colleagues (2005) of course is a major source, because it compiled virtually comprehensive data from unpublished sources as of its issue date. Project staff visited Tempiute (Johnson and Wagner 2005:33–34, 37). Johnson and Haarklau's (2005:Figure 6.2) summary of obsidian distributions in regional archaeological samples revealed Modena as the most common source in southern Nevada, Tempiute occurring at modest rates. In general, known obsidian sources in order of descending occurrence in Haarklau and colleagues' study area were Modena, Saline Range (CA), Wild-horse Canyon (UT), Obsidian Butte (NV), Coso (CA), Kane Springs, Montezuma Range (NV), Black Rock (UT), Fish Springs (CA), Shoshone Mountain (NV), Queen/Truman Meadows (CA/NV) Oak Springs Butte (NV), and Tempiute, followed by seven other sources.

As part of the Fingerprints project, Skinner and Thatcher (2005) reported sourcing data, while Haarklau (2005) compiled metric data and obsidian identification for approximately 2,000 previously reported diagnostic points. These data are invaluable for distributional studies and in order to contextualize the assemblages of individual sites. Besides Haarklau and colleagues' (2005) massive report and published sources that were relatively easy to obtain, web searches yielded additional sources. Relevant data from these sources also was compiled (Appendix B). (Detailed data on the UNEV Pipeline Project were not available until this report was approaching completion. McKee et al. [2013:Table 30] found modest quantities of Modena obsidian, but reported no Tempiute obsidian [McKee et al. 2013:Table 30; see also Yoder et al. 2012].) Other sources that reported occurrences of Modena obsidian (Curewitz 2001:257; Menocal 2010:149–151) were obtained only after data collection and analysis were completed.

Data Limitations

A dataset of such size, compiled from so many sources, inevitably has limitations. Some involve the detail or quality of data documentation, some the history of regional archaeological research, and some the circumstances of study. Most sources consulted were reasonably de-

tailed but not all reported the size of sourced artifact assemblages, or whether sourced artifacts were flakes or tools. That is, most consulted sources reported sourced artifacts as points, preforms, or flakes. Some, however, reported simply that x artifacts were sourced to Modena or Tempiute, but not whether the artifacts were points, preforms, or flakes, nor, in some cases, the larger population X from which sourced Modena or Tempiute artifacts were identified. As a result, sums in Appendix B for number of sourced artifacts are not necessarily sums of separate numbers of sourced points, preforms, or flakes.

Few sources reported the technological character of sourced flakes, such as presence/absence of cortex, flake size, platform type, or exterior-surface scar density that might bear upon both the spatial scale of distribution (e.g., Basgall 1990; Eerkens et al. 2007; McKee 2009) and the discard processes that governed it. Accordingly, although it is possible in many cases to calibrate sourced artifacts to assemblage size—essentially, to express incidence as a percentage or proportion—it is impossible in this dataset to consistently distinguish between (presumably small) flakes detached in the resharpening of curated tools from (presumably variable but large) flakes generated in core reduction or early stages of tool production. If calibrating quantity and gauging technological quality are equally important in analysis, as suggested above, then data compiled here often accomplish the former but never the latter.

Archaeological research in the southern Great Basin began in the 1870s (Fowler et al. 1973:4–6). Yet as recently as 30 years ago, few obsidian sources were documented in southern Nevada (Skinner 1983:15); sources in this study, especially Modena and Tempiute, were documented even more recently. Consequently, obsidian artifacts could be sourced definitively to Modena only since the mid-1980s (e.g., Nelson 1984) and to Tempiute only within the last 15 years. Sources written or published before approximately 2000 are unlikely to identify those obsidians. Material collected earlier sometimes (e.g., Conaway and O'Malley [Skinner and Thatcher 2005]) has been restudied for sourcing, but not always (e.g., Civa II and Slivovitz Shelters [Busby 1979], Stuart Rockshelter [Shutler et al. 1960]). Many unsourced artifacts probably derive from Modena or Tempiute, but this cannot be determined in the absence of analysis.

42WS3636, for instance, has a sizeable obsidian assemblage whose "nearest and most commonly used obsidian source was...Modena" (Roberts and Eskenazi 2006:97). Almost certainly some, probably most, obsidian at that site originated at Modena, but the absence of sourcing data precludes certainty. Although obsidian is an important constituent of both flake and tool assemblages at Sunshine Locality in Long Valley (Beck and Jones 2009a, 2009b), specific obsidian sources are not identified there. Unsourced obsidian also was found at Quail Creek, well southeast of Modena (Walling et al. 1988:Table 46). Shackley (1986; cited in Roberts 2008:62) suspected that then-unidentifiable obsidian from six artifacts in Kaibab National Forest of northern Arizona, about 500 km to the southeast, were from Modena. Obsidian occurred in modest quantities in the Groom Range south of Rachel, but has not been sourced (Reno and Pippin 1986:86, 109). If not local, much of this obsidian may be from Tempiute considering the source's proximity to that survey area. Obsidian artifacts are common in Altschul and colleagues' (2006:19) Black Mountain survey area on the NTTR, but none were sourced.

Circumstances do not always allow for instrumental sourcing. Tuohy (1982), for instance, could only borrow a looted assemblage from NC Cave in northwestern Lincoln County that contained several obsidian artifacts, including an Elko Corner-Notched point. All were made of a "banded gray" (1982:83) obsidian whose description matches Modena but other sources as well. Although they were unable to conduct any instrumental sourcing, Kremkau and colleagues (2011:163) reported one flake of "red-banded obsidian" from each of two sites in the Pine and Mathews Canyon reservoirs. They tentatively associated these flakes with Modena, although red-banded variants likewise occur in other obsidian sources. Conversely, even when material is reliably sourced, its lack of provenience documentation may render it useless for distribu-

tional studies. For instance, one Idaho private collector reported two Clovis points sourced to Modena, that the collector could provenience only to "Oregon, Nevada, Idaho, or Arizona" (F. Lytle and C. Skinner, personal communication 12 June 2011).

Toolstone distributions can be compiled only from reports of archaeological fieldwork. Over the geographic scale of the Modena and Tempiute terranes, the archaeological record is not uniformly documented. Patterns in the distribution of toolstones certainly owe to prehistoric behavior, but they owe to geographic patterns of archaeological fieldwork as well. Until the archaeological landscape of these terranes—an area that encompasses southern Nevada, western Utah, eastern California, and northwestern Arizona—is mapped and measured for patterns of archaeological fieldwork, it is impossible to separate the effects of prehistoric behavior and organization from the effects of sample vagaries.

Most Great Basin toolstone distribution studies are site-centered, focused on the occurrence and proportional frequency of two or more toolstones across a landscape of occupation sites (e.g., G. T. Jones et al. 2003; Jones et al. 2012; Estes 2009; Hauer 2005). Such studies often make inferences to the scale and pattern of prehistoric land use involving large areas and several toolstones, with an eye to overall patterns of land use that the site documents and/or modes of toolstone acquisition or distribution. From this perspective, toolstone sourcing gives insight into the scale and placement of areas over which Great Basin foragers ranged. A legitimate alternative is to focus upon toolstone quarries, not prehistoric land-use systems, as units of analysis and to map the distribution and abundance of their products and by-products across the landscape. Given the focus and orientation of UA research, this source-centric perspective is the best option.

Limitations are unavoidable in a dataset compiled from so many original sources. Nevertheless, consulted sources sampled a considerable number of artifacts from a range of sites. Overall, sources reported 2,003 Modena artifacts and 377 from Tempiute (Shott 2016:Table 10.1);

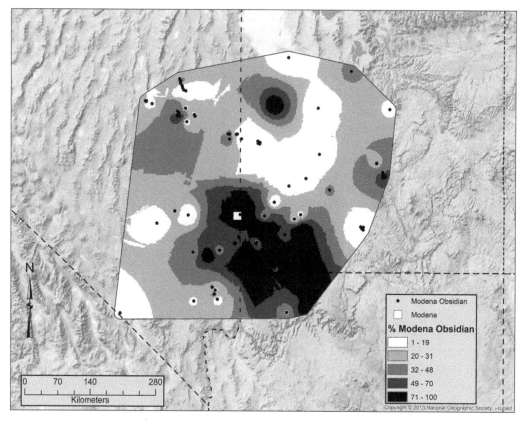

FIGURE 10.1. Density-contour map of the Modena terrane, all artifact categories.

Modena obsidian was the most common among points, preforms, and flakes alike. Appendix B data were used to generate density-contour maps that express the frequency of a source as a proportion of all sourced obsidian artifacts at the site of occurrence.

Modena

The Modena terrane was mapped and measured as the smallest polygon that encompassed all sourced material. Recalling that a few documented occurrences at relatively great distance (e.g., several noted in Chapter 2, two in Inyo County, California [Zeanah and Leigh 2002], two on the Wasatch Plateau [Curewitz 2001] and, although fairly large samples of sourced points from Danger Cave included no Modena or Tempiute obsidian [Hughes 2014], Umshler [1975:Figure 6] evidently reported Modena from either Hogup or Danger Cave, and other sources

cited in Chapter 3) were omitted as outliers that would exaggerate the scale of a source's distribution (Smith and Harvey 2018:834), the documented Modena terrane measures about 163,000 km² (Figure 10.1).

Like most Great Basin obsidians, Modena is most abundant near the source. Yet among obsidian sources common in the UNEV project area, Modena showed "the greatest likelihood to be found at sites distant from the source area" (McKee et al. 2013:97 and Table 32). McKee and colleagues' (2013:78–80) cost-surface model (essentially, distance between sources and places of use weighted by physiographic features like elevation and streams) for the UNEV project area in western Utah defined the terranes of major obsidian sources in and near that region. Modena's terrane as defined by the cost-surface model and by straight-line distance largely coincided and occupied the southwestern corner of Utah

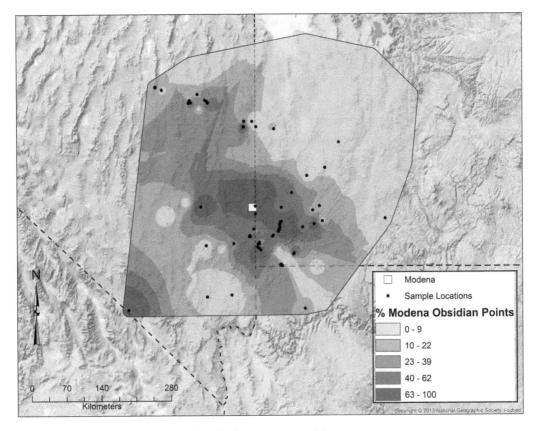

FIGURE 10.2. Density-contour map of the Modena terrane, points.

(McKee et al. 2013:Figure 14). Despite the predominant local scale of obsidian distributions documented in the literature, some reports suggest at least the possibility of occasional transport over longer distances (e.g., Johnson and McQueen 2012).

The Modena terrane map documents the source's broad distribution in the southern Great Basin. However, the strong skew toward occurrences in southwestern Utah also suggests that the concentration of fieldwork there affected results. This possible geographic bias may also involve chronological sampling error, because most occurrences in southwestern Utah are late prehistoric in age. Modena was transported in quantity over considerable distance. Modena's proportional contribution to sourced point assemblages show similar patterns (Figure 10.2), with high point proportions at several occurrences to the west and southwest owing

partly to small overall assemblage size. Yet the point map lacks the heavy concentration in southwestern Utah visible in the overall terrane map. Preforms of the Modena terrane are considerably fewer in number, which complicates their comparison to points; generally, though, they show a similar pattern to the overall and point maps over a more restricted geographic range (Shott 2016:Figure 10.8). The small size of the sourced preform sample probably owes to some combination of the comparatively low frequencies of preforms with distance from sources and an archaeological preference to source diagnostic points rather than preforms. Nevertheless, consulted sources document both some frequency and the considerable scale of export of preforms from the Modena source on which analysis in Chapters 7 and 8 was premised.

Following Basgall (1990), the distribution of Modena points might be expected to be wider

230   CHAPTER 10

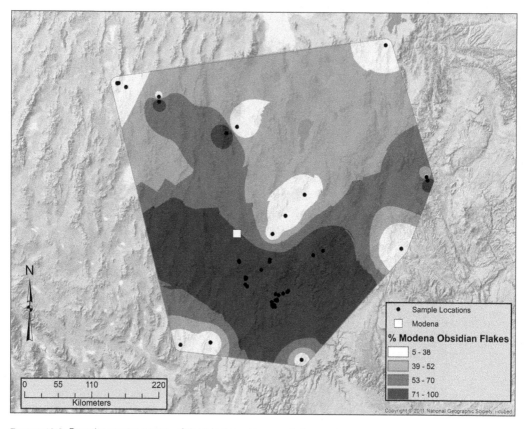

FIGURE 10.3. Density-contour map of the Modena terrane, flakes.

than that of Modena flakes, although Panich and colleagues (2015) saw no such difference in their Baja California study. Indeed, the point distribution seems slightly larger (Figures 10.2–10.3). Besides the difference in scale, the Modena point distribution is more complex, showing relatively abrupt changes in density and high-density modes both near the source and also at Ash Meadows NWR to the southwest (admittedly, n = 1 there). Modena's flake distribution is less complex, and more of it is occupied by the highest density mode. Appendix B data lacking systematic information about flakes' technological character, unfortunately, it is impossible to distinguish in Modena's flake distribution between, for instance, large cortical flakes and small resharpening ones. At face value, comparison of Modena's point and flake distributions supports Basgall's (1990) expecta-

tion and suggests embeddedness as the dominant procurement mode for Modena obsidian.

The flake distribution (Figure 10.3) is more strongly patterned to the south. As above, most occurrences in southwestern Utah are late prehistoric. Flake proportions to the southeast being much higher than point and preform ones, Modena may have been accessed and exploited differently in later prehistory, raw cobbles exported for processing elsewhere rather than the partial processing at the source that probably characterized the source's use for most of prehistory. This possibility—Chapter 9's second scenario—suggests that the FPM may not have governed late prehistoric use of the source, and may help explain the difference between OHD production curves for the source itself and Modena's terrane except to the southeast. If late prehistoric knappers merely collected and

TABLE 10.1. Sourced Occurrences of Modena and Tempiute Obsidians by Diagnostic Point Type or Series.

Source	Elko						
	LP/EH[a]	Humboldt	Series	G/RS/RG[b]	Cott.[c]	DSN[d]	PBN[e]
Modena	min. 12[f]	53	39	85	36	21	56
Temp.	10	1	6	9	5	2	2

Types of minor occurrence omitted.
[a] Late Pleistocene/Early Holocene, including Clovis and Great Basin Series
[b] Gatecliff/Rose Springs/Rosegate
[c] Cottonwood Series
[d] Desert Side-Notched
[e] Parowan Basal-Notched
[f] One entry reported "various" GBS

exported raw cobbles, they would leave no trace of their use in OHD data.

About two-thirds of sourced Modena artifacts that can be tentatively dated using Seddon's (2005a) OHD intervals fall in his "Confidently Archaic," (i.e., Pleistocene through mid-Holocene) interval. Appendix B denotes these occurrences as "Time Period 1." Remaining dated artifacts are divided about equally between the later Holocene and late prehistoric intervals (Time Periods 2 and 3, respectively). Thus, the documented Modena terrane skews toward earlier prehistoric intervals. Only 57 of 210 documented Modena occurrences can be dated to Seddon's OHD intervals. The 57 artifacts account for less than one-sixth of all Modena and other sourced obsidians, a sample too small for reliable inference.

As discussed in Chapter 9, no reliable OHD chronologies exist for Tempiute obsidian. However, Tempiute points can be dated typologically. To facilitate comparison, the Modena dataset can be characterized the same way (Table 10.1), taking type assignments as reported and acknowledging the chronological ambiguity of Elko Series points and the typological range of the Great Basin Series and Gatecliff/Rose Springs/Rosegate series. Briefly, Modena occurrences are fairly evenly distributed across defined point types. Modena was selected for far more Humboldt and aggregate Late Pleistocene or Early Holocene (LP/EH) types than was Tempiute. Elko Series dating is ambiguous,

but later Archaic Gatecliff/Rose Springs/Rosegate points are the most common series among Modena material. Later prehistoric types, most presumably arrow points, also are well represented.

Tempiute

Mapped in the same way as Modena, the Tempiute terrane measures nearly 102,000 km² (Figure 10.4). Although Tempiute obsidian is well represented to the north in east-central Nevada, overall it dominates another area of fairly high concentration lying immediately to its south, though the assemblages are admittedly comparatively small.

Tempiute distributions show a clear tendency to highest proportions immediately south of the source and in east-central Nevada, consistent with earlier studies that documented its prevalence in the latter area (e.g., G. T. Jones et al. 2003). The small point assemblage likewise largely skews north, although in small assemblages (Figure 10.5), as does the small sample of sourced Tempiute preforms (Shott 2016:Figure 10.15), and the larger flake sample (Figure 10.6).

Tempiute maps clearly show a wider distribution for points than for preforms or flakes. Although the terrane scales of the respective maps are identical, the point distribution shows significant high modes south of the source, where preform and flake distributions show low density (Figures 10.5–10.6). As in the case of Modena, this comparison somewhat implicates

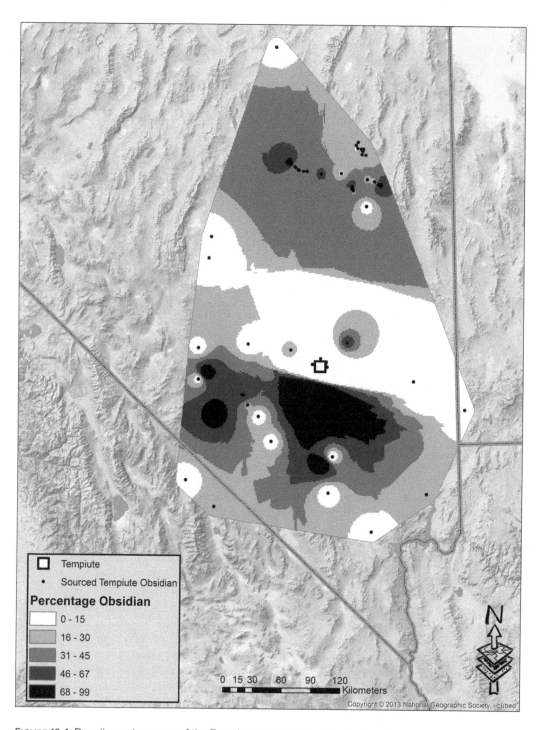

FIGURE 10.4. Density-contour map of the Tempiute terrane, all artifact categories.

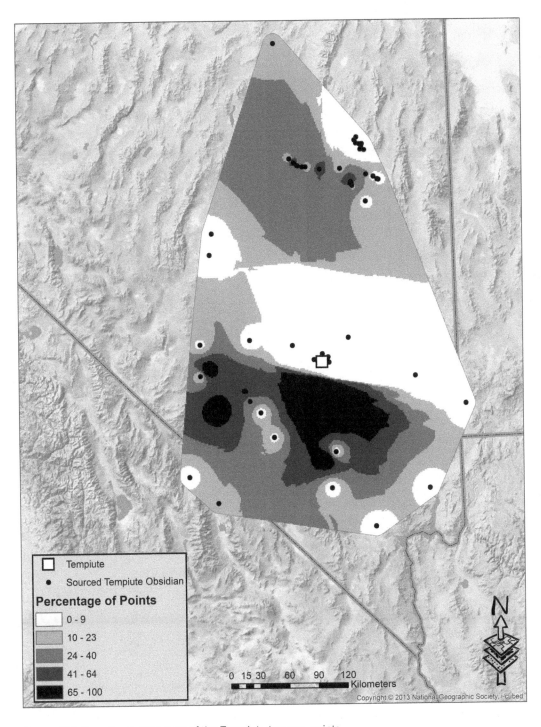

FIGURE 10.5. Density-contour map of the Tempiute terrane, points.

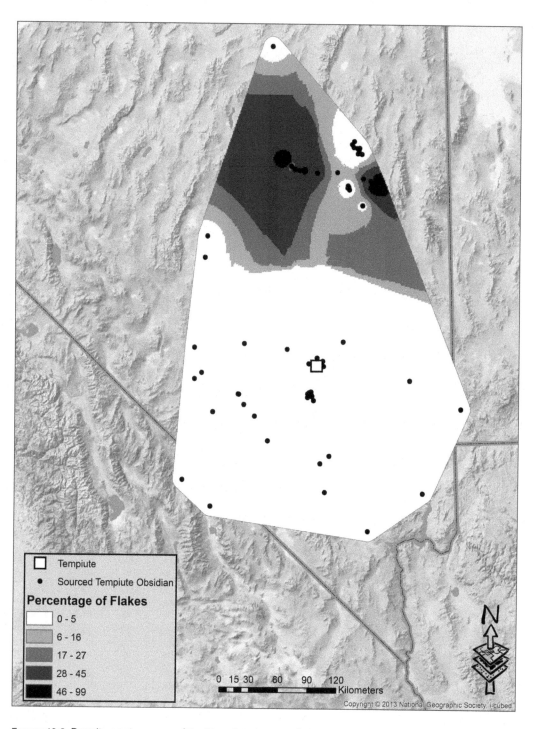

FIGURE 10.6. Density-contour map of the Tempiute terrane, flakes.

embedded procurement over the likelihood of exchange as the most common acquisition mode for Tempiute obsidian (Basgall 1990).

Overall, Tempiute shows a fairly limited distribution in its immediate environs and, except for points, to the south; it was used much more extensively by people who transported it northward. Either this owes to variation in population density, possibly lower in the southern than central Great Basin, to land-use patterns of forager groups that scheduled their exploitation of the source around other activities, or to concentration of fieldwork in G. T. Jones and colleagues' (2003) area. Tempiute's northern distribution largely coincides with Modena's northern mode. Possibly, Tempiute's limited occurrence east of the source owes to the greater popularity and local abundance of Modena and other obsidians there.

By point typology, the Tempiute dataset is dominated mostly by LP/EH WST/GBSS types, and by later Archaic types like Gatecliff/Rose Springs/Rosegate (Table 10.1). Like Modena's, the chronological distribution of sourced Tempiute occurrences skews to early prehistory. This reflects either prehistoric exploitation trends, source depletion, or vagaries of archaeological sampling that, for instance, include considerable quantities of sourced Tempiute in several early Holocene datasets from east-central Nevada. Whatever the explanation, the sample of typologically dated Tempiute occurrences is too small to justify separate treatment and interpretation.

Discussion

Strictly, the distribution maps presented in this chapter do not exhibit source terranes, which Elston (1992a:35) defined as areas over which particular toolstones are dominant. Instead, they show the overall distribution of each source, excepting extreme outliers, and accordingly include areas in which the toolstone is second or lower in rank among sourced toolstones. The distribution of Modena and other sources along the UNEV project route (McKee et al. 2013:Figure 14) is, in that stricter sense, a depiction of each source's terrane as it intersected that project area. Yet the distinction may amount to little difference.

A source's terrane in the strictest sense depends not upon the abundance, quality, and accessibility of its toolstone in isolation, but in comparison to other sources. All else equal, a source's terrane may be large where other toolstones are few and small when they are many. Relative to the scales of most major toolstone terranes and Great Basin hunter-gatherer land use, Modena and Tempiute are fairly closely spaced. Therefore, it is inevitable that their separate distributions would overlap considerably.

Distribution maps are dependent to unknown degree on sample vagaries, for example geographic patterns of archaeological fieldwork and the unwitting neglect of possibly important datasets. They also are dependent, again to unknown degree, upon the disposition of archaeologists to source toolstones and the further vagaries of funds available for sourcing, which affect the size and possibly the composition and source-diversity of resulting datasets. For instance, it is clear that first points and then flakes are more popular sourcing subjects than are preforms (Shott 2016:Table 10.1). This preference almost certainly is deliberate rather than a reflection of relative abundances in the archaeological record. Points are favored because of their intrinsic information content, particularly concerning age, and flakes as a default option when points are few or absent because of their abundance. In contrast, preforms are not popular, being possibly only slightly more common than points and much less abundant than flakes, and lacking the intrinsic chronological content that points possess.

Given the limitations and the uncontrolled sources of variation embedded in the OHD dataset, interpretation of these data must be conservative. Taking this approach, Modena and Tempiute terranes are considerably smaller than the conveyance or broad distribution zones defined by G. T. Jones and colleagues (2003) and Jones and others (2012). This is primarily because several toolstones contributed to all zones mapped in those studies. That is, such distribution zones defined for limited sets of occupation sites are composites of sources. By comparison, the distribution/terrane maps presented here are source-centric. Nevertheless, this chapter's Modena and Tempiute terrane maps agree fairly closely with the distribution zones mapped by Jones and others (2012:Figure 7) for Paleoarchaic occupation, and with McKee and colleagues' (2013:Figure 14) narrowly defined terrane map for southwestern Utah, whose record both in McKee and colleagues (2013) and here bears a strong late prehistoric occupational signal. Broadly at least, terrane patterning is visible and fairly persistent over long periods of time.

More broadly still, overall patterns in source terranes are evident. The Modena terrane is roughly symmetrical around the source (admittedly, Modena's preform distribution map is narrower, but this may owe to small sample size). The Tempiute terrane is noticeably elongated north to south, and narrow to the point of convergence to the north while broader to the south. The latter characteristic probably is a robust reflection of prehistoric land use, but the northern convergence of Tempiute's terranes may owe to limited archaeological sampling of the central Great Basin.

Another salient consideration is the relatively modest scale of production inferred for Modena and especially Tempiute. As discussed in Chapter 8, available but limited estimates of annual per capita toolstone consumption combined with the probable time span of exploitation suggest that a relative handful of people could account for Modena's and Tempiute's aggregate consumption. Of course such estimates may be biased as well as limited. At least at face value, however, one implication of modest consumption rate is that very small populations could account for source distributions and, by extension, the scale and form of terranes. In that perspective, it may be inadvisable to attempt broad inferences to the scale and pattern of prehistoric land use or the mode of acquisition of obsidians if the populations capable of generating them were so small.

Over 13 millennia or more of human occupation, of course source distributions in the archaeological record are noisy, complex palimpsests. Still, an overall pattern seems evident, in which Modena, not surprisingly, dominates within a roughly 75 km radius in general but extends over 150 km to the east and southeast. Tempiute is somewhat displaced toward the margins of Modena's distribution but is very common to its north and Modena's northwest. To some unknown extent, this crude geographic pattern has at once a chronological dimension. As above, typologically datable Tempiute occurrences are mostly LP/EH, and typological and OHD Modena occurrences somewhat more broadly distributed.

As Holmes (1892) and later archaeologists recognized, semifinished and sometimes finished tools were exported from quarries for use across much larger regions. Viewed from an archaeological perspective, the landscapes of these export zones become terranes, like those of Modena and Tempiute. Regional sourcing data consulted in this chapter document merely the crude outlines of the Modena and Tempiute terranes. For progress in research, cost-surface models (e.g., McKee et al. 2010; Putzi et al. 2015) should be devised for these terranes, taking into account the roughly north-south trending uplands of the Great Basin's basin-and-range province as possible barriers to straight-line travel and access.

But future research will better document and explain terranes' scale and pattern of toolstone occurrence only when the flakes that so often are sourced are better characterized for their technological properties. At a minimum, salient attributes of sourced flakes include weight and perhaps longest dimension, their thickness, presence/absence of cortex, exterior-surface scar density, and platform characteristics when present. Archaeologists also should source more preforms where available, not just points, because the distance and direction that preforms travelled are at least as informative about scale and pattern of land use as are points. Like flakes, sourced preforms should be recorded using some minimal standard attribute set, including Callahan Stage where possible to determine, weight and major linear dimensions of intact specimens, and perhaps technological characteristics like edge sinuosity and exterior-surface scar density. Finally, points themselves, the clear favorite of archaeologists in sourcing studies, might be characterized by their degree of reduction using, for instance, methods applied to WST/GBSS bifaces (Beck and Jones 2009b:183–192; Duke 2011) or to hafted points more generally (e.g., Lerner 2015).

There is also the question of obsidian toolstone quality. This property can be gauged using various physical-science methods (e.g., Luedtke 1992:Table 6.2). A. Nelson and colleagues (2012) used the inverse coefficient of variation of between inner and outer fracture diameters of specimens subjected to controlled laboratory fracture as a measure of toolstone consistency or predictability. They found considerable difference among Idaho obsidians (2012:Figure 5), which partly explained the popularity and resulting distribution scale of sources. Similar analysis of Modena and Tempiute obsidians, ideally including nearby Utah sources like Wild Horse Canyon and Topaz as well, would correct or calibrate source distributions and terranes to the intrinsic workability of their toolstones.

With such data, analysis can become finer-grained and more nuanced than was possible here. The distance fall-off curves of flakes can be calibrated to various flake attributes. We may find that flakes of similar placement in reduction continua (as measured, for instance, by the %-completeness methods used in Chapter 5) are more or less widely distributed at different times, or their abundance with distance from source may implicate different acquisition modes. We may find, as suggested in Chapter 7, not only that preforms generally become more advanced with distance from source, but that

the relationship between distance and degree of advancement varies over time in ways that the FPM can explain. We may find that finished points of different types and, by extension, time periods have different fall-off distributions from sources but also that the realized curation rate (Shott 1996a) varies by type and over time, again in ways that implicate different models of land use and modes of acquisition.

Finally, however formulaic archaeologists are when they call for more data, it is clear that more data would help gauge the robusticity of the scale and pattern of documented toolstone distributions. Of course we never will find, let alone source, all artifacts made of Modena or Tempiute obsidians. But it underscores the limited quality of the current sample to note that the 583 sourced points to Modena (Shott 2016:Table 10.1) comprise roughly 1.5% of the estimated 40,000 or more preforms exported from the quarry. Even if only half of exported preforms became points, the sample amounts to barely 3% of all Modena points. And the Modena sample is considerably larger than Tempiute's. It is optimistic to assume that an aggregate corpus compiled from so many reports that vary so greatly in degree and kind of documentation somehow is a representative sample by point type, land-use scale and pattern, and type of behavior.

Clearly, data of the quality compiled for this analysis can be improved. When it is, the scope of inference to prehistoric Great Basin land-use models from better contextualized archaeological data will be greatly expanded. Until then, we know merely the broadest outlines of the cultural practices that governed the Modena and Tempiute terranes.

11

Conclusion

Since Holmes, archaeologists have appreciated both the great volume of evidence that toolstone quarries possess and, by virtue of that volume, how challenging is their study. UA investigations documented considerable evidence of prehistoric use of the Modena and Tempiute obsidian quarries and do not encourage optimism about the ease of its analysis. But they suggest ways both to efficiently sample the immense abundance of quarry debris and to effectively, and in some ways originally, analyze those samples. Toolstone quarries never will be easy subjects of analysis. However, this and other recent studies offer hope that the great potential of quarry sites can begin to be matched by analytical methods at our command.

If it still needed it, UA's investigations further validate the effectiveness of probabilistic sampling of complex archaeological deposits. Valid estimates of the size and character of such deposits is possible only when they are sampled properly, not casually. UA's sample design efficiently estimated the size and distribution of flake-debris deposits there. Projecting from our probabilistic samples, Modena contains something in the neighborhood of 25–30 million flakes. In this way, we can legitimately conclude that quarries like Modena indeed are impressive in scale—no one who has visited them could doubt that—but, more importantly, now also can attach grounded if provisional parameters to its size, as well as its scale of production, number of products, and efficiency of production.

Questions Posed, and Some Tentative Answers

UA's approach to flake debris emphasized attribute and mass analysis. It employed a range of approaches and analytical methods and tested some ideas about the nature of reduction and sources of variation in debris assemblages. On balance, the size and character of the Modena and Tempiute debris assemblages strongly suggest that they are the by-product of reduction of cobbles to unfinished, intermediate-stage preforms. Analysis reinforces the growing consensus that reduction is best understood as a continuous process, not a set of successive stages. Virtually all flake assemblages that accumulate over significant lengths of time are of technologically mixed character. But an innovative form of CLSR analysis allowed us to apportion varying proportions of these assemblages to different reduction modes or segments, possibly the first time that such allocation methods have been applied to large archaeological assemblages.

Another result of UA investigation is covariation between flake and biface assemblages as, for instance, in the correlation revealed between proportions of flake-assemblage stage assignments and proportions of Callahan-stage preforms among areas at Modena. Other dimensions of covariation probably reside in the flake and tool datasets analyzed in such detail, which future work can explore. Too often flake and tool assemblages are analyzed in isolation.

Closer attention to how patterning in one might be explained by patterning in the other is warranted by UA results.

Converting flakes to cobbles worked is complicated by variation in original cobble size. Carr and Bradbury's (2001:142–143) concept of analytical core units (ACU) expresses flake quantity relative to weight loss of cobbles. With reasonable assumptions about original size of raw cobbles and their degree of reduction at the source, the Modena assemblage may represent about 30,000–50,000 ACU reductions. More than 80,000 preforms probably were produced at Modena, at least to intermediate state, half or more of which were exported for completion and use elsewhere. This makes Modena's production efficiency (*sensu* Root 1997) at least comparable to that of other analyzed quarry assemblages. When similar analysis is conducted at other quarries, we can begin to gauge how common such efficiency rates are.

Testing of the FPM in preform data was a major goal of UA research. Following pioneering work by Elston (1992a) and Beck and colleagues (2002), it seems likely that most reduction at Modena and Tempiute was for the production of intermediate-stage preforms, that reduction terminated usually in the vicinity of Callahan's Stage 3, and that semifinished preforms were the most common products exported from the sites. Besides the methods used in earlier studies, Chapter 7 demonstrated some methods original to this study, notably involving the slope of preform weight-upon-size plots and the detailed studied of debris size distributions. These might prove useful in the analysis of other quarry assemblages, in the Great Basin and elsewhere.

In analytical perspective, the impressive scale of obsidian deposits and production at Tempiute and especially Modena are qualified somewhat by demand or usage estimates. Whatever the spatial extent of Modena's debris fields, particularly at Areas A, B, and F, in the aggregate they account for relatively modest rates of toolstone consumption over the source's approximately 7,000 years of chief use; again, span

and intensity of Tempiute's exploitation are unknown. If demand estimates are reasonably accurate, as rough as they admittedly are, it would not take many people very long, in archaeological terms, to deplete Modena nor, presumably, Tempiute considering its much smaller production estimates.

As discussed in Chapter 3, prehistoric depletion is the inferred fate of several Great Basin obsidian quarries. These include not just sources considerably smaller than Modena or even Tempiute (e.g., Buckboard Mesa [Amick 1991:80–81]; the Highland chert quarry [Reno and Pippin 1986:126]) but larger ones as well (e.g., the Coso Field [Hartwell et al. 1996:57]). While Rowley and colleagues (2002) suggested Modena was depleted during prehistory, of course depletion is not absolute; even now, by careful searching useful nodules can be found at Modena. But a toolstone quarry need not be absolutely exhausted to lose much of its value. Once a point of diminishing return is reached between time available for search and toolstone acquired, a quarry ceases to be a reliable source of supply. It passes from destination to place of opportunity if travels otherwise draw people to its vicinity. That transformation may have been the fate of Modena and almost certainly of Tempiute before the end of Great Basin prehistory.

Yet sourcing data show clearly that Modena remained a popular toolstone in late prehistory, possibly via the exploitation of secondary sources. Generally, sourcing data show that Modena and Tempiute obsidians were fairly widely distributed. So, despite small supplies and limited potential to supply prehistoric users, these toolstones circulated over a considerable time-space range.

Questions for Future Research

Research projects can be gauged not just by questions posed and the tentative answers proposed to them, but also by the questions they prompt to guide future research. This concluding section poses several for consideration.

Quarries abound in flake debris. Assemblages that accumulate on the surface over long periods are subject to taphonomic bias that must be gauged and controlled for before analysis. Types of taphonomic bias were identified in this study and magnitude of bias estimated using comparative data from southern Nevada. Besides analyzing debris assemblages for the values and patterns of association between attributes, or making high-level inferences about the general character or purpose of reduction, future analyses must continue to confront the mixing problem—the likelihood that assemblage aggregates are the mixed product of different reduction modes and different segments of reduction modes to different degrees. In previous research, the problem mostly was invoked to preclude some forms of analysis or was acknowledged without effective resolution. However, earlier studies (e.g., Ahler 1989a; Root 1994; Stahle and Dunn 1982) suggested two possible approaches. Efforts here to confront rather than avoid the mixing problem were guided by these studies. Tentative solutions are reported in Chapter 5, which, for possibly the first time, uses a systematic method to infer kind and degree of mixing of flake assemblages.

Despite this, much more work is needed. One critical need is further experimental work to explore possible differences between even similar toolstones like Modena and Tempiute. We also need more experimental studies that mimic the archaeological record's complexity in kind and degree of mixing among reduction modes. Equally as important are further studies, both archaeological and experimental, to gauge the best set of categorical and continuous attributes of individual flakes and the best strategies for sampling of large flake assemblages for attribute analysis (e.g., Milne 2009). Essential to progress in this respect is analysis like that reported in Chapter 7 for flake assemblages across a range of distance and occupational context in the Modena and Tempiute terranes. Only then can we determine if the kinds and amounts of reduction-mode mixing at sources complement those found at end-user sites, and how and to what extent flake assemblages at consumer sites vary in inferred mixing as a function of distance from sources.

Chapter 7 concluded with suggestions for future research and testing that are worth brief synthesis here. As important as was formal testing of the FPM model at quarry sources like Modena, progress requires similar testing of both flake and preform data at consumer sites over a range of distance from the source. To accomplish this goal will require probabilistic sample designs for regional survey, in-field sourcing by portable XRF, and in-field measurement and coding of individual flakes and preforms. The result would be a test of the FPM model against a large, systematic, contextualized dataset. Lines of analysis could include ratio-scale regression slope of weight upon PC1 in preform assemblages and in plots of ln-cumulative flake counts by size class at successive distances from Modena, subdivided by definable time when possible using OHD data. Such research would test the FPM, not merely in the valid but necessarily limited qualitative ways accomplished in earlier studies, but more precisely and robustly in continuous data as in this study.

Chapter 8 made an initial assay at converting crude quantities of flake debris to standardized measures of quantity like ACUs. Of course more experimental data on the relationship between cobble size and extent of reduction, on the one hand, and kind and amount of flake debris, on the other hand, will be useful. At least for Modena, targeted survey of the source's immediate environs and possibly limited excavation to gauge the range of size and the remaining abundance of original cobbles is needed as well.

Seddon (2005a) and especially A. Rogers and Duke (2014) established good calibrations of Modena's hydration rate. Uncertainty in OHD calibration never can be eliminated, both because a source's geochemistry may vary across its natural terrane in ways that affect hydration, and because elevation, depositional context, and other uncontrollable factors also bear upon results. Initial efforts to calibrate Tempiute obsidian were unsuccessful, but a well-grounded calibration for that source likewise would be useful.

For sourcing studies, we need more and better data on the technological character of flakes sourced to Modena and Tempiute. Such data can come from restudy of extant collections or, as suggested above and in Chapter 7, by new fieldwork. Only when distance from source is calibrated to various technological attributes—flake size, cortex presence/absence, platform type or faceting, exterior-surface scar density—in order to distinguish production-stage from resharpening debris can models like Basgall's (1990) be tested in the detail they deserve. Furthermore, we need more data from sourced artifacts analyzed for OHD, so that chronological patterns of variation in Modena's distribution scale and mode(s) of acquisition can be estimated. In this process, it may be useful to compare Modena distribution data by OHD time intervals to A. White's (2012:273–280) model linking hunter-gatherer toolstone distributions to baseline de-

mographic and ecological contexts. It may be that Modena's early Holocene terrane resembles White's mobility setting B, while later ones mimic other land-use parameters.

In these and other ways merely sketched above, continued research in the terranes of Modena and Tempiute will limn the details of local prehistory. It also is poised, if designed carefully, to contribute to important unresolved questions in the long-term adaptations of hunter-gatherers to challenging environments. Rocks can tell us how prehistoric knappers reduced them, trivially. But if interrogated properly, rocks can also tell us why knappers did so, thereby providing insight into the logic and organization of prehistoric cultures. That conviction animated this study, whose methods and results perhaps might inform future ones.

References

Abrahams, Athol D., Anthony J. Parsons, and P. J. Hirsch

1985 Hillslope Gradient-particle Size Relations: Evidence for the Formation of Debris Slopes by Hydraulic Processes in the Mojave Desert. *Journal of Geology* 93:3437–357.

Adams, Jacob S., and Douglas H. MacDonald

2015 Differential Selection of Lithic Raw Materials by Prehistoric Hunter-Gatherers in the Upper Yellowstone River Valley, Montana/Wyoming. In *Toolstone Geography of the Pacific Northwest*, edited by T. Ozbun and R. Adams, pp. 208–217. Archaeology Press, Simon Fraser University, Burnaby, BC, Canada.

Ahler, Stanley A.

1975 Pattern and Variety in Extended Coalescent Lithic Technology. PhD dissertation, Department of Anthropology, University of Missouri, Columbia, MO.

1986 *The Knife River Flint Quarries: Excavations at Site 32DU508.* State Historical Society of North Dakota, Bismarck, ND.

1989a Mass Analysis of Flaking Debris: Studying the Forest Rather Than the Tree. In *Alternative Approaches to Lithic Analysis*, edited by D. Henry and G. Odell, pp. 85–118. Archeological Papers of the American Anthropological Association No. 1.

1989b Experimental Knapping with KRF and Midcontinent Cherts: Overview and Applications. In *Experiments in Lithic Technology*, edited by D. Amick and R. Mauldin, pp. 199–233. British Archaeological Reports International Series No. 528, Oxford, UK.

1992 Use-Phase Classification and Manufacturing Technology in Plains Village Arrowpoints. In *Piecing Together the Past: Application of Refitting Studies in Archaeology*, edited by J. Hofman and J. Enloe, pp. 36–62. BAR International Series 578, Oxford, UK.

Allard, Pierre, and Laurence Burnez-Lanotte

2008 An Economy of Surplus Production in the Early Neolithic of Hesbaya (Belgium): Bankeramik Blade Debitage at Verlaine 'Petit Paradis.' In *Flint Mining in Prehistoric Europe: Interpreting the Archaeological Records*, edited by P. Allard, F. Bostyn, F. Giligny, and J. Lech, pp. 31–39. BAR International Series 1891, Oxford, UK.

Allen, M. J.

1991 Analysing the Landscape: A Geographic Approach to Archaeological Problems. In *Interpreting Artefact Scatters: Contributions to Ploughzone Archaeology*, edited by A. Schofield, pp. 39–58. Oxbow Monograph 4, Oxbow Books, Oxford, UK.

Altschul, Jeffery H., Michael K. Lerch, Kathleen L. Hull, Margaret Beck, and Robert M. Wegener

2006 *A Glimpse at the Archaeological Landscape of Black Mountain and Upper Thirsty Canyon, Nevada Test and Training Range, Nellis Air Force Base, Nevada.* Statistical Research, Inc., Technical Report 05-50, Tucson, AZ.

Ames, Kenneth M., Kristen A. Fuld, and Sara Davis

2010 Dart and Arrow Points on the Columbia Plateau of Western North America. *American Antiquity* 75:287–325.

Amick, Daniel S.

1985 Late Archaic Fort Payne Biface Manufacture at the Topsy Site (40WY204), Buffalo River Basin, Tennessee. *Southeastern Archaeology* 4:134–151.

1991 Site 26NY2894: An Obsidian Nodule Quarry. In *Archaeological Investigations on the Buckboard Mesa Road Project*, edited by D. Amick, G. Henton and L. Pippin, pp. 31–92. Desert Research Institute Technical Report 69. University of Nevada, Reno, NV.

2004 A Possible Ritual Cache of Great Basin Stemmed Bifaces from the Terminal Pleistocene–Early Holocene Occupation of NW Nevada, USA. *Lithic Technology* 29:119–145.

2007 Investigating the Behavioral Causes and Archaeological Effects of Lithic Recycling. In *Tools Versus Cores: Alternative Approaches to Stone Tool Analysis*, edited by S. McPherron, pp. 223–252. Cambridge Scholars Press, Newcastle.

Ammerman, Albert J. and William Andrefsky
1982   Reduction Sequences and the Exchange of Obsidian in Neolilthic Calabria. In *Contexts for Prehistoric Exchange*, edited by J. Ericson and T. Earle, pp. 149–172. Academic Press, New York City, NY.

Anderson, Duane C., Joseph A. Tiffany, and Fred W. Nelson
1986   Recent Research on Obsidian from Iowa Archaeological Sites. *American Antiquity* 51:837–852.

Anderson, Jacob M., and Lisa M. Hodgetts
2007   Pre-Dorset Technological Organization and Land Use in Southwestern Hudson Bay. *Canadian Journal of Archaeology* 31:224–249.

Andrefsky, William
1998   *Lithics: Macroscopic Approaches to Analysis.* Cambridge University Press, Cambridge, UK.

2007   The Application and Misapplication of Mass Analysis in Lithic Debitage Studies. *Journal of Archaeological Science* 34:392–402.

2008   Projectile Point Provisioning Strategies and Human Land-use. In *Lithic Technology: Measures of Production, Use and Curation*, edited by W. Andrefsky, pp. 195–216. Cambridge University Press, Cambridge, UK.

Andrefsky, William, editor
2001   *Lithic Debitage: Context, Form, Meaning.* University of Utah Press, Salt Lake City, UT.

Andrews, Bradford W.
2005   Lithic Technology and Mobility: A Comparative Diachronic Perspective from the Kern River Expansion Project. In *Kern River 2003 Expansion Project, Utah, Vol. IV: Prehistoric Synthesis, Part 1*, edited by A. Reed, M. Seddon, and H. Stettler, pp. 665–685. SWCA Environmental Consultants, Salt Lake City, UT.

Andrews, Bradford W., Timothy M. Murtha, and Barry Scheetz
2004   Approaching the Hatch Jasper Quarry from a Technological Perspective: A Study of Prehistoric Stone Tool Production in Central Pennsylvania. *Midcontinental Journal of Archaeology* 29:63–101.

Arkush, Brooke S., and Bonnie L. Pitblado
2000   Paleoarchaic Surface Assemblages in the Great Salt Lake Desert, Northwestern Utah. *Journal of California and Great Basin Anthropology* 22:12–42.

Ataman, Kathryn, and William W. Bloomer
1992   Cores and Modified Chunks. In *Archaeological Investigations at Tosawihi, a Great Basin Quarry, Part 1: The Periphery (Volume 1)*, edited by R. Elston and C. Raven, pp. 217–227. Intermountain Research, Silver City, NV.

Austin, Robert J.
1999   Technological Characterization of Lithic Waste-flake Assemblages: Multivariate Analysis of Experimental and Archaeological Data. *Lithic Technology* 24:53–68.

Ball, Sydney
1941   The Mining of Gems and Ornamental Stones by American Indians. *Bureau of American Ethnology Bulletin* 128:ix–78. Smithsonian Institution, Washington, DC.

Ballenger, Jesse A., and John D. Hall
2010   Obsidian Procurement, Technology, and Exchange in the Vicinity of Superior, Arizona. In *Queen Valley to Queen Creek Prehistoric Analyses*, edited by R. Wegener and R. Ciolek-Torrello, pp. 137–156. The U.S. 60 Archaeological Project Formative and Historical-Period Use of the Upper Queen Creek Region, vol. 4. Technical Series 92. Statistical Research, Inc., Tucson, AZ.

Bamforth, D. B., and Ronald I. Dorn
1988   On the Nature and Antiquity of the Manix Lake Industry. *Journal of California and Great Basin Anthropology* 10:209–226.

Barbarena, Ramiro, María V. Fernández, Agustina A. Rughini, Karen Borrazzo, Raven Garvey, Gustavo Lucero, Claudia Della Negra, Guadalupe Romero Villanueva, Víctor Durán, Valeria Cortegoso, Martín Giesso, Catherine Klesner, Brandi L. MacDonald, and Michael D. Glascock
2018   Deconstructing a Complex Obsidian "Source-scape": A Geoarchaeological and Geochemical Approach in Northwestern Patagonia. *Geoarchaeology* DOI: 10.1002/gea.21701.

Barnes, Robin B.
2000   Prehistoric Caches in an Intermittent Wetlands Environment: An Analysis of the Nicolarsen Cache Collection, Washoe County, Nevada. PhD dissertation, Department of Anthropology, University of Texas, Austin, TX.

Barton, Huw
2001   Mobilising Lithic Studies: An Application of
       Evolutionary Ecology to Understand Pre-
       historic Patterns of Human Behaviour in the
       Simpson Desert, Far Western Queensland."
       PhD dissertation, Department of Archaeol-
       ogy, University of Sydney, Sydney, Australia.
2008   Expedient Technologies and Curated
       Tools within a System of High Residential
       Mobility: An Example Using Mass Analysis
       of Flakes from the Simpson Desert, Central
       Australia. *Lithic Technology* 33:51–71.
Basgall, Mark E.
1990   Obsidian Acquisition and Use in Prehistoric
       Central Eastern California: A Preliminary
       Assessment. In *Current Directions in Califor-
       nia Obsidian Studies*, edited by R. E. Hughes,
       pp. 111–126. Contributions of the Univer-
       sity of California Archaeological Research
       Facility No. 48. University of California,
       Berkeley, CA.
Baumler, Mark F. and Christian E. Downum
1989   Between Micro and Macro: A Study in
       the Interpretation of Small-sized Lithic
       Debitage. In *Experiments in Lithic Technol-
       ogy*, edited by D. Amick and R. Mauldin,
       pp. 101–116. BAR International Series 528,
       Oxford, UK.
Beardsall, Robert J.
2013   Mass and Attribute Analysis of the Quartz
       Lithic Assemblage from the Grandfather
       Quarry (HbMd-4), near Granville Lake,
       Northern Manitoba. PhD dissertation,
       Department of Anthropology, University
       of Manitoba, Winnipeg, MB, Canada.
Beck, Charlotte
1999   Dating the Archaeological Record and
       Modeling Chronology. In *Models for the
       Millennium: Great Basin Anthropology
       Today*, edited by C. Beck, pp. 171–181. Uni-
       versity of Utah Press, Salt Lake City, UT.
Beck, Charlotte, and George T. Jones
1994   Dating Surface Assemblages Using Obsidian
       Hydration. In *Dating in Exposed and Surface
       Contexts*, edited by C. Beck, pp. 47–76.
       University of New Mexico Press, Albuquer-
       que, NM.
2009a Artifact Analysis. In *The Archaeology of the
       Eastern Nevada Paleoarchaic, Part I: The
       Sunshine Locality*, edited by C. Beck and
       G. Jones, pp. 77–144. University of Utah

Anthropological Papers No. 126, Salt Lake
City, UT.
2009b Projectile Points. In *The Archaeology of the
       Eastern Nevada Paleoarchaic, Part I: The
       Sunshine Locality*, edited by C. Beck and
       G. Jones, pp. 145–217. University of Utah
       Anthropological Papers No. 126, Salt Lake
       City, UT.
Beck, Charlotte, A. Taylor, George T. Jones,
C. Fadem, C. Cook, and S. Millward
2002   Rocks Are Heavy: Transport Costs and
       Paleoarchaic Quarry Behavior in the Great
       Basin. *Journal of Anthropological Archaeol-
       ogy* 21:481–507.
Beck, R. Kelly
2008   Transport Distance and Debitage Assem-
       blage Diversity: An Application of the
       Field Processing Model to Southern Utah
       Toolstone Procurement Sites. *American
       Antiquity* 73:759–780.
Behm, Jeffrey A.
1983   Flake Concentrations: Distinguishing be-
       tween Flintworking Activity Areas and Sec-
       ondary Deposits. *Lithic Technology* 12:9–16.
Bellifemine, Viviana I.
1992   Flakes vs. Projectile Points: Changes in
       Obsidian Procurement in Prehistoric
       Mendocino County, California, Suggested by
       Hydration Analysis. *International Associa-
       tion for Obsidian Studies Newsletter* 7:4–5.
Benson, Michael P.
1980   The Sitterud Bundle: A Prehistoric Cache
       from Central Utah. Report on file, Division
       of Utah State History, Antiquities Section,
       Salt Lake City, UT.
Bernatchez, Jocelyn, Michael J. Boley, and Brian R.
McKee
2013   Chronological Considerations for the
       UNEV Pipeline Prehistoric Sites. In *Data
       Recovery Along the UNEV Pipeline Utah
       Segment—Davis, Salt Lake, Tooele, Juab,
       Millard, Beaver, Iron and Washington Counts,
       Vol. VI: Prehistoric Synthesis and Concluding
       Thoughts on Prehistoric Research*, edited by
       M. Medeiros, J. Bernatchez, and J. Ravesloot,
       pp. 19–54. Technical Report No. 2011-29,
       WSA, Tucson, AZ.
Bertran, Passcal, E. Claud, L. Detrain, Arnaud
Lenoble, Bertrand Masson, and Luc Vallin
2006   Composition Granulométrique des As-
       semblages Lithiques: Application à l'Etude

Taphonomique des Sites Paléolithques. *Paleo* 18:7–36.

Bertran, Passcal, Arnaud Lenoble, Dominique Todisco, Pierre M. Desrosiers, and Mikkel Sørensen

2012   Particle Size Distribution of Lithic Assemblages and Taphonomy of Paleolithic Sites. *Journal of Archaeological Science* 39:3148–3166.

Best, Myron G., Eric H. Christiansen, and Richard H. Blank

1989   Oligocene Caldera Complex and Calc-alkaline Tuffs and Lavas of the Indian Peak Volcanic Field, Nevada and Utah. *Geological Society of American Bulletin* 101:1076–1090.

Bettinger, Robert L.

1982   Aboriginal Exchange and Territoriality in Owens Valley, California. In *Contexts for Prehistoric Exchange*, edited by J. Ericson and T. Earle, pp. 103–127. Academic, New York, NY.

2009   *Hunter-Gatherer Foraging: Five Simple Models.* Eliot Werner, Clinton Corners, NY.

2015   *Orderly Anarchy: Sociopolitical Evolution in Aboriginal California.* University of California Press, Berkeley, CA.

Bettinger, Robert L., R. Malhi, and H. McCarthy

1997   Central Place Models of Acorn and Mussel Processing. *Journal of Archaeological Science* 24:887–899.

Bickler, Simon H., and Marianne Turner

2002   Food to Stone: Investigations at the Suloga Adze Manufacturing Sites, Woodlark Island, Papua New Guinea. *Journal of the Polynesian Society* 111:11–44.

Binford, Lewis R.

1979 Organization and Formation Processes: Looking at Curated Technologies. *Journal of Anthropological Research* 35:255–273.

Binford, Lewis R., and James F. O'Connell

1984   An Alyawara Day: The Stone Quarry. *Journal of Anthropological Research* 40:406–432.

Bird, Douglas W., and Rebecca L. Bliege Bird

1997   Contemporary Shellfish Gathering Strategies among the Meriam of the Torres Strait Islands, Australia: Testing Predictions of a Central Place Foraging Model. *Journal of Archaeological Science* 24:39–63.

Bird, Douglas W., and James F. O'Connell

2006   Behavioral Ecology and Archaeology. *Journal of Archaeological Research* 14:143–188.

Birnie, Robert I., Gregory H. Miller, Betsy L. Tipps, Alan R. Schroedl, and B. Christopher Tapscott

2003   *Class III Cultural Resource Inventory of the Eagle Fire Emergency Stabilization Rehabilitation Project Area (Y133), Lincoln County, Nevada.* P-III Associates, Cultural Resources Report 5194-01-20304, Salt Lake City, UT.

Blitz, John H.

1988   Adoption of the Bow in Prehistoric North America. *North American Archaeologist* 9:123–145.

Bloomer, William W., Kathryn Ataman, and Eric E. Ingbar

1992   Bifaces. In *Archaeological Investigations at Tosawihi, a Great Basin Quarry, Part 1: The Periphery (Volume 1)*, edited by R. Elston and C. Raven, pp. 81–132. Intermountain Research, Silver City, NV.

Bloomer, William W., and Eric E. Ingbar

1992   Debitage Analysis. In *Archaeological Investigations at Tosawihi, a Great Basin Quarry, Part 1: The Periphery (Volume 1)*, ed. by R. Elston and C. Raven, pp. 229–270. Intermountain Research, Silver City, NV.

Bloomer, William W., and Denise Jaffke

2008   A High Sierran Nexus: Hot Obsidian Data from Donner Memorial State Park. *Proceedings of the Society for California Archaeology* 21:109–115.

Bosch, Peter W.

1979   A Neolithic Flint Mine. *Scientific American* 240(6):126–132.

Boulanger, Matthew T., Michael D. Glascock, M. Steven Shackley, and Craig Skinner

2013   Likely Source Attribution for a Paleoindian Obsidian Graver from Northwest Louisiana. *International Association of Obsidian Studies Bulletin* 49:4–7.

Boulanger, Matthew T., Thomas R. Jamison, Craig Skinner, and Michael D. Glascock

2007   Analysis of an Obsidian Biface Reportedly Found in the Connecticut River Valley of Vermont. *Archaeology of Eastern North America* 35:81–92.

Bowers, Alfred W., and C. N. Savage

1962   *Primitive Man on Browns Bench: His Environment and His Record.* Idaho Bureau of Mines and Geology, Information Circular No. 16, Moscow, ID.

Bradbury, Andrew P.

2010   Bipolar Reduction Experiments and the Examination of Middle Archaic Bipolar Technologies in West-Central Illinois. *North American Archaeologist* 31:67–116.

Bradbury, Andrew P., and Philip J. Carr

1995   Flake Typologies and Alternative Approaches:

An Experimental Assessment. *Lithic Technology* 20:100–115.

1999 Examining Stage and Continuum Models of Flake Debris Analysis. *Journal of Archaeological Science* 26:105–116.

2004 Combining Aggregate and Individual Methods of Flake Debris Analysis: Aggregate Trend Analysis. *North American Archaeologist* 25:65–90.

2009 Hit and Misses When Throwing Stones at Mass Analysis. *Journal of Archaeological Science* 26:2788–2796.

2014 Non-metric Continuum-based Flake Analysis. *Lithic Technology* 39:20–38.

Bradbury, Andrew P, and Jay D. Franklin

2000 Raw Material Variability, Package Size, and Mass Analysis. *Lithic Technology* 25:42–58.

Bradley, Bruce, and C. Garth Sampson

1986 Analysis by Replication of Two Acheulian Artefact Assemblages. In *Stone Age Prehistory: Studies in Memory of Charles McBurney,* edited by G. N. Bailey, and P. Callow, pp. 29–45. Cambridge University Press, Cambridge, UK.

Brantingham, P. Jeffrey

2003 A Neutral Model of Stone Raw Material Procurement. *American Antiquity* 68:487–509.

Braun, David R., Joanne C. Tactikos, Joseph V. Ferraro, Shira L. Arnow, and John W. Harris

2008 Oldowan Reduction Sequences: Methodological Considerations. *Journal of Archaeological Science* 35:2153–2163.

Brown, Clifford T.

2001 The Fractal Dimensions of Lithic Reduction. *Journal of Archaeological Science* 28:619–631.

Browne, Constance L., and Lucy Wilson

2013 Evaluating Inputs to Models of Hominin Raw Material Selection: Map Resolution and Path Choices. *Journal of Archaeological Science* 40:3955–3962.

Bryan, Kirk

1950 *Flint-Quarries: The Source of Tools and at the Same Time the Factories of the American Indian.* Peabody Museum of American Archaeology and Ethnology Papers 17(3). Harvard University, Cambridge, MA.

Buck, Paul E., Daniel S. Amick, and William T. Hartwell

1994 *The Midway Valley Site (26NY4759): A Prehistoric Lithic Quarry near Yucca Mountain, Nye County, Nevada.* Desert Research Institute Topics in Yucca Mountain Archaeology No. 1, University of Nevada, Las Vegas, NV.

Bucy, Douglas R.

1974 A Technological Analysis of a Basalt Quarry in Western Idaho. *Tebiwa* 16(2):1–45.

Buenger, Brent A.

2003 The Impact of Wildland and Prescribed Fire on Archaeological Resources. PhD dissertation, Department of Anthropology, University of Kansas, Lawrence, KS.

Burke, Adrian L.

2007 Quartzite Source Areas and the Organization of Stone Tool Technology: A View from Quebec. *Archaeology of Eastern North America* 35:63–80.

Burton, John

1984 Quarrying in a Tribal Society. *World Archaeology* 16:234–247.

Busby, Colin I.

1979 *The Prehistory and Human Ecology of Garden and Coal Valleys: A Contribution to the Prehistory of Southeastern Nevada.* Contributions of the University of California Archaeological Research Facility, No. 39, Berkeley, CA.

Bush, Clarence M.

2004 The Working Qualities of Great Basin Obsidians. Ms. on file, Bureau of Land Management, Ely District, Ely, NV.

Butler, B. Robert

1980 The 1968 Excavations at the Braden Site (10-WN-117), An Early Archaic Cemetery in Western Idaho. In *Anthropological Papers in Memory of Earl H. Swanson, Jr.,* edited by L. Harten, C. Warren, and D. Tuohy, pp. 117–129. Idaho Museum of Natural History, Pocatello, ID.

Byers, David A., Elise Hargiss, and Judson B. Finley

2015 Flake Morphology, Fluvial Dynamics, and Debitage Transport Potential. *Geoarchaeology* 30:379–392.

Byram, R. Scott, Thomas J. Connolly, and Robert R. Musil

1999 Newberry Crater Debitage Analysis. In *Newberry Crater: A Ten-Thousand-Year Record of Human Occupation and Environmental Change in the Basin-Plateau Borderlands,* edited by T. Connolly, pp. 131–150. University of Utah Anthropological Papers No. 121, Salt Lake City, UT.

Cadieux, Nicolas

2013 Size Matters: Measuring Debitage Area and Getting It Right with a Digital Scanner. *Lithic Technology* 38:46–70.

Callahan, Errett

1979   The Basics of Biface Knapping in the Eastern
       Fluted Point Tradition: A Manual for Flint
       Knappers and Lithic Analysts. *Archaeology of
       North America* 7:1–179.

Cameron, David, Peter White, Ronald Lampert,
and Stan Florek

1990   Blowing in the Wind: Site Destruction and
       Site Creation at Hawker Lagoon, South
       Australia. *Australian Archaeology* 30:
       58–69.

Carr, Philip J., and Andrew P. Bradbury

2001   Flake Debris Analysis, Levels of Production,
       and the Organization of Technology. In
       Lithic Debitage: Context, Form, Meaning,
       edited by W. Andrefsky, pp.126–146. Univer-
       sity of Utah Press, Salt Lake City, UT.

2004   Exploring Mass Analysis, Screens, and
       Attributes. In *Aggregate Analysis in Chipped
       Stone*, edited by C. Hall and M. L. Larson,
       pp. 21–44. University of Utah Press, Salt Lake
       City, UT.

Cessford, Craig, and Tristan Carter

2005   Quantifying the Consumption of Obsidian
       at Neolithic Çatalhöyük, Turkey. *Journal of
       Field Archaeology* 30:305–315.

Charnov, Eric L.

1976   Optimal Foraging: The Marginal Value
       Theorem. *Theoretical Population Biology*
       9:129–136.

Cherry, John F., Elissa Z. Faro, and Leah Minc

2010   Field Survey and Geochemical Characteri-
       zation of the Southern Armenian Obsidian
       Sources. *Journal of Field Archaeology* 35:
       147–163.

Church, Tim

2000   Distribution and Sources of Obsidian in the
       Rio Grande Gravels of New Mexico. *Geo-
       archaeology* 15:649–678.

Clark, John E.

1986   Another Look at Small Debitage and Micro-
       debitage. *Lithic Technology* 15:21–33.

1989   Hacia una Definición de Talleres. In *La
       Obsidiana en Mesoamerica*, edited by
       M. Gaxiola G., and J. Clark, pp. 213–217.
       INAH Serie Arqueológico, Mexico City.

Clarkson, Chris

2007   *Lithics in the Land of the Lightning Brothers:
       The Archaeology of Wardaman Country,
       Northern Territory*. Terra Australis 25. Aus-
       tralian National University Press, Canberra,
       Australia.

Cobb, Charles R.

2000   *From Quarry to Cornfield: The Political
       Economy of Mississippian Hoe Production*.
       University of Alabama Press, Tuscalo-
       osa, AL.

Cole, Clint

2006   Prehistoric Obsidian Use in the Upper
       Reaches of Meadow Valley Wash, Eastern
       Nevada. *In-Situ: Newsletter of the Nevada
       Archaeological Association* 10(1):24–30.

2012   Prehistoric Archaeology and the Fremont
       Frontier at North Meadow Valley Wash,
       Eastern Nevada. PhD dissertation, Depart-
       ment of Anthropology, University of Califor-
       nia, Davis, CA.

Collins, Michael B.

1975   Lithic Technology as a Means of Processual
       Inference. In *Lithic Technology: Making and
       Using Stone Tools*, edited by E. Swanson,
       pp. 15–34. Mouton, The Hague, Holland.

Connolly, Thomas J., editor

1999   *Newberry Crater: A Ten-Thousand-Year Rec-
       ord of Human Occupation and Environmen-
       tal Change in the Basin-Plateau Borderland*.
       University of Utah Anthropological Papers
       No. 121, Salt Lake City, UT.

Connolly, Thomas J., William L. Cornett, and
Richard D. Cheatham

1999   The Hot Springs Boat Ramp Site (35DS219).
       In *Newberry Crater: A Ten-Thousand-Year
       Record of Human Occupation and Envi-
       ronmental Change in the Basin-Plateau
       Borderland*, edited by T. Connolly, pp. 53–66.
       University of Utah Anthropological Papers
       No. 121, Salt Lake City, UT.

Connolly, Thomas J., and R. Scott Byram

1999   Obsidian Hydration Analysis. In *Newberry
       Crater: A Ten-Thousand-Year Record of
       Human Occupation and Environmental
       Change in the Basin-Plateau Borderlands*,
       edited by T. Connolly, pp. 175–188. Univer-
       sity of Utah Anthropological Papers No. 121,
       Salt Lake City, UT.

Connolly, Thomas J., Craig E. Skinner, and Paul W.
Baxter

2015   Ancient Trade Routes for Obsidian Cliffs
       and Newberry Volcano Toolstone in the
       Pacific Northwest. In *Toolstone Geography
       of the Pacific Northwest*, edited by T. Ozbun
       and R. Adams, pp. 180–192. Archaeology
       Press, Simon Fraser University, Burnaby, BC,
       Canada.

Copeland, James M., and Richard E. Fike
1988   Fluted Projectile Points in Utah. *Utah Archaeology 1988*:5–28.

Cottrell, Marie G.
1985   Tomato Springs: The Identification of a Jasper Trade and Production Center in Southern California. *American Antiquity* 50:833–849.

Crabtree, Don E.
1972   *An Introduction to Flintworking.* Occasional Papers of the Idaho State University Museum, Pocatello, ID.

Crabtree, R. H., and D. D. Ferraro
1980   *Artifact Assemblages from the Pahranagat, Lincoln County, Nevada.* Technical Report No. 4, Bureau of Land Management, Reno, NV.

Cressman, Luther S.
1937   The Wickiup Damsite No. 1 Knives. *American Antiquity* 3:53–67.

Curewitz, Diane C.
2001   High Elevation Land-Use on the Northern Wasatch Plateau, Manti-La Sal National Forest, Utah. *Journal of California and Great Basin Anthropology* 23:249–272.

Dahlstrom, Bruce, and David G. Bieling
1991   A Morpho-functional Classification System for Bifaces. *Proceedings of the Society for California Archaeology* 4:67–75.

Dames and Moore, Inc.
1994   *Kern River Pipeline Cultural Resources Data Recovery Report, Utah—Volume II: Archaeological Sites along the Pipeline Corridor in Utah.* Ms. on file, Bureau of Land Management Utah State Office.

Davidson, Iain
1988   The Naming of the Parts: Ethnography and the Interpretation of Australian Prehistory. In *Archaeology with Ethnography: An Australian Perspective*, edited by B. Meehan and R. Jones, pp. 17–32. Department of Prehistory, Australian National University, Canberra.

Davis, Leslie B., Stephen A. Aaberg, and James G. Schmitt
1995   *The Obsidian Cliff Plateau Prehistoric Lithic Source, Yellowstone National Park, Wyoming.* United States Department of the Interior, National Park Service, Rocky Mountain Region, Division of Cultural Resources, Selections Series No. 6, Denver, CO.

Davis, Loren G., Alex J. Nyers, and Samuel C. Willis
2014   Context, Provenance and Technology of a Western Stemmed Tradition Artifact Cache from the Cooper's Ferry Site, Idaho. *American Antiquity* 79:596–615.

Delacorte, Michael G.
1985   The George T. Hunting Complex, Deep Springs Valley, California. *Journal of California and Great Basin Anthropology* 7:225–239.

Dickerson, Robert P., Paul R. Bierman, and Gregory Cocks
2015   Alluvial Fan Surfaces and an Age-related Stability for Cultural Resource Preservation: Nevada Test and Training Range, Nellis Air Force Base, Nevada, USA. *Journal of Archaeological Science: Reports* 2:551–568.

Dillian, Carolyn D.
2002   More than Toolstone: Differential Utilization of Glass Mountain Obsidian. PhD dissertation, Department of Anthropology, University of California, Berkeley, CA.

Dillian, Carolyn D., Charles A. Bello, and M. Steven Shackley
2007   Crossing the Delaware: Documenting Super-Long Distance Obsidian Exchange in the Mid-Atlantic. *Archaeology of Eastern North America* 35:93–104.

Doelman, Trudy
2008   *Time to Quarry: The Archaeology of Stone Procurement in Northwestern New South Wales, Australia.* British Archaeological Reports International Series 1801. Archaeopress, Oxford, UK.

Douglass, Matthew J., Simon J. Holdaway, Patricia C. Fanning, and Justin I. Shiner
2008   An Assessment and Archaeological Application of Cortex Measurement in Lithic Assemblages. *American Antiquity* 73:513–526.

Downs, James F.
1966   *The Two Worlds of the Washo: An Indian Tribe of California and Nevada.* Holt, Rinehart, and Winston, New York, NY.

Duke, Daron D.
2008   Obsidian Hydration Chronologies for the Great Salk Lake Desert. In *The Archaeology of Shifting Environments in the Great Salt Lake Desert: A Geoarchaeological Sensitivity Model and Relative Chronology for the Cultural Resources of the U.S. Air Force Utah Testing and Training Range,* edited by D. C. Young, pp. 73–98. Far Western Anthropological Research Group, Davis, CA.

2011   If the Desert Blooms: A Technological Per-
       spective on Paleoindian Ecology in the Great
       Basin from the Old River Bed, Utah. PhD
       dissertation, Department of Anthropology,
       University of Nevada, Reno, NV.

2013   The Exploded Fine-grained Volcanic
       Sources of the Desert West and the Primacy
       of Tool Function in Material Selection.
       North American Archaeologist 34:323–354.

Duke, Daron D., and Ryan M. Byerly

2014   *On the Co-occurrence of Fremont and Late
       Prehistoric Archaeology in Lincoln County,
       Nevada: An Examination of Ceramic and
       Obsidian Data.* BLM Report No. 8111 CRR
       NV 040-13-2062. Far Western Anthropologi-
       cal Research Group, Davis, CA.

Duke, Daron D., and Gregory Haynes

2009   Asking Why in Great Basin Lithic Studies. In
       *Past, Present and Future Issues in Great Basin
       Archaeology: Papers in Honor of Don D.
       Fowler,* edited by B. Hockett, pp. 146–168.
       Bureau of Land Management Nevada
       Cultural Resource Series No. 20, Carson
       City, NV.

Duke, Daron D., and D. Craig Young

2007   Episodic Permanence in Paleoarchaic Basin
       Selection and Settlement. In *Paleoindian or
       Paleoarchaic? Great Basin Human Ecology at
       the Pleistocene/Holocene Transition,* edited
       by K. Graf and D. Schmitt, pp. 123–138. Uni-
       versity of Utah Press, Salt Lake City, UT.

Duff, Andrew I., Jeremy M. Moss, Thomas C.
Windes, John Kantner, and M. Steven Shackley

2012   Patterning in Procurement of Obsidian in
       Chaco Canyon and in Chaco-era Commu-
       nities in New Mexico as Revealed by X-ray
       Fluorescence. *Journal of Archaeological
       Science* 39:2995–3007.

Earl, Dale R.

2010   Toolstone Quarry Exploitation Decisions in
       the Northeastern Great Basin. *Utah Archae-
       ology* 23:85–100.

Eerkens, Jelmer, Jeffrey R. Ferguson, Michael D.
Glascock, Craig E. Skinner, and Sharon A. Waechter

2007   Reduction Strategies and Geochemical
       Characterization of Lithic Assemblages: A
       Comparison of Three Case Studies from
       Western North America. *American Antiquity*
       72:585–597.

Eerkens, Jelmer W., Jerome King, and Eric
Wohlgemuth

2004   The Prehistoric Development of Intensive

       Green-Cone Piñon Processing in Eastern
       California. *Journal of Field Archaeology*
       29(1–2):17–27.

Eerkens, Jelmer W., and J. S. Rosenthal

2004   Are Obsidian Subsources Meaningful Units
       of Analysis? Temporal and Spatial Patterning
       of Subsources in the Coso Volcanic Field,
       Southeastern California. *Journal of Archaeo-
       logical Science* 31:21–29.

Ellis, Chris

1997   Factors Influencing the Use of Stone Projec-
       tile Tips: An Ethnographic Perspective. In
       Prehistoric Technology, edited by H. Knecht,
       pp. 37–74. Plenum, New York, NY.

Elston, Robert G.

1990a A Cost-Benefit Model of Lithic Assemblage
       Variability. In *The Archaeology of James
       Creek Shelter,* edited by R. Elston and
       E. Budy, pp. 153–164. University of Utah
       Anthropological Papers No. 115, Salt Lake
       City, UT.

1990b Lithic Raw Materials: Sources and Utility.
       In *The Archaeology of James Creek Shelter,*
       edited by R. Elston and E. Budy, pp. 165–174.
       University of Utah Anthropological Papers
       No. 115, Salt Lake City, UT.

1992a Modeling the Economics and Organization
       of Lithic Procurement. In *Archaeological
       Investigations at Tosawihi, a Great Basin
       Quarry* (Vol. 1), edited by R. Elston, pp. 31–
       47. Intermountain Research, Silver City, NV.

1992b Introduction to the Tosawihi Quarries. In
       *Archaeological Investigations at Tosawihi,
       a Great Basin Quarry* (Vol. 1), edited by
       R. Elston, pp. 1–6. Intermountain Research,
       Silver City, NV.

1992c Economics and Strategies of Lithic Produc-
       tion at Tosawihi. In *Archaeological Investi-
       gations at Tosawihi, a Great Basin Quarry*
       (Vol. 1), edited by R. Elston, pp. 775–801.
       Intermountain Research, Silver City, NV.

2005   Flakes- and Battered-Stone Artifacts. In
       Camels Back Cave, edited by D. Schmitt and
       D. Madsen, pp. 92–119. University of Utah
       Anthropological Papers No. 125, Salt Lake
       City, UT.

Elston, Robert G., editor

1992   *Archaeological Investigations at Tosawihi, a
       Great Basin Quarry* (Vol. 1). Intermountain
       Research, Silver City, NV.

Elston, Robert G., and Kenneth Juell

1987   *Archaeological Investigations at Panaca Sum-*

mit. Bureau of Land Management Cultural
Resource Series No. 10, Carson City, NV.

Elston, Robert G., and David W. Zeanah

2002   Thinking Outside the Box: A New Perspec-
tive on Diet Breadth and Sexual Division of
Labor in the Prearchaic Great Basin. *World
Archaeology* 34:103–130.

Elston, Robert G., David W. Zeanah, and
B. F. Codding

2014   Living Outside the Box: An Updated
Perspective on Diet Breadth and Sexual
Division of Labor in the Prearchaic Great
Basin. *Quaternary International* 352:200–211.

Elston, Robert G., and Charles D. Zeier

1984   *The Sugarloaf Obsidian Quarry.* Naval
Weapons Center Administrative Publication
313. China Lake, CA.

Environmental Protection Agency

2012   Escalante Desert Watershed—16030006.
http://cfpub.epa.gov/surf/huc.cfm?huc
_code=16030006 (accessed 14 May 2012).

Ericson, Jonathon E.

1977   Egalitarian Exchange Systems in California:
A Preliminary View. In *Exchange Systems in
Prehistory,* edited by T. Earle and J. Ericson,
pp. 109–126. Academic, New York, NY.

1982   Production for Obsidian Exchange in California. In *Contexts for Prehistoric Exchange,*
edited by J. E. Ericson and T. K. Earle,
pp. 129–148. Academic, New York, NY.

1984   Toward the Analysis of Lithic Produc-
tion Systems. In *Prehistoric Quarries and
Lithic Production,* edited by J. Ericson and
B. Purdy, pp. 1–9. University of Cambridge
Press, Cambridge, UK.

Ericson, Jonathon E., and Michael D. Glascock

2004   Subsource Characterization: Obsidian Uti-
lization of Subsources of the Coso Volcanic
Field, Coso Junction, California, USA.
Geoarchaeology 19:779–805.

Estes, Mark B.

2009   Paleoindian Occupations in the Great Basin:
A Comparative Study of Lithic Technologi-
cal Organization, Mobility, and Landscape
Use from Jakes Valley, Nevada. MA Thesis,
Department of Anthropology, University of
Nevada, Reno, NV.

Fanning, Patricia, and Simon Holdaway

2001   Stone Artifact Scatters in Western NSW,
Australia: Geomorphic Controls on Artifact
Size and Distribution. *Geoarchaeology*
16:667–686.

Farrell, Mary M., and Jeffery F. Burton

2010   Plum Family Mammoth Lakes Partnership
Mammoth Lakes, California (TPM 10-01)
Archaeological Survey and Evaluation.
Contributions to Trans-sierran Archaeology
No. 68, Tucson, AZ.

Faull, Mark R.

2006   Emerging Efforts to Define the Coso Obsid-
ian Economic Exchange System in the Rose,
Fremont and Antelope Valleys of the Western
Mojave Desert, California. *Proceedings of the
Society for California Archaeology* 19:159–167.

Féblot-Augustins, Jehanne

2009   Revisiting European Upper Paleolithic
Raw Material Transfers: The Demise of the
Cultural Ecological Paradigm? In *Lithic
Materials and Paleolithic Societies,* edited by
B. Adams and B. Blades, pp. 25–46. Black-
well, Oxford, UK.

Fish, Paul R.

1981   Beyond Tools: Middle Paleolithic Debitage
Analysis and Cultural Inference. *Journal of
Anthropological Research* 37:374–386.

Fladmark, Knut R.

1982   Microdebitage Analysis: Initial Considerations. *Journal of Archaeological Science*
9:205–220.

1984   Mountains of Glass: Archaeology of the
Mount Edziza Obsidian Source, British
Columbia, Canada. *World Archaeology*
16:139–156.

Flenniken, J. Jeffrey

1981   *Replicative Systems Analysis: A Model
Applied to the Vein Quartz Artifacts from the
Hoko River Site.* Laboratory of Anthropology
Report of Investigations No. 59, Washington
State University, Pullman, WA.

2003   Flake Lithic Analysis. In *The Coral Canyon
Project: Archaeological Investigations in the
St. George Basin, Southwestern Utah,* edited
by H. Roberts and R. Ahlstrom, pp. 117–168.
HRA Papers in Archaeology No. 3. HRA
Conservation Archaeology, Las Vegas, NV.

2006   Technological Analyses of the Flaked Stone
Artifacts. In *The Coral Canyon II Project
in the St. George Basin, Southwestern Utah,*
edited by H. Roberts and S. Eskenazi, pp. 99–
119. HRA Archaeological Report 02-09, HRA
Conservation Archaeology, Las Vegas, NV.

Flenniken, J. Jeffrey, and Terry L. Ozbun

1988   Archaeological Investigations in Newberry
Crater, Deschutes National Forest, Central

Oregon. Report No. 4, Lithic Analysts, Pullman, WA.

Foley, Robert A., and Marta Mirazón Lahr
2015   Lithic Landscapes: Early Human Impact from Stone Tool Production on the Central Saharan Environment. *PLoS ONE* 10(3):e0116482.doi:10.1371/journal.pone.0116482.

Fowler, Benjamin L.
2014   Obsidian Toolstone Conveyance: Southern Idaho Forager Mobility. MA thesis, Department of Anthropology, Utah State University, Logan, UT.

Fowler, Catherine S.
1989   *Willard Z. Park's Ethnographic Notes on the Northern Paiute of Western Nevada, 1933–1940, Volume I.* University of Utah Anthropological Papers No. 114, Salt Lake City, UT.

Fowler, Don D., David B. Madsen, and Eugene M. Hattori
1973   *Prehistory of Southeastern Nevada.* Desert Research Institute Publications in the Social Sciences No. 6. Reno, NV.

Frahm, Ellery
2012   What Constitutes an Obsidian "Source"?: Landscape and Geochemical Considerations and Their Archaeological Implications. *International Association of Obsidian Studies Bulletin* 46:16–28.
2016   Can I Get Chips with That? Sourcing Small Obsidian Artifacts Down to Microdebitage Scales with Portable XRF. *Journal of Archaeological Sciences: Reports* 9:448–467.

Garfinkel, Alan P.
2007   Rose Spring Point Chronology and Numic Population Movements in Eastern California. *Pacific Coast Archaeological Society Quarterly* 43:42–49.

Garfinkel, Alan P., Jeanne D. Binning, Elva Younkin, Craig Skinner, Tom Origer, Rob Jackson, Jan Lawson, and Tim Carpenter
2004   The Little Lake Biface Cache, Inyo County, California. *Proceedings of the Society for California Archaeology* 17:87–101.

Gary, Mark A., and Deborah L. McLear-Gary
1990   The Caballo Blanco Biface Cache, Mendocino County, California (CA-MEN-1608). *Journal of California and Great Basin Anthropology* 12:19–27.

Geib, Phil R., and Peter W. Bungart
1989   Implications of Early Bow Use in Glen Canyon. *Utah Archaeology 1989*:32–47.

Geneste, Jean-Michel
1988   Systems d'Approvisionnement en Matieres Premieres au Paleolithique Moyen et au Paleolithique Superieru en Aquitaine. In *L'Homme de Néandertal, Vol. 8, La Mutation,* edited by J. Kozlowski, pp. 61–70. Etudes et Recherches Archéologie de l'Université de Liège, No. 35. Liege, Belgium.

Giambastini, Mark A.
2004   Prehistoric Obsidian Use on the Volcanic Tableland and its Implications for Settlement Patterns and Technological Change in the Western Great Basin. PhD dissertation, Department of Anthropology, University of California, Davis, CA.

Giambastini, Mark A., and Dayna R. Tinsley
2002   *Archaeology Beyond the Virgin Valley: Class III Survey, Testing and Data Recovery for the Lincoln County Land Act, Mesquite, Nevada, Volume I: Technical Report.* Albion Environmental, Santa Cruz, CA.

Gilreath, Amy J. and William R. Hildebrandt
1997   *Prehistoric Use of the Coso Volcanic Field.* Contributions of the University of California Archaeological Research Facility No. 56. Berkeley, CA.
2011   Current Perspectives on the Production and Conveyance of Coso Obsidian. In *Perspectives on Prehistoric Trade and Exchange in California and the Great Basin,* edited by R. Hughes, pp. 171–188. University of Utah Press, Salt Lake City, UT.

Goldstein, Steven
2018   Picking Up the Pieces: Reconstructing Lithic Production Strategies at a Late Holocene Obsidian Quarry in Southern Kenya. *Journal of Field Archaeology* 43:85–101.

Gould, Richard A.
1980   *Living Archaeology.* Cambridge University Press, Cambridge, UK.

Gould, Richard A., and Sherry Saggers
1985   Lithic Procurement in Central Australia: A Closer Look at Binford's Idea of Embeddedness in Archaeology. *American Antiquity* 50:117–136.

Gramly, R. M.
1984   Mount Jasper: A Direct-access Lithic Source Area in the White Mountains of New Hampshire. In *Prehistoric Quarries and Lithic Production,* edited by J. Ericson and B. Purdy, pp. 11–21. Cambridge University Press, Cambridge, UK.

Grayson, Donald K.

2011   *The Great Basin: A Natural Prehistory.* University of California Press, Berkeley, CA.

Greubel, Rand A.

2005   Investigations at Hunchback Shelter (42BE751). In *Kern River 2003 Expansion Project, Utah—Volume III: Prehistoric Excavated Sites and Discoveries,* edited by A. Reed, M. Seddon, and H. Stettler, pp. 195–720. SWCA Environmental Consultants, Salt Lake City, UT.

Greubel, Rand A., and Bradford W. Andrews

2008   Hunchback Shelter: A Fremont Lithic Production Site in the Mineral Mountains of Eastern Utah. *Journal of California and Great Basin Anthropology* 28:43–61.

Griffin, S. Joe

2013   Toward an Understanding of Prehistoric Mobility in the Tahoe Sierra: Optimization Theories and Chipped Stone. MA thesis, Department of Anthropology, California State University, Sacramento, CA.

Haarklau, Lynn

2001   *Investigation of Geochemical Variability in Obsidian Raw Material Sources and Artifacts on the North Nellis Air Force Range, Nevada.* United States Air Force, Nellis AFB, NV, USA.

2005   Table of Point Metrics and Point Graphics. In *Fingerprints in the Great Basin: The Nellis Air Force Base Regional Obsidian Sourcing Study,* edited by L. Haarklau, L. Johnson, and D. Wagner, Appendix C. United States Air Force, Nellis AFB, NV.

Haarklau, Lynn, Lynn Johnson, and David L. Wagner

2005   *Fingerprints in the Great Basin: The Nellis Air Force Base Regional Obsidian Sourcing Study.* United States Air Force, Nellis AFB, NV, USA.

Hafey, R. L.

2003   Archaeology of Sand Spring Valley: Source of Butte Valley Group B Located. Ms. on file, Deptartment of Anthropology and Classical Studies, University of Akron, Akron, OH.

Halford, F. Kirk

2001   New Evidence for Early Holocene Acquisition and Production of Bodie Hills Obsidian. *Society for California Archaeology Newsletter* 35(1):32–37.

2008   *The Coleville and Bodie Hills NRCS Soil Inventory, Walker and Bridgeport, California: A Reevaluation of the Bodie Hills Obsidian Source (CA-MNo-4527) and its Spatial and Chronological Use.* Cultural Resources Report CA-170-07-08, U.S. Dept. of the Interior, Bureau of Land Management, Bishop Field Office, Bishop, CA.

Hall, David R.

1998   Tsini Tsini: A Technological Analysis of a Biface Production Centre in the Talchako River Valley, British Columbia. MA thesis, Department of Archaeology, Simon Fraser University, Burnbaby, BC, Canada.

Hamusek, Blossom, Eric W. Ritter, and Julie Burcell

1997   *Archaeological Explorations in Shasta Valley, California.* United States Bureau of Land Management, Redding Field Office, Cultural Resources Publications, Redding, CA.

Hanson, P. V., and B. Madsen

1983   Flint Axe Manufacture in the Neolithic: An Experimental Investigation of a Flint Axe Manufacture Site at Hastrup Vœnget, East Zealand. *Journal of Danish Archaeology* 2:43–59.

Harper, Christopher, editor

2006   *A Room with a View: Data Recovery of an Early Historic Rockshelter Site Located in the Upper Moapa Valley, Clark County, Nevada.* HRA Papers in Archaeology No. 5. HRA Conservation Archaeology, Las Vegas, NV.

Harrington, Mark R.

1933   *Gypsum Cave, Nevada.* Southwest Museum Papers No. 8. Los Angeles, CA.

Hartley, Ralph J.

1991   Experiments on Artifact Displacement in Canyonlands National Park. *Utah Archaeology* 1991:55–68.

Hartwell, William T., Gregory M. Haynes, and David Rhode

1996   Early Obsidian use and Depletion at Yucca Mountain, Southern Nevada: Evidence from Obsidian Hydration Studies. *Current Research in the Pleistocene* 13:57–59.

Harvey, D. W.

1966   Geographical Processes and the Analysis of Point Patterns: Testing Models of Diffusion by Quadrat Sampling. *Transactions and Papers of the Institute of British Geographers* 40:81–95.

Hatch, James W., Joseph W. Michels, Christopher Stevenson, Barry E. Scheetz, and Richard A. Geidel

1990   Hopewell Obsidian Studies: Behavioral Implications of Recent Sourcing and Dating. *American Antiquity* 55:461–479.

Hatch, John B.

1998   Archaeological Investigation and Techno-
        logical Analysis of the Quartz Mountain
        Obsidian Quarry, Central Oregon. MA
        thesis, Department of Anthropology, Oregon
        State University, Corvallis, OR.

Hauer, A. Craig

2005   An Examination of Shifts in Archaic Mo-
        bility Patterns in the Central Great Basin.
        MA thesis, Department of Anthropology,
        California State University, Chico, CA.

Hayden, Brian

1977   Stone Tool Functions in the Western Desert.
        In *Stone Tools as Cultural Markers,* edited by
        R. Wright, pp. 178–188. Australian Institute of
        Aboriginal Studies, Canberra.

Haynes, Gregory M.

1996   Evaluating Flake Assemblages and Stone
        Tool Distributions at a Large Western
        Stemmed Tradition Site near Yucca Moun-
        tain, Nevada. *Journal of California and Great
        Basin Anthropology* 18:104–130.

Heizer, Robert F., and Adan E. Treganza

1944   Mines and Quarries of the Indians of
        California. *California Journal of Mines and
        Geology* 40:292–330.

Hiscock, Peter, and Scott Mitchell

1993   *Stone Artefact Quarries and Reduction
        Sites in Australia: Towards a Type Profile.*
        Australian Heritage Commission, Technical
        Publications Series No. 4. Canberra.

Hockett, Bryan S.

2009   13,000 Years of Large Game Hunting in the
        Great Basin. In *Past, Present and Future
        Issues in Great Basin Archaeology: Papers in
        Honor of Don D. Fowler,* edited by B. Hock-
        ett, pp. 169–204. United States Department
        of the Interior, Bureau of Land Management
        Nevada Office, Cultural Resource Series
        No. 20.

Hocking, Sara M.

2013   If Rocks Could Talk: Using Central Place
        Foraging Theory in Lithic Production and
        Utilization Research. MA thesis, Department
        of Anthropology, University of Montana,
        Missoula, MT.

Hollenbach, Kandace D.

2009   *Foraging in the Tennessee River Valley, 12,500
        to 8,000 Years Ago.* University of Alabama
        Press, Tuscaloosa, AL.

Holmes, William H.

1892   Modern Quarry Refuse and the Palaeolithic
        Theory. *Science* 20:295–297.

1894a   Natural History of Flaked Stone Implements.
        In *Memoirs of the International Congress
        of Anthropology,* edited by C. S. Wake,
        pp. 120–139. Schulte, Chicago, IL.

1894b   *An Ancient Quarry in Indian Territory.* Bu-
        reau of American Ethnology Bulletin No. 21.
        Smithsonian Institution, Washington, DC.

1900   The Obsidian Mines of Hidalgo, Mexico.
        American Anthropologist 2:405–416.

Houston, Alasdair I.

2011   Central-place Foraging by Humans: Trans-
        port and Processing. *Behavioral Ecology and
        Sociobiology* 65:525–535.

Howell, Ryan

1996   Searching for Standardization: Research
        Toward Replicable Systems of Lithic Deb-
        itage Analysis. Paper presented at the 54th
        Plains Anthropology Conference, Iowa
        City, IA.

Hughes, Richard E.

1984   Mosaic Patterning in Prehistoric California-
        Great Basin Exchange. In *Prehistoric
        Exchange Systems in North America,* edited
        by T. Baugh and J. E. Ericson, pp. 363–383.
        Plenum, New York, NY.

1990   A New Look at Mono Basin Obsidians. In
        *Current Directions in California Obsidian
        Studies,* edited by R. E. Hughes, pp. 1–12.
        Contributions of the University of California
        Archaeological Research Facility No. 48.
        University of California, Berkeley, CA.

2005   Description of Geologic Obsidian Collection
        Locations, 2001 and 2003. In *Fingerprints
        in the Desert: The Nellis Air Force Base
        Regional Obsidian Sourcing Study,* edited by
        L. Haarklau, L. Johnson, and D. L. Wagner,
        Appendix B. United States Air Force, Nellis
        AFB, NV.

2010   Trace Element Characterization of Archae-
        ologically Significant Volcanic Glasses from
        the Southern Great Basin of North America.
        In *Crossing the Straits: Prehistoric Obsidian
        Source Exploitation in the North Pacific
        Rim,* edited by Y. Kuzmin and M. Glascock,
        pp. 165–181. BAR International Series 2152.
        Archaeopress, Oxford, UK.

2012   Field Reconnaissance, Collection, and En-
        ergy Dispersive X-ray Fluorescence Analysis
        of Geologic Obsidian Samples from Lincoln
        County, Nevada. December 18. In *Hydra-
        tion Rates for Four Obsidians in Lincoln
        County, Nevada: Panaca Summit, Meadow
        Valley Mountains, Delamar Mountains, and*

Timpahute Range, edited by A. Rogers and D. Duke, Appendix C. Far Western Anthropological Research Group, Davis, CA.

2014   Long-term Continuity and Change in Obsidian Conveyance at Danger Cave, Utah. In *Archaeology in the Great Basin and Southwest: Papers in Honor of Don D. Fowler*, edited by N. Parezo and J. Janetski, pp. 210–225. University of Utah Press, Salt Lake City, UT.

Hughes, Richard E., and James A. Bennyhoff

1986   Early Trade. In *Handbook of North American Indians, Volume 11, Great Basin*, edited by W. d'Azevedo, pp. 238–255. Smithsonian Institution, Washington, DC.

Hull, Kathleen L

1994   Obsidian Studies. In *Kern River Pipeline Cultural Resources Data Recovery Report: Utah, Vol. I, Research Context and Data Analysis*, pp. 7-1–7-63. Dames and Moore, Las Vegas, NV.

2010   *Research Design for Obsidian Hydration Chronology-building in Lincoln County, Nevada*. University of California-Merced, School of Social Sciences, Humanities, and Arts, Merced, CA.

Humphreys, Kristin H.

1994   Description and Analysis of the Glen Aulin and Pate Valley Obsidian Biface Caches. MA thesis, Department of Anthropology, California State University, Sacramento, CA.

Ingbar, Eric E.

1992   Distribution Studies. In *Archaeological Investigations at Tosawihi, A Great Basin Quarry, Part 3: A Perspective from Locality 36*, edited by R. Elston and C. Raven, pp. 189–221. Intermountain Research, Silver City, NV.

1994   Lithic Material Selection and Technological Organization. In *The Organization of North American Prehistoric Chipped Stone Tool Technologies*, edited by P. Carr, pp. 45–56. International Monographs in Prehistory, Archaeological Series 7, Ann Arbor, MI.

Ingbar, Eric E., Kathryn Ataman, and Mark W. Moore

1992   Debitage. In *Archaeological Investigations at Tosawihi, A Great Basin Quarry, Part 3: A Perspective from Locality 36*, edited by R. Elston and C. Raven, pp. 49–82. Intermountain Research, Silver City, NV.

Ingbar, Eric E., Mary Lou Larson, and Bruce A. Bradley

1989   A Nontypological Approach to Debitage Analysis. In *Experiments in Lithic Technology*, edited by D. Amick and R. Mauldin, pp. 117–136. British Archaeological Reports International Series No. 528, Archaeopress, Oxford, UK.

Isaac, Glynn L.

1967   Towards the Interpretation of Occupation Debris: Some Experiments and Observations. *Kroeber Anthropological Society Papers* 37:31–57.

Jackson, Robert, Jason Spidell, Deirdre Kennelly-Spidell, and Amy Kovak

2009   *A Historic Context for Native American Procurement of Obsidian in the State of Utah*. Pacific Legacy, Cameron Park, CA., for Logan Simpson Design, Inc., Salt Lake City, UT.

Jackson, Thomas L.

1984   A Reassessment of Obsidian Production Analyses for the Bodie Hills and Casa Diablo Quarry Areas. In *Obsidian Studies in the Great Basin*, edited by R. Hughes, pp. 117–134. Contributions of the University of California Archaeological Research Facility, Berkeley, CA.

1988   Amending Models of Trans-Sierran Obsidian Tool Production and Exchange. *Journal of California and Great Basin Anthropology* 10:62–72.

1990   Late Prehistoric Obsidian Production and Exchange in the North Coast Ranges, California. In *Current Directions in California Obsidian Studies*, edited by R. E. Hughes, pp. 79–84. Contributions of the University of California Archaeological Research Facility No. 48. University of California, Berkeley, CA.

Janetski, Joel C.

1981   *Prehistoric and Historic Settlement in the Escalante Desert: A Report of a Class II Cultural Resources Survey of the Proposed MX Missile Operating Base Sites in the Escalante Desert*. University of Utah Archaeological Center Report of Investigations No. 81-10, University of Utah, Salt Lake City, UT.

Janetski, Joel C., Fred Nelson, and James D. Wilde

1988   The Loa Obsidian Cache. *Utah Archaeology* 1:57–65.

Johnson, Ann M., Leslie B. Davis, and Stephen A. Aaberg

1995   Obsidian Cliff National Historic Landmark Nomination. Ms. on file, National Park Center Rocky Mountain Region, Denver, CO.

Johnson, Erika, and Robert McQueen
2012 Mitigation of Cortez Gold Mines' Cortez Hills Expansion Project, Lander and Eureka Counties, Nevada, Volume II, Part 2: Prehistoric Artifacts and Research Issues. Draft report, Summit Envirosolutions, Reno, NV.

Johnson, Jay
1979 Archaic Biface Manufacture: Production Failures, a Chronicle of the Misbegotten. *Lithic Technology* 8:25–35.
1981 *Yellow Creek Archaeological Project, Volume 2.* Tennessee Valley Authority Publications in Anthropology No. 28. Jackson, MS.
1993 North American Biface Production Trajectory Modeling in Historic Perspective. *Plains Anthropologist* 38:151–162.

Johnson, Lynn, and Lynn Haarklau
2005 Results of the Regional Obsidian Projectile Point Sourcing Study. In *Fingerprints in the Desert: The Nellis Air Force Base Regional Obsidian Sourcing Study*, edited by L. Haarklau, L. Johnson, and D. L. Wagner, pp. 115–150. United States Air Force, Nellis AFB, NV, USA.

Johnson, Lynn, and David L. Wagner
2005 Obsidian Source Characterization Study. In *Fingerprints in the Desert: The Nellis Air Force Base Regional Obsidian Sourcing Study*, edited by L. Haarklau, L. Johnson, and D. L. Wagner, pp. 25–50. United States Air Force, Nellis AFB, NV.

Jones, G. T., C. Beck, E. Jones, and R. Hughes
2003 Lithic Source Use and Paleoarchaic Foraging Territories in the Great Basin. *American Antiquity* 68:5–38.

Jones, G. T., L. M. Fontes, R. A. Horowitz, C. Beck, and D. G. Bailey
2012 Reconsidering Paleoarchaic Mobility in the Central Great Basin. *American Antiquity* 77:351–367.

Jones, Rhys, and Neville White
1988 Point Blank: Stone Tool Manufacture at the Ngilipitji Quarry, Arnhem Land, 1981. In *Archaeology with Ethnography: An Australian Perspective,* edited by B. Meehan and R. Jones, pp. 51–87. Australian National University Press, Canberra.

Jones, Robert C., A. BuBarton, S. Edwards, Lonnie C. Pippin, and Colleen M. Beck
2003 *Archaeological Investigations at a Toolstone Source Area and Temporary Camp: Sample Unit 19-25, Nevada Test Site, Nye County, Nevada.* Technical Report No. 77, Quaternary Sciences Center, Desert Research Institute, Las Vegas, NV.

Joseph, Suzanne
2002 Anthropological Evolutionary Ecology: A Critique. *Journal of Ecological Anthropology* 4:6–30.

Kahn, Jennifer G., Peter Mills, Steve Lundblad, John Holson, and Patrick V. Kirch
2009 Tool Production at the Nuʻu Quarry, Maui, Hawaiian Islands: Manufacturing Sequences and Energy-Dispersive X-Ray Fluorescence Analyses. *New Zealand Journal of Archaeology* 30:135–165.

Kelly, Robert L.
1983 Hunter-Gatherer Mobility Strategies. *Journal of Anthropological Research* 39:277–306.

Kessler, Rebecca A., Charlotte Beck, and George T. Jones
2009 Trash: The Structure of Great Basin Paleoarchaic Debitage Assemblages in Western North America. In *Lithic Materials and Paleolithic Societies*, edited by B. Adams and B. Blades, pp. 144–159. Blackwell, Oxford, UK.

King, Jerome
2004 Re-examining Coso Obsidian Hydration Rates. *Proceedings of the Society for California Archaeology* 14:135–142.

King, Jerome, William R. Hildebrandt, and Jeffrey S. Rosenthal
2011 Evaluating Alternative Models for the Conveyance of Bodie Hills Obsidian into Central California. In *Perspectives on Prehistoric Trade and Exchange in California and the Great Basin,* edited by R. Hughes, pp. 148–170. University of Utah Press, Salt Lake City, UT.

Klimowicz, Janis
1991 Obsidian Hydration Analysis of the Buckboard Mesa Road Project Surface Collected Artifacts. In *Archaeological Investigations on the Buckboard Mesa Road Project*, edited by D. Amick, G. Henton and L. C. Pippin, pp. 98–109. Desert Research Institute Technical Report 69. University of Nevada, Reno, NV.

Knell, Edward J.
2014 Terminal Pleistocene-Early Holocene Lithic Technological Organization around Lake Mojave, California. *Journal of Field Archaeology* 39:213–229.

Kodack, Marc
1997   Environmental Structure and its Effect on Hunter-Gatherer Organizational Strategies in Eastern Nevada. PhD dissertation, Department of Anthropology, University of California, Santa Barbara, CA.

Kohler, Timothy A., and Eric Blinman
1987   Solving Mixture Problems in Archaeology: Analysis of Ceramic Materials for Dating and Demographic Reconstruction. *Journal of Anthropological Archaeology* 6:1–28.

Kohntopp, Steve W.
2001   Summary of Four Lithic Caches on the South Central Snake River Plain of Idaho: Their Possible Purposes and Relationships. MA thesis, School of Archaeological Studies, University of Leicester, Leicester, UK.

Kotcho, James P.
2009   The Lithic Technology of a Late Woodland Occupation on the Delaware Bay Kimble's Beach Site (28CM36A), Cape May County, New Jersey. MA thesis, Department of Anthropology, Rutgers University, New Brunswick, NJ.

Kremkau, Scott H., William M. Graves, and Robert M. Wegener
2011   Prehistoric Land Use at Pine and Mathews Canyon Reservoirs: A Class I Overview and Class III Cultural Resources inventory of Pine and Mathews Canyons Dams, Lincoln County, Nevada. Statistical Research, Inc., Technical Report 10-57. Tucson, AZ.

Kuhn, Steven L.
1994   A Formal Approach to the Design and Assembly of Mobile Toolkits. *American Antiquity* 59:426–442.

Kuhn, Steven L., and D. Shane Miller
2015   Artifacts as patches: The Marginal Value Theorem and Stone Tool Life Histories. *Lithic Technological Systems and Evolutionary Theory* 172.

La Pierre, Kish D.
2007   A Preliminary Report of a Rock Feature Complex on the East Side of Searles Lake (CA-SBR-12134/H), Western Mojave Desert, San Bernardino County, California. *Pacific Coast Archaeological Society Quarterly* 43:84–100.

Lafayette, Linsie M., and Geoffrey M. Smith
2012   Use-Wear Traces on Experimental (Replicated) and Prehistoric Stemmed Points from the Great Basin. *Journal of California and Great Basin Anthropology* 32:141–160.

Lavachery, Phillippe, and Els Cornelissen
2000   Natural and Spatial Patterning in the Late Holocene Deposits of Shum Lake Rock Shelter, Cameroon. *Journal of Field Archaeology* 27:153–168.

LaValley, Stephen J.
2011   Continuity in Biface Reduction Strategies at Paiute Creek Shelter (26Hu147), Humboldt County, Nevada. *Nevada Archaeologist* 24:37–46.

Lawrence, Kenneth, Alan Hutchinson, Matthew T. Seddon, Sonia Hutmacher, Clint Lindsay, James Hasbargen, Scott Edmisten, and Krislyn Taite
2005   Site 42WS2453—The ROW Site. In *Kern River 2003 Expansion Project, Utah, Volume III: Prehistoric Excavated Sites and Discoveries*, edited by A. Reed, M. Seddon, and H. Stettler, pp. 1845–1933. SWCA Environmental Consultants, Salt Lake City, UT.

Le Roux, C. T.
1979   Stone Axes of Brittany and the Marches. In *Stone Axe Studies,* edited by T. McK. Clough and W. A. Cummins, pp. 49–56. Council for British Archaeology Research Report 23, London.

Lee, Craig M., and Michael D. Metcalf
2011   Ancient Export or Seasonal Transhumance? A Role for Snake River Plain Obsidian in the Lives of the Ancient Peoples of Northwest Colorado and Southwest Wyoming. *Idaho Archaeologist* 34:13–18.

Lerner, Harry J.
2015   Dynamic Variables and the Use-Related Reduction of Southern Huron Projectile Points. In *Works in Stone: Contemporary Perspectives on Lithic Analysis*, edited by M. Shott, pp. 143–161. University of Utah Press, Salt Lake City, UT.

Liljeblad, Sven
1957   *Indian Peoples in Idaho.* Idaho State University Press, Pocatello, ID.

Liritzis, Ioannis, and Nikolaos Laskaris
2011   Fifty Years of Obsidian Hydration Dating in Archaeology. *Journal of Non-Crystalline Solids* 357:2011–2023.

Lohse, E. S., C. Moser, and D. Sammons
2008   The Smith Cache: A Look into a Knapper's Bag c. 1200 BP. Poster presented at the 2008 Plains Anthropological Conference, Laramie, WY.

Loosle, Byron

2000   The Acquisition of Nonlocal Lithic Material by the Uinta Fremont. *Journal of California and Great Basin Anthropology* 22:277–294.

Lothrop, Jonathan C.

1988   The Organization of Paleoindian Lithic Technology at the Potts Site. PhD dissertation, Department of Anthropology, State University of New York, Binghamton, NY.

Luedtke, Barbara E.

1984   Lithic Material Demand and Quarry Production. In *Prehistoric Quarries and Lithic Production*, edited by J. Ericson and B. Purdy, pp. 65–76. Cambridge University Press, Cambridge, UK.

1992   *An Archaeologist's Guide to Chert and Flint.* Institute of Archaeology, University of California, Los Angeles, Archaeological Research Tools 7. Los Angeles, CA.

Lytle, Farrel W.

2003   Research on Obsidian Artifacts in Lincoln County. Ms. on file, EXAFS Co., Pioche, NV.

2010   Discussion of Lincoln County Obsidian Hydration Data. Ms. on file, EXAFS Co., Pioche, NV.

Lytle, Farrel W., and Nicholas E. Pingitore

2004   Iron Valence in the Hydration Layer of Obsidian: Characterization by X-ray Absorption Spectroscopy. *Microchemical Journal* 71:185–191.

Mackay, Glen R.

2004   The Nii'ii Hunting Stand Site: Understanding Technological Practice as Social Practice in Subarctic Prehistory. MA thesis, Department of Anthropology, University of Victoria, Victoria, BC, Canada.

Madsen, David B.

2007   The Paleoarchaic to Archaic Transition in the Great Basin. In *Paleoindian or Paleoarchaic? Great Basin Human Ecolety at the Pleistocene/Holocene Transition*, edited by K. Graf and D. Schmitt, pp. 3–20. University of Utah Press, Salt Lake City, UT.

Magne, Martin P.

1985   *Lithics and Livelihood: Stone Tool Technologies of Central and Southern Interior British Columbia.* National Museum of Man, Archaeological Survey of Canada Paper No. 133. Ottawa, Canada.

Magne, Martin P., and David Pokotylo

1981   A Pilot Study in Bifacial Lithic Reduction Sequences. *Lithic Technology* 10:34–47.

Marschall, Mary E.

2004   A Preliminary Regional Analysis of Lithic Cache Sites in Central Oregon. MA thesis, Department of Anthropology, Oregon State University, Corvallis, OR.

Martin, Cheryl M.

2009   Analysis of Flaked Stone Lithics from Virgin Anasazi Sites near Mt. Trumbull, Arizona Strip. MA thesis, Department of Anthropology, University of Nevada, Las Vegas, NV.

Martinez, Jesse E.

1999   An Archaeological Investigation of the Mt. Hicks Obsidian Source, Mineral County, Nevada. MA thesis, Department of Anthropology, California State University, Sacramento, CA.

Marwick, Ben

2013   Multiple Optima in Hoabinhian Flaked Stone Artefact Palaeoeconomics and Palaeoecology at Two Archaeological Sites in Northwest Thailand. *Journal of Anthropological Archaeology* 32:553–564.

Mauldin, Raymond P., and Daniel S. Amick

1989   Investigating Patterning in Debitage from Experimental Bifacial Core Reduction. In *Experiments in Lithic Technology*, edited by D. Amick and R. Mauldin, pp. 67–88. British Archaeological Reports International Series No. 528, Oxford, UK.

McCutcheon, Patrick T., and Robert C. Dunnell

1998   Variability in Crowley's Ridge Gravel. In *Changing Perspectives on the Archaeology of the Central Mississippi Valley*, edited by M. O'Brien and R. Dunnell, pp. 258–280. University of Alabama, Tuscaloosa, AL.

McGuire, Kelly, and Richard V. Ahlstrom

2012   Gray, Buff, and Brown: Untangling Chronology, Trade and Culture in the Las Vegas Valley, Southern Nevada. In *Meetings at the Margins: Prehistoric Cultural Interactions in the Intermountain West*, edited by D. Rhode, pp. 211–228. University of Utah Press, Salt Lake City, UT.

McGuire, Kelly, Kimberley L. Carpenter, and Jeffrey Rosenthal

2012   Great Basin Hunters of the Sierra Nevada. In *Meetings at the Margins: Prehistoric Cultural Interactions in the Intermountain West*, edited by D. Rhode, pp. 124–141. University of Utah Press, Salt Lake City, UT.

McGuire, Kelly, William Hildebrandt, Amy Gilreath, Jerome King, and John Berg

2014   *The Prehistory of Gold Butte: A Virgin River Hinterland, Clark County, Nevada.* University of Utah Anthropological Papers No. 127, Salt Lake City, UT.

McKee, Brian R.

2009   Obsidian Sourcing, Curation, and Mobility in Western Utah. Poster presented at the 74th Annual Meeting of the Society for American Archaeology, Atlanta, GA.

McKee, Brian R., Brandon M. Gabler, Damon Stone, and Jocelyn Bernatchez

2013   The Lithic Landscape and Cultural Use of Stone along the UNEV Pipeline Corridor. In *Data Recovery Along the UNEV Pipeline Utah Segment—Davis, Salt Lake, Tooele, Juab, Millard, Beaver, Iron and Washington Counties, Vol. VI: Prehistoric Synthesis and Concluding Thoughts on Prehistoric Research*, edited by M. Medeiros, J. Bernatchez, and J. Ravesloot, pp. 77–120. Technical Report No. 2011-29, WSA, Tucson, AZ.

McKee, Brian R., Brandon M. Gabler, Damon Stone, and Michael J. Boley

2010   Great Basin Raw Material Selection in a Redundant Lithic Landscape. Poster presented at the 33rd Great Basin Anthropological Conference, Layton, UT.

McLaren, D., and N. Smith

2008   The Stratigraphy of Bifacial Implements at the Richardson Island Site, Haida Gwaii. In *Projectile Point Sequences in Northwestern North America*, edited by R. Carlson and M. Magne, pp. 41–60. Archaeological Press Simon Fraser University, Burnaby, BC, Canada.

Menocal, Tatianna

2010   Chipped Stone Analysis of the Yamashita Sites in Moapa Valley, Nevada: A Technological Organization Approach. Unpublished MA thesis, Department of Anthropology, University of Nevada, Las Vegas, NV.

Metcalfe, Duncan and K. R. Barlow

1992   A Model for Exploring the Optimal Trade-off between Field Processing and Transport. *American Anthropologist* 94:340–356.

Michie, James L.

1990   Bioturbation and Gravity as Potential Site Formation Processes: The Open Area Site, 38GE261, Georgetown County, South Carolina. *South Carolina Antiquities* 22:27–46.

Miller, D. Shane

2018   *From Colonization to Domestication: Population, Environment, and the Origins of Agriculture in Eastern North America.* University of Utah Press, Salt Lake City, UT.

Miller, D. Shane, and Ashley M. Smallwood

2012   Modeling Clovis Biface Production at the Topper Site, South Carolina. In *Contemporary Lithic Analysis in the Southeast: Problems, Solutions, and Interpretations*, edited by P. Carr, A. Bradbury and S. Price, pp. 28–42. University of Alabama Press, Tuscaloosa, AL.

Mills, William C.

1921   Flint Ridge. *Ohio Archaeological and Historical Publications* 30:91–161.

Milne, S. Brooke

2009   Debitage Sample Size and its Implications for Understanding Lithic Assemblage Variability. *Canadian Journal of Archaeology* 33:4–64.

Mone, Sheila, and Cynthia Adams

1988   CA-MNO-574 and -833: A Look at Casa Diablo Obsidian Production at Stoneworking Sites in Long Valley, Mono County. *Proceedings of the Society for California Archaeology* 1:17–37.

Moore, Joe

2009   Great Basin Tool-Stone Sources: The NDOT Obsidian and Tool-Stone Sourcing Project: 2002 Progress Report. Nevada Department of Transportation, Carson City, NV. (Originally issued in 2002).

Morrison, Donna M.

1994   Validity in Lithic Debitage Analysis: An Experimental Assessment Comparing Quartzite to Obsidian. MA thesis, Department of Archaeology, Simon Fraser University, Burnaby, BC, Canada.

Morrow, Toby A.

1997   A Chip Off the Old Block: Alternative Approaches to Debitage Analysis. *Lithic Technology* 22:51–69.

Moutsiou, Theodora

2014   *The Obsidian Evidence for the Scale of Social Life during the Palaeolithic.* BAR International Series 2613. Archaeopress, Oxford, UK.

Musil, Robert R.

2004   If It Ain't Fixed Don't Flute It: Form and Context in the Classification of Early Projectile Points in the Far West. In *Early and Middle Holocene Archaeology of the Northern Great Basin*, edited by D. Jenkins,

T. Connolly, and C. Aikens, pp. 271–280.
University of Oregon Anthropological
Papers 62. Eugene, OR.

Muto, Guy R.
1971   A Stage Analysis of the Manufacture of
        Stone Tools. In *Great Basin Anthropological
        Conference 1970: Selected Papers*, edited by
        M. Aikens, pp.109–118. University of Oregon
        Anthropological Papers No. 1. Eugene, OR.

Nance, Jack
1981   Statistical Fact and Archaeological Faith:
        Two Models in Small-Sites Sampling. *Jour-
        nal of Field Archaeology* 8:151–165.
1983   Regional Sampling in Archaeological Sur-
        vey: The Statistical Perspective. *Advances
        in Archaeological Method and Theory* 6:
        289–356.

Natoli, Amelia, Cannon Daughtrey, Scott Kremkau,
and Rita Sulkosky.
2011   Land Use and Subsistence Patterns in South-
        eastern Nevada: Projectile Point Analysis
        in Pine and Mathews Canyons, Lincoln
        County. Poster presented at the 76th Annual
        Meeting of the Society for American Archae-
        ology, Sacramento, CA.

Nelson, Aimee M., Dinesh Bastakoti, and John V.
Dudgeon
2012   Do Performance Characteristics Explain
        Variation in Archaeological Selection
        and Use of Snake River Obsidian? Paper
        presented at the 77th Annual Meeting of
        the Society for American Archaeology,
        Memphis, TN.

Nelson, Fred
1984   X-ray Fluorescence of Some Western North
        American Obsidians. In *Obsidian Studies
        in the Great Basin*, edited by R. E. Hughes,
        pp. 27–62. Contributions of the University of
        California Archaeological Research Facility
        No. 45, Berkeley, CA.

Nelson, Fred, and Richard D. Holmes
1978   Trace Element Analysis of Obsidian Sources
        and Artifacts from Western Utah. *Antiquities
        Section Selected Papers*, Vol. 6(15). Salt Lake
        City, UT.

Nelson, Margaret C.
1987   Site Content and Structure: Metate Quarries
        and Workshops in the Maya Highlands.
        In *Lithic Studies Among the Contemporary
        Highland Maya*, edited by B. Hayden,
        pp. 120–147. University of Arizona,
        Tucson, AZ.

Nelson, Zachary
2000   Analysis of an Obsidian Workshop at
        Hacienda Metepec, Teotihuacán, Mexico,
        AD 700–800. MA thesis, Department of
        Anthropology, Brigham Young University,
        Provo, UT.

Nevada Bureau of Mines
1964   *Mineral and Water Resources of Nevada.*
        Nevada Bureau of Mines Bulletin 65, Mackay
        School of Mines, University of Nevada,
        Reno, NV.

Newcomer, Mark H.
1971   Some Quantitative Experiments in Handaxe
        Manufacture. *World Archaeology* 3:85–94.

Newcomer, Mark H., and G. de G. Sieveking
1980   Experimental Flake Scatter-Patterns: A New
        Interpretative Technique. *Journal of Field
        Archaeology* 7:345–52.

Newlander, Khori S.
2012   Exchange, Embedded Procurement, and
        Hunter-Gatherer Mobility: A Case Study
        from the North American Great Basin. PhD
        dissertation, Department of Anthropology,
        University of Michigan, Ann Arbor, MI.
2018   Imagining the Cultural Landscapes of
        Paleoindians. *Journal of Archaeological
        Sciences: Reports* 19:836–845.

Noll, Christopher D.
2012   The Development of Lithic Extraction Areas
        in the Okanogan Highlands during the Late
        Holocene: Evidence from Curlew Lake,
        Washington. *Journal of Northwest Anthro-
        pology* 46:227–242.

Northwest Research Obsidian Studies Laboratory
Source Catalog
2012   http://www.sourcecatalog.com/ut/s_ut.html.
        Accessed 6 March 2012.

Norton, Mark R.
2008   Obsidian Research in Tennessee and Ala-
        bama. *Tennessee Archaeology* 3:123–130.

Origer, Thomas
2012   Letter report to Far Western Anthropological
        Research Group, Inc. Origer's Obsidian Lab-
        oratory, Rohnert Park, CA. August 28. In *Hy-
        dration Rates for Four Obsidians in Lincoln
        County, Nevada: Panaca Summit, Meadow
        Valley Mountains, Delamar Mountains, and
        Timpahute Range*, edited by A. Rogers and
        D. Duke, Appendix D. Far Western Anthro-
        pological Research Group, Davis, CA.

Ozbun, Terry L.
2011   The Inadequacy of ¼ Inch Mesh Screen in

Archaeology. *Journal of Northwest Anthropology* 45:235–242.

Panich, Lee M., Érika M. Mondragón, and Antonio P. Michelini
2015   Exploring Patterns of Obsidian Conveyance in Baja California, Mexico. *Journal of California and Great Basin Anthropology* 35:257–274.

Park, Robin J.
2010   A Culture of Convenience? Obsidian Source Selection in Yellowstone National Park. MA thesis, Department of Archaeology and Anthropology, University of Saskatchewan, Saskatoon, Canada.

Parkman, E. Breck
1983   A Note Concerning the Archaeology of Annadel State Park. *Journal of California and Great Basin Archaeology* 5:255–259.

Parsons, Anthony J., Athol D. Abrahams, and Alan D. Howard
2009   Rock-Mantled Slopes. In *Geomorphology of Desert Environments*, edited by A. Parsons and A. Abrahams, pp. 233–263. Springer, Berlin, Germany.

Patterson, Leland
1990   Characteristics of Bifacial-reduction Flake-size Distributions. *American Antiquity* 55:550–558.

Pavesic, Max G.
1966   A Projectile Point "Blank" Cache from Southeastern Idaho. *Tebiwa* 9:52–57.

Pedrick, Kathryn E.
1985   *The Lake Range Quarry, Washoe County, Nevada.* Bureau of Land Management Nevada Office, Technical Report No. 14. Reno, NV.

Pelcin, Andrew W.
1996   Controlled Experiments in the Production of Flake Attributes. PhD dissertation, Department of Anthropology, University of Pennsylvania, Philadelphia, PA.

Pelegrin, Jacques, and Claude Chauchat
1993   Tecnología y Función de las Puntas de Paiján: El Aporte de la Experimentación. *Latin American Antiquity* 4:367–382.

Pendleton, Lorann S.
1979   Lithic Technology in Early Nevada Assemblages. MA thesis, Department of Anthropology, California State University, Long Beach, CA.

Perreault, Charles, and P. Jeffrey Brantingham
2011   Mobility-driven Cultural Transmission along the Forager-Collector Continuum. *Journal of Anthropological Archaeology* 30:62–68.

Petraglia, Michael D., and David T. Nash
1987   The Impact of Fluvial Processes on Experimental Sites. In *Natural Formation Processes and the Archaeological Record,* edited by D. Nash and M. Petraglia, pp. 108–130. British Archaeological Reports International Series 352. BAR, Oxford, UK.

Petraglia, Michael D., and Richard Potts
1994   Water Flow and the Formation of Early Pleistocene Artifact Sites in Olduvai Gorge, Tanzania. *Journal of Anthropological Anthropology* 13:228–254.

Pitblado, Bonnie L.
2003   *Late Paleoindian Occupation of the Southern Rocky Mountains: Early Holocene Projectile Points and Land Use in the High Country.* University Press of Colorado, Boulder, CO.

Poesen, Jean W. Bas van Wesemael, Kristin Bunte, and Albert S. Benet
1998   Variation of Rock Fragment Cover and Size along Semiarid Hillslopes: A Case-Study from Southeast Spain. *Geomorphology* 23:323–335.

Pope, Saxton T.
1923   *A Study of Bows and Arrows.* University of California Press, Berkeley, CA.

Premo, L. S.
2012   The Shift to a Predominantly Logistical Mobility Strategy Can Inhibit Rather than Enhance Forager Interaction. *Human Ecology* 40:647–649.

Prentiss, William C.
1998   The Reliability and Validity of a Lithic Debitage Typology: Implications for Archaeological Interpretation. *American Antiquity* 63:635–650.

Presnyakova, Darya, Will Archer, David R. Braun, and Wesley Flear
2015   Documenting Differences between Early Stone Age Flake Production Systems: An Experimental Model and Archaeological Verification. *PLoS One* 10(6):e0130732.

Price, B. A., A. G. Gold, B. S. Tejada, D. D. Earle, S. Griset, J. B. Lloyd, M. Baloian, N. Valente, V. S. Popper, and L. Anderson
2009   The Archaeology of CA-LAN-192: Lovejoy Springs and Western Mojave Desert Prehistory. Applied EarthWorks, Fresno, CA.

Putzi, Jeffrey L., Nathaniel J. DiVito, Carl E. Sholin, Peter R. Mills, Steven Lundblad, Bobby Camara, and Thomas S. Dye

2015   Alternative Models of Volcanic Glass Quarrying and Exchange in Hawai'i. *Journal of Archaeological Science: Reports* 2:341–352.

R Core Team

2013   R: A Language and Environment for Statistical Computing. R Foundation for Statistical Computing, Vienna, Austria. http://www.R-project.org/.

Railey, Jim, and Eric J. Gonzales

2015   The Problem with Flake Types and the Case for Attribute Analysis of Debitage Assemblages. In *Works in Stone: Contemporary Perspectives on Lithic Analysis,* edited by M. J. Shott, pp. 11–32. University of Utah Press, Salt Lake City, UT.

Redman, Kimberly L.

1997   An Experiment-based Evaluation of the Debitage Attributes Associated with "Hard" and "Soft" Hammer Percussion. MA Thesis, Department of Anthropology, Washington State University, Pullman, WA.

Reed, Alan D., Matthew T. Seddon, and Heather K. Stettler

2005a   *Kern River 2003 Expansion Project, Utah: Cultural Resources Mitigation Report Vol. II: A Synthesis of Archaeological Research along the Kern River Pipeline Corridor.* SWCA Environmental Consultants, Salt Lake City, UT, USA.

2005b   *Kern River 2003 Expansion Project, Utah-Volume III: Prehistoric Excavated Sites and Discoveries.* SWCA Environmental Consultants, Salt Lake City, UT.

Rego, Justin P.

2010   A Lithic Technological Analysis of the Nunnery Collection Bifaces from the Toby-Thornhill Site in Lauderdale County, Mississippi. MA Thesis, Department of Anthropology, University of Mississippi. Oxford, MS.

Reid, Ian, and Lynne E. Frostick

1985   Arid Zone Slopes and Their Archaeological Materials. In *Themes in Geomorphology,* edited by A. Pitty, pp. 141–157. Croom Helm, London.

Renfrew, Colin

1984   *Approaches to Social Archaeology.* Harvard University Press, Cambridge, MA.

Reno, Ronald L., and Lonnie C. Pippin

1986   *An Archaeological Reconnaissance of the Groom Range, Lincoln County, Nevada.* Desert Research Institute Social Sciences Center Technical Report No. 46. Las Vegas, NV.

Riciputi, Lee R., J. Michael Elam, Larry M. Anovitz, and David R. Cole

2002   Obsidian Diffusion Dating by Secondary Ion Mass Spectrometry: A Test Using Results from Mound 65, Chalco, Mexico. *Journal of Archaeological Science* 29:1055–1075.

Rick, John W.

1976   Downslope Movement and Archaeological Intrasite Spatial Analysis. *American Antiquity* 41:133–144.

Rick, John W., and Thomas L. Jackson

1992   A Funny Thing Happened on the Way from the Quarry…Analysis of the Great Blades Cache of Northern California. In *Stone Tool Procurement, Production, and Distribution in California Prehistory,* edited by J. Arnold, pp. 5–62. Perspectives in California Archaeology, Volume 2. Institute of Archaeology, University of California, Los Angeles, CA.

Ridings, Rosanna

1996   Where in the World Does Obsidian Hydration Dating Work? *American Antiquity* 61:136–148.

Riley, Lynn, David C. Bachman, Glen Mellin, JoAnn E. Jamison, Barbara H. Silber, J. F. Custer, and David J. Grettler

1994   Phase II Archaeological Excavation of All Prehistoric Sites in the Early Action Segment of the Delaware Route 1 Corridor, New Castle and Kent Counties. Archaeological Series No. 101. Delaware Department of Transportation, Dover, DE.

Roberts, Heidi, and Suzanne Eskenazi

2006   The Coral Canyon II Project in the St. George Basin, Southwestern Utah. HRA Archaeological Report 02-09. HRA Conservation Archaeology, Las Vegas, NV.

Roberts, Heidi, and J. Jeffrey Flenniken

2008   New Methods of Analyzing Flaked Stone Quarries. *Nevada Archaeologist* 23:45–56.

Roberts, Theodore

2008   Footprints and "Fingerprints": A Northern Arizona Geochemical Study of Archaic Period Lithic Procurement and Mobility. MA Thesis, Department of Anthropology, Northern Arizona University, Flagstaff, AZ.

Robins, Richard

1999   Lessons Learnt from a Taphonomic Study of Stone Artefact Movement in an Arid

Environment. In *Taphonomy: The Analysis of Processes from Phytoliths to Megafauna*, edited by M-J Mountain and D. Bowdery, pp. 93–106. Papers in Archaeology and Natural History No. 30, Department of Archaeology and Natural History, Australian National University, Canberra.

Rogers, Alexander K.
2003   A Reassessment of Obsidian Hydration Ages of Projectile Point Types from the Coso Volcanic Field. *Pacific Coast Archaeological Society Quarterly* 39:23–38.
2007   Effective Hydration Temperature of Obsidian: A Diffusion Theory Analysis of Time-Dependent Hydration Rates. *Journal of Archaeological Science* 34:656–665.
2008   Obsidian Hydration Dating: Accuracy and Resolution Limitations Imposed by Intrinsic Water Variability. *Journal of Archaeological Science* 35:2009–2016.

Rogers, Alexander K., and Daron G. Duke
2014   Hydration Rates for Four Obsidians in Lincoln County, Nevada: Panaca Summit, Meadow Valley Mountains, Delamar Mountains, and Timpahute Range. Far Western Anthropological Research Group, Davis, CA.

Rogers, J. Daniel
1982   The Experimental Determination of Lithic Tool Manufacturing Goals. In *Spiro Archaeology: 1980 Research*, edited by J. D. Rogers, pp. 93–115. Oklahoma Archaeological Survey, Studies in Oklahoma's Past No. 9, Norman, OK.

Root, Matthew J.
1992   The Knife River Flint Quarries: The Organization of Stone Tool Production. PhD dissertation, Department of Anthropology, Washington State University, Pullman, WA.
1997   Production for Exchange at the Knife River Flint Quarries, North Dakota. *Lithic Technology* 22:33–50.
2004   Technological Analysis of Flake Debris and the Limitations of Size-Grade Techniques. In *Aggregate Analysis in Chipped Stone*, edited by C. Hall and M. L. Larson, pp. 65–93. University of Utah Press, Salt Lake City, UT.

Rowan, Robert R., and David H. Thomas
1982   Microwear Analysis of Gatecliff Lithics. In *The Archaeology of Monitor Valley 2: Gatecliff Shelter*, edited by D. Thomas, pp. 320–331. Anthropological Papers of the American Museum of Natural History Vol. 59, Part 1. New York, NY.

Rowley, Peter D., Farrel W. Lytle, Manetta B. Lytle, and Keith R. Stever
2002   *Geology of the Modena Obsidian Source, Lincoln County, Nevada*. Geological Mapping, Inc., New Harmony, UT, and the EXAFS Co., Pioche, NV.

Rusco, Mary K. and Jeanne Muñoz
1983   *An Archaeological Survey in the Mormon Mountains, Lincoln County, Nevada*. Bureau of Land Management, Contributions to the Study of Cultural Resources, Technical Report No. 11. Reno, NV.

Sanders, Thomas N.
1983   The Manufacturing of Chipped Stone Tools at a Paleo-Indian Site in Western Kentucky. MA thesis, Department of Anthropology, University of Kentucky, Lexington, KY.

Sappington, R. L.
1984   Procurement without Quarry Production: Examples from Southwestern Idaho. In *Prehistoric Quarries and Lithic Production*, edited by J. Ericson and B. Purdy, pp. 23–34. Cambridge University Press, Cambridge, UK.

Schick, Kathy D.
1986   *Stone Age Sites in the Making: Experiments in the Formation and Transformation of Archaeological Occurrences*. BAR International Series 319, BAR, Oxford, UK.
1987   Experimentally-derived Criteria for Assessing Hydrologic Disturbance of Archaeological Sites. In *Natural Formation Processes and the Archaeological Record,* edited by D. Nash and M. Petraglia, pp. 86–107. British Archaeological Reports International Series 352, BAR, Oxford, UK.
1992   Geoarchaeological Analysis of an Acheulean Site at Kalambo Falls, Zambia. *Geoarchaeology* 7:1–26.

Schiffer, Michael B.
1975   The Effects of Occupation Span on Site Content. In *The Cache River Archeological Project: An Experiment in Contract Archeology*, edited by M. B. Schiffer and J. House, pp. 265–269. Arkansas Archeological Survey Research Series No. 8, Fayetteville, AR.

Schweitzer, Robert
2001   Site 26LN6: Nine Mile Hill Site. In *Playa to Panaca: Results of Archaeological Investigations for the Level (3) Communications Fiber Optic Line from Las Vegas to the Utah/Nevada Border, Clark and Lincoln Counties, Nevada, Vol. IV: Methods and Results of Data Recovery at Eleven Prehistoric Sites*, edited

by M. T. Seddon, C. Kelly, A. Wright, and
K. Taite, pp. 54–63. SWCA Environmental
Consultants, Report No. 01-153, Salt Lake
City, UT.

Schweitzer, Robert, Alan Hutchinson, Sonia Hutmacher, James Hasbargen, Clint Lindsay, Matthew T.
Seddon, Scott Edmisten, and Krislyn Taite

2005a   Site 42WS1460—The Monkey's Paw Site. In
        *Kern River 2003 Expansion Project, Utah,
        Vol. III: Prehistoric Excavated Sites and Dis-
        coveries*, edited by A. Reed, M. Seddon and
        H. Stettler, pp. 1325–1469. SWCA Environ-
        mental Consultants, Salt Lake City, UT.

Schweitzer, Robert, Alan Hutchinson, Sonia
Hutmacher, Matthew T. Seddon, Scott Edmisten,
Clint Lindsay, James Hasbargen, and Krislyn Taite

2005b   Site 42WS1579—The Crucible Site. In *Kern
        River 2003 Expansion Project, Utah, Vol. III:
        Prehistoric Excavated Sites and Discover-
        ies*, edited by A. Reed, M. Seddon and H.
        Stettler, pp. 1503–1617. SWCA Environmental
        Consultants, Salt Lake City, UT.

Schweitzer, Robert, and Matthew T. Seddon

2001   Sailing an Obsidian Sea: The Panaca
        Summit Archeological District. In *Playa to
        Panaca: Results of Archaeological Investi-
        gations for the Level (3) Communications
        Fiber Optic Line from Las Vegas to the Utah/
        Nevada Border, Clark and Lincoln Counties,
        Nevada, Vol. IV: Methods and Results of Data
        Recovery at Eleven Prehistoric Sites*, edited
        by M. T. Seddon, C. Kelly, A. Wright, and
        K. Taite, pp. 356–361. SWCA Environmental
        Consultants, Report No. 01-153, Salt Lake
        City, UT.

Schyle, Daniel

2007   *Ramat Tamar and Metzad Mazal: The
        Early Neolithic Economy of Flint Mining and
        Production of Bifacials Southwest of the Dead
        Sea*. Ex oriente, Berlin, Germany.

Scott, Sara A.

1991   Problems with the Use of Flake Size in
        Inferring Stages of Lithic Reduction. *Journal
        of California and Great Basin Anthropology*
        13:172–179.

Scott, Sara A., Carl M. Davis, and J. Jeffrey Flenniken

1986   The Pahoehoe Site: A Lanceolate Biface
        Cache in Central Oregon. *Journal of Califor-
        nia and Great Basin Anthropology* 8:7–23.

Seddon, Matthew T.

2001a   A Preliminary Relative Obsidian Hydration
        Chronology for Panaca Summit/Modena

Area Obsidian in Southeast Nevada. In *Playa
to Panaca: Results of Archaeological Inves-
tigations for the Level (3) Communications
Fiber Optic Line from Las Vegas to the Utah/
Nevada Border, Clark and Lincoln Counties,
Nevada, Vol. IV: Methods and Results of Data
Recovery at Eleven Prehistoric Sites*, edited
by M. T. Seddon, C. Kelly, A. Wright, and
K. Taite, pp. 42–53. SWCA Environmental
Consultants, Report No. 01-153, Salt Lake
City, UT.

2001b   Searching for Home Base: Evaluating
        Site Type Models for the Panaca Summit
        Archeological District. In *Playa to Panaca:
        Results of Archaeological Investigations for
        the Level (3) Communications Fiber Optic
        Line from Las Vegas to the Utah/Nevada
        Border, Clark and Lincoln Counties, Nevada,
        Vol. IV: Methods and Results of Data Recov-
        ery at Eleven Prehistoric Sites*, edited by M. T.
        Seddon, C. Kelly, A. Wright, and K. Taite,
        pp. 337–355. SWCA Environmental Consul-
        tants, Report No. 01-153, Salt Lake City, UT.

2005a   A Revised Relative Obsidian Hydration
        Chronology for Wild Horse Canyon, Black
        Rock Area, and Panaca Summit/Modena
        Obsidian. In *Kern River 2003 Expansion
        Project, Utah, Vol. IV: Prehistoric Synthesis,
        Part 2*, edited by A. Reed, M. Seddon, and
        H. Stettler, pp. 447–497. SWCA Environ-
        mental Consultants, Salt Lake City, UT.

2005b   Interpreting Obsidian Hydration Re-
        sults within the Framework of a Relative
        Chronology. In *Kern River 2003 Expansion
        Project, Utah, Vol. IV: Prehistoric Synthesis,
        Part 2*, edited by A. Reed, M. Seddon and
        H. Stettler, pp. 499–524. SWCA Environ-
        mental Consultants, Salt Lake City, UT.

2005c   A Revised Model of Obsidian Procurement
        and Use in the Eastern Great Basin. In *Kern
        River 2003 Expansion Project, Utah, Vol. IV:
        Prehistoric Synthesis, Part 2*, edited by
        A. Reed, M. Seddon and H. Stettler, pp. 687–
        707. SWCA Environmental Consultants, Salt
        Lake City, UT.

Seddon, Matthew, Christina Kelly, Alyssa Wright,
and Krislyn Taite

2001   *Playa to Panaca: Results of Archaeological In-
        vestigations for the Level (3) Communications
        Fiber Optic Line from Las Vegas to the Utah/
        Nevada Border, Clark and Lincoln Counties,
        Nevada, Vol. IV: Methods and Results of Data*

Recovery at Eleven Prehistoric Sites. SWCA Environmental Consultants, Report No. 01-153, Salt Lake City, UT.

Shackley, M. Steven

1994 Intersource and Intrasource Geochemical Variability in Two Newly Discovered Archaeological Obsidian Sources in the Southern Great Basin. *Journal of California and Great Basin Anthropology* 16:118–129.

2002 More than Exchange: Pre-Ceramic through Ceramic Period Obsidian Studies in the Greater North American Southwest. In *Geochemical Evidence for Long-Distance Exchange*, edited by M. Glascock, pp. 53–87. Bergin & Garvey, Westport, CT.

2005 *Obsidian: Geology and Archaeology in the North American Southwest.* University of Arizona Press, Tucson, AZ.

Shafer, Harry J., and Thomas R. Hester

1983 Ancient Maya Chert Workshops in Northern Belize, Central America. *American Antiquity* 48:519–543.

Sharrock, Floyd W.

1966 *Prehistoric Occupation Patterns in Southwest Wyoming and Cultural Relationships with the Great Basin and Plains Culture Areas.* Anthropological Papers No. 77, Department of Anthropology, University of Utah. Salt Lake City, UT.

Sheppard, Peter J., and Maxine R. Kleindienst

1996 Technological Change in the Earlier and Middle Stone Age of Kalambo Falls (Zambia). *African Archaeological Review* 13:171–196.

Shott, Michael J.

1986 Technological Organization and Settlement Mobility: An Ethnographic Examination. *Journal of Anthropological Research* 42:15–51.

1989 Bipolar Reduction: Ethnographic Evidence and Archaeological Implications. *North American Archaeologist* 10:1–24.

1994 Size and Form in the Analysis of Flake Debris: Review and Recent Approaches. *Journal of Archaeological Method and Theory* 1:69–110.

1995 How Much Is a Scraper? Curation, Use Rates, and the Formation of Scraper Assemblages. *Lithic Technology* 20:53–72.

1996a An Exegesis of the Curation Concept. *Journal of Anthropological Research* 52:259–280.

1996b Stage Versus Continuum in the Debris Assemblage from Production of a Fluted Biface. *Lithic Technology* 21:6–22.

1997a Lithic Reduction at 13HA365, a Middle Woodland Occupation in Hardin County. *Journal of the Iowa Archaeological Society* 44:109–120.

1997b Stones and Shafts Redux: The Metric Discrimination of Chipped-Stone Dart and Arrow Points. *American Antiquity* 62:86–102.

2000 The Quantification Problem in Stone Tool Assemblages. *American Antiquity* 65:725–738.

2003 Reduction Sequence and *Chaîne Opèratoire. Lithic Technology* 28:95–105.

2010 Size-dependence in Assemblage Measures: Essentialism, Materialism, and 'SHE' Analysis in Archaeology. *American Antiquity* 75:886–906.

2015 Glass Is Heavy Too: Testing the Field-Processing Model at the Modena Obsidian Quarry, Lincoln County, Southeastern Nevada. *American Antiquity* 80:548–570.

2016 *Quarries and Terranes: Mapping and Analysis of the Modena, Tempiute and Kane Springs Obsidian Sources, Lincoln County, Nevada.* Report of Lincoln County Archaeological Initiative Grant no. 2008 V040 5844FD B005 411C, Department of Anthropology, University of Akron, Akron, OH.

2017 Stage and Continuum Approaches in Prehistoric Biface Production: A North American Perspective. *PLoS One* 12(3)e0170947. doi.org/10.1371/journal.pone.0170947.

Shott, Michael J., Andrew Bradbury, Philip Carr, and George Odell

2000 Flake Size from Platform Attributes: Predictive and Empirical Approaches. *Journal of Archaeological Science* 27:877–894.

Shott, Michael J., and Desale Habtzghi

2016 Toward Disentangling Stages in Mixed Assemblages of Flake Debris from Biface Reduction: An Experimental Approach. *Journal of Archaeological Science* 70:172–180.

2019 The Mixture Problem in Flake Analysis: Allocating Flake Samples to Segments of Reduction using CLSR Methods. *Journal of Archaeological Science* 103:46–56.

Shott, Michael J., and Eric Olson

2015 Scale of Production at Prehistoric Quarries: A Pilot Study in Extending the "Analytical Core Unit" Concept. *Lithic Technology* 40:218–230.

Shurack, Nichol

2001 Site 26LN1775: Bitter Knob Site. In *Playa to Panaca: Results of Archaeological*

Investigations for the Level (3) Communications Fiber Optic Line from Las Vegas to the Utah/Nevada Border, Clark and Lincoln Counties, Nevada, Vol. IV: Methods and Results of Data Recovery at Eleven Prehistoric Sites, edited by M. T. Seddon, C. Kelly, A. Wright, and K. Taite, pp. 64–110. SWCA Environmental Consultants, Report No. 01-153, Salt Lake City, UT.

Shutler, Dick, Mary E. Shutler, and James S. Griffith
1960   *Stuart Rockshelter: A Stratified Site in Southern Nevada*. Nevada State Museum Anthropological Paper No. 3, Carson City, NV.

Simms, Steven R.
1989   The Structure of the Bustos Wickiup Site, Eastern Nevada. *Journal of California and Great Basin Anthropology* 11:2–34.
2008   *Ancient Peoples of the Great Basin and Colorado Plateau*. Left Coast Press, Walnut Creek, CA.

Singer, Clay A.
1984   The 63-kilometer Fit. In *Prehistoric Quarries and Lithic Production*, edited by J. Ericson and B. Purdy, pp. 35–48. Cambridge University Press, Cambridge, UK.

Singer, Clay A., and Jonathon E. Ericson
1977   Quarry Analysis at Bodie Hills, Mono County, California: A Case Study. In *Exchange Systems in Prehistory*, edited by T. Earle and J. Ericson, pp. 171–188. Academic, New York, NY.

Skinner, Craig E.
1983   Obsidian Studies in Oregon: An Introduction to Obsidian and an Investigation of Selected Methods of Obsidian Characterization Utilizing Obsidian Collected at Prehistory Quarry Sites in Oregon, Volume I. MA thesis, Department of Interdisciplinary Studies, University of Oregon, Eugene, OR.

Skinner, Craig E., and Jennifer J. Thatcher
2005   Results of X-Ray Fluorescence Trace Element Analysis of Project Obsidian Artifacts. In *Fingerprints in the Great Basin: The Nellis Air Force Base Regional Obsidian Sourcing Study*, edited by L. Harklau, L. Johnson and D. Wagner, Appendix D. United States Air Force, Nellis AFB, NV.

Skinner, Elizabeth, and Peter Ainsworth
1991   Unifacial Bifaces: More Than One Way to Thin a Biface. *Journal of California and Great Basin Anthropology* 13:160–171.

Slaughter, Suzan, and Diane L. Winslow
2004   Kern River 2003 Expansion Project, Nevada—Volume I: Results of Obsidian Hydration Dating, Geochemical Sourcing of Obsidian, and Thermoluminescence Dating of Ceramics from Selected Sites in Nevada. Harry Reid Center Report 5-150-14(28), University of Nevada, Las Vegas, NV.

Smith, Charles M.
1885   A Sketch of Flint Ridge, Licking County, Ohio. *Smithsonian Annual Report for the Year 1884*, pp. 851–873. Smithsonian Institution, Washington, DC.

Smith, Geoffrey M.
2010   Footprints Across the Black Rock: Temporal Variability in Prehistoric Foraging Territories and Toolstone Procurement Strategies in the Western Great Basin. *American Antiquity* 75:865–885.
2011   Shifting Stones and Changing Homes: Using Toolstone Ratios to Consider Relative Occupation Span in the Northwestern Great Basin. *Journal of Archaeological Science* 38:461–489.
2015   Modeling the Influences of Raw Material Availability and Functional Efficiency on Obsidian Projectile Point Curation: A Great Basin Example. *Journal of Archaeological Science: Reports* 3:112–121.

Smith, Geoffrey M., Pat Barker, Eugene M. Hattori, Anan Raymond, and Ted Goebel
2013   Points in Time: Direct Radiocarbon Dates on Great Basin Projectile Points. *American Antiquity* 78:580–594.

Smith, Geoffrey M., and David C. Harvey
2018   Reconstructing Prehistoric Landscape Use at a Regional Scale: A Critical Review of the Lithic Conveyance Zone Concept with a Focus on Its Limitations. *Journal of Archaeological Science: Reports* 19:828–835.

Smith, Moody F., and William A. Pond
1994   Broken Knives: Complete Implements in the Lake Mohave Tool Kit. *Nevada Archaeologist* 12:11–17.

Smith, Shannon C.
2001   Soil Erosion and Transport of Archaeological Sites and Artifacts on a Small Watershed in Northern New Mexico. MA thesis, Department of Anthropology, Colorado State University, Fort Collins, CO.

Solomon, Madeline
2002   Fire and Glass: Effects of Prescribed Burning

on Obsidian Hydration Bands. In *The Effects of Fire and Heat on Obsidian*, edited by J. Loyd, T. Origer, and D. Fredrickson, pp. 69–94. Society for California Archaeology, Sacramento, CA.

Spinden, Herbert J.

1908 *The Nez Percé Indians.* Memoirs of the American Anthropological Association, Vol. II, Part 3.

Stahle, David W., and J. E. Dunn

1982 An Analysis and Application of the Size Distribution of Waste Flakes from the Manufacture of Bifacial Stone Tools. *World Archaeology* 14:84–97.

1984 *An Experimental Analysis of the Size Distribution of Waste Flakes from Biface Reduction.* Arkansas Archeological Survey, Technical Paper No. 2, Fayetteville, AR.

Steffen, Anastasia

2005 The Dome Fire Obsidian Study: Investigating the Interaction of Heat, Hydration, and Glass Geochemistry. PhD dissertation, Department of Anthropology, University of New Mexico, Albuquerque, NM.

Steffen, Anastasia, Elizabeth J. Skinner, and Peter W. Ainsworth

1998 A View to the Core: Technological Units and Debitage Analysis. In *Unit Issues in Archaeology: Measuring Time, Space, and Material*, edited by A. Ramenofsky and A. Steffen, pp. 131–146. University of New Mexico Press, Albuquerque, NM.

Stevenson, Alexander E.

2008 Lithic Procurement Strategies through Time: A Study of Obsidian Source Utilization in Washington County, Utah. Poster presented at the 31st Great Basin Anthropological Conference, Portland, OR.

Stevenson, Christopher M., Ihab Abdelrehim, and Steven W. Novak

2004 High Precision Measurement of Obsidian Hydration Layers on Artifacts from the Hopewell Site Using Secondary Ion Mass Spectometry. *American Antiquity* 69:555–568.

Steward, Julian H.

1933 Ethnography of the Owens Valley Paiute. *University of California Publications in American Archaeology and Ethnology* 33:233–350.

Stoffle, Richard W., Kathleen A. Van Vlack, Hannah Z. Johnson, Phillip T. Dukes, Stephanie C. De Sola, and Kristen L. Simmons

2011 Tribally Approved American Indian Ethno-

graphic Analysis of the Proposed Escalante Valley Solar Energy Zone. Bureau of Applied Research in Anthropology, University of Arizona, Tucson, AZ.

Stokes, Wendy L., Danny Mullins, Rob Herrmann, Sonia Hutmacher, Rob Schweitzer, Jonathan Baxer, David Crowley, and Jason Bright

2001 Site 26LN3357: Buckeye Site. In *Playa to Panaca: Results of Archaeological Investigations for the Level (3) Communications Fiber Optic Line from Las Vegas to the Utah/Nevada Border, Clark and Lincoln Counties, Nevada, Vol. IV: Methods and Results of Data Recovery at Eleven Prehistoric Sites*, edited by M. T. Seddon, C. Kelly, A. Wright, and K. Taite, pp. 111–151. SWCA Environmental Consultants, Report No. 01-153, Salt Lake City, UT.

Stoltman, James B., and Richard E. Hughes

2004 Obsidian in Early Woodland Contexts in the Upper Mississippi Valley. *American Antiquity* 69:751–759.

Stoner, Edward J., Mary K. Rusco, Charles W. Wheeler, and Fred Niles

2002 The Archaeology of Two Upland Paleoarchaic Sites in Giroux Wash, White Pine County, Nevada, Volume I. Western Cultural Resource Management, Inc., Sparks, NV.

Sturgess, Matthew D.

1999 Size Matters: Intrasite Variability of Lithic Debitage Assemblages from Tasiarulik, a Late Dorset Habitation Site. MA thesis, Department of Archaeology, University of Calgary, AB, Canada.

Sundström, Lars, and Jan Apel

1998 An Early Neolithic Axe Production and Distribution System within a Semi-sedentary Farming Society in Eastern Central Sweden, c. 3500 BC. In *Proceedings from the Third Flint Alternatives Conference at Uppsala, Sweden, October 18–20, 1996*, edited by L. Holm and K. Knutsson, pp. 155–191. Occasional Papers in Archaeology 16, University of Uppsala Department of Archaeology and Ancient History, Uppsala, Sweden.

Sullivan, Alan P., and Kenneth C. Rozen

1985 Debitage Analysis and Archaeological Interpretation. *American Antiquity* 50:755–779.

Surovell, Todd A.

2009 *Toward a Behavioral Ecology of Lithic Technology: Cases from Paleoindian Archaeology.* University of Arizona Press, Tucson, AZ.

Surovell, Todd A., Judson B. Finley, Geoffrey M. Smith, P. Jeffrey Brantingham, and Robert Kelly
2009   Correcting Temporal Frequency Distributions for Taphonomic Bias. *Journal of Archaeological Science* 36:1715–1724.

Suyuc Ley, Edgar
2011   The Extraction of Obsidian at El Chayal, Guatemala. In *The Technology of Maya Civilization: Political Economy and Beyond in Lithic Studies*, edited by Z. Hruby, G. Braswell, and O. Chinchilla Mazariegos, pp. 130–139. Equinox Publishing, Sheffield.

Syncrude Canada, Ltd.
1974   *The Beaver Creek Site: A Prehistoric Stone Quarry on Syncrude Lease #22.* Environmental Research Monograph 1974-2. Syncrude Canada, Ltd., Edmonton, AB, Canada.

Talbot, Richard K., and Lane D. Richens
2012   Obsidian Crossroads: An Archaeological Investigation of the Panaca Summit/Modena Obsidian Source in Lincoln County, Nevada: Year 1 Draft Report. Ms. on file, Office of Public Archaeology, Brigham Young University, Provo, UT.

Talbot, Richard K., Lane D. Richens, James D. Wilde, Joel C. Janetski, and Deborah E. Newman
2000   *Excavations at Five Finger Ridge, Clear Creek Canyon, Central Utah.* Museum of Peoples and Cultures, Occasional Paper No. 5. Brigham Young University, Provo, UT.

Tarasov, Alexey, and Sergey Stafeev
2014   Estimating the Scale of Stone Axe Production: A Case Study from Onega Lake, Russian Karelia. *Journal of Lithic Studies* 4:239–261.

Thatcher, Jennifer
2000   The Distribution of Geologic and Artifact Obsidian from the Silver Lake/Sycan Marsh Geochemical Source Group, South-Central Oregon. MA thesis, Department of Interdisciplinary Studies, Oregon State University, Corvallis, OR.

Thomas, David H.
1981   How to Classify the Projectile Points from Monitor Valley, Nevada. *Journal of California and Great Basin Anthropology* 3:7–43.
1983   *The Archaeology of Monitor Valley 2: Gatecliff Shelter.* Anthropological Papers of the American Museum of Natural History Vol. 59, Part 1. New York, NY.
1985   *The Archaeology of Hidden Cave, Nevada.* Anthropological Papers of the American

Museum of Natural History, Vol. 61. New York, NY.
2014   The Chert Core and the Obsidian Rim: Some Long-term Implications for the Central Great Basin. In *Meetings at the Margins: Prehistoric Cultural Interactions in the Intermountain West*, edited by D. Rhode, pp. 254–270. University of Utah Press, Salt Lake City, UT.

Thomsen, Knud
2004   Numericana. Web page, http://www.numericana.com/answer/ellipsoid.htm, accessed 26 August 2012.

Tomka, Steven A.
1989   Differentiating Lithic Reduction Techniques: An Experimental Approach. In *Experiments in Lithic Technology*, edited by D. Amick and R. Mauldin, pp. 137–162. BAR International Series 528, Oxford, UK.

Toohey, Jason L.
1999   Taller de San José: A Prehistoric Quarry Near San José del Cabo, Baja California Sur, Mexico. *Pacific Coast Archaeological Society Quarterly* 39:38–52.

Torrence, Robin
1986   *Production and Exchange of Stone Tools: Prehistoric Obsidian in the Aegean.* Cambridge University Press, Cambridge, UK.
1989   Tools as Optimal Solutions. In *Time, Energy, and Stone Tools,* edited by R. Torrence, pp. 1–6. Cambridge University Press, Cambridge, UK.

Trubitt, Mary Beth
2007   The Organization of Novaculite Tool Production: Quarry-workshop Debitage Components. *Caddo Archaeology Journal* 16:71–89.

Tschanz, C. M., and E. H. Pampeyan
1970   *Geology and Mineral Deposits of Lincoln County, Nevada.* Nevada Bureau of Mines Bulletin 73. Mackay School of Mines, University of Nevada, Reno, NV.

Tuohy, Donald R.
1982   Another Great Basin Atlatl with Dart Foreshafts and Other Artifacts: Implications and Ramifications. *Journal of California and Great Basin Anthropology* 4:80–106.

Turner, Marianne, and Dante Bonica
1994   Following the Flake Trail: Adze Production on the Coromandel East Coast, New Zealand. *New Zealand Journal of Archaeology* 16:5–32.

Umshler, D. B.

1975   Source of the Evan's Mound Obsidian. Un-
        published MS Thesis, New Mexico Institute
        of Mining and Technology, Socorro, NM.

United States Geological Survey

2011   Gap Analysis Program, National Land
        Cover, version 2. http://gis1.usgs.gov/csas
        /gap/viewer/land_cover/Map.aspx, accessed
        4 June 2012.

Vicari, Mary Ann

2013   Investigating Bias in the Survey Visibility
        of Prehistoric Great Basin Sites. Poster
        presented at the 78th Annual Meeting of the
        Society for American Archaeology, Hono-
        lulu, HI.

Walling, Barbara A., Richard A. Thompson,
Gardiner F. Dalley, and Dennis G. Weder

1988   *Excavations at Quail Creek.* United States
        Bureau of Land Management Utah State
        Office, Cultural Resource Series No. 20, Salt
        Lake City, UT.

Walsh, Laurie E.

1991   The 18-03 Road Sites: Obsidian Quarry
        Scatters. In *Archaeological Investigations
        on the Buckboard Mesa Road Project*, edited
        by D. Amick, G. Henton, and L. Pippin,
        pp. 95–97. Desert Research Institute Tech-
        nical Report 69. University of Nevada,
        Reno, NV.

Wells, Susan J.

1993   *Archeological Investigations at Great Basin
        National Park: Testing and Site Recording in
        Support of the General Management Plan.*
        Western Archeological and Conservation
        Center, Publications in Anthropology 64,
        Tucson, AZ.

Weide, David L.

1970   Appendix III: The Geology and Geography
        of the Parowan and Cedar Valley Region,
        Iron County, Utah. In *Median Village and
        Fremont Culture Regional Variation*, edited
        by J. P. Marwitt, pp. 173–193. University of
        Utah Anthropological Papers No. 95, Salt
        Lake City, UT.

Weide, Margaret L., and Davlid L. Weide

1969   A Cache from Warner Valley, Oregon.
        Tebiwa 12:28–34.

Westfall, Deborah A., William E. Davis, and Eric
Blinman

1987   *Green Spring: An Anasazi and Southern
        Paiute Encampment in the St. George Basin
        of Utah.* Bureau of Land Management—Utah

State Office, Cultural Resource Series No. 21.
Salt Lake City, UT.

Wheeler, Samuel M.

1973   *The Archeology of Etna Cave, Lincoln
        County, Nevada.* Desert Research Institute
        Publications in the Social Sciences No. 7.
        Reno, NV.

White, Andrew

2012   The Social Networks of Early Hunter-
        Gatherers in Midcontinental North America.
        PhD dissertation, Department of Anthropol-
        ogy, University of Michigan, Ann Arbor, MI.

White, Nancy Marie, and Richard A. Weinstein

2008   The Mexican Connection and the Far West
        of the U.S. Southeast. *American Antiquity*
        73(2):227–277.

Whittaker, John C., and Eric J. Kaldahl

2001   Where the Waste Went: A Knappers' Dump
        at Grasshopper Pueblo. In *Lithic Debitage:
        Context, Form, Meaning*, edited by W. An-
        drefsky, pp. 32–60. University of Utah Press,
        Salt Lake City, UT.

Wilke, Phillip, and A. B. Schroth

1989   Lithic Raw Material Prospects in the Mojave
        Desert, California. *Journal of California and
        Great Basin Anthropology* 11:146–174.

Williams, Van S., Myron G. Best, and Jeffrey D.
Keith

1997   *Geologic Map of the Ursine-Panaca Summit-
        Deer Lodge Area, Lincoln County, Nevada
        and Iron County, Utah.* United States Geo-
        logical Survey Miscellaneous Investigations
        Series Map I-2479. Washington, DC.

Wills, Wesley

2013   A Home in the Yosemite Wilderness: An
        Archaeological Investigation of Prehistory at
        Laurel Lake, Site CA-TUO-4818, Toulume
        County, California. MA thesis, Department
        of Anthropology, Calilfornia State University
        Sonoma, Sonoma, CA.

Wilmsen, Edwin N.

1970   *Lithic Analysis and Cultural Inference:
        A Paleo-Indian Case.* Anthropological
        Papers of the University of Arizona No. 16.
        Tucson, AZ.

Wilson, Jennifer, and William Andrefsky

2008   Exploring Retouch on Bifaces: Unpacking
        Production, Resharpening, and Hammer
        Type. In *Lithic Technology: Measures of
        Production, Use, and Curation*, edited by
        W. Andrefsky, pp. 86–105. Cambridge Uni-
        versity Press, Cambridge, UK.

Wilson, Lucy
2007   Understanding Prehistoric Lithic Raw
        Material Selection: Application of a Gravity
        Model. *Journal of Archaeological Method and
        Theory* 14:388–411.
Wobst, H. Martin
1976   Locational Relationships in Paleolithic
        Society. *Journal of Human Evolution*
        5:49–58.
Womack, Bruce R.
1977   An Archaeological Investigation and Tech-
        nological Analysis of the Stockhoff Basalt
        Quarry, Northeastern Oregon. MA thesis,
        Department of Anthropology, Washington
        State University, Pullman, WA.
Wright, Christopher A.
1980   A Comparative Analysis of Debitage from a
        Late Archaic Settlement and Workshop in
        Northwestern Missouri. In *Archaic Prehis-
        tory on the Prairie-Plains Border,* edited by
        A. Johnson, pp. 43–55. University of Kansas
        Publications in Anthropology No. 12. Law-
        rence, KS.
Yoder, David T., Brandon M. Gabler, Melanie A.
Medeiros, and Brian R. McKee
2012   The Lithic Landscape: Studies of Obsidian
        from UNEV Archaeological Sites. http://
        www.utaharchunev.com/special-topics
        /studies-of-obsidian-from-the-unev

-archaeological-sites. Accessed 20 March
        2015.
Young, D. Craig, Daron G. Duke, and Teresa
Wriston
2006   Cultural Resources Inventory of High
        Probability Lands near Wildcat Mountain:
        The 2005 Field Season on the US Air Force
        Utah Test and Training Range-South, Tooele
        County, Utah. Far Western Associates, Salt
        Lake City, UT.
Zeanah, D. W., and A. T. Leigh
2002   Appendix D: Obsidian Sourcing and
        Hydration Data. In *Final Report on Phase II
        Investigations at 26 Archaeological Sites for
        the Aberdeen-Blackrock Four-Lane Project
        on Highway 395, Inyo County, California.
        Volume III.* Report on file, California
        Department of Transportation, District 09,
        Bishop, CA.
Zeier, Charles D., and Ron Reno
2012   Deer Lodge and Fay, Lincoln County,
        Nevada: A Historic Overview and an Ar-
        chaeological Inventory. Report on file, Zeier
        & Assoc., Clinton, TN.
Zeigler, K. E., P. Hogan, C. Hughes, and A. Kurota
2011   Native American Lithic Procurement along
        the International Border in the Boot Heel
        Region of Southwestern New Mexico. *Solid
        Earth* 2:75–93.

Index

Geographic locations and site names are located in the Great Basin unless a different area is indicated (i.e., Flint Ridge Quarry [Ohio]). Page numbers in italics and Arabic numerals refer to images or tables.